# Traffic Calming
## State of the Practice

Reid Ewing

*Prepared for*

U.S. Department of Transportation
**Federal Highway Administration**

Office of Human Environment and
Office of Safety Research and Development

*Prepared by*

Institute of Transportation Engineers
1099 14th Street, NW
Suite 300 West
Washington, DC 20005-3438


August 1999

*Traffic Calming: State of the Practice* is an Informational Report of the Institute of Transportation Engineers (ITE) and the Federal Highway Administration (FHWA). The information in this document has been obtained from the research and experiences of transportation engineering and planning professionals. The report was prepared by ITE on behalf of FHWA for informational purposes only and does not include recommendations on the best course of action or the preferred application of the data.

ITE is an international educational and scientific association of transportation and traffic engineers and other professionals who are responsible for meeting mobility and safety needs. The Institute facilitates the application of technology and scientific principles to research, planning, functional design, implementation, operation, policy development, and management for any mode of transportation by promoting professional development of members, supporting and encouraging education, stimulating research, developing public awareness, and exchanging professional information; and by maintaining a central point of reference and action.

Founded in 1930, the Institute serves as a gateway to knowledge and advancement through meetings, seminars, and publications; and through our network of more than 15,000 members working in some 80 countries. The Institute also has more than 70 local and regional chapters and more than 90 student chapters that provide additional opportunities for information exchange, participation, and networking.

## Sponsored by:

Office of Safety Research and Development
Federal Highway Administration
6300 Georgetown Pike
McLean, VA 22102-2296

Office of Human Environment
Federal Highway Administration
400 7th Street, S.W.
Washington, DC 20590

## Notice

This document is disseminated under the sponsorship of the Department of Transportation in the interest of information exchange. The United States Government assumes no liability for its contents or the use thereof. This report does not constitute a standard, specification, or regulation. The United States Government and ITE do not endorse products or manufacturers. Trade and manufacturers' names appear in this report only because they are considered essential to the object of the document.

FHWA-RD-99-135

Institute of Transportation Engineers
1099 14th Street, NW
Suite 300 West
Washington, DC 20005-3438
Telephone: +1 (202) 289-0222
Fax: +1 (202) 289-7722
ITE on the Web: http://www.ite.org


**Library of Congress Cataloging-in-Publication Data**

Ewing, Reid H.
    Traffic calming: state of the practice / Reid Ewing.
        p.  cm.       --(publication: no. IR-098)
    "Prepared for the U.S. Department of Transportation, Federal Highway Administration, Office of Safety Research and Development and Office of Human Environment; prepared by Institute of Transportation Engineers."
    "August, 1999."
    "FHWA-RD-99-135"—Copr. p.
    ISBN 0-935403-36-1
    1. Traffic safety—United States—Case studies. 2. Traffic engineering—United States—Case studies. 3. Speed limits—United States—Case studies. I. Institute of Transportation Engineers. II. Title. III. Series: Publication (Institute of Tranportation Engineers): IR-098.
    HE5614.2.E97 1999
    363.12'57—dc21




Printed in the United States of America.

# Table of Contents

# Acknowledgments

FHWA and ITE wish to particularly thank the traffic managers of featured communities, who spent hours in interviews, guided the author around to photograph traffic calming measures, and supplied program documents by the dozens. Many of the tours coincidentally fell on weekends or holidays, which made their time commitment all the more remarkable. With their permission, names and telephone numbers are listed on page vii, and several of them are shown in their element below. These managers of innovative programs are literally inventing the practice of traffic calming in the United States, from which the rest of us can learn.

Also, appreciation is offered to the ITE members who reviewed the draft report and offered comments and suggestions. The final product is more readable, balanced, and technically sound as a result of their input. The ITE Traffic Calming Advisory Committee consisted of David G. Gerard, Chair; Crysttal Atkins; John D. Edwards; John J. Kennedy; and Susan McMillian. Other ITE reviewers included Gian C. Aggarwal; Brian S. Bochner; W. Martin Bretherton, Jr.; Anthony J. Castellone; Angela M. Christo; Edward Cline; Steven B. Colman; Rafael Cruz; Raymond Davis; Frederick C. Dock; Kay Fitzpatrick; Ian M. Lockwood; Ellis K. McCoy; Patricia Noyes; Dale Picha; Thomas A. Sohrweide; Howard S. Stein; and John Van Winkle.

Regarding authorship, Reid Ewing was the original author. Charles Kooshian, then a graduate student at Florida International University, wrote portions of chapters 2 ("Brief History of Traffic Calming") and 9 ("Beyond Residential Traffic Calming"). Mark White, an attorney with the firm of Freilich, Leitner & Carlisle, contributed to legal analyses in chapter 6 ("Legal Authority and Liability").

ITE also wishes to acknowledge Kevin Hooper, who served as the Technical Editor for this publication. As such, his responsibilities were to refine the draft document prepared by the author as follows: identify the need for and provide as necessary clarification of technical text; remove language which to some readers could constitute recommendations for a specific practice methodology or approach; and reorganize several chapters and text.

Also noted for project management, technical and editorial review, and coordination throughout the development of this publication are ITE staff members Lisa M. Fontana, Shannon Gore Peters, and Mark R. Norman.

Crysttal Atkins

W. Martin Bretherton, Jr.

Charles E. DeLeuw, Jr.

Randy A. Dittberner

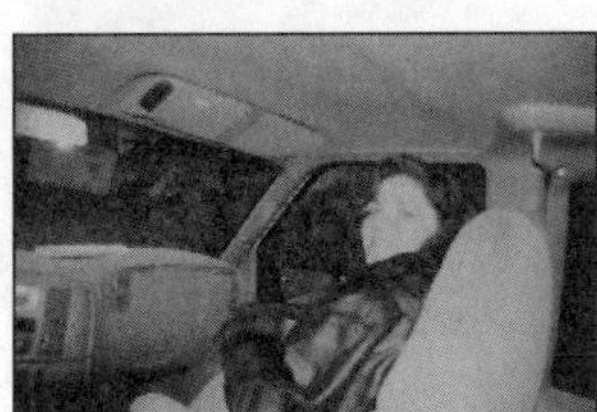

Karen L. Gonzalez

Ian Lockwood

David A. Loughery

Jay Millikin

# Featured Traffic Calming Programs

| Community | Traffic Manager | Telephone | Web Site |
| --- | --- | --- | --- |
| Austin, TX | David Gerard<br>Samileh Mozafari | 512-499-7129 | www.ci.austin.tx.us/roadworks |
| Bellevue, WA | Karen L. Gonzalez | 425-452-4598 | www.ci.bellevue.wa.us/bellevue |
| Berkeley, CA | Charles E. DeLeuw, Jr. | 510-665-3400 | www.ci.berkeley.ca.us/PW/Traffic/traffic.html |
| Boulder, CO | Noreen Walsh | 303-441-3266 | www.publicworks.ci.boulder.co.us/DEPTS/<br>TRANS/NTMP/ntmp_information.htm |
| Charlotte, NC | R. Douglas Gillis | 704-336-3926 | www.charmeck.nc.us/citransportation/<br>programs/trafcalm.html |
| Dayton, OH | Kerry Lawson | 937-443-4075 | — |
| Eugene, OR | Gary McNeel<br>Jay Millikin | 541-682-8451<br>541-682-5082 | under development |
| Ft. Lauderdale, FL | Peter Partington | 954-761-5761 | — |
| Gainesville, FL | Brian Kanely<br>Philip Mann | 352-334-5074 | — |
| Gwinnett County, GA | W. Martin Bretherton, Jr.<br>Vince Edwards | 770-822-7412 | under development |
| Howard County, MD | Buck Bohmer | 410-313-2430 | www.co.ho.md.us/spdcntrl.htm |
| Montgomery County, MD | David A. Loughery | 301-217-2190 | www.dpwt.com/TraffPkgDiv/triage.htm |
| Phoenix, AZ | Randy A. Dittberner | 602-534-9529 | — |
| Portland, OR | Ellis McCoy<br>Crysttal Atkins | 503-823-5214 | www.trans.ci.portland.or.us/Traffic_Management/<br>trafficcalming |
| San Diego, CA | Allen Holden, Jr. | 619-533-3012 | — |
| San Jose, CA | James Helmer<br>Lawrence Moore | 408-277-4304 | — |
| Sarasota, FL | Ellen Cranos | 941-954-4180 | www.ci.sarasota.fl.us/eng.nsf/pages/calming+home |
| Seattle, WA | Jim Mundell | 206-684-0814 | www.ci.seattle.wa.us/td |
| Tallahassee, FL | Monica Heller | 850-891-8261 | — |
| West Palm Beach, FL | Ian Lockwood | 561-659-8031 | — |

## Abbreviations

This document reports the state of traffic calming programs in the United States. It also includes historical information about programs in other countries. Although speed and distance measurements are provided primarily in U.S. customary units, some metric measurements appear. The following abbreviations are used in the text.

dB(A) = decibel (ampere)
ft = feet
g = acceleration of gravity
hr = hour
in = inch
kph = kilometers per hour
mph = miles per hour
sec = second
vmt = vehicle-miles of travel
vpd = vehicles per day
vph = vehicles per hour

## Metric Conversions

The following common factors represent the appropriate magnitude of conversion. This is because the quantities given in U.S. customary units in the text, tables, or figures, represent a precision level that in practice typically does not exceed two significant figures. In making conversions, it is important to not falsely imply a greater accuracy in the product than existed in the original dimension or quantity. However, certain applications such as surveying, structures, curve offset calculations, and so forth, may require great precision. Conversions for such purposes are given in parentheses.

Length
1 inch = 25 millimeters (25.4)
1 inch = 2.5 centimeters (2.54)
1 foot = 0.3 meters (0.3048)
1 yard = 0.91 meters (0.914)
1 mile = 1.6 kilometers (1.609)

Speed
1 foot/sec = 0.3 meters/second (0.3048)
1 mile/hour = 1.6 kilometers/hour (1.609)

For other units refer to the American Society for Testing and Materials, 100 Barr Harbor Drive, West Conshohoken, PA 19428-2959, USA; *Standard for Metric Practice E380*.

# CHAPTER 1

# Introduction

In his pioneering publication *Livable Streets,* Don Appleyard called streets the "most important part of our urban environment."[1] Appleyard goes on to say:

> [W]e should raise our sights for the moment. What could a residential street—a street on which our children are brought up, adults live, and old people spend their last days—what could such a street be like?

Such questions are being asked with increasing frequency. For some transportation professionals, public officials, and citizens, the answer involves traffic calming. For others, it does not. The purpose of this report is not to advocate for or against traffic calming but rather to provide balanced information so readers can make their own informed decisions.

Nationally, traffic calming is part of a marked change in the way transportation systems are viewed. With passage of the Intermodal Surface Transportation Efficiency Act of 1991 (ISTEA), transportation planning and engineering have become more multimodal and sensitive to the social costs of automobile use.[2] The once single-minded pursuit of speed, capacity, and traffic safety is being tempered by other concerns.[3] The legislative successor to ISTEA, the Transportation Equity Act for the 21st Century (TEA-21), continues and expands ISTEA programs, and creates a $120-million "Transportation and Community and System Preservation Pilot Program." The legislation refers to traffic calming by name as an eligible activity under this new program. Prior to TEA-21, traffic calming projects were eligible for federal funding only under the Hazard Elimination Program (part of the Surface Transportation Program's safety set-aside).

At the local level, traffic calming responds to public concerns about speeding and cut-through traffic, particularly on neighborhood streets (see figure 1.1). Citizens look to their elected officials for leadership in this area, and elected officials look to transportation professionals for technical solutions. The Federal Highway Administration (FHWA) has responded by launching a national traffic calming technical assistance project in partnership with the Institute of Transportation Engineers (ITE). This report is one work product.

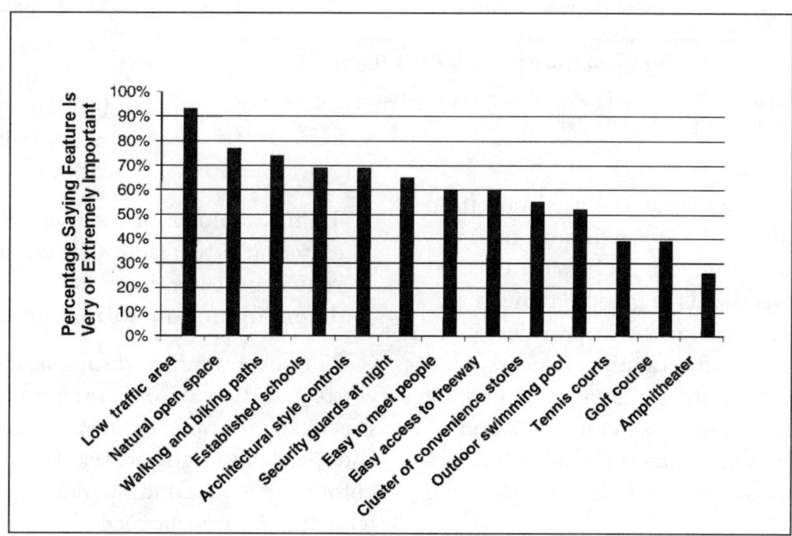


**Figure 1.1. Concern About Traffic in One Public Survey.**

Source: Adapted from B. Warrick and T. Alexander, "Looking for Hometown America," *Urban Land,* February 1997, p. 28.

## Related Studies

The last federally funded study of traffic calming dates back to 1979–1981, before any meaningful history had been established in the United States.[4] That pioneering study explored residential preferences related to traffic, collected performance data on speed humps, and reviewed legal issues.[5] It documented the adverse impact of high traffic volumes and speeds on quality of life in residential areas (an example is illustrated in figure 1.2). Appleyard's *Livable Streets* grew out of that project.

Almost 20 years later, with a track record in place, there is much to learn from the U.S. experience. Compared to the 1980 study, this report goes beyond residential streets to major thoroughfares, beyond speed humps to a toolbox of calming measures, and beyond legal issues to policy, procedural, and political challenges.

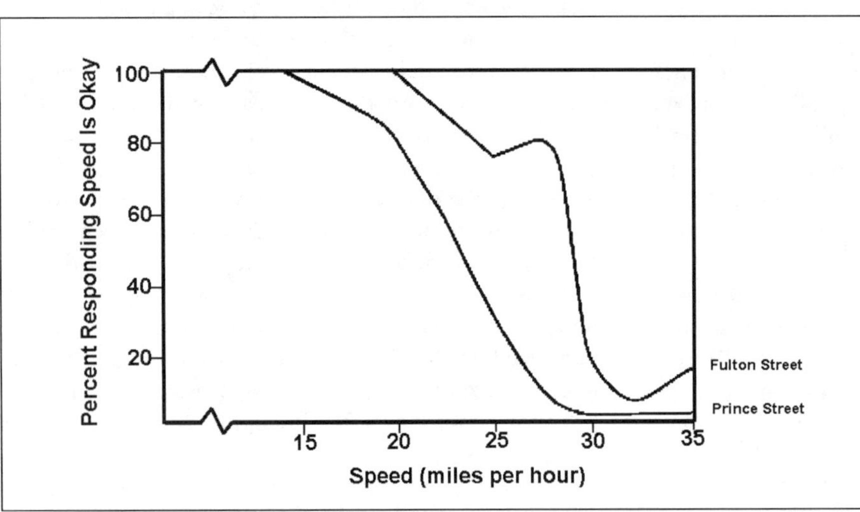


**Figure 1.2. Resident Acceptance versus Traffic Speed. (From the Early FHWA Study)**

Source: D.T. Smith and D. Appleyard, *Improving the Residential Street Environment—Final Report*, Federal Highway Administration, Washington, DC, 1981, p. 117.

In a parallel effort to this one, the Transportation Association of Canada and the Canadian Institute of Transportation Engineers have produced a *Canadian Guide to Neighbourhood Traffic Calming*.[6] That guide outlines a recommended process of public involvement, provides guidelines for the selection of traffic calming measures, and provides guidelines for geometrics, signing, and marking of different measures. The desired outcome is "a consistent approach to traffic calming across Canada, eliminating the need for local municipalities to develop their own guidelines."[7]

Examples of suggested designs from the Canadian manual are reproduced in chapter 4 of this report, "Engineering and Aesthetic Issues." These designs, plus Canadian process guidelines, will prove useful to transportation engineers who want off-the-shelf guidance. The approach taken in this report is less prescriptive, outlining principles and presenting case studies for those who choose to design their own programs and projects.

## What Traffic Calming Is and Is Not

What this report calls traffic calming has many names across the country. In San Jose, CA, its official name is "neighborhood traffic management." An ordinance in Boulder, CO, refers to "traffic mitigation." Until recently, it was called "traffic abatement" in Sarasota, FL. "Neighborhood traffic control" is another common name for traffic calming.

The term "traffic calming" has such descriptive power that even places with other official names for their programs revert to this English translation of the German term "verkehrsberuhigung." Sarasota is not the first, nor will it be the last, to change the official name of its program to the more descriptive term (as illustrated in figures 1.3 and 1.4).

### An Elusive Definition

Reaching consensus on a definition of traffic calming has proved difficult. After much debate, a subcommittee of ITE came up with the following:

> Traffic calming is the combination of mainly physical measures that reduce the negative effects of motor vehicle use, alter driver behavior and improve conditions for non-motorized street users.[8]

The subcommittee distinguished traffic calming from route modification, traffic control devices, and streetscaping. Traffic control devices, notably STOP signs and speed limit signs, are regulatory measures that require enforcement. By contrast, traffic calming measures are intended to be *self-enforcing*.

**Figure 1.3. Original Name. (Sarasota, FL)**

**Figure 1.4. More Descriptive Term. (Sarasota, FL)**



Second, as defined by the ITE subcommittee, traffic calming measures rely on the laws of physics rather than human psychology to slow down traffic. Street trees, street lighting, street furniture, and other streetscape elements, while complementary to traffic calming, do not directly compel drivers to slow down.

The ITE subcommittee made a third distinction. Route modification measures, such as diverters, street closures, and turn restrictions, were placed outside the umbrella of traffic calming. They were said not to change driver behavior (i.e., speed) but simply to modify driver routing options.

This third distinction is harder to justify than the first two. In terms of their ultimate effects on traffic speeds and volumes, as will be demonstrated in "Traffic Calming Impacts" (chapter 5), a single-lane choker is not very different from a half street closure, nor is a sharp bend designed into a new street network very different from a diagonal diverter inserted into an old street grid. All affect volumes and speeds of traffic. All are largely self-enforcing. All are engineered.

### Scope of This Report

For the purposes of this report, traffic calming involves changes in street alignment, installation of barriers, and other physical measures to reduce traffic speeds and cut-through volumes in the interest of street safety, livability, and other public purposes. The Canadian definition of traffic calming is similar.[9]

The concept of traffic calming as presented in this report is narrow compared to those of some surveyed communities, whose traffic calming programs are structured around the "3Es"—education, enforcement, and engineering. The definition used by Montgomery County, MD, for example, includes "operational measures such as enhanced police enforcement, speed displays, and a community speed watch program, as well as such physical measures as edgelines, chokers, chicanes, traffic circles, and (for the past 4 years) speed humps and raised crosswalks."[10]

This report takes the middle ground, focusing mainly on physical measures, including street closures and other volume controls under the traffic calming umbrella. Education and enforcement activities, such as neighborhood speed watch and neighborhood traffic safety campaigns (as illustrated in figure 1.5), fall outside the umbrella but will also be mentioned where relevant.

## Multiple Purposes of Traffic Calming

The immediate purpose of traffic calming is to reduce the speed and volume of traffic to acceptable levels ("acceptable" for the functional class of a street and the nature of bordering activity). Reductions in traffic speed and volume, however, are just means to other ends such as traffic safety and active street life. Different localities have un-

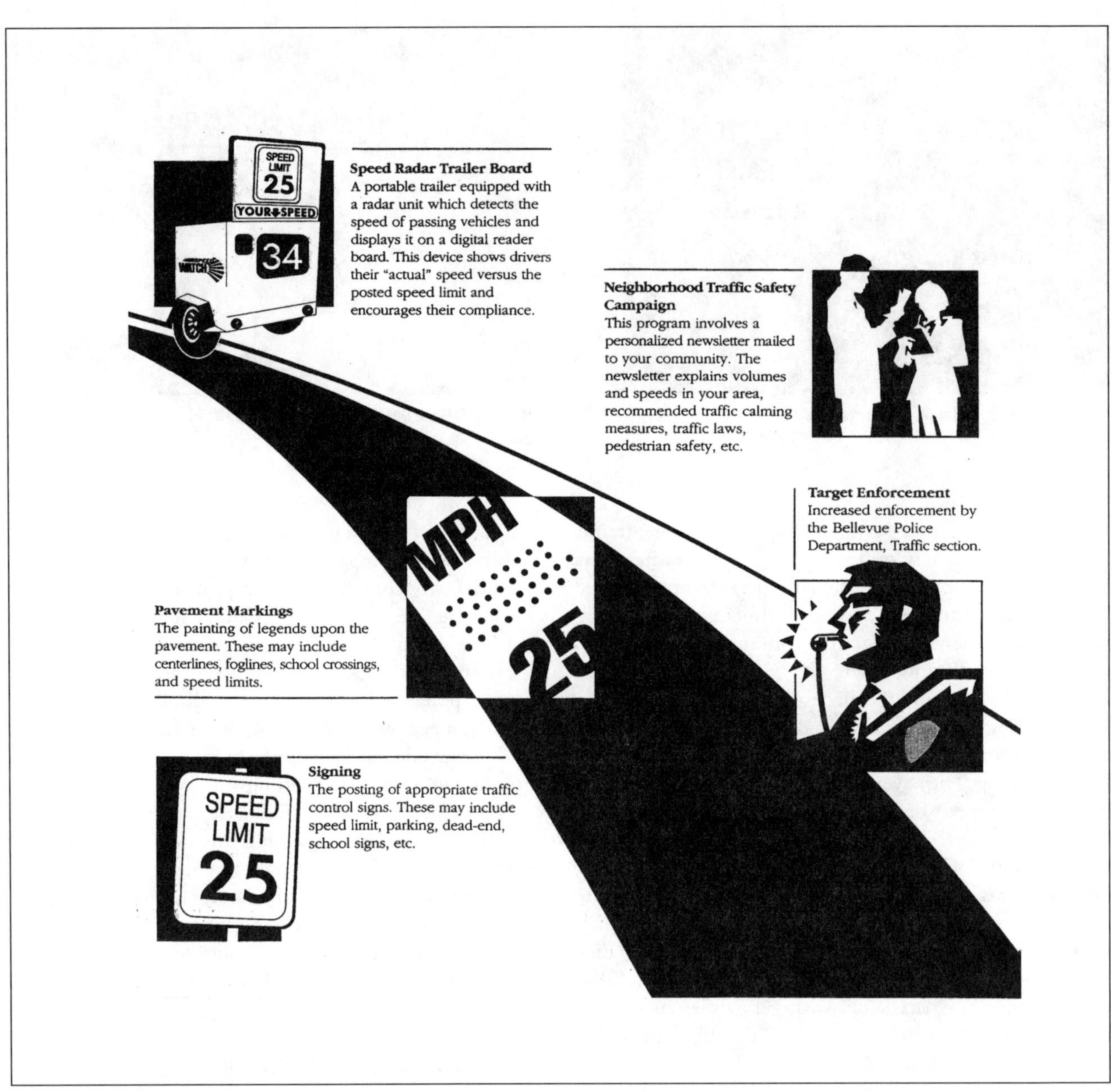


**Figure 1.5. Examples of Education and Enforcement Activities. (Bellevue, WA)**

Source: City of Bellevue, Transportation Department, "Neighborhood Traffic Control Program," Bellevue, WA, 1996.

dertaken traffic calming for different reasons, three of which are now given as examples.

## Neighborhood Livability—San Jose, CA

A neighborhood traffic calming project in San Jose, CA, defined the following objectives:

- Reduce through traffic
- Reduce truck traffic
- Reduce occurrence of excessive speeding
- Reduce noise, vibration, and air pollution
- Reduce accidents
- Provide safer environment for pedestrians and children

Objective measurements such as a reduction in collisions—from 47 in the 9 months before treatment to 27 in the 9 months after—demonstrated the effect of traffic calming on neighborhood livability. So did attitudinal changes captured in a resident survey, which are summarized in table 1.1.

## Crime Prevention—Dayton, OH

Traffic calming measures that limit motor vehicle access are a common strategy in the field of crime prevention through environmental design (CPTED). One crime-ridden neighborhood in Dayton, OH, underwent street and alley closures to transform an open grid into a series of mini-neighborhoods, each with a single entry portal off an arterial (illustrated in figure 1.6).[11] Through streets were treated with speed humps. With street closures in place, violent crime within the neighborhood dropped from 111 reported incidents in 1992 to 56 reported incidents in the same 11-month period of 1993, a 50 percent

**Table 1.1. Resident Opinion Survey Results. (San Jose, CA)**

| Problem Reported | % Residents Reporting Problem Before Traffic Calming | % Residents Reporting Problem After Traffic Calming |
|---|---|---|
| Air pollution from traffic | 54 | 44 |
| Noise from traffic | 52 | 34 |
| Safety of children | 39 | 30 |
| Pedestrian safety | 43 | 28 |

Source: Department of Transportation Operations, "Naglee Park Traffic Plan—Final Project Report," City of San Jose, CA, August 1984.

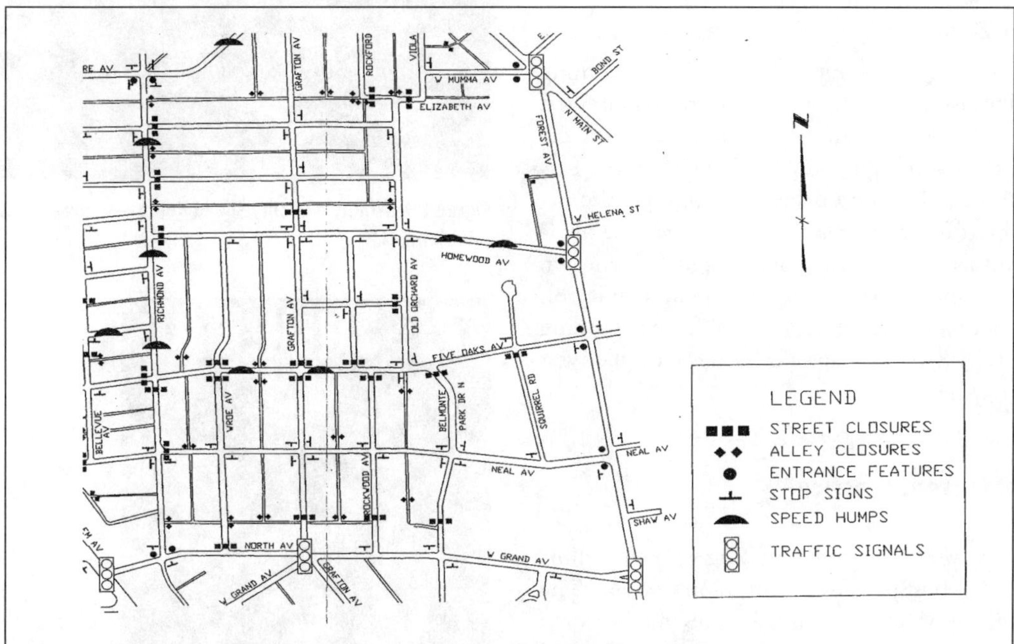


**Figure 1.6. Traffic Calming in the Five Oaks Neighborhood. (Dayton, OH)**

Source: Department of Urban Development, City of Dayton, OH, 1995.

**Figure 1.7. Before, During, and After Neighborhood Redevelopment. (West Palm Beach, FL)**

**Figure 1.8. Before, During, and After Commercial Area Revitalization. (West Palm Beach, FL)**

reduction; nonviolent crime within the neighborhood dropped from 969 to 741 reported incidents in the same time period, a 24 percent reduction. Traffic volumes, collisions, and speeds within the neighborhood were down as well—by 36, 40, and 18 percent, respectively.

### Urban Redevelopment— West Palm Beach, FL

Probably nowhere in the United States is traffic calming more central to overall redevelopment efforts than in West Palm Beach, FL. "Traffic calming has gone beyond the usual speeding, cut-through, and safety benefits by increasing inner city neighborhood pride, attracting private investment, supporting other programs involving home ownership and historic preservation, and helping downtown businesses."[12] From the level of reinvestment activity on traffic-calmed streets, the strategy seems to be working (figures 1.7 and 1.8). (See chapter 5 for more on the West Palm Beach experience.)

## Overview of Current Practice

Until only a few years ago, traffic calming was but a glimmer on the U.S. transportation profession's screen. The 1991 ITE Annual Meeting included a presentation on a novel 22-foot, flat-topped speed hump designed and tested by Seminole County, FL (see figure 1.9). Because its 85th percentile speed (the speed below which 85 percent of the vehicles travel) was higher than that for the common

**Figure 1.9. Seminole County Speed Hump—Innovation Circa 1991. (Maitland, FL)**

**Figure 1.10. Special Issue of the *ITE Journal*.**

12-foot rounded hump, this new hump was successfully applied to a collector road with a daily volume of 12,000 vehicles. There was also a presentation on roundabouts, which are both intersection control devices and traffic calming measures. There were two presentations on neotraditional neighborhood design, whose goals include traffic calming, and mention of the fledgling neighborhood traffic management program in Austin, TX. But that was all, among 124 professional presentations.

Just 6 years later, traffic calming was declared a priority by ITE's International Board of Direction. Two special issues of the *ITE Journal* (figure 1.10), one of three tracks at the 1997 ITE International Conference, and a newly formed Traffic Calming Committee all signaled burgeoning professional interest in the subject.

## ITE District 6 Survey

U.S. traffic calming practice has evolved in ways that would have been hard to imagine only a few years ago. While the precise number is unknown, jurisdictions with active traffic calming programs certainly number in the hundreds. Of 153 cities and counties located in the 13 western U.S. States that responded to a 1996 ITE District 6 survey, 110 reported the use of one or more engineering measures.[13] Others had educational and enforcement ac-

**Table 1.2. Prevalence of Selected Measures in 153 Cities and Counties. (ITE District 6 Survey)**

| Measure | Number of Jurisdictions |
| --- | --- |
| Speed humps | 79 |
| Diverters/closures | 67 |
| Traffic circles | 46 |
| Chokers | 35 |
| Engineering measures (any kind) | 110 |

tivities that would fall under a broader definition of traffic calming. The numbers of jurisdictions in each category are shown in table 1.2.

## University of California at Berkeley Survey

A literature search by researchers at the University of California at Berkeley uncovered about 350 U.S. cities and counties that had engaged in some form of traffic calming over the past 30 years. The study's definition of traffic calming included nonengineering measures.[14] In a random sample of 43 communities, 40 reported taking steps beyond the standard enforcement of traffic laws. The initial survey was supplemented by interviews with an additional 20 cities whose traffic calming programs appeared to be particularly ambitious. The survey covered a host of hard and soft subjects, from funding levels to political conflict.

## For Every Action...

For every action there is often an opposite reaction. As traffic calming measures have proliferated, political support and political opposition have grown. The more traffic calming occurs in a locality, the more controversy seems to erupt (see figure 1.11). The more it expands beyond local streets to major thoroughfares, the more heated the controversy becomes. The following is a brief status report as of mid-1998.

Montgomery County, MD, first witnessed a lawsuit challenging the legality of its speed hump program and then an antihump petition drive. The lawsuit was dismissed, and the petition was disqualified from the ballot by the courts. Later, the county council imposed a moratorium on new speed hump applications, and after lifting the moratorium adopted such stringent eligibility requirements that a virtual moratorium still exists. The county council also decreed that 12-foot speed humps be replaced

Figure 1.11. Controversy Surrounding Traffic Calming.

by 22-foot speed tables on all emergency response routes, potentially a very costly requirement.

The experience of Portland, OR, has paralleled that of Montgomery County. First, a moratorium was applied to the installation of humps and circles on emergency response routes. Then, when the moratorium was lifted, funding was withheld from the Neighborhood Collector Program aimed at just such routes. Portland has been sued as well. The lawsuit, won by the city at the trial court level, is under appeal.

San Diego, CA, imposed a moratorium on all speed hump projects while new warrants were being developed. The old warrants had been violated under political pressure from city council members, and the resulting installation of humps on collector roads outraged both fire officials and residents of local streets to which traffic was diverted.

Boulder, CO, imposed a large budget cut (from $900,000 annually to $250,000 and finally to $100,000) as part of a general retrenchment of traffic calming. Only demonstration projects, plus education and enforcement activities, are permitted until emergency response issues have been resolved.

When Gwinnett County, GA, expanded its notification area, residents of neighboring streets began appearing at county commission meetings in opposition to speed table applications. The board interpreted their sudden appearance as a revolt against the program, and has placed otherwise qualified applications on hold until public support for the program can be reassessed.

Sarasota, FL, has been sued, and lost; the decision is being appealed. Berkeley, CA, has a total moratorium in effect. Eugene, OR, has a moratorium on speed humps, while Howard County, MD, has a moratorium on speed humps and most other vertical measures. San Jose, CA, has stopped funding comprehensive neighborhood traffic calming plans. Austin, TX, has a limited moratorium in effect while new measures are being pilot tested.

The various types of traffic calming measures referenced above are described in "Toolbox of Traffic Calming Measures" (chapter 3). Moratoria, lawsuits, and political controversies are discussed in "Legal Authority and Liability" (chapter 6), "Emergency Response and Other Agency Concerns" (chapter 7), and "Warrants, Project Selection Procedures, and Public Involvement" (chapter 8). Let it suffice to say that this is a critical time in the evolution of U.S. traffic calming, one filled with perils and possibilities.

## Featured Programs

Twenty traffic calming programs are featured in this report (see list on page vii). Traffic managers were interviewed by telephone several times, and sites were visited and photographed at least once; in some cases, two or three times. Another 30 programs were surveyed less extensively, and many others provided before-and-after studies, photographs, and occasional anecdotes.[15]

Selection criteria were informal. A program experimenting with a variety of measures, defending itself in a lawsuit, beginning to treat major thoroughfares, using traffic calming to help revitalize low-income neighborhoods, or facing a funding crisis was an obvious choice for in-depth study. A big residential speed hump program with no institutional issues was less likely to be selected. The former had much to teach us; the latter did not.

Admittedly, a Florida bias crept into the selection process, for it is close to home for the author. But even the featured Florida programs had to be exemplary. The 20 featured programs are among the most innovative in the United States. Because they are pushing the envelope, the

**Figure 1.12. One of the More Complete Web Sites (www.trans.ci. portland.or.us/Traffic_Management/trafficcalming). (Portland, OR)**

featured communities often face complex institutional issues, which adds to their interest. For those wishing to learn more about the featured programs, several web sites are well worth visiting (see p. vii for list, and figure 1.12).

## Endnotes

1. D. Appleyard, *Livable Streets,* University of California Press, Berkeley, 1981, p. 243.

2. R. Ewing, *Transportation and Land Use Innovations—When You Can't Pave Your Way Out of Congestion,* American Planning Association (in cooperation with the Surface Transportation Policy Project), Chicago, IL, 1998, pp. 5–8.

3. R. Ewing, "Beyond Speed—The Next Generation of Transportation Performance Measures," in D. Porter (ed.), *Performance Standards for Growth Management,* American Planning Association, Chicago, IL, 1996, pp. 31–40.

4. D.T. Smith and D. Appleyard, *State-of-the-Art: Residential Traffic Management,* Federal Highway Administration, Washington, DC, 1980; and D.T. Smith and D. Appleyard, *Improving the Residential Street Environment—Final Report,* Federal Highway Administration, Washington, DC, 1981.

5. There have been modest efforts since the early 1980's, consisting of literature surveys and European site visits, in connection with the National Bicycling and Walking Study of the Federal Highway Administration. See, in particular, A. Clarke and M.J. Dornfeld, *National Bicycling and Walking Study: Case Study No. 19, Traffic Calming, Auto-Restricted Zones and Other Traffic Management Techniques: Their Effects on Bicycling and Pedestrians,* Federal Highway Administration, Washington, DC, 1994.

6. Transportation Association of Canada, *Canadian Guide to Neighbourhood Traffic Calming,* Ottawa, ON, Canada, December 1998.

7. G. Chartier and Diane G. Erickson, "Canada's Guide to Neighbourhood Traffic Calming—CITE/TAC Project 208," in *Compendium of Technical Papers for the 67th ITE Annual Meeting* (Boston, MA, 1997), Institute of Transportation Engineers, Washington, DC, 1997, CD-ROM.

8. I.M. Lockwood, "ITE Traffic Calming Definition," *ITE Journal,* Vol. 67, July 1997, pp. 22–24.

9. The *Canadian Guide to Neighbourhood Traffic Calming* wrestled with the distinction between speed and volume control, and came to favor an inclusive definition of traffic calming:

   > Traffic calming involves altering of motorist behaviour on a single street or on a street network. It also includes traffic management, which involves changing traffic routes or flows within a neighbourhood.

   Transportation Association of Canada, op. cit., p. 1–1.

10. D.A. Loughery and M. Katzman, *Montgomery County, Maryland—Speed Hump Program Evaluation Report,* Montgomery County Council, January 1998, p. 1.

11. Oscar Newman, a recognized expert in the field of CPTED, developed the Five Oaks Neighborhood Stabilization Plan for a crime-ridden neighborhood in Dayton, OH.

12. I.M. Lockwood, "Meeting Community Objectives Through Street Design (The West Palm Beach Approach)," paper presented at the ITE International Conference in Monterey, CA, Institute of Transportation Engineers, Washington, DC, 1998.

13. R.S. McCourt, *Neighborhood Traffic Management Survey, ITE District 6,* available through DKS Associates, Portland, OR, 1996.

14. The University of California at Berkeley defined traffic calming as "physical retrofitting or changes in operations or management strategies on existing streets, designed to reduce adverse impacts such as speeding and excessive volumes and to improve safety and amenity." A. Weinstein and E. Deakin, "A Survey of Traffic Calming Programs in the United States," paper presented at the ITE International Conference in Monterey, CA, Institute of Transportation Engineers, Washington, DC, 1998.

15. A shorter survey included Ada County, ID; Albuquerque, NM; Arlington County, VA; Beaverton, OR; Boca Raton, FL; Brookline, MA; Cambridge, MA; Dallas, TX; Greensboro, NC; Houston, TX; Lee County, FL; Madison, WI; Minneapolis, MN; Naples, FL; North Little Rock, AR; Omaha, NE; Orlando, FL; Plano, TX; Reno, NV; Sacramento, CA; San Antonio, TX; Santa Monica, CA; Tampa, FL; Tucson, AZ; and Yakima, WA.

# CHAPTER 2

# Brief History of Traffic Calming

This chapter gives an abbreviated history of European and Australian traffic calming. It then describes the early U.S. experience, focusing on Seattle, WA, a leader in the field.

## International Origins of Traffic Calming

### Dutch Woonerven and Other Experiments

European traffic calming began as a grassroots movement in the late 1960's.[1] Angry residents of the Dutch city of Delft fought cut-through traffic by turning their streets into "woonerven," or "living yards."[2] What were once channels for the movement of cars became shared areas, outfitted with tables, benches, sand boxes, and parking bays jutting into the street. The effect was to turn the street into an obstacle course for motor vehicles, and an extension of home for residents (see figure 2.1).

Woonerven were officially endorsed by the Dutch government in 1976. Over the next decade, the idea spread to many other countries. Laws and regulations were changed to permit woonerf designs in Germany, Sweden, Denmark, England, France, Japan, Israel, Austria, and Switzerland. By 1990, there were more than 3,500 shared streets in the Netherlands and Germany, 300 in Japan, and 600 in Israel.[3]

Woonerven were no cure-all. The woonerf design was meant for streets with low traffic volumes. Extensive use of street furniture made converted woonerven about 50 percent costlier than normal reconstructed streets. The twists and turns, plus brick pavement and periodic raised areas, brought motorists down to "walking speeds," meaning about 15 kph or 9 mph. Such low speeds were sustainable only for short distances on local access streets.

The Dutch wanted to see if the design principles of woonerven could be adapted to a wider range of streets at a lower cost to the government. They experimentally compared the effectiveness of woonerven to treatments of two types:

**Figure 2.1. Dutch Woonerf. (Delft, The Netherlands)**

Source: L. Herrstedt et al., *An Improved Traffic Environment—A Catalogue of Ideas*, Danish Road Directorate, Copenhagen, Denmark, 1993, p. 11.

- Diversion schemes involving street closures and one-way streets
- Now-standard traffic calming treatments involving humps and other physical measures

Of the three approaches, the traffic calming alternative was judged the most cost-effective for neighborhood streets. It was officially endorsed by the Dutch government in 1983. Other nations followed suit, calling their traffic-calmed streets and areas "stille veje" (translated as "silent roads") in Denmark, "Tempo 30" zones in Germany, and 20-mph zones in Britain.

### European "Environmentally Adapted Through Roads"

In the early 1980's Norway needed a policy to deal with intercity traffic speeding through its many small towns. Due to budget constraints, the nation could not afford to build bypasses around all of them. The government decided its one viable option was traffic calming.

Inspired by Norway, Denmark undertook a test of traffic calming measures applied to highways through three small towns.[4] Pre-warnings or gateways were placed at the town entries, and chicanes, roundabouts, chokers, and other mea-

**Figure 2.2. Danish Environmentally Adapted Through Road. (Vinderup, Denmark)**

Source: L. Herrstedt et al., *An Improved Traffic Environment— A Catalogue of Ideas,* Danish Road Directorate, Copenhagen, Denmark, 1993, p. 117.

sures were installed in the town centers. The results included a drop in speeds, decline in accidents, and improvement in air quality, all at one-fourth to one-third the cost of constructing a bypass. This led to a series of similar projects on main roads throughout Denmark (see figure 2.2).

Germany conducted a related test in the state of Nordrhein-Westfalen. Twenty-eight villages located on intercity highways were traffic calmed with narrowings, roundabouts, textured surfaces, and redesigned street spaces. Significant speed reductions were recorded for most highways as they ran through town centers and for nearly all highways as they entered towns.

## German Areawide Traffic Calming

Germany experimented in the late 1970's with neighborhood traffic calming.[5] This was the era when the term "verkehrsberuhigung" (translated as traffic calming) was coined. The Germans quickly learned that calming individual streets resulted in traffic diversion. Already quiet streets became quieter as traffic moved to already congested streets. The Germans decided to test the feasibility of areawide traffic calming, where calming principles were extended to main roads.

In the 1980's, a long-term demonstration was conducted in six German towns (see figure 2.3). A 30-kph speed limit was imposed over large areas; local streets and collectors were treated with speed tables, chicanes, and pinch points; and one-way streets were converted to two-way operation. Ring roads and arterials were narrowed in some cases. Alternative travel modes were given higher priority. The demonstration had these results:

- Volumes were unchanged.
- Speeds were reduced.

- Frequency of accidents was unchanged, but severity was reduced.
- Air pollution was reduced.
- Noise was reduced.
- Fuel use increased or decreased depending on the location.

These positive results helped encourage many cities across the globe to adopt areawide traffic calming programs. Notable examples include Odense in Denmark; Goteburg and Malmö in Sweden; Gronignen, Delft, Tilburg, The Hague, and Amsterdam in the Netherlands; Bologna and Parma in Italy; Zurich and Basel in Switzerland; and Osaka, Tokyo, and Nagoya in Japan.[6]

Germany's Green Party has argued that, even with areawide traffic calming, heavy traffic ends up somewhere in cities. Their view is gaining currency and, now in the late 1990's, citywide policies are being adopted to restrain automobile use. Traffic restraint is called the "third generation" of traffic calming, coming as it does after the neighborhood and areawide approaches. Although similar to travel demand management in the United States, traffic restraint in Germany is being pursued much more vigorously.[7]

## British "Environmental Traffic Management"

A 1963 British government document, *Traffic in Towns,*[8] is often credited with launching the modern traffic calming movement. The report's author, Colin Buchanan, is considered the father of traffic calming by many Europeans. Thus it is surprising that Britain has only recently begun to implement the range of measures used, the extension of traffic calming to main roads, and the redesign of street environments to create people places.[9]

The Buchanan report was the first official document to recognize that growth of traffic threatened the quality of urban life. However, compared with current thinking on the subject, the solutions offered in the report were shortsighted. Urban areas were to be reconstructed to accommodate the automobile. Neighborhoods were to be protected largely by closing streets and using short one-way segments to prevent through trips. *Volume control measures* were emphasized to the virtual exclusion of *speed control measures* (see chapter 3).

Buchanan-inspired traffic calming plans were implemented throughout Britain under the 1969 Housing Act and a 1977 street design manual (*Design Bulletin 32,* updated in 1992).[10] The Urban Safety Project, a traffic calming initiative launched in 1982 to reduce accidents, also featured Buchanan-like volume controls. It had a relatively modest impact on collision rates compared with German, Dutch, and Danish demonstrations. Comparing

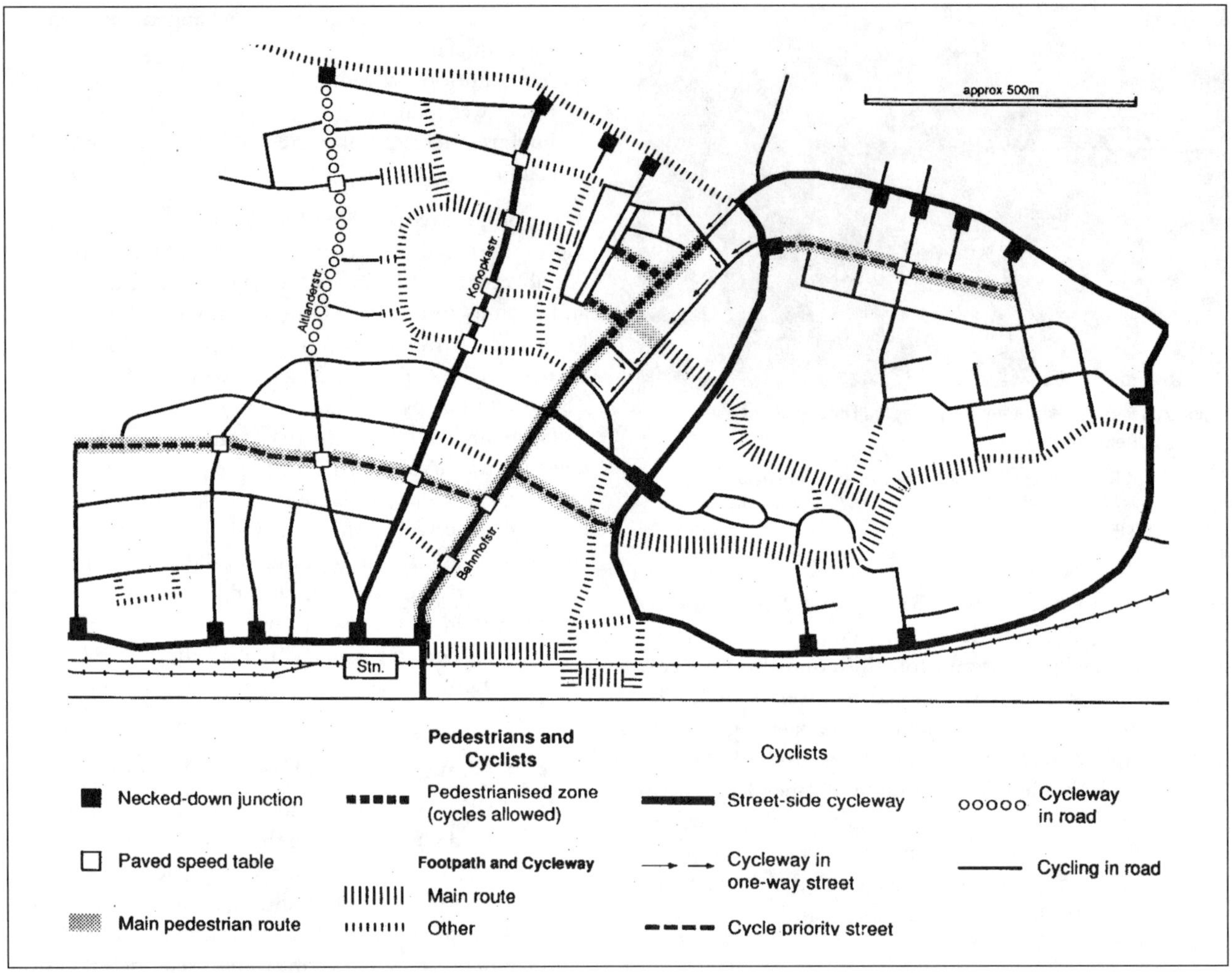

**Figure 2.3. One of Six German Towns in a Test of Areawide Traffic Calming. (Buxtehude, Germany)**

Source: R. Tolley, *Calming Traffic in Residential Areas*, Brefi Press, Brefi, England, 1990, p. 44.

these countries, one critic writing in 1989 declared that the "application of traffic calming in Britain has…been almost imperceptible, implemented here and there on new housing estates, and usually in a very diluted and faint-hearted manner."[11]

Changes in law and regulation, and a new edition of the street design manual, have brought Britain into line with the rest of Europe. Regulations were liberalized in 1986 and 1990 to permit the use of vertical measures other than rounded 12-foot humps, a profile developed by the British and useful in many applications but ill-suited for raised crosswalks, raised intersections, and midblock locations on major roads. The "Children and Road Safety" campaign launched in 1990 and an accompanying regulation permitted for the first time the designation of 20-mph zones (see figure 2.4). The 1992 Traffic Calming Act

**Figure 2.4. Raised Intersection in a 20-mph Zone. (Manchester, England)**

Source: County Surveyors Society, *Traffic Calming in Practice*, Landor Publishing, Ltd., London, England, 1994, p. 114. Reprinted with permission.

and 1993 Traffic Calming Regulations expanded the range of authorized measures to include almost any vertical or horizontal feature imaginable. The 1992 edition of *Design Bulletin 32* shifted from advocating a tree-like hierarchy of roads to a hierarchical network of traffic-calmed streets.

## Australian "Local Area Traffic Management"

Following the Buchanan model, Australia began its traffic calming efforts with street closures and conversions to one-way streets, but soon progressed beyond these measures. By the 1980's, Adelaide, Melbourne, and Sydney had full-blown "local area traffic management" programs in place, concentrating on residential streets.[12] A 1988 survey identified hundreds of speed control measures in the Sydney Metropolitan Area alone.[13]

The emphasis in Australian traffic calming shifted again in 1989, with a campaign by the Committee Against Route Twenty. This community group developed a plan offering traffic calming as an alternative to a major highway project. The plan, and the resulting publicity, drew attention to problems of higher order roadways.[14]

Today, one can find many types of traffic calming measures on Australian streets that have not yet appeared in the United States (see figure 2.5). One can also find an extraordinary number of roundabouts, almost 2,000 at last count. Australia has been a leader in the use of modern roundabouts for traffic calming and intersection control. It has also been a leader in roundabout capacity research and analysis.

## Lessons from Abroad

Having a considerable head start, Europe and Australia have much to share with the United States about traffic calming. Several trends are evident, such as the shift from volume controls to speed controls, from simple to diverse programs, and from spot to areawide treatments. These trends are just beginning to show up in the United States (see chapter 3). The advantage of supportive legislation is evident from the European experience. U.S. traffic calm-

**Driveway Link**

**Diamond Choker**

**Angle Point**

**Impeller**

**Figure 2.5. Australian Calming Measures.**
Photo Credit: Joseph P. Perone, Melbourne, Victoria, Australia

ing is proceeding without any official sanction, to its legal detriment (see chapter 6). The Europeans have conducted several large-scale controlled demonstrations to better assess the benefits and costs of traffic calming. U.S. programs have generated before-and-after speed, volume, and collision data, but nothing equivalent in scope or rigor to the European studies (see chapter 5). Some European communities have long since concluded that traffic calming must encompass higher order roads if traffic safety, livability, and walkability are to be achieved outside isolated pockets. Given the controversies described in chapters 1, 7, and 9, a similar conclusion may never be reached in the United States.

## U.S. Beginnings

Use of street closures and traffic diverters in the United States dates back to the late 1940's or early 1950's, when Montclair, NJ, and Grand Rapids, MI, treated problem streets with these measures.[15] Berkeley, CA, was probably first to establish a full-blown program of traffic calming, when it adopted a citywide traffic management plan in 1975. Seattle, WA, may have been first to do areawide planning, when it conducted neighborhood-wide demonstrations in the early 1970's. Seattle has more experience implementing more traffic calming measures than any other community in the United States.

Seattle's early success was due, in part, to its ability to get funding in place. A $12-million bond issue for neigh-

borhood street improvements passed in 1968. Bond proceeds were used for a series of traffic calming demonstrations.

## Stevens Neighborhood Demonstration

The first demonstration, in the Stevens neighborhood, rivals in sophistication some of today's best projects. It began in 1971 and involved a 12-square-block area of gridded streets that were used as cut-through routes. Although bordering arterials had excess capacity, outsiders apparently found internal streets more convenient for certain trips. To discourage through traffic, the initial demonstration involved a series of temporary diagonal diverters constructed with 50-gallon drums. Diverters were placed at both ends of streets, creating very indirect trips for the neighborhood's own residents (see figure 2.6a). This inconvenience was corrected following a favorable neighborhood vote to modify the demonstration. Traffic circles replaced diverters at one end of each street (see figure 2.6b). A half street closure was installed, and a diagonal diverter was redesigned to permit an additional turning movement. This was Seattle's first test of what became the workhorse of its traffic calming program—the traffic circle. It was also the first test of its preferred alternative to a full street closure (i.e., a half closure that blocked traffic in one direction).

Finally, in early 1973, permanent landscaped circles and diverters were installed to replace the temporary ones. Before-and-after traffic counts showed a reduction in in-

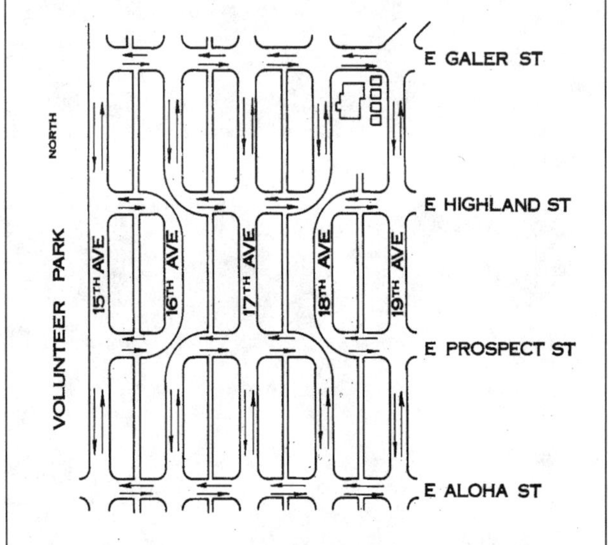


**Figure 2.6a. Original Demonstration. (Seattle's Stevens Neighborhood)**

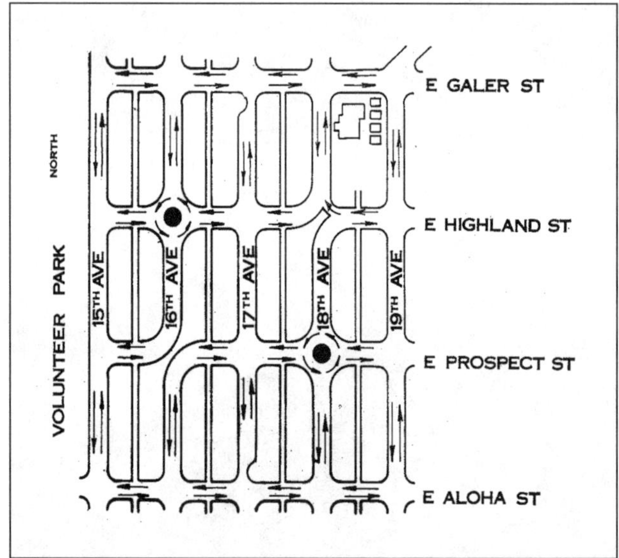


**Figure 2.6b. Permanent Installation. (Seattle's Stevens Neighborhood)**

Source: Traffic and Transportation Division, "A Study in Traffic Diversion in the Stevens Neighborhood," City of Seattle, WA, 1974.

ternal traffic volume of 56 percent. Traffic accidents, which had averaged 12 per year, fell to zero during the 2 years of the demonstration. A follow-up survey of residents found general satisfaction with the treatment.

Serious concern was raised by the Seattle Fire Department. Emergency response would be affected, particularly by the one full diagonal diverter. The solution was to place fire hydrants on each side of that diverter and design it to be traversable by emergency vehicles (see figure 2.7).

## Lessons from Seattle

This early demonstration illustrates the wisdom of several practices:

- Testing complex areawide treatments before implementing them permanently
- Assessing public support for the treatment
- Conducting before-and-after studies of traffic impacts
- Including traffic accidents among the impacts studied

- Working with emergency services to address their concerns
- Opting for the most conservative designs that will do the job

Seattle's selective replacement of volume controls (diagonal diverters) with speed controls (traffic circles) was particularly enlightened for its time.

## Other Early Programs

Seattle and Berkeley were followed by other communities. Most experimented with traffic calming measures in an isolated case or two before establishing formal programs. Indeed, it was the citywide demand created by these isolated examples that prompted the creation of full-blown programs. The communities in table 2.1 were among the first to establish programs. Communities that experimented with street closures, diverters, or other measures but stopped at that—and there were many such places—are not listed.[16]

**Traffic Circle**

**Half Closure**

**Truncated Diverter**

**Traversable Diverter**

**Figure 2.7. Early Innovations in the Stevens Neighborhood. (Seattle, WA)**

**Table 2.1. Approximate Start Dates of Other Early U.S. Traffic Calming Initiatives.**

| Community | Year |
|---|---|
| Austin, TX | 1986 |
| Bellevue, WA | 1985 |
| Charlotte, NC | 1978 |
| Eugene, OR | 1974 |
| Gainesville, FL | 1984 |
| Montgomery County, MD | 1978 |
| Portland, OR | 1984 |
| San Jose, CA | 1978 |

## Endnotes

1. For a general history of European traffic calming, see K. Kjemtrup and L. Herrstedt, "Speed Management and Traffic Calming in Europe: A Historical View," *Accident Analysis & Prevention,* Vol. 24, 1992, pp. 57–65; A. Clarke and M.J. Dornfeld, *National Bicycling and Walking Study: Case Study No. 19, Traffic Calming, Auto-Restricted Zones and Other Traffic Management Techniques: Their Effects on Bicycling and Pedestrians,* Federal Highway Administration, Washington, DC, 1994, pp. 3–24; and K. Schlabbach, "Traffic Calming in Europe," *ITE Journal,* Vol. 67, July 1997, pp. 38–40.

2. For the history of Dutch traffic calming, see J.H. Kraay, "Woonerven and Other Experiments in the Netherlands," *Built Environment,* Vol. 12, 1986, pp. 20–29; R. Tolley, *Calming Traffic in Residential Areas,* Brefi Press, Brefi, England, 1990, pp. 19–27; S.T. Janssen, "Road Safety in Urban Districts: Final Results of Accident Studies in the Dutch Demonstration Projects of the 1970s," *Traffic Engineering + Control,* Vol. 32, 1991, pp. 292–296; and C. Hass-Klau et al., *Civilised Streets—A Guide to Traffic Calming, Environment & Transport Planning,* Brighton, England, 1992, pp. 103–114.

3. E. Ben-Joseph, "Changing the Residential Street Scene: Adapting the Shared Street (Woonerf) Concept to the Suburban Environment," *Journal of the American Planning Association,* Vol. 61, 1995, pp. 504–515.

4. For the history of Danish traffic calming, see Hass-Klau et al., op. cit., pp. 115–119; L. Herrstedt, "Traffic Calming Design: A Speed Management Method—Danish Experience on Environmentally Adapted Through Roads," *Accident Analysis & Prevention,* Vol. 24, 1992, pp. 3–16; and L. Herrstedt et al., *An Improved Traffic Environment—A Catalogue of Ideas,* Danish Road Directorate, Copenhagen, Denmark, 1993, pp. 11–12.

5. For the history of German traffic calming, see Hass-Klau et al., op. cit., pp. 85–102; Tolley, op. cit., pp. 29–57; P.H. Bowers, "Environmental Traffic Restraint: German Approaches to Traffic Management by Design," *Built Environment,* Vol. 12, 1986, pp. 60–73; H.H. Keller, "Environmental Traffic Restraints on Major Roads in the Federal Republic of Germany," *Built Environment,* Vol. 12, 1986, pp. 44–57; H.H. Keller, "Three Generations of Traffic Calming in the Federal Republic of Germany," Environmental Issues, PTRC Education and Research Services, Sussex, England, 1989, pp. 15–31; and R. Schnull and J. Lange, "Speed Reduction on Through Roads in Nordrhein-Westfalen," *Accident Analysis & Prevention,* Vol. 24, 1992, pp. 67–74.

6. H. Monheim, "Area-Wide Traffic Restraint: A Concept for Better Urban Transport," *Built Environment,* Vol. 12, 1986, pp. 74–82.

7. See, for example, J. Pucher and S. Clorer, "Taming the Automobile in Germany," *Transportation Quarterly,* Vol. 46, 1992, pp. 383–395.

8. C. Buchanan, *Traffic in Towns: A Study of the Long Term Problems of Traffic in Urban Areas,* Her Majesty's Stationery Office, London, England, 1963.

9. For the history of British traffic calming, see Hass-Klau et al., op. cit., pp. 61–83; Tolley, op. cit., pp. 13–18, 59–71; C. Hass-Klau, "Environmental Traffic Management in Britain—Does It Exist?" *Built Environment,* Vol. 12, 1986, pp. 7–19; and County Surveyors Society, *Traffic Calming in Practice,* Landor Publishing, London, England, 1994, p. 9.

10. J. Noble and A. Smith, *Residential Roads and Footpaths—Layout Considerations—Design Bulletin 32,* Her Majesty's Stationery Office, London, England, 1992.

11. Tolley, op. cit., p. 61.

12. For the history of Australian traffic calming, see W.B. Hagan and S.E. Amamoo, "Residential Street Management in South Australia," *ITE Journal,* Vol. 58, March 1988, pp. 35–41; R. Brindle, "Local Street Speed Management in Australia—Is It 'Traffic Calming'?" *Accident Analysis & Prevention,* Vol. 24, No. 1, 1992, pp. 29–38; and R. Brindle, "Traffic Calming in Australia—More Than Neighborhood Traffic Management," *ITE Journal,* Vol. 67, July 1997, pp. 26–31.

13. Brindle, op. cit., 1992.

14. Citizens Against Route Twenty (CART), *The Solution to Route 20 and a New Vision for Brisbane,* available from Sensible Transportation Options for People, Tigard, OR, 1989.

15. W.S. Homburger et al., *Residential Street Design and Traffic Control,* Prentice Hall, Englewood Cliffs, NJ, 1989, p. 10.

16. The original traffic calming project of the Federal Highway Administration, undertaken circa 1980, found 120 jurisdictions in North America that had taken some action to control speeding. D.T. Smith and D. Appleyard, *Improving the Residential Street Environment—Final Report,* Federal Highway Administration, Washington, DC, 1981, table 1.

# CHAPTER 3

# Toolbox of Traffic Calming Measures

In the past, ITE has used the analogy of a toolbox in its informational documents. (For congestion management, ITE published *A Toolbox for Alleviating Traffic Congestion*.[1] For traffic safety, ITE published *The Traffic Safety Toolbox*.[2]) This chapter provides a toolbox of traffic calming measures. For reasons indicated in chapter 1, traffic control devices and streetscape improvements are missing from this toolbox, as are education and enforcement activities that some communities classify as traffic calming. These other measures are defined and discussed in "Traffic Calming Impacts" (chapter 5).

## A "Simple" Matter of Choosing the Right Tools

Any job is made easier with the right tools. It is an over-simplification, but not much of one, to say that traffic calming boils down to two things:

- Identifying the nature and extent of traffic-related problems on a given street or in a given area
- Selecting and implementing cost-effective measures for solving identified problems

If cut-through traffic is the problem (as determined by traffic counts), it suggests one set of measures. If speeding is the problem (as determined by speed measurements), it suggests another set. High collision rates, crime, or urban blight may suggest a third set.

This linear (problem → solution) view of traffic calming breaks down when it runs into legal, procedural, and political constraints. These are the subjects of "Legal Authority and Liability" (chapter 6), "Emergency Response and Other Agency Concerns" (chapter 7), and "Warrants, Project Selection Procedures, and Public Involvement" (chapter 8). Here the focus is on performance.

## Effective and Ineffective Measures—San Diego, CA, Case Studies

Two case studies from San Diego—the Mira Mesa and Royal Highlands communities—illustrate effective and ineffective choices of traffic calming measures.

### Collectors in Mira Mesa

Motorists use Mira Mesa streets to travel between inland and coastal communities (figure 3.1). There are few east-west arterials in that part of San Diego, and those few had become congested enough to cause motorists to divert to alternative routes. Five residential collectors had become problematic, affected not only by high traffic volumes but also by the excessive speeds that often accompany through traffic.

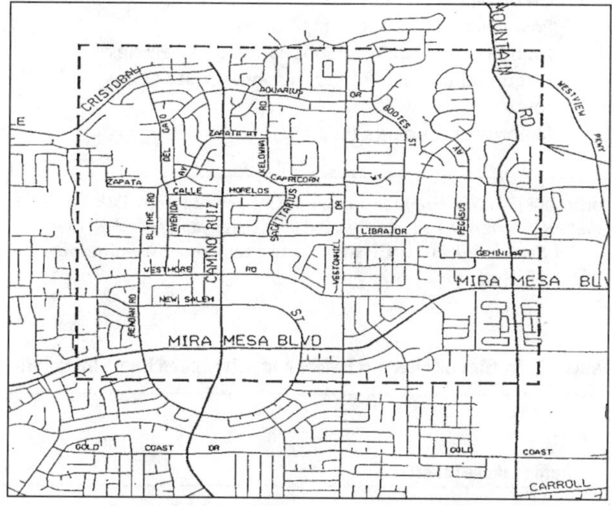


**Figure 3.1. Street Network Inviting Cut-Through Traffic. (Mira Mesa, CA)**
Source: Traffic Engineering Division, City of San Diego, CA.

At the request of the Mira Mesa Community Planning Committee, the city first tried peak-hour turn restrictions to discourage shortcutting. The restrictions did not work. Motorists found ways to circumvent them through U-turns and other maneuvers.

The city then installed speed humps. The hump profile chosen was the 12-foot parabolic hump (described later in this chapter). ITE guidelines suggest that these humps be used only on local streets, and not be used on primary emergency response routes or bus routes.[3] One or more of the ITE guidelines were violated on each collector treated with 12-foot speed humps (table 3.1).

The humps were successful in the limited sense of reducing through traffic on four collectors and reducing vehicle speeds on all five (table 3.2). They were not successful in a more general sense, however, because new problems were created. Fire response times were degraded by the treatment of Capicorn Way (see chapter 7). Traffic was diverted from collectors to parallel local streets that were less well designed to deal with it. The one local street for which before-and-after data were available experienced a 34 percent rise in traffic volume and a 9 percent increase in its 85th percentile speed (the speed below which 85 percent of vehicles travel).

## Local Streets in Royal Highlands

The Royal Highlands neighborhood, sandwiched between two arterials and a freeway in San Diego, also had a cut-through traffic problem (see figure 3.2). Traffic would cut through the neighborhood on one of four local residential streets. The first attempt at traffic calming was the installation of 12-foot speed humps. While closely spaced and severe in profile, the humps were not sufficient to counter the strong incentive to cut through the neighborhood. The main effect of the humps was to divert traffic to the local street closest to the neighborhood's northern entry point, Dellwood Street (see table 3.3). The Dellwood route offered the fewest humps end-to-end.

**Table 3.1. 12-foot Speed Hump Guidelines.**

Use only where:

- Streets classified as "local"
- No more than two travel lanes or 40-foot pavement width
- Horizontal curve of 300-foot radius or more
- Vertical curve with adequate stopping sight distance
- Grade of 8 percent or less
- Posted speed limit of 30 mph or less
- No more than 5 percent long-wheelbase vehicles
- Not on primary emergency response route or bus route
- Majority of residents support

Source: ITE Traffic Engineering Council Speed Humps Task Force, *Guidelines for the Design and Application of Speed Humps—A Recommended Practice,* Institute of Transportation Engineers, Washington, DC, 1997, pp. 8–10.

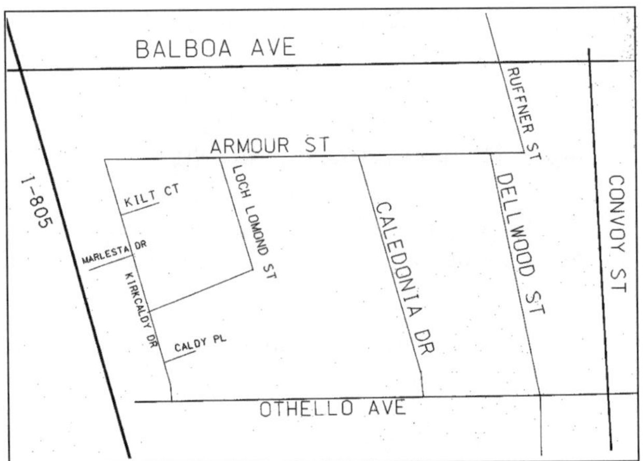


**Figure 3.2. Street Network that Once Invited Cut-Through Traffic— Royal Highlands. (San Diego, CA)**
Source: Traffic Engineering Division, City of San Diego, CA.

**Table 3.2. Traffic on Collectors Before and After Speed Hump Installation. (Mira Mesa, CA)**

| Traffic-Calmed Collector | Daily Volume (vehicles per day) | | 85th Percentile Speed (miles per hour) | |
|---|---|---|---|---|
| | Before | After | Before | After |
| Aquarius Drive | 5,940 | 3,250 | 38 | 25 |
| Avenida Del Gato | 2,960 | 1,250 | 38 | 25 |
| Bootes Street | 5,710 | 4,660 | 36 | 30 |
| Capicorn Way (Camino Ruiz–Orion Way) | 6,870 | 6,860 | 34 | 25 |
| Capicorn Way (Orion Way–Black Mountain Road) | 11,540 | 11,040 | 36 | 25 |
| Libra Drive | 5,580 | 2,660 | 38 | 27 |

Source: Traffic Engineering Division, "Mira Mesa Road Humps Analysis/Report," City of San Diego, CA, undated.

The second attempt at traffic calming was more successful. After closing the northern entry point at Armour Street (see figure 3.3), traffic volumes on all local streets fell below their initial levels (table 3.3). The neighborhood now has speed controls (which did not solve the cut-through problem) and a volume control (which apparently was effective).

## Measures Defined and Illustrated

Although most traffic calming measures have some effect on both volume and speed, they are usually classified according to their dominant effect. Full and half street closures, diverters of various types, median barriers, and forced turn islands are classified as *volume control measures*. Their primary purpose is to discourage or eliminate through traffic.

Speed humps, speed tables, raised intersections, traffic circles, chicanes, chokers, lateral shifts, and realigned intersections are classified as *speed control measures*. Their primary purpose is to slow traffic.

The pros and cons of different traffic calming measures have been cited in many reports and manuals.[4] These generalized assessments have limited relevance to specific problem streets, each being unique. See, for example, table 3.4. Rather than repeating or attempting to refine earlier assessments, this report will focus on four specific areas:

- Beginning to standardize traffic calming nomenclature
- Presenting photos of exemplary measures for illustrative purposes
- Enumerating measures used in the most innovative U.S. programs
- Identifying trends in the choice of measures as a guide to future practice

### Volume Control Measures

*Full street closures* are barriers placed across a street to close the street completely to through traffic, usually leaving only sidewalks or bicycle paths open. They are also called *cul-de-sacs* or *dead ends*. The barriers may consist of landscaped islands, walls, gates, side-by-side bollards, or

**12-foot Speed Humps**

**Street Closure**

**Figure 3.3. Traffic Calming Measures in Royal Highlands. (San Diego, CA)**

**Table 3.3. Traffic Before Humps, After Humps, and After Closure—Royal Highlands. (San Diego, CA)**

| | Vehicles Per Day | | |
|---|---|---|---|
| | **Before Speed Humps** | **After Speed Humps** | **After Street Closure** |
| Armour Street | 525 | 350 | 280 |
| Caledonia Street | 215 | 240 | 210 |
| Dellwood Street | 1,065 | 1,260 | 370 |
| Kirkcaldy Street | 1,350 | 820 | 260 |
| Lochlomond Street | 140 | 180 | 90 |
| **Total traffic within neighborhood** | 3,295 | 2,850 | 1,210 |
| **% change in total traffic** | base | −14% | − 63% |

Source: Traffic Engineering Division, City of San Diego, CA.

**Table 3.4. Generalized Assessment of Traffic Calming Measures. (Phoenix, AZ)**

| Traffic Management Device | Traffic Reduction | Speed Reduction | Noise and Pollution | Safety | Traffic Access Restrictions | Emergency Vehicle Access | Maintenance Problems | Level of Violation | Cost |
|---|---|---|---|---|---|---|---|---|---|
| Speed Humps | Possible | Limited | Increase Noise | No Documented Problems | None | Minor Problems | None | Not Applicable | Low |
| STOP Signs | Unlikely | None | Increase | Unclear | None | No Problems | None | Potentially High | Low |
| NO LEFT/RIGHT TURN Signs | Yes | None | Decrease | Improved | No Turn(s) | No Problems | Vandalism | Potentially High | Low |
| One-Way Street | Yes | None | Decrease | Improved | One Direction | One Direction | None | Low | Low |
| Chokers | Unlikely | Minor | No Change | Improved For Pedestrians | None | No Problems | Trucks Hit Curbs | Not Applicable | Moderate |
| Traffic Circle | Possible | Likely | No Change | Unclear | None | Some Constraint | Vandalism | Low | Moderate |
| Median Barrier | Yes | None | Decrease | Improved | Right Turn Only | Minor Constraint | None | Low | Moderate |
| Forced Turn Channelization | Yes | Possible | Decrease | Improved | Some | Minor Constraint | Vandalism | Potentially High | Moderate |
| Semi-Diverter | Yes | Likely | Decrease | Improved | One Direction | Minor Constraint | Vandalism | Potentially High | Moderate |
| Diagonal Diverters | Yes | Likely | Decrease | Improved | Thru Traffic | Some Constraint | Vandalism | Low | Moderate |
| Cul-de-Sac | Yes | Likely | Decrease | Improved | Total | Some Constraint | Vandalism | Low | High |

Source: Street Transportation Division, City of Phoenix, AZ.

any other obstructions that leave an opening smaller than the width of a passenger car.

Street closures are the most commonly used cure for cut-through traffic. They are also the most controversial.[5] Table 3.5 summarizes street closure policies of featured communities. Nearly all oppose closures in principle. Some no longer permit street closures, or permit them only after other measures have failed. Other communities have set up procedural barriers to discourage street closures. All featured communities worry about the effects of closures on emergency response, street network connectivity and capacity, and parallel local streets that carry diverted traffic. Yet nearly all featured communities can cite a case or two where a street was closed, as a last resort, and it was justified.

Two examples illustrate the potential problem associated with overuse of street closures. West Palm Beach, FL, was closing streets at such a rate in the Old Northwood neighborhood that the connectivity of the street network was threatened. A moratorium was placed on closures, and a neighborhood-wide plan of traffic circles, neckdowns, chokers, and speed humps was instead put in place for the remainder of the Old Northwood neighborhood and the neighborhood to the north, Northboro Park (see figure 3.4).

Ft. Lauderdale, FL, undertook numerous full street closures in the mid 1990's. The extent of the street closures was controversial enough for the city to now require two public hearings and a 65 percent resident approval rating for any measure that diverts traffic (but not for those that merely slow it down). It has been 4 years since Ft. Lauderdale's last permanent street closure. The only closures since then have been temporary measures for crime prevention (see figure 3.5).

*Half closures* are barriers that block travel in one direction for a short distance on otherwise two-way streets. They are also sometimes called *partial closures* or *one-way closures*. When two half closures are placed across from one another at an intersection, the result is a *semi-diverter*.

Half closures are the most common volume control measure after full street closures. Half closures are often used in sets to make travel through neighborhoods with gridded streets circuitous rather than direct. That is, half closures are not lined up along a border, which would preclude through movement, but instead are staggered, which leaves through movement possible but less attrac-

**Table 3.5. Sample Street Closure Policies and Procedures.**

| Community | Policies and Procedures |
| --- | --- |
| Austin, TX | Closures discouraged but not ruled out as part of neighborhood-wide plans |
| Bellevue, WA | Closures considered only on residential streets with 20 percent or more cut-through traffic and at least 3,000 vehicles per day |
| Berkeley, CA | Closures discouraged where other measures will address problem—closures and other traffic diversion schemes must be referred by city council or city manager |
| Boulder, CO | Closures discouraged but listed among program options—planning board policy against additional closures due to effect on network connectivity |
| Charlotte, NC | Closures not listed among program options—barriers occasionally erected without abandoning street right-of-way |
| Dayton, OH | Neutral |
| Eugene, OR | Special study required for closures and other volume control measures |
| Ft. Lauderdale, FL | Permanent closures discouraged—two public hearings and super-majority of resident support required—temporary closures allowed for crime prevention |
| Gainesville, FL | Closures discouraged |
| Gwinnett County, GA | Neutral |
| Howard County, MD | Unofficial ban on street closures |
| Montgomery County, MD | Closures difficult to effect under county code |
| Phoenix, AZ | Closures discouraged but listed among program options—street abandonment process inhibited by a filing fee, public hearing, and likelihood of no action—residents redirected to other options |
| Portland, OR | Closures discouraged but listed among program options |
| San Diego, CA | Closures discouraged |
| San Jose, CA | Closures discouraged |
| Sarasota, FL | Closures not listed among program options—considered only as a last resort, if an alternative route exists |
| Seattle, WA | Closures discouraged but listed among program options—larger impact area from which petition signatures must be obtained for volume controls than for speed controls |
| Tallahassee, FL | Closures discouraged—no closures planned—no formal policy |
| West Palm Beach, FL | Moratorium in effect |

Source: Interviews with staffs of traffic calming programs.

**Figure 3.4. Early Closure and Later Traffic Circle. (West Palm Beach, FL)**

**Figure 3.5. Full Street Closure for Crime Prevention. (Ft. Lauderdale, FL)**

tive than alternative routes. While usually located at intersections, half closures are sometimes located internal to blocks between residential and nonresidential land uses. Placing them there has the advantage of buffering residences from business traffic. It is analogous to placing street closures between residences and businesses, a common practice. However, a half closure at midblock is far less effective than a full closure at midblock. If blocked from entering a street entirely, drivers tend to comply with the closure. Once on a street, the strong tendency is to go around a short barrier. This has been a particular problem in Seattle, which has many half closures at midblock. According to a Seattle police officer, drivers violate half closures even when they see police cars (see figure 3.6).

**Figure 3.6. Half Closure Requiring Diligent Enforcement. (Seattle, WA)**

**Figure 3.7. Half Closures Designed for Compliance.**

Wherever half closures are located, at an intersection or midblock, effective design is the key to compliance (see figure 3.7). When drivers routinely went around narrow barriers at its intersections, Ft. Lauderdale built a half closure that extended 30 feet upstream of an intersection. Drivers are reluctant to travel in the wrong direction for such a distance. Ft. Lauderdale also began to angle its barriers for right turns out of the neighborhood, making turns into the neighborhood awkward and threatening. Half closures elsewhere have been designed with opposing center islands to make through movements more awkward, as well as with extensive signage and markings to make prohibited movements more apparent.

Other volume control measures are much less common. **Diagonal diverters** are barriers placed diagonally across an intersection, blocking through movement. They are also called *full diverters* or *diagonal road closures.* Like half closures, diagonal diverters are usually staggered to create circuitous routes through neighborhoods. **Median barriers** are raised islands located along the centerline of a street and continuing through an intersection so as to block through movement at a cross street. They are also referred to as *median diverters* or occasionally as *island diverters.* **Forced turn islands** are raised islands that block certain movements on approaches to an intersection. They are sometimes called *forced turn channelizations, pork chops,* or in their most common incarnation, *right turn islands.* Finally, there are a few unusual measures such as *star diverters* and *truncated diagonal diverters.*

Because of perennial concerns about traffic being diverted from streets that are calmed to parallel streets that are not, less restrictive forms of volume control are increasingly favored over the more restrictive full street closures. However, less restrictive forms are more easily violated, as when motorists drive around forced turn islands.

## Gallery of Volume Control Measures

To help readers picture the various volume control measures, line drawings and photographs are provided on the following seven pages. The line drawings were adapted from the Boulder, CO, *Neighborhood Traffic Mitigation Program Toolkit.*[6] The photographs were chosen to illustrate a range of design options.

# FULL CLOSURES
## (cul-de-sacs, dead ends)

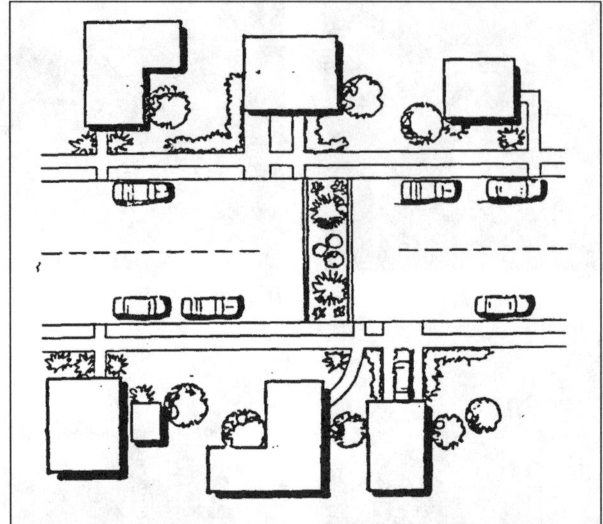

Berkeley, CA

Palo Alto, CA

Gainesville, FL

Coral Gables, FL

# HALF CLOSURES
## (partial closures, one-way closures)

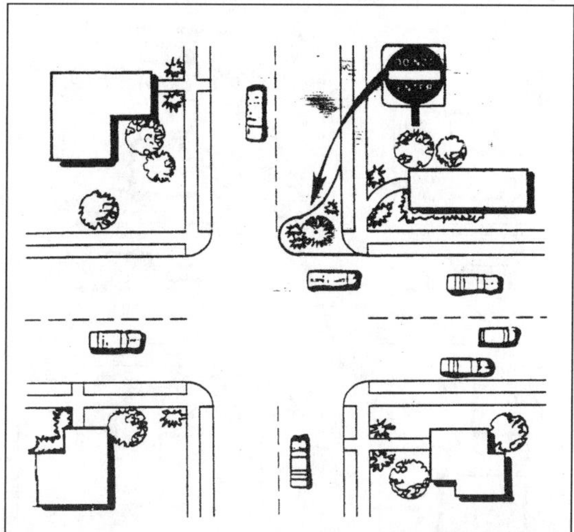

San Jose, CA

Bellevue, WA

Eugene, OR

Phoenix, AZ

# SEMI-DIVERTERS

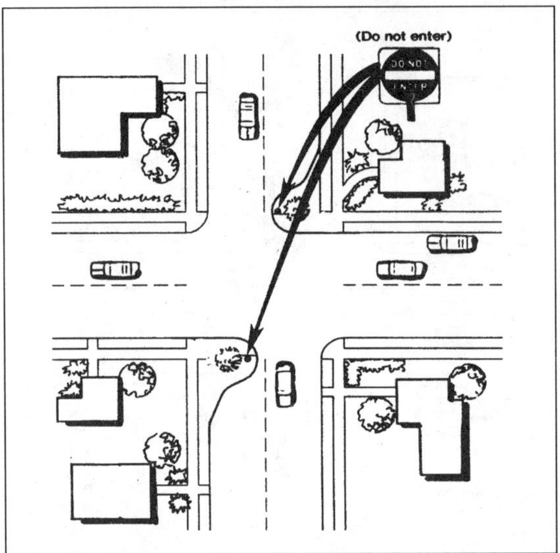

Sarasota, FL

Gainesville, FL

# DIAGONAL DIVERTERS
## (full diverters, diagonal road closures)

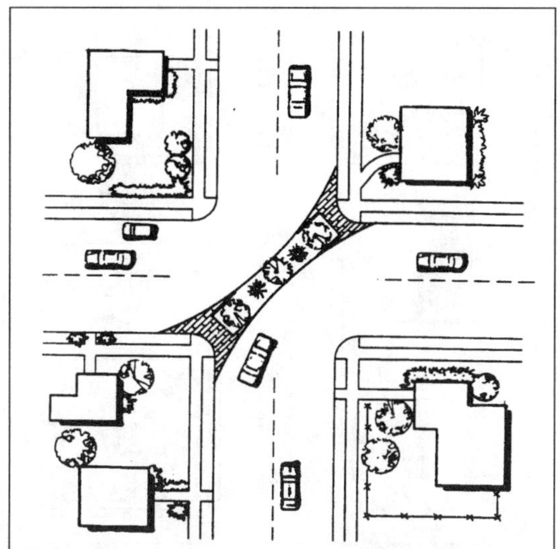

Ft. Lauderdale, FL

Boulder, CO

Berkeley, CA

Seattle, WA

# MEDIAN BARRIERS
## (median diverters, forced turn islands, island diverters)

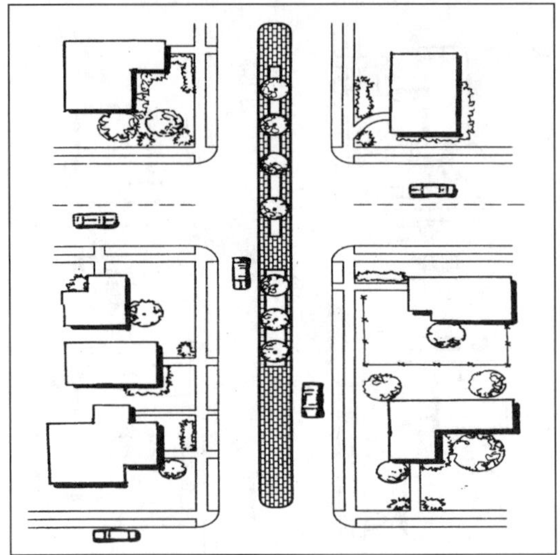

San Diego, CA

Phoenix, AZ

Montgomery County, MD

Berkeley, CA

# FORCED TURN ISLANDS
## (forced turn channelizations, pork chops, right turn islands)

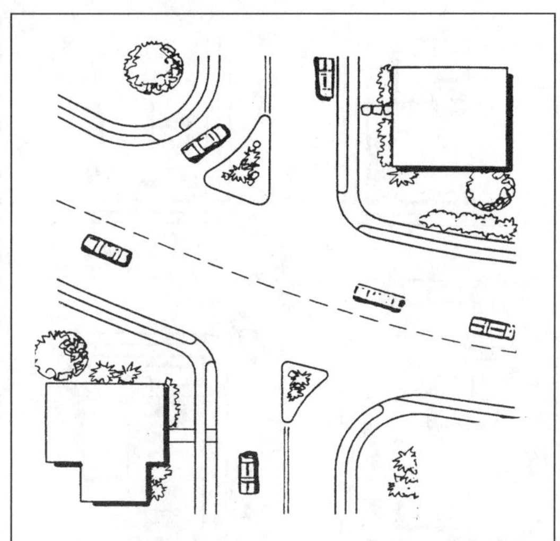

Orlando, FL

Phoenix, AZ

San Jose, CA

Montgomery County, MD

# OTHER VOLUME CONTROL MEASURES
## (various names and designs)

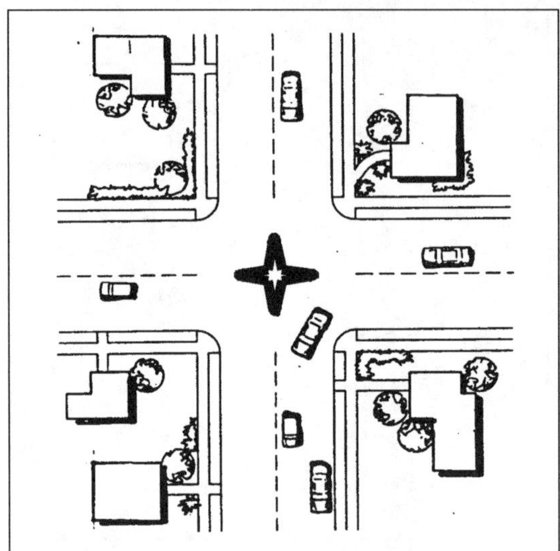

**Star Diverter. (Seattle, WA)**

**One Way–Two Way. (Boulder, CO)**

**Truncated Diagonal Diverter. (Seattle, WA)**

**One Way–Two Way. (Montgomery County, MD)**

## Speed Control Measures

Speed control measures are of three types: *vertical measures,* which use forces of vertical acceleration to discourage speeding; *horizontal measures,* which use forces of lateral acceleration to discourage speeding; and *narrowings,* which use a psycho-perceptive sense of enclosure to discourage speeding. Because physical forces are more compelling, vertical and horizontal devices tend to be more effective in reducing speeds. Indeed, some traffic calming programs do not even classify narrowings that maintain standard lane widths in each direction as traffic calming measures (see figure 3.8). For example, curb extensions, which shorten pedestrian crossing distances, are often classified and funded as pedestrian improvements rather than traffic calming measures.

## Vertical Measures

*Speed humps* are rounded raised areas placed across the road. They are also referred to as *road humps* and *undula-*

**Figure 3.8. Roadway Narrowings—Traffic Calming Measures?**

*tions.* The Watts profile hump, developed and tested by Britain's Transport Research Laboratory, is the most common speed control measure in the United States. ITE has a recommended practice for the design and application of speed humps.[7] Its guidelines specify a speed hump that is 12 feet long (in the direction of travel), 3 to 4 inches high, and parabolic in shape, and that has a design speed of 15 to 20 mph. It is usually constructed with a taper on each side to allow unimpeded drainage between the hump and curb. In some European countries, the space between the hump and curb is wide enough to accommodate bicycles. In the United States, this space is typically kept narrower to discourage motorists from crossing a hump with one wheel on the hump and the other in the gutter.

The 12-foot length guarantees that a passenger vehicle cannot straddle a hump, thereby reducing the likelihood of bottoming out. While humps as short as 6 to 8 feet have been tested, they tend to function more like speed bumps. Bumps produce their greatest driver discomfort at relatively low speeds. At higher speeds, the suspension quickly absorbs all impact before the vehicle body has time to react. Also at higher speeds, damage to the suspension or loss of control can result (not a problem with common humps). See "Legal Authority and Liability" (chapter 6) for more on humps versus bumps.

In a survey by the *Urban Transportation Monitor,* speed humps were rated both the "best" traffic control technique and the "worst," depending on who was responding.[8] They were rated best for their relatively low cost and their effectiveness in reducing vehicle operating speed (typically by 5 to 10 mph, if properly spaced). They were rated worst for various reasons, including appearance (see figures 3.9 and 3.10). Orlando, FL, has removed humps from two streets, and no longer considers them an option. Their appearance was believed to detract from the value of residential property. Appearance of humps can be improved with landscaped street edges and moderate marking and signage. With colored and stamped asphalt, humps may even improve on the appearance of uninterrrupted asphalt. The issue of aesthetics is covered in "Engineering and Aesthetic Issues" (chapter 4).

Liability is another issue. A 1986 survey of 407 urban traffic agencies found legal liability to be their greatest concern about speed humps.[9] Lee County and Tampa, FL, have stopped installing speed humps because of liability concerns. Until recently, Gainesville, FL, avoided speed humps at the advice of its city attorney. As shown in chapter 6, no special liability attaches to speed humps.

The rough ride caused by the 4-inch-high, 12-foot-long humps is another issue. Most communities now limit the height to 3 to 3.5 inches. The lower height is less abrupt. Several communities require an extraordinary level

**Figure 3.9. Speed Hump. (Ft. Lauderdale, FL)**

**Figure 3.10. Speed Hump. (Austin, TX)**

of neighborhood support before they will consider humps. Sacramento, CA, for example, requires majority support for other traffic calming measures, but a super-majority (two-thirds) for speed humps. The rough ride has an upside—effectiveness in slowing traffic.

The 12-foot hump is one of many hump profiles, varying in height, length, and shape. In 1992 Portland, OR, conducted field tests of different profiles. The 12-foot hump was judged too abrupt. Portland opted instead for 14-foot parabolic humps and 22-foot, flat-topped humps (called speed tables in this report).

Other profiles include a 12-foot hump with a sinusoidal rise being tested in Toronto, ON (see figure 3.11); a 30-foot rounded hump with a textured surface in Beaverton, OR; a 22-foot parabolic hump in Ft. Lauderdale; and a 10-foot rounded hump in New Castle County, DE (all of which typically have heights ranging between 3 and 3.5 inches). The sinusoidal design has long been used in Continental Europe, and the *Canadian Guide to Neighbourhood Traffic Calming* recommends this profile. At least one source expects a proliferation of hump profiles in the United States.[10]

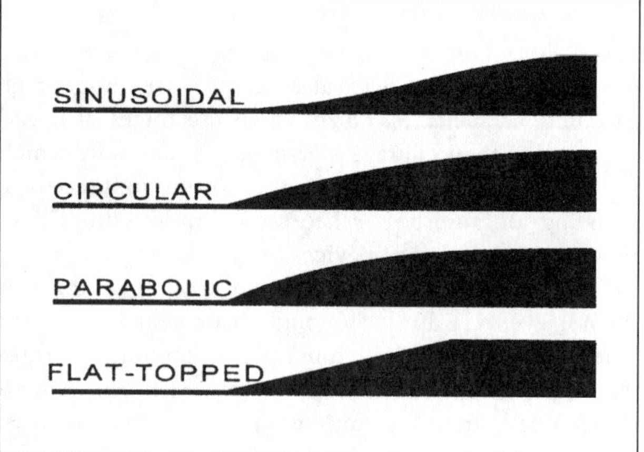


**Figure 3.11. Different Hump Profiles.**

Source: City of Toronto, "Installation of Speed Humps on City Streets," Toronto, ON, Canada, July 1997.

*Speed tables* are essentially flat-topped speed humps often constructed with brick or other textured materials on the flat section. They are also called *trapezoidal humps, speed platforms,* and, if marked for pedestrian crossing, *raised crosswalks* or *raised crossings.* Speed tables are typically long enough for the entire wheelbase of a passenger car to rest on top. Their long flat fields, plus ramps that are sometimes more gently sloped than speed humps, give speed tables higher design speeds than humps. The brick or other textured materials improve the appearance of speed tables, draw attention to them, and may enhance safety and speed reduction (a theory, as yet unproven).

The most common type of speed table is the one designed by Seminole County, FL (see figure 3.12). The Seminole County table is 3 to 4 inches high and 22 feet long in the direction of travel, with 6-foot ramps at the ends and a 10-foot field on top. It has an 85th percentile speed of 25 to 30 mph, is less jarring than the standard

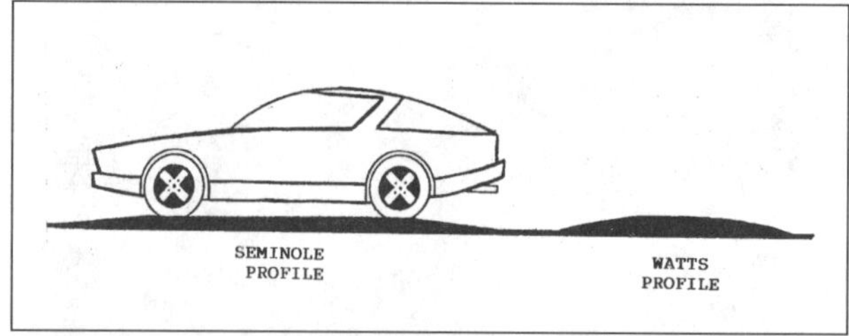


**Figure 3.12. Seminole 22-foot Speed Table versus Watts 12-foot Speed Hump.**

Source: D.A. Nicodemus, "Safe and Effective Roadway Humps —The Seminole County Profile," *Compendium of Technical Papers 61st Annual Meeting,* Institute of Transportation Engineers, Washington, DC, 1991, pp. 102-105.

12-foot hump, and is considered to be better proportioned for aesthetics.

In Florida, there seems to be a shift from 12-foot humps to 22-foot speed tables. Tallahassee has installed only 22-foot speed tables. Naples is using only this profile with a brick paver top and concrete ramps. Sarasota is so pleased with its speed table design, similar to that of Naples, that it has stopped building humps in favor of speed tables. Ft. Lauderdale now restricts 12-foot humps to streets carrying 500 to 3,000 vehicles per day, while 22-foot tables are currently used on streets carrying up to 6,000 vehicles per day.

Outside Florida, the same shift to speed tables is occurring. Among featured communities, Gwinnett County, GA, has always used only 22-foot tables. Austin, TX, now uses only 22-foot tables after experience with both tables and standard humps. Howard County, MD, favors Seminole County tables, except where limited sight distances demand lower speeds.

The shift from humps to longer speed tables is, in part, to accommodate other public agencies. Austin, Gwinnett County, and Portland are responding to the preferences of their fire departments (see chapter 7, "Emergency Response and Other Agency Concerns"). The shift could also represent attempts to move beyond local streets to collectors and even arterials, where volumes and speeds are too high for standard humps. ITE guidelines limit 12-foot humps to local streets with posted speed limits of 30 mph or less. In Portland, only 22-foot tables (with a 3-inch height) are even considered for use on collector streets.

A third reason for the shift to speed tables is their ability, where appropriately marked and extended from curb to curb, to serve as raised crosswalks. Raised crosswalks bring the street up to sidewalk level, making it pedestrian territory. Slower traffic and better pedestrian visibility add to pedestrian safety. Standard humps are too rounded and too sloped to perform this function. Speed tables are used this way in Bellevue, WA; Boulder; Eugene, OR; Montgomery County, MD; Howard County; and Tallahassee; plus several places not featured in this report.

Lest speed tables appear too good to be true, two drawbacks must be acknowledged. Speed tables are more expensive than standard humps, by about $500 per table when constructed of asphalt. Brickwork, stamped asphalt, concrete ramps, concrete headers, and other add-ons to plain asphalt further inflate the price. Sarasota's speed tables, with concrete pavers and concrete ramps, run close to $10,000 apiece. By using asphalt ramps and stamped asphalt fields, Sarasota hopes to maintain the same look at half the price (see figures 3.13 and 3.14).

Figure 3.13. $10,000 Speed Table. (Sarasota, FL)

Figure 3.14. Plain (above) and Stamped (below) Asphalt Tables with Cost Estimates. (Charlotte, NC)

Also, 22-foot speed tables may be too gentle to solve certain speeding problems. This was the conclusion in Ft. Lauderdale, after experimentation with a 22-foot speed table (with 3-inch height) in one application. A third profile was subsequently developed, a hump as long as this speed table but with a 4-inch vertical rise and a roughly parabolic profile.

Like speed humps, speed tables have been designed to different specifications. Boulder has designed its speed tables with heights of 5 to 6 inches, ramps of 7.5 to 10 feet, and fields of 18 to 23 feet. By varying dimensions, Boulder is able to achieve a desired target speed for a given application. It can also better accommodate fire trucks with long wheelbases. To accommodate transit buses, Minneapolis, MN, has designed its speed tables with 6-foot ramps and 20-foot fields. (Geometric design is dealt with in chapter 4; emergency response, in chapter 7.)

Other *vertical* traffic calming measures include raised intersections, textured pavements, and several anomalies such as raised crosswalk headers and intersection jiggle bumps. **Raised intersections** are flat raised areas covering entire intersections, with ramps on all approaches and often with brick or other textured materials on the flat section (see figure 3.15). They are also called *raised junctions, intersection humps,* or *plateaus.* They usually rise to sidewalk level, or slightly below to provide a "lip" for the visually impaired. They make entire intersections, crosswalks and all, pedestrian territory. They are particularly useful in dense urban areas, where the loss of on-street parking associated with other traffic calming measures is considered unacceptable.

**Textured pavements** are roadway surfaces paved with brick, concrete pavers, stamped asphalt, or other surface materials that produce constant small changes in vertical alignment. Though including textured pavements among vertical features may appear a stretch to some readers, one need only observe travel speeds on old cobblestone and brick streets to appreciate the rationale (see figure 3.16). A noted limitation to textured pavements such as cobblestone is that they may present difficulties for pedestrians and bicycles, particularly in wet conditions.

## Horizontal Measures

Horizontal measures achieve their speed reductions by forcing drivers around horizontal curves and by blocking long views of the road ahead. By far the most common horizontal measure is the traffic circle. **Traffic circles** are raised islands, placed in intersections, around which traffic circulates. They are sometimes called *intersection islands.* They are usually circular in shape and landscaped in their center islands, though not always. They are typically controlled by YIELD signs on all approaches.

**Figure 3.15. Raised Intersection. (West Palm Beach, FL)**

**Charleston, SC**

**Gainesville, FL**

**Figure 3.16. Cobblestone and Brick Streets that Discourage Speeding.**

Circles prevent drivers from speeding through inter-sections by impeding the straight-through movement (see figure 3.17) and forcing drivers to slow down to yield. Drivers must first turn to the right, then to the left as they pass the circle, and then back to the right again after clearing the circle.

While not as controversial as speed humps, traffic circles also raise concerns. One is the inability of large vehicles to turn around small-radius curves. One solution used in the featured communities is to make circles partially or wholly mountable by adding outer rings (called truck aprons), building conical-shaped center islands (with "lips"), or paving over the tops of islands with concrete or asphalt (as in figure 3.18). Alternatively, center islands can be designed with cutouts for buses and trucks with wide turning radii (as in figure 3.19).

Figure 3.18. Mountable Traffic Circles. (Bellevue, WA, and Howard County, MD)

Figure 3.17. Blocking the Straight-Through Movement. (Tallahassee, FL)

Figure 3.19. Traffic Circles with Cutouts for Transit Vehicles. (Seattle, WA, and Dayton, OH)

Other concerns relate to bicyclists and pedestrians. The horizontal deflection that occurs at circles may force motor vehicles into pedestrian crossing areas on cross streets or into travel paths of cyclists on main streets. Where streets are designed with separate bicycle lanes, cyclists tend to get cut off or squeezed as these lanes merge with motor vehicle lanes at traffic circles. Signs instructing motorists to yield to merging cyclists are not always heeded. It is such concerns that cause some communities to avoid traffic circles in the vicinity of parks, schools, and other pedestrian and bicyclist traffic generators.

An organized cycling group in Boulder, a mecca of cycling activity, has taken positions on traffic calming measures. Circles rank low on their list of acceptable measures (see table 3.6). More than one-third of all near-accidents reported to Boulder's "Close Call Hotline" in 1996 were at traffic circles on a particular collector, Pine Street (shown in figure 3.20). Most of those near-accidents involved bicyclists.

Yet Boulder and Pine Street are not exactly typical of the national experience. Boulder is known for its political activism and bicycle advocacy. Pine Street has high volumes of both motor vehicle and bicycle traffic (about 9,000 motor vehicles per day and an unknown but large number of cyclists). On other streets outfitted with circles, in

**Figure 3.20. Pine Street, with Circles that Were Opposed by Bicyclists. (Boulder, CO)**

Boulder and elsewhere, the occasional cyclist seems to comfortably coexist with low-volume, low-speed motor vehicle traffic.

Another concern about circles is their cost (see figure 3.21). Traffic circles generally cost several times as much as speed humps or speed tables. The added cost is due to the size of the features, use of concrete rather than asphalt, need for landscaping, and frequent need for new curb lines at corners. The cost can be brought more in line with

**Table 3.6 Boulder Bicycle Commuters' Views on Traffic Calming Measures.**

| Measure | Views |
| --- | --- |
| Street closures | Mildly in favor as long as efficient through connections are maintained for bicyclists |
| Speed humps | Strongly in favor as long as cross sections are not sloped across bike lanes |
| Raised crosswalks (speed tables) | Strongly in favor as long as cross sections are not sloped across bike lanes and crosswalks are not textured |
| Raised intersections | Opposed due to their high cost |
| Traffic circles | Opposed due to their high cost, danger to merging cyclists, and confusion for motorists—somewhat tolerable at low traffic volumes |
| Neckdowns | Mildly in favor as long as cyclists are not forced to merge with cars |
| Medians (center islands) | No consensus—opposed if cyclists are crowded together with fast-moving cars |
| STOP signs | Mildly in favor |
| Speed radar trailer | Mildly in favor |
| Photo-radar | Strongly in favor |

Source: Boulder Bicycle Commuter (BCC) meeting minutes, 2 October 1997.

costs of humps and tables by getting neighbors to supply landscape materials, using pre-cast or extruded curbs epoxied in place, and fitting circles to intersection dimensions. Also, the cost may not appear so excessive when compared with raised intersections. This is an appropriate comparison since both circles and raised intersections calm traffic on two streets at once, at the crossing point.

There are concerns about the effectiveness of traffic circles in controlling vehicle operating speeds. Seattle systematically monitors the performance of traffic circles through before-and-after speed studies. Midblock speeds seldom decline greatly, and occasionally even rise. Unlike humps and tables, circles are restricted to intersections, and intersections may be widely spaced. Their areas of influence tend to be limited to a couple hundred feet upstream and downstream of circles. The Seattle studies are a reminder that the main benefit of circles is not midblock speed reduction but intersection safety. Seattle has achieved a 95 percent reduction in intersection collisions (where most collisions occur) with traffic circles (see "Traffic Calming Impacts," chapter 5).

A final concern relating to circles was mentioned in three different featured communities. Where intersections are very tight, too tight for large vehicles to circulate counterclockwise around center islands, left turns must be made in front of center islands. Seattle was the first to allow this practice. Gainesville does as well now, and Dayton allows it selectively, adding a small sign to its circulating arrow (KEEP RIGHT) sign, exempting vehicles over 22 feet in length (see figure 3.22). With its hundreds of traffic circles and decades of experience, Seattle reports only one collision involving a left-turn maneuver. Yet such circles may create confusion for motorists when combined with large traffic circles or roundabouts that require counterclockwise circulation by all vehicles.

Related to neighborhood traffic circles are **roundabouts.** Like neighborhood traffic circles, roundabouts require traffic to circulate counterclockwise around a center island. But unlike circles, roundabouts are used on higher volume streets to allocate rights-of-way among competing movements. They are found primarily on arterial and collector streets, often substituting for traffic signals or all-way STOP signs. They are larger than neighborhood traffic circles and typically have raised splitter islands to channel approaching traffic to the right. Roundabouts are one of the alternatives for traffic calming major thoroughfares featured in "Beyond Residential Traffic Calming" (chapter 9).

There is some debate about whether roundabouts are a traffic calming measure or just another form of intersection control. Because they involve deflection at the entry point (which limits speed) and counterclockwise circula-

**Figure 3.21. Basic (above) and Enhanced (below) Circles with Cost Estimates. (Gainesville and Naples, FL)**

**Figure 3.22. KEEP RIGHT—EXCEPT VEHICLES OVER 22 FT. (Dayton, OH)**

tion around a center island (which also limits speed), they calm traffic. Roundabouts are to neighborhood traffic circles what long speed tables are to 12-foot humps— essentially the same geometric feature adapted to higher speeds and higher volumes. The stellar safety record of roundabouts is further evidence that roundabouts calm traffic.[11, 12]

Note that modern roundabouts are distinct from the large traffic circles and rotaries once common in the northeastern United States but out of favor since the 1950's (see figure 3.23). With a modern roundabout, approaching traffic must wait for a gap in the traffic flow before entering the intersection; in contrast, traffic enters an old-fashioned traffic circle at high speeds and then must merge and weave, a more hazardous operation. Also, a modern roundabout always requires yield-at-entry (yield-to-left), while some large traffic circles still operate on yield-to-entering traffic (yield-to-right) basis. Unless such circles are very large, providing long storage distances between successive entries and exits, they tend to "lock up" at high traffic volumes. Finally, modern roundabouts are more compact (e.g., 100-foot outside diameter for a single-lane roundabout) than old traffic circles and rotaries.

Other *horizontal* traffic calming measures include chicanes, realigned intersections, lateral shifts, and uncommon measures such as midblock deflector islands and half circles. **Chicanes** are curb extensions that alternate from one side of the street to the other, forming S-shaped curves. They are also referred to as *deviations, serpentines, reversing curves,* or *twists.* They are less common than circles, partly because of the high costs of curb realignment and landscaping. Also, unless well-designed, chicanes may still permit speeding by drivers cutting straight paths across the center line or testing their skills on the curves. European manuals recommend shifts in alignment of at least one-lane width, deflection angles of at least 45 degrees, and center islands to prevent drivers from taking a straight "racing line" through the feature (see figure 3.24).

A chicane-like effect can be achieved, at a fraction of the cost, by alternating on-street parking from one side of the street to the other. Parallel parking, angled parking, or a combination may be used. This treatment can be as simple as restriping to delineate parking bays. Or it can include landscaped curb extensions to beautify the street, screen unsightly parking, and create protected parking bays (see figure 3.25). Even this more expensive treatment, popular now in Main Street projects, involves less curb work than a standard chicane.

**Figure 3.23. Modern Roundabout (left) versus Old-Fashioned Traffic Circle (right). (Dallas, TX, and Sarasota, FL)**

**Figure 3.24. Driver Following a Straight "Racing Line" Through a Chicane. (Boulder, CO)**

**Figure 3.25. Chicane Created with Protected Parking Bays. (Fernadina Beach, FL)**

*Lateral shifts* are curb extensions on otherwise straight streets that cause travel lanes to bend one way and then bend back the other way to the original direction of travel. They are occasionally referred to as *axial shifts, staggerings, or jogs*. Lateral shifts, with just the right degree of deflection, are one of the few measures that have been used on collectors or even arterials, where high traffic volumes and high posted speeds preclude more abrupt measures. They are a standard measure in Europe, and have been adopted by U.S. programs—such as those in Beaverton and West Palm Beach—that wish to calm major thoroughfares. Lateral shifts are like chicanes in that they can be created at moderate cost using protected parking bays. Center islands have been added to keep drivers from cutting straight paths across the center line (see figure 3.26). For significant speed reduction, lateral shifts of at least one-lane width and angles of deflection of at least 45 degrees have been used.

*Realigned intersections* are changes in alignment that convert T-intersections with straight approaches into curving streets that meet at right angles. A former "straight-through" movement along the top of the T becomes a turning movement. Realigned intersections are sometimes called *modified intersections*. While not commonly used, they are one of the few traffic calming measures for T-intersections, because the straight top of the T makes deflection difficult to achieve, as needed for traffic circles.

## Narrowings

The final set of traffic calming measures uses roadway narrowing to achieve speed reductions. Narrowing is usually accompanied by plantings, street furniture, or other vertical elements to draw attention to the constriction and visually bound the space. *Neckdowns* are curb extensions at intersections that reduce roadway width curb to curb. They are sometimes called *nubs, bulbouts, knuckles,* or *intersection narrowings*. If coupled with crosswalks, they are referred to as *safe crosses*. Neckdowns are the most common type of street narrowing. As already noted, their effect on vehicle speeds is limited by the absence of pronounced vertical or horizontal deflection. Instead, their primary purpose is to "pedestrianize" intersections. They do this by shortening crossing distances for pedestrians and drawing attention to pedestrians via raised peninsulas (see figure 3.27). By tightening curb radii at the corner, the pedestrian crossing distance is reduced and the speeds of turning vehicles are reduced (see figures 3.28 and 3.29). This increases pedestrian comfort and safety at cross streets.

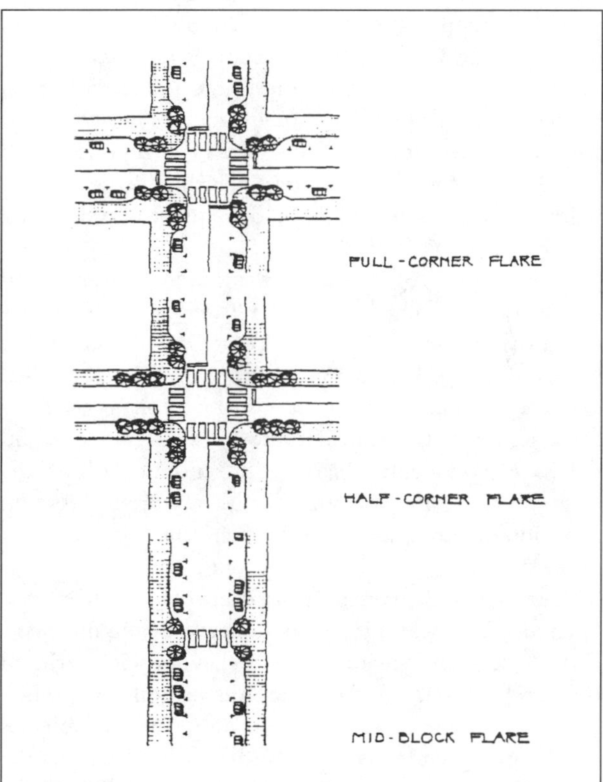


**Figure 3.27. Sidewalks Flared to Create Safe Crosses.**

Source: City of Toronto, *Urban Design Guidebook—Draft for Discussion,* Toronto, ON, Canada, 1995, p. 25.

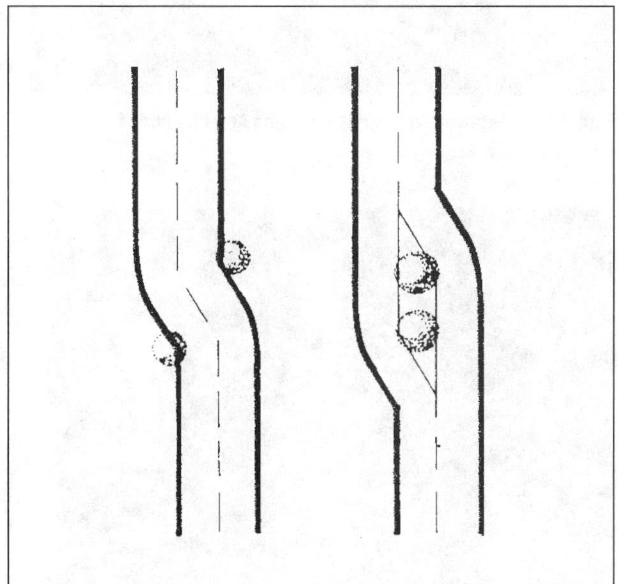

**Figure 3.26. Lateral Shifts that Encourage  (left) or Discourage (right) Shortcuts.**

Source: Devon County Council, *Traffic Calming Guidelines,* Exeter, England, 1991, p. 37.

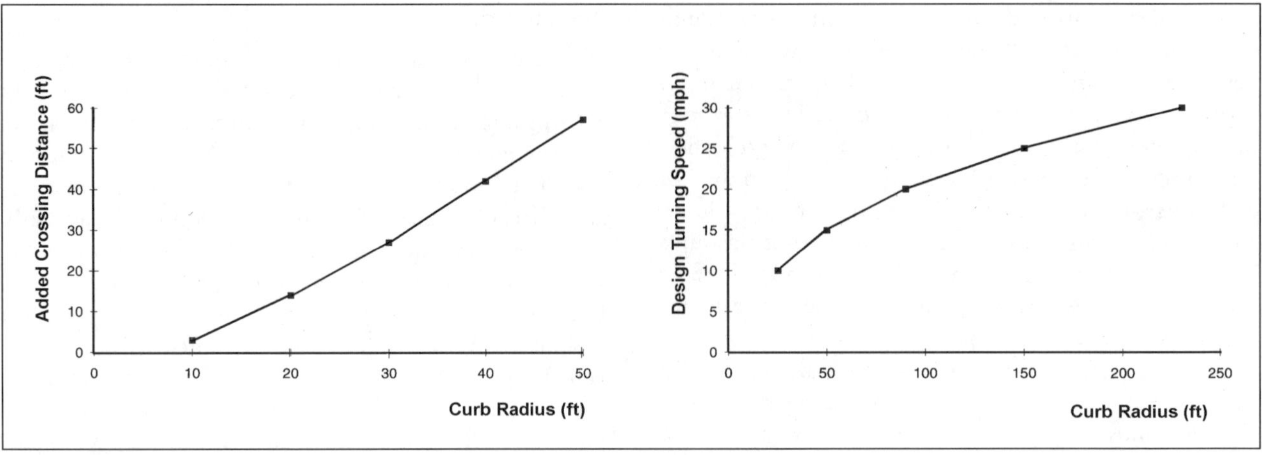

Figures 3.28 and 3.29. Crossing Distance and Turning Speed versus Curb Radius.

Source: American Association of State Highway and Transportation Officials, *A Policy on Geometric Design of Highways and Streets*, Washington, DC, Copyright 1990 [1994 (metric)], p. 714 (left) and p. 197 (right). Used by permission.

Not surprisingly, the great majority of neckdowns are part of downtown redevelopment projects. Neckdowns go hand-in-hand with on-street parking bays and crosswalks for shoppers (in "safe cross" designs). In a few places, neckdowns are used in residential settings. Howard County, for example, has redesigned some large-radius corners to reduce crossing distances from as much as 66 feet to 30 feet or less. Very few problems have been reported with neckdowns other than the relatively high cost of curb work, drainage modifications, and, frequently, landscaping or decorative pavements.

Other types of narrowings include center island narrowings and chokers. ***Center island narrowings*** are raised islands located along the centerline of a street that narrow the travel lanes at that location. They are also called *midblock medians, median slow points,* or *median chokers.* They often are nicely landscaped to provide visual amenity and neighborhood identity. Placed at the entrance to a neighborhood, and often combined with textured pavement and monument signs, they are often called *gateways* (see figure 3.30).

Center islands have been used effectively on curves. Such an island was installed on a curve where motorists had a history of speeding in a Bellevue neighborhood (see figure 3.31). Center islands are also effective when placed just downstream of intersections. Turning vehicles cannot swing wide because islands channel them to the right. The Northboro Park neighborhood of West Palm Beach has a center island that was placed at a particular intersection because cut-through drivers were making right turns at high speeds (see figure 3.32).

Center islands may be more effective when they are short interruptions to an otherwise open street cross sec-

Figure 3.30. Gateway Treatment Providing Amenity and Identity. (Ft. Lauderdale, FL)

Figure 3.31. Center Island Discouraging Speeding on a Curve. (Bellevue, WA)

**Figure 3.32. Center Island Discouraging High-Speed Turns. (West Palm Beach, FL)**

**Figure 3.33. Center Island Narrowing with a Break for a Crosswalk. (Montgomery County, MD)**

**Figure 3.34. Unsuccessful One and One-Half Lane Choker. (Sarasota, FL)**

tion, rather than long median islands that channelize traffic and separate opposing flows. The latter have been found to sometimes result in increased running speeds, while the former (perhaps because they appear as obstacles to approaching traffic) reportedly result in slower traffic.

Like other narrowings, center islands can help pedestrianize streets. Center islands provide a refuge for pedestrians crossing half way, waiting for a break in the traffic, and then crossing the other half. They are even more pedestrian-friendly when combined with crosswalks and divided to provide a crossing entirely at street level (as in figure 3.33). This minimizes the number of level changes for walkers, bicyclists, and wheelchair users.

*Chokers* are curb extensions at midblock that narrow a street by widening the sidewalk or planting strip. In different configurations, they are called *pinch points, midblock narrowings, midblock yield points,* or *constrictions*. If marked as crosswalks, they are also called *safe crosses*. Chokers can leave the street cross section with two lanes, albeit narrower lanes than before, or take it down to one lane. If the roadway is narrowed down to one lane, the lane may be parallel to the alignment or angled to the alignment. The former is called a *parallel choker,* the latter an *angled choker, twisted choker,* or *angle point*.

One-lane chokers are common in other countries; but in the United States, city attorneys, police chiefs, and residents have sometimes opposed them. They are perceived to be unsafe because opposing traffic is vying for space in a single lane. In most cases, this perception either discourages testing one-lane chokers or leads to removal of one-lane chokers after brief tests. In a few cases, it leads to a confusing compromise: a choker too wide for one vehicle but not wide enough for two. These one and one-half lane chokers leave opposing drivers uncertain whether they can squeeze through at the same time. One street in Sarasota, with one and one-half lane chokers, is being widened again to two full lanes and outfitted with speed tables instead (see figure 3.34).

## Gallery of Speed Control Measures

To help readers picture the various speed control measures just described, line drawings and photographs are provided on the following 16 pages. The line drawings were adapted from the city of Boulder's *Neighborhood Traffic Mitigation Program Toolkit*.[13] The photographs were chosen to illustrate a range of design options.

## SPEED HUMPS
### (road humps, undulations)

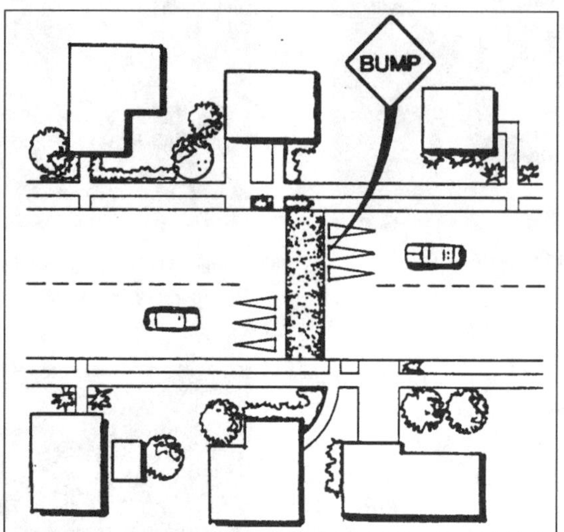

14-foot Hump. (Portland, OR)

12-foot Hump. (West Palm Beach, FL)

22-foot Hump. (Ft. Lauderdale, FL)

30-foot Hump. (Beaverton, OR)

# SPEED TABLES
## (trapezoidal humps, speed platforms)

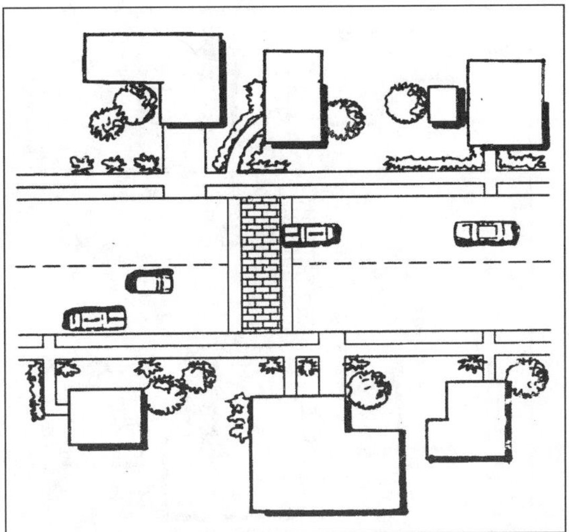

**Bellevue, WA**

**Charlotte, NC**

**Portland, OR**

**Naples, FL**

# RAISED CROSSWALKS
## (raised crossings, sidewalk extensions)

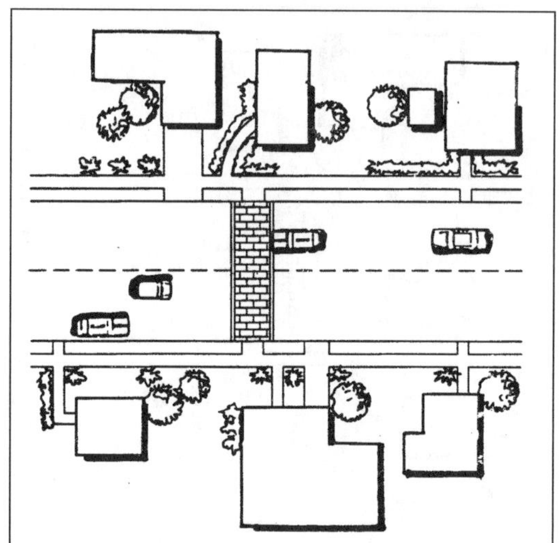

**Beaverton, OR**

**Eugene, OR**

**Montgomery County, MD**

**Tallahassee, FL**

# RAISED INTERSECTIONS
## (raised junctions, intersection humps, plateaus)

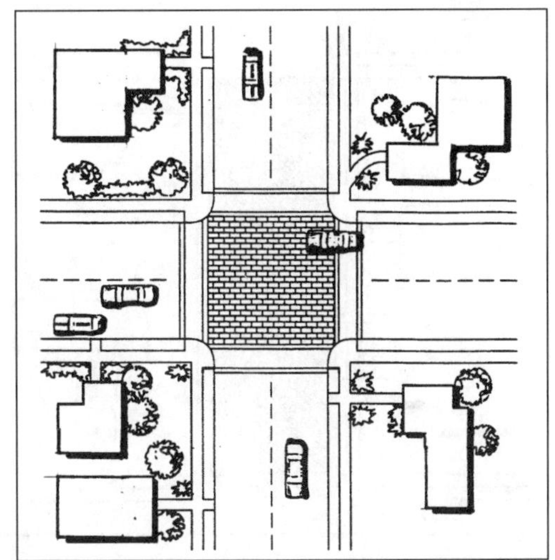

**Beaverton, OR**

**Columbia, MD**

**Cambridge, MA**

**West Palm Beach, FL**

# TEXTURED PAVEMENTS

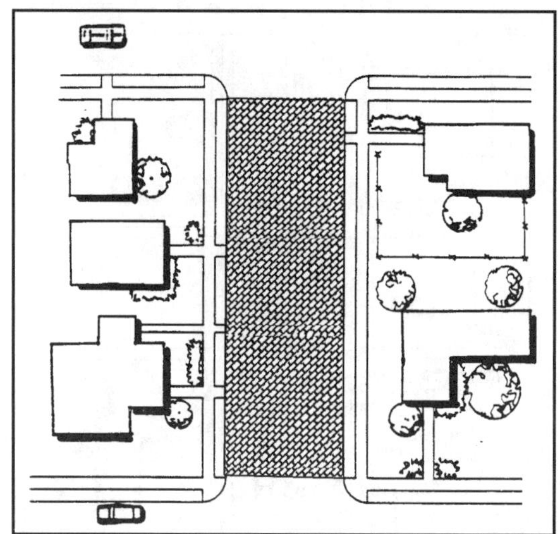

**Gainesville, FL**

**Seattle, WA**

**Winter Park, FL**

**Montgomery County, MD**

# NEIGHBORHOOD TRAFFIC CIRCLES
## *(intersection islands)*

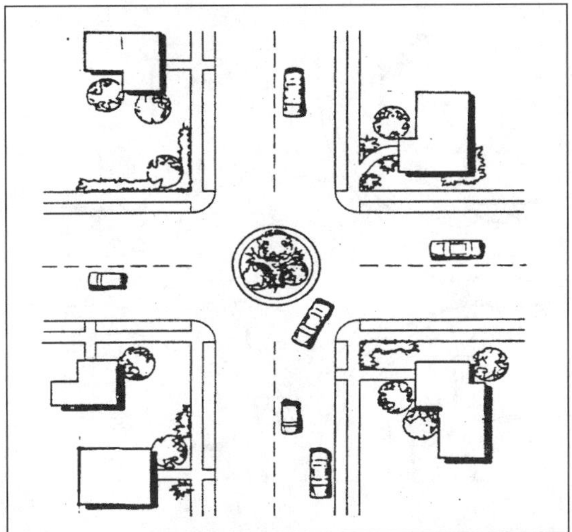

Boulder, CO

Portland, OR

San Jose, CA

Eugene, OR

# ROUNDABOUTS
## (rotaries)

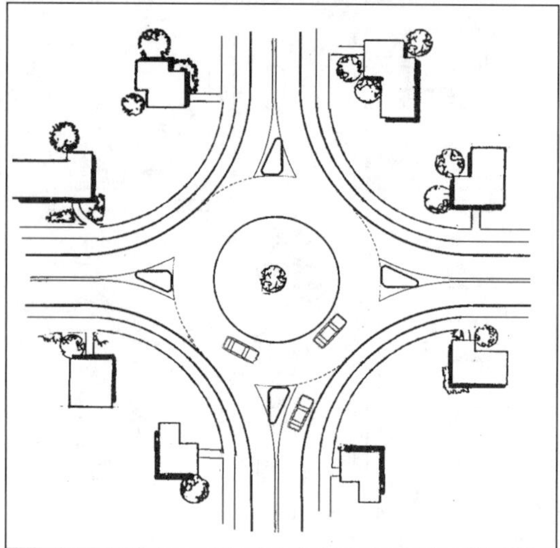

Beaverton, OR

Tallahassee, FL

West Palm Beach, FL

Las Vegas, NV

# CHICANES
## (deviations, serpentines, reversing curves, twists)

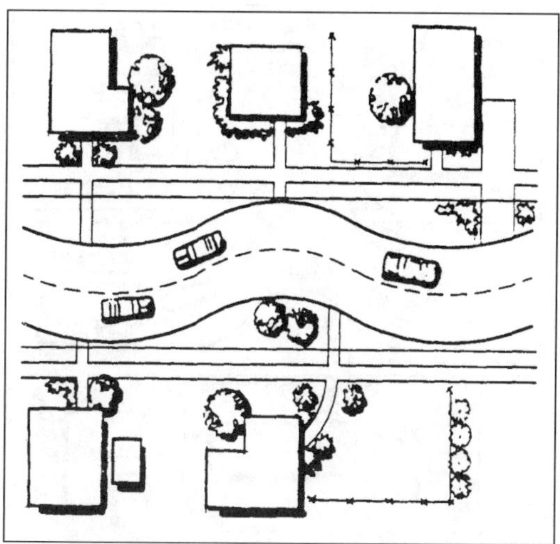

**Seattle, WA**

**Alachua, FL**

**Tallahassee, FL**

**Montgomery County, MD**

# REALIGNED INTERSECTIONS
## (modified intersections)

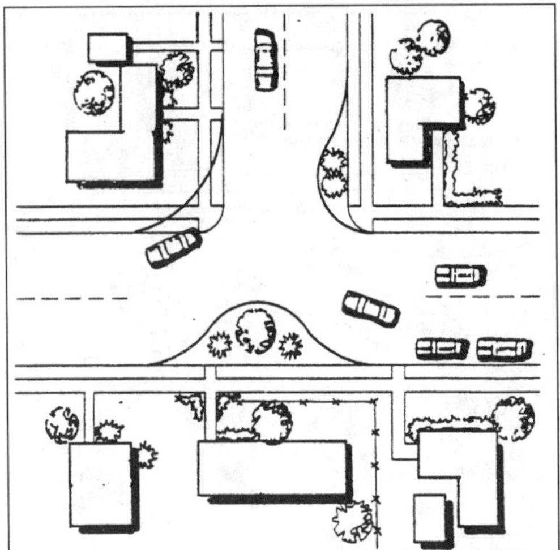

Boulder, CO

Deerfield Beach, FL

Seattle, WA

Tampa, FL

# NECKDOWNS
## (nubs, bulbouts, knuckles, intersection narrowings, corner bulges, safe crosses)

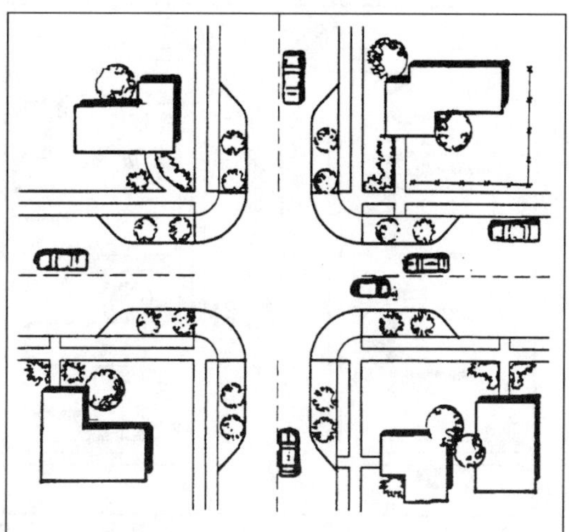

Eugene, OR

Cambridge, MA

Jacksonville, FL

Sarasota, FL

# CENTER ISLAND NARROWINGS
## (midblock medians, median slowpoints, median chokers)

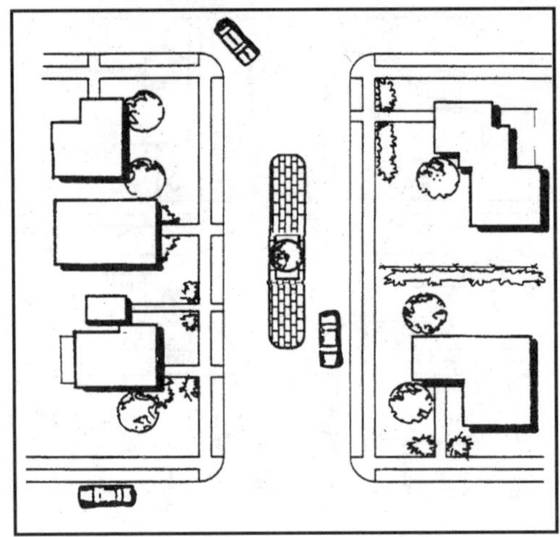

**Montgomery County, MD**

**Tallahassee, FL**

**Portland, OR**

**Ft. Lauderdale, FL**

# CHOKERS
## (pinch points, midblock narrowings, midblock yield points, constrictions)

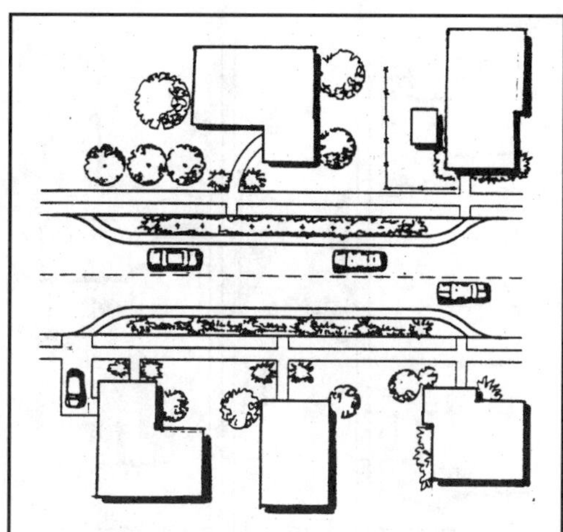

Winter Park, FL

Montgomery County, MD

Howard County, MD

Sarasota, FL

# OTHER SPEED CONTROL MEASURES
## (various names and designs)

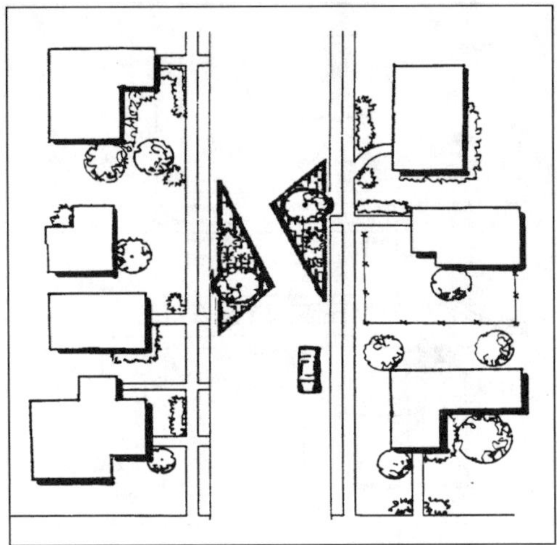

Intersection Jiggle Bumps. (Dayton, OH)

Hammerhead. (Beaverton, OR)

Angle Point. (Bellevue, WA)

Lateral Shift. (West Palm Beach, FL)

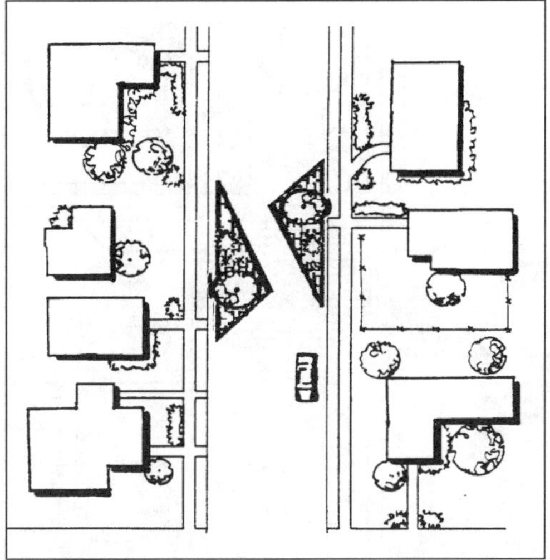

**Midblock Deflector Island. (Eugene, OR)**

**Median Choker. (San Jose, CA)**

**Split Median. (Portland, OR)**

**Half Circle. (Williamsburg, VA)**

# COMBINED MEASURES

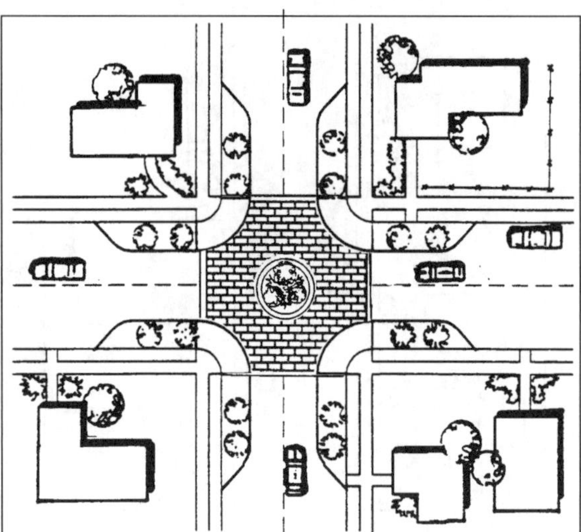

**Speed Hump with Choker. (Bellevue, WA)**

**Diverter-Closure. (San Jose, CA)**

**Center Island with Neckdown. (Eugene, OR)**

**Raised Intersection with Neckdown. (Toronto, ON, Canada)**

# COMBINED MEASURES
## (continued)

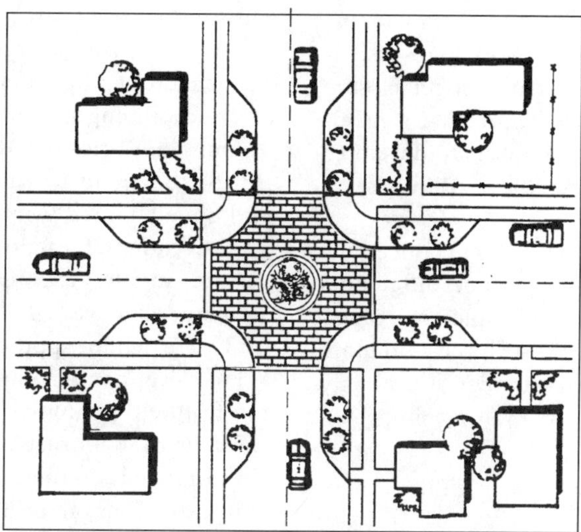

**Center Island with Chokers. (Tallahassee, FL)**

**Center Island with Tables. (Boulder, CO)**

**Raised Crosswalk with Choker. (West Palm Beach, FL)**

**Center Island with Humps. (Montgomery County, MD)**

## Cost of Traffic Calming Measures

Table 3.7 provides sample cost estimates for various traffic calming measures as reported by selected jurisdictions. These estimates cannot replace detailed cost estimates using quantities and local unit prices for work items associated with specific projects. The cost of a street closure may range from a couple thousand dollars to install a guardrail to well over a hundred thousand dollars to develop a landscaped cul-de-sac. In this sense, there are no "standard" costs.

The estimates in table 3.7 may be useful in conceptual planning, as they show order-of-magnitude differences among measures. Speed humps, for example, are consistently the least expensive option and usually cost no more than a couple thousand dollars. Costs increase quickly when measures require landscaping, drainage improvements, or land acquisition.

## Important Trends

This section describes trends in the design and application of traffic calming measures as information for use for future practice.

### From Simple to Diverse Programs

One traffic manager from a surveyed community noted a curious pattern in the spread of traffic calming across the United States. Communities in the west started with horizontal speed control measures (principally circles) and eventually added vertical measures (principally humps) to their repertoire. Communities in the east did the opposite.

This pattern reflects growing diversification as traffic calming programs mature. Programs seem to start with one or two favorite measures. Through experience, the limitations of the favorites become apparent and other measures are tried. Streets are not all the same. Neighborhood preferences are not all the same. Traffic problems being addressed by traffic calming are not all the same.

By classifying measures in broad categories—such as "humps" and "closures/diverters"—national surveys have missed this trend toward diversification. Longer humps and speed tables were developed as substitutes for 12-foot humps. Realigned intersections were devised, in part, because less expensive options such as traffic circles were not effective at T-intersections.

The search for appropriate, customized treatments has led to clever combinations of traffic calming measures by the featured communities (see table 3.8). For example, Bellevue thought that a standard traffic circle would not control speeds on the top of a T-intersection, so it added curb extensions on the approaches to achieve some horizontal deflection (see figure 3.35). Beaverton thought a choker would not control speeds in the absence of opposing traffic, so it placed a speed table in the gap between the curb extensions (see figure 3.36). Boulder thought that a chicane would not control speeds sufficiently, so it placed a speed table on the tangent (see figure 3.37). Sarasota thought that a center island narrowing would not control speeds on a long tangent section, so it added a speed table alongside (see figure 3.38).

The search for appropriate treatments has also led to combinations of measures at different points along the same street. Streets with at least two measures, and some-

**Table 3.7. Sample Cost Estimates for Individual Traffic Calming Measures.**

| Measure | Sample Cost Estimates ($) | | |
| --- | --- | --- | --- |
| | Portland, OR (1997) | Sarasota, FL (1997) | Seattle, WA (1998) |
| Speed humps | 2,000–2,500 | 2,000 | 2,000 |
| Speed tables | — | 2,500 | — |
| Raised intersections | — | 12,500 | — |
| Traffic circles | 10,000–15,000 | 3,500 | 6,000 |
| Chicanes | — | — | 14,000 |
| Chokers | 7,000–10,000 | — | — |
| Center islands | 8,000–15,000 | 5,000 | — |
| Median barriers | 10,000–20,000 | — | — |
| Half closures | 40,000 | — | 35,000 |
| Diagonal diverters | — | — | 85,000 |
| Full closures | — | — | 120,000 |

Sources: Staffs of the respective traffic calming programs.

**Table 3.8. Combined Measures in Featured Communities.**

| Community | Measures |
| --- | --- |
| Bellevue, WA | Humps and chokers<br>Circles and neckdowns |
| Boulder, CO | Tables and center islands<br>Tables and chicanes |
| Eugene, OR | Center island and neckdown |
| Howard County, MD | Tables and chokers (planned) |
| Montgomery County, MD | Center islands and humps |
| Portland, OR | Center islands and chokers |
| San Jose, CA | Diverter and closure<br>Forced turn island and half closure |
| Sarasota, FL | Center island and speed table |
| Seattle, WA | Circles and neckdowns<br>Raised intersection and neckdown<br>Circle and half closure |
| Tallahassee, FL | Center island and chokers |
| West Palm Beach, FL | Raised crosswalks and chokers<br>Raised intersections and neckdowns |

**Figure 3.35. Traffic Circle Combined with Neckdowns. (Bellevue, WA)**

**Figure 3.36. Speed Table Combined with a Choker. (Beaverton, OR)**

**Figure 3.37. Speed Table Combined with a Chicane. (Boulder, CO)**

**Figure 3.38. Speed Table Combined with a Center Island Narrowing. (Sarasota, FL)**

times many more, along their lengths include Norwood
Avenue in Boulder; Huntington Parkway in Montgomery County; Northwood Road in West Palm Beach; SW
155th Avenue in Beaverton; Berkshire Street in Cambridge, MA; and Balliol Street in Toronto. Milvia Street in
Berkeley, CA, six blocks long, has a mix of neckdowns,
chicanes, speed humps, and center islands (see figure 3.39).

## From Volume to Speed Controls

Early traffic calming initiatives in the United States relied
almost exclusively on volume control measures. The Seattle case study presented in chapter 2 is illustrative. Seattle's
original demonstration made use of diagonal diverters,
and nothing else. Only after the diverters proved unwork-
able, when paired on the same street, were two of the
diverters replaced with less restrictive traffic circles. In
Florida, early efforts were limited to street closures in West
Palm Beach; to semi-diverters in Gainesville; and to full
closures, half closures, and diagonal diverters in Ft. Lauderdale.

All of these communities, and others, now rely primarily on speed control measures. In places with traditional
street grids, like Seattle, there is justified concern about
diversion of traffic to parallel local streets. While some
diversion often accompanies speed control measures, it is
not their primary purpose.

On NW 55th Street in Seattle, a cut-through problem
was initially addressed with a street closure. When residents of parallel local streets complained of diverted traffic, the closure was replaced by a severe speed control
measure, but a speed control measure nonetheless. Installation of one-lane chicanes on NW 55th Street (and con-
currently on NW 56th Street) led to some diversion to
parallel streets. However, the effect of the chicanes was to
balance traffic volumes somewhat across parallel local
streets (see figure 3.40).

In places with curvilinear street networks, such as
Seattle's neighbor Bellevue, there is usually little need for
volume controls. Branching street hierarchies ending in
cul-de-sacs keep cut-through traffic off local streets. Yet,
even in such places, speeding can be a problem. Residential subcollectors and collectors, in particular, are long
enough, straight enough, and wide enough to accommodate excessive speeds in many cases, thereby resulting
in requests for speed control measures (see figure 3.41).

On 128th Avenue NE in Bellevue, a half closure was
replaced by a one-lane angled choker (angle point). Traffic volumes are actually lower with the speed control measure (the choker) than with the earlier volume control
measure (the half closure) because the latter was violated
so frequently (see table 3.9).

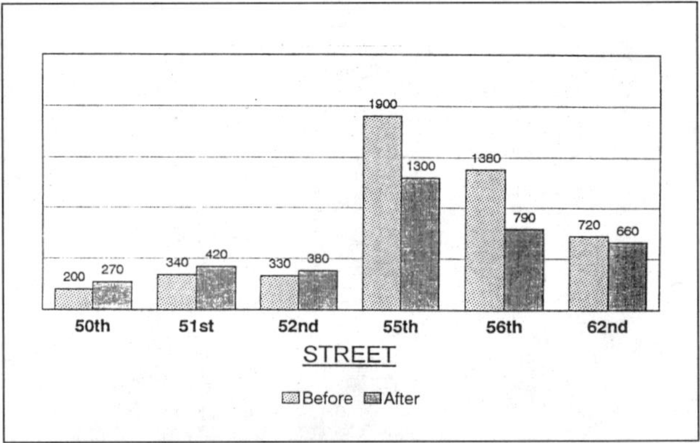


**Figure 3.40. Traffic Volumes Before and After Installation of a
One-Lane Chicane on NW 55th Street. (Seattle, WA)**

Source: Seattle Engineering Department, "Phinney Ridge
Traffic Control Project," Seattle, WA, May 1993.

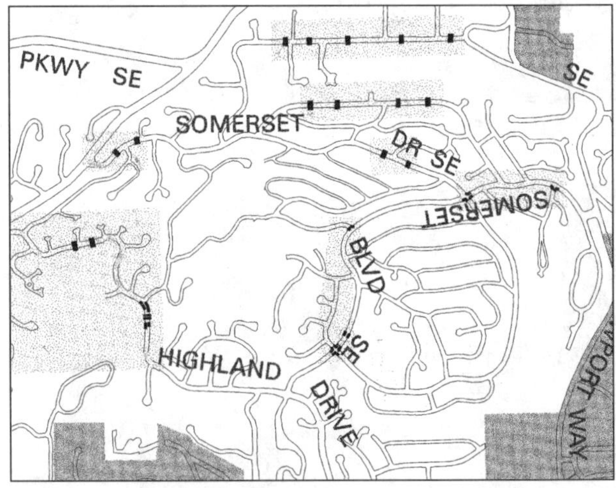


**Figure 3.41. Curvilinear Network Generating Excessive Speeds.
(Bellevue, WA)**

Source: City of Bellevue, Transportation Department, Bellevue, WA.

**Figure 3.39. Milvia "Slow" Street. (Berkeley, CA)**

**Table 3.9. Traffic Volumes Before and After Installation of a Half Closure  and a One-Lane Angled Choker. (Bellevue, WA)**

|  | Before | After Half Closure | After One-Lane Choker |
|---|---|---|---|
| Northbound traffic | 439 vpd | 91 vpd | 145 vpd |
| Southbound traffic | 331 vpd | 351 vpd | 186 vpd |
| Daily traffic volume | 770 vpd | 442 vpd | 331 vpd |
| 85th percentile speed | 31–32 mph | Not available | 27–30 mph |

vpd=vehicles per day; mph=miles per hour

Source: City of Bellevue, Transportation Department, Bellevue, WA.

## From Random to Predictable Treatments

Some early traffic calming plans had an element of randomness about them, as if testing many new ideas in a single application. This raises an issue: whether to *mix* or to *match* traffic calming measures on a given street or in a given neighborhood. One view is that each application should employ only one type of measure spaced at regular intervals. The Gwinnett County speed hump program is based on the idea that uniformity aids in the recognition and understanding of traffic calming measures. A single vertical profile is used throughout the county, always designed to the same specifications (see figure 3.42).

The alternative view is that familiarity encourages excessive speeds. Bellevue intentionally mixes and modifies measures to "keep drivers on their toes." The plan for SE 46th Way was based on two concepts (see figure 3.43). The first is to space traffic calming measures at short in-

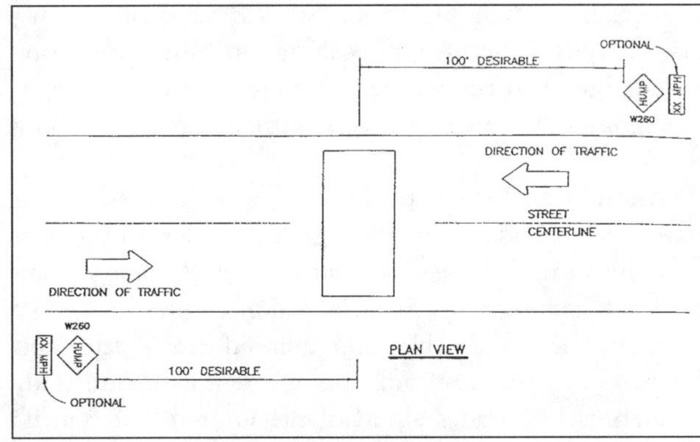

**Figure 3.42. Standard Speed Hump Plan. (Gwinnett County, GA)**

Source: County Traffic Engineer, "Standard Plan—22' Speed Hump," Gwinnett County, GA.

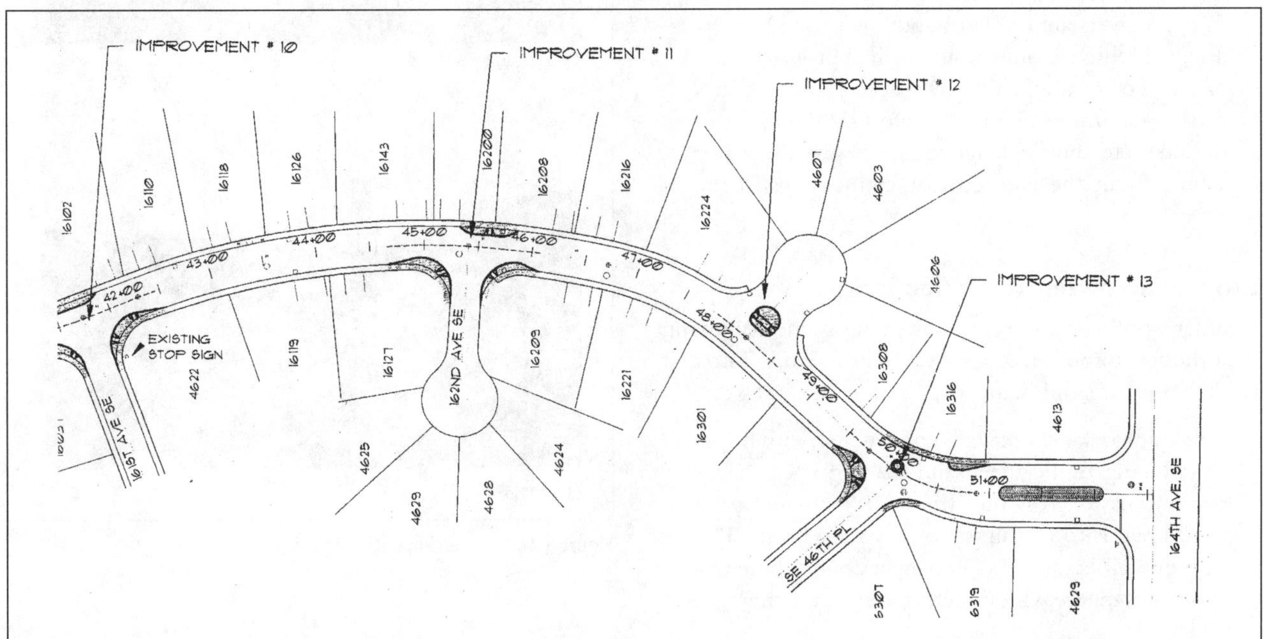

**Figure 3.43. Varied Measures Along SE 46th Way. (Bellevue, WA)**

Source: KPG, Inc., *Design Report for SE 46th Way Traffic Control Improvements*, City of Bellevue, WA, 1994.

tervals to discourage speeding between them. That was not controversial. The second concept is to vary the types of devices so that the driver cannot become accustomed to the same movement at each slow point.

In the absence of empirical evidence, an analogy to the treatment of sight distances has led some practitioners to the conclusion that predictability is preferable to surprise. Restricting sight distances may cause responsible drivers to use more caution because of the possibility of striking a pedestrian previously hidden by landscaping or hitting a vehicle pulling out on a blind curve. But such changes may invite problems with less responsible drivers. Many feel that if traffic calming measures are properly designed, forces of acceleration produced by changes in alignment should give drivers sufficient reason to slow down.

Another analogy is to traffic control devices, which have been standardized through the Federal Highway Administration's *Manual on Uniform Traffic Control Devices for Streets and Highways.* Standardization ensures that every installation is recognizable and requires the same action on the part of motorists, regardless of where it is encountered.

Denmark, decades ahead of the United States in its application of traffic calming measures, advocates "a reasonable balance between uniformity and variation."[14] The balance it supports seems slightly tipped toward uniformity.

> A certain consistency is also important as regards the technical content of the traffic calming. The speed reducing elements should be of the same kinds so that drivers are not constantly surprised by new designs, which would result in inappropriate behavior. For example, the first speed reducer that a driver encounters on his way into a local traffic area should preferably be designed so as to give the driver a hint about the nature of other measures in the area.[15]

### From Narrowing to Deflection

Boulder's traffic calming toolkit presents the following hypothetical responses to a speeding problem.[16] The first is labeled unsafe and ineffective:

> One midblock neckdown is constructed, with hopes of reducing traffic speed and making it easier for pedestrians to cross the street. Unfortunately, the neckdown is too small to actually slow traffic. The neckdown becomes a new danger zone, where cyclists must merge with vehicles traveling much faster.

An alternative response is labeled safe and effective:

> A midblock neckdown is constructed, with speed humps installed approximately 100 feet before and after. The speed humps slow the motor vehicles so that the cyclists can merge more safely.

These hypothetical situations illustrate an important point. Any narrowing that provides adequate clearance may not bring speeds down appreciably. For this reason, there seems to be a trend from straight narrowings to hybrid measures that involve both narrowing and deflection. Circles at T-intersections are being designed with curb indentations at the top of the T to make them function more like circles at cross streets. Center islands are being designed wider, with corresponding widening at the street edges, to make them function more like traffic circles. Chokers and center islands are being used in series to make them function more like chicanes (see figure 3.44).

Seattle, WA

Eugene, OR

**Figure 3.44. Introducing Deflection.**

## Spacing of Measures

Early traffic calming initiatives in the United States tended to space slow points far apart. Humps were often spaced at intervals of well over 500 feet. An early study of speed humps in Phoenix found almost no midblock speed reduction when humps were spaced so far apart.

There were also a few early cases of spacing slow points close together, to the dismay of even residents who usually support speed control measures on their streets. Traffic managers must remember that residents are also motorists and are inconvenienced by traffic calming measures many times over for every time the targeted cut-through driver is inconvenienced.

Bellevue provides good examples of both spacing problems. Every other hump originally spaced 150 feet apart on Somerset Drive had to be removed to produce a more satisfactory 300-foot spacing. Conversely, humps spaced 1,000 feet apart on SE 63rd Street had to be supplemented to bring the spacing down to 500 feet.

Figure 3.45, based on data from outside the United States, shows midpoint speeds plotted as a function of the spacing of slow points. For a midpoint speed of 20 mph, slow points were typically spaced no more than 200 to 250 feet apart. For 25 mph, the typical spacing increased to about 400 feet, and for 30 mph, typical spacing was 600 feet or greater. The types of roadways (local versus collector) and the types of traffic calming measures were not specified.

Spacing guidelines of featured communities are presented in table 3.10. They can be compared with points in figure 3.45 to see what speeds will likely result. The likely speeds are generally consistent with posted speed limits in these same communities.

Gwinnett County goes beyond basic spacing guidelines to consider sequencing. The county wants to avoid having the first hump in a series approached at high speeds. Therefore, the county positions the first hump at a point 100 to 200 feet downstream of a tight curve or a STOP sign.

## From Spot to Areawide Treatments

Traffic calming efforts in most communities begin with spot treatments of problem streets. When problems reappear at nearby locations, traffic managers often switch from volume to speed controls, or from speed controls with more diversion potential (standard humps) to those with less diversion potential (traffic circles, for example). When even the speed control measures produce diversion, program managers begin to rethink their whole approach.

The national experience suggests that traffic calming should be planned on an areawide basis, but not over such a wide area that it becomes difficult to achieve consensus on a plan. Having prepared plans for individual streets and for large subareas of the city, Portland has settled on the individual neighborhood as the optimal scale for planning purposes.

The case for areawide traffic calming is clear from several examples. In Gainesville, all-way STOP signs were installed on one neighborhood street. They created a problem by diverting cut-through traffic to another street as drivers sought to avoid the STOP signs. Many drivers also ran the STOP signs, a common problem when unwarranted STOP signs are used simply to slow traffic. The cut-through problem was solved only by closing another street to create a circuitous route through the neighborhood. Austin, Bellevue, Sarasota (see figure 3.46), Seattle, West Palm Beach, and other featured communities have experience with both spot and areawide traffic calming. Lessons from these places are reviewed in "Warrants, Project Selection Procedures, and Public Involvement" (chapter 8).

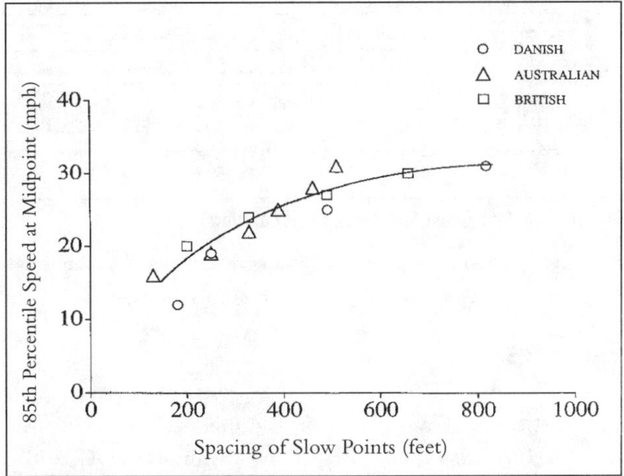


**Figure 3.45. Midpoint Speed versus Distance Between Slow Points.**

Source: R. Ewing, *Best Development Practices*, American Planning Association (in cooperation with the Urban Land Institute), Chicago, IL, 1996, p.64.

**Table 3.10. Spacing Guidelines for Speed Humps in Featured Communities.**

| Community | Spacing (feet) |
| --- | --- |
| Bellevue, WA | 200–300 |
| Berkeley, CA | 150–400 |
| Boulder, CO | 150–800 |
| Gwinnett County, GA | 350–500 |
| Howard County, MD | 400–600 |
| Montgomery County, MD | 400–600 |
| Phoenix, AZ | 500 or less |
| Portland, OR | 300–600 |

Sources: Memos and reports of respective traffic calming programs; interviews with staffs.

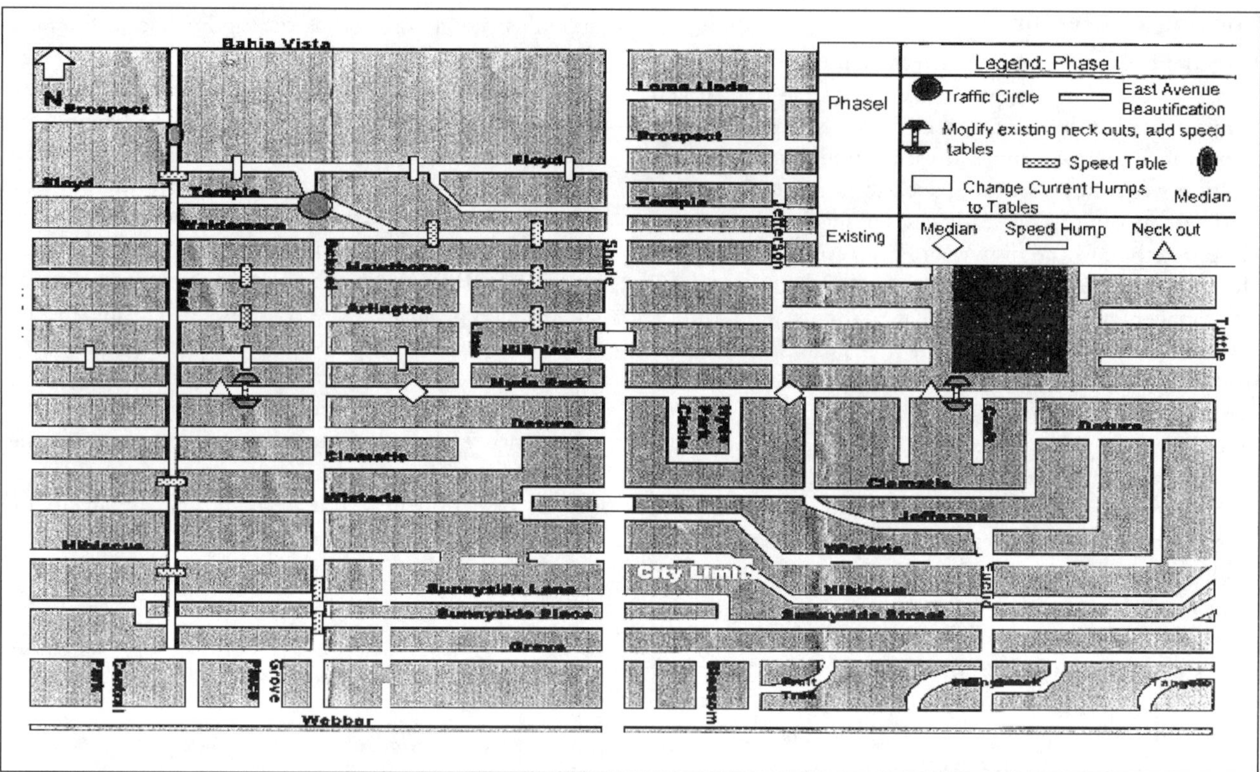

**Figure 3.46. Southeast Sarasota Traffic Calming Plan.**

Source: Engineering Department, "Southeast Sarasota Neighborhood Traffic Calming Project," City of Sarasota, FL, undated.

## Endnotes


1. Institute of Transportation Engineers (ITE), *A Toolbox for Alleviating Traffic Congestion,* Washington, DC, 1989.

2. Institute of Transportation Engineers (ITE), *The Traffic Safety Toolbox: A Primer on Traffic Safety,* Washington, DC, 1993.

3. ITE Traffic Engineering Council Speed Humps Task Force, *Guidelines for the Design and Application of Speed Humps—A Recommended Practice,* Institute of Transportation Engineers, Washington, DC, 1997.

4. Generalized assessments are available from Boulder, CO; Charlotte, NC; Madison, WI; Naples, FL ; Phoenix, AZ; Portland, OR; Salt Lake City, UT; San Buenaventura, CA; San Diego, CA; and Sunnyvale, CA. Similar published assessments include *Canadian Guide to Neighbourhood Traffic Calming,* Transportation Association of Canada, December 1998, Chapter 3; J.P. Savage, R.D. MacDonald, and J. Ewell, *A Guidebook for Residential Traffic Management,* Washington Department of Transportation, Olympia, WA, 1994, Chapter 4; G.L. Ullman, "Neighborhood Speed Control: U.S. Practices," in *Compendium of Technical Papers for the 66th ITE Annual Meeting* (Minneapolis, MN, 1996), Institute of Transportation Engineers, Washington, DC, 1996, pp. 111–115; and M.J. Wallwork, "Traffic Calming," in *The Traffic Safety Toolbox,* Institute of Transportation Engineers, Washington, DC, 1993, pp. 235–245.

5. A.J. Castellone and M.M. Hasan, "Neighborhood Traffic Management: Dade County Florida's Street Closure Experience," in *Harmonizing Transportation & Community Goals,* (ITE International Conference, Monterey, CA, 1998), Institute of Transportation Engineers, Washington, DC, 1998, CD-ROM.

6. Boulder, CO, *Neighborhood Traffic Mitigation Program Toolkit,* undated.

7. ITE Traffic Engineering Council, op. cit.

8. *Urban Transportation Monitor,* Vol. 10, May 10, 1996, pp. 10–11.

9. ITE Technical Council Committee 5B-15, "Road Bumps—Appropriate for Use on Public Streets," *ITE Journal,* Vol. 56, November 1986, pp. 18–21.

10. D. Zaidel, A.S. Hakkert, and A.H. Pistiner, "The Use of Road Humps for Moderating Speeds on Urban Streets," *Accident Analysis & Prevention,* Vol. 24, 1992, pp. 45–56.

11. G. Jacquemart, *Modern Roundabout Practice in the United States,* Synthesis of Highway Practice 264, Transportation Research Board, Washington, DC, 1998. This source provides a detailed discussion of safety and other issues related to pedestrians and bicyclists.

12. Jacquemart, op. cit., pp. 25–29; C. Schoon and J. van Minnen, "The Safety of Roundabouts in the Netherlands," *Traffic Engineering + Control,* Vol. 35, 1994, pp. 142–147; L. Ourston and J.G. Bared, "Roundabouts: A Direct Way to Safer Highways," *Public Roads,* Vol. 59, Autumn 1995, pp. 41–49; A. Flannery and T.K. Datta, "Modern Roundabouts and Traffic Crash Experience in the United States," *Transportation Research Record 1553,* 1996, pp. 103–109; M.E. Niederhauser, B.A. Collins, and E.J. Myers, "The Use of Roundabouts: Comparison of Alternate Design Solutions," in *Compendium of Technical Papers for the 67th ITE Annual Meeting* (Boston, MA, 1997), Institute of Transportation Engineers, Washington, DC, 1997, CD-ROM; and A. Flannery et al., "Safety, Delay and Capacity of Single-Lane Roundabouts in the United States," paper presented at the 77th Annual Meeting, Transportation Research Board, Washington, DC, 1998.

13. Boulder, CO, op. cit.

14. L. Herrstedt et al., *An Improved Traffic Environment— A Catalogue of Ideas,* Danish Road Directorate, Copenhagen, Denmark, 1993, p. 31.

15. Herrstedt et al., op. cit., p. 58.

16. Boulder, CO, op. cit.

# CHAPTER 4

# Engineering and Aesthetic Issues

This chapter addresses engineering issues, specifically geometrics, signing, and marking, of traffic calming measures. It also deals with aesthetic issues, including the use of landscaping and the disadvantages of temporary measures.

In one application in Bellevue, WA, the importance of aesthetics was made clear. In this example, reflective thermoplastic markings were placed on the humps themselves, and pavement legends were placed in front of the humps. Reflective raised pavement markers also lined the markings, to increase nighttime visibility.

However, in a public opinion survey conducted by the city, although the humps received high marks for speed control, they were criticized for their aesthetics. In response, Bellevue has eliminated the raised pavement markers (see figure 4.1).

In some applications, aesthetics, safety, and speed control may be complementary. Taking another Bellevue example, the city found that by combining speed humps with landscaped curb extensions, it could not only improve the appearance of humps but also draw attention to them for added safety and speed reduction (see figure 4.2). Any vertical element such as a tree or shrub is more visible from the driver's angle of vision than is a horizontal element such as a speed hump. While the enhanced hump

costs considerably more than a simple hump ($5,000 versus $1,500 for this particular application), speed reduction and neighborhood approval may also be greater with this design.

This chapter demonstrates the success of a balance between aesthetics and other objectives of traffic calming, since no traffic calming program can succeed without community support. It also explores ways in which aesthetics, safety, and speed control may be mutually supportive in traffic calming applications.

## Design Principles

### Horizontal Curvature versus Vehicle Speed

The sharper the horizontal curvature at a circle, chicane, or other slow point, the slower motorists will travel around or through it. Once the desired speed of a street is set, some slow points are designed with enough horizontal curvature to maintain something less than this speed at the points themselves, so that acceleration between slow points does not result in midpoint speeds well above the desired speed.

Graphs and tables from the American Association of State Highway and Transportation Officials' *A Policy on Geometric Design of Highways and Streets* (commonly re-

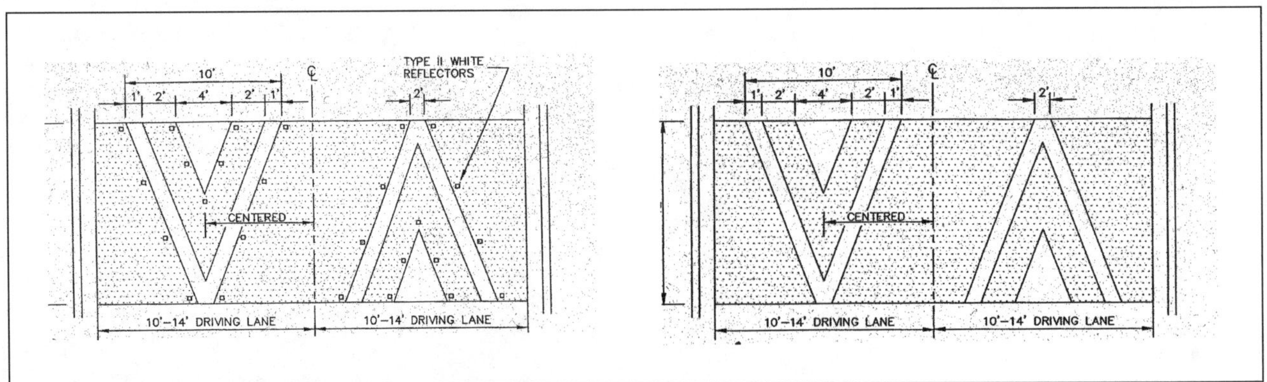


**Figure 4.1. Old (left) and New (right) Hump Marking Patterns. (Bellevue, WA)**

Source: City of Bellevue, "Speed Hump: Design, Pavement Marking, and Signing," November 1995 and December 1997.

**Figure 4.2. Speed Hump Enhanced by a Landscaped Choker. (Bellevue, WA)**

ferred to as the AASHTO Green Book) relate horizontal curvature to operating speed. All are based on the formula from mechanics

$$R = V^2/15(e + f)$$

where $R$ is the horizontal curve radius (in feet), $V$ is the speed of travel around a curve (in miles per hour), $e$ is the superelevation rate, and $f$ is the side-friction factor.[1]

Based on the design speed concept used in traditional design, $R$ represents the *minimum* horizontal radius for a defined design speed $V$, with larger radii being preferred. For traffic calming purposes, $R$ could represent the *maximum* horizontal radius, since any greater radius will fail to produce a centrifugal force sufficient to cause driver discomfort. It is this discomfort that keeps drivers from exceeding the desired speed.

Table 4.1 presents the product of sample calculations for maximum radii for horizontal curves, given desired maximum turning speeds and using AASHTO's side friction factors. These side-friction factors "are based on a tolerable degree of discomfort and provide a reasonable margin of safety against skidding under normal driving conditions in the urban environment."[2] Negligible superelevation is also assumed, as is common on low-speed urban and suburban streets. On streets with superelevation, the above equation can be used to reestimate horizontal curve radii.

The physics of vehicular movement becomes more complex when reverse curves are involved, as in a chicane, lateral shift, or traffic circle. Neither AASHTO's Green Book nor any other standard highway design reference provides much insight into comfortable speeds on such curves. So it may be necessary to treat more complex traffic calming measures to a first approximation, such as a series of simple curves.

An additional constraint on horizontal curvature is the presence of long wheelbase vehicles. All streets have at least an occasional moving van, garbage truck, or emergency vehicle negotiate their curves. Many serve schoolbuses. These vehicles can be assumed to take sharp curves at such low speeds, well below 10 mph, that a primary issue of concern is the turning radii of the vehicles and their path widths (refer to Chapter 7, "Emergency Response and Other Agency Concerns," for a discussion of other important concerns). In some cases, where traffic volumes are low, such vehicles may be able to swing into the opposing lane briefly and thereby increase the effective radius of a horizontal curve (see figure 4.3). Or they may be able to mount a curb that other smaller vehicles will go around and thereby finesse a tight curve. But in general, horizontal traffic calming measures are typically designed with radii sufficient to accommodate large vehicles.

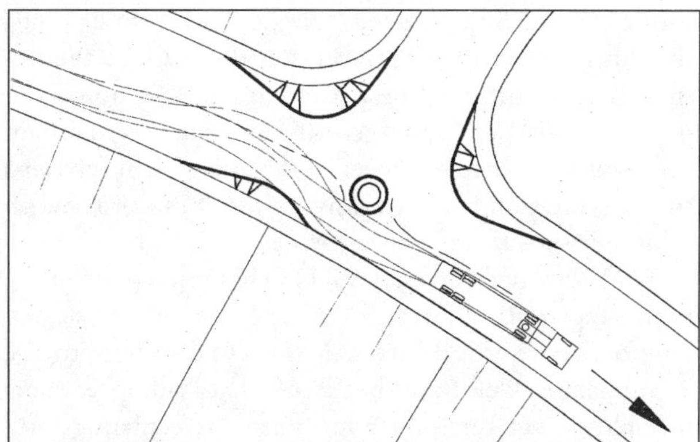

**Figure 4.3. Traffic Circle with Neckdowns Designed for a WB-40 Truck. (Bellevue, WA)**

Source: KPG, Inc., *Design Report for SE 46th Way Traffic Control Improvements*, City of Bellevue, WA, 1994.

**Table 4.1. Sample Maximum Curve Radii for Different Maximum Speeds.**

| Desired Maximum Speed (mph) | Assumed Side Friction Factor* | Assumed Superelevation | Maximum Curve Radius (feet) |
|---|---|---|---|
| 15 | 0.35 | 0.00 | 43 |
| 20 | 0.30 | 0.00 | 88 |
| 25 | 0.25 | 0.00 | 167 |
| 30 | 0.22 | 0.00 | 273 |

* Side friction factors are based on American Association of State Highway and Transportation Officials, *A Policy on Geometric Design of Highways and Streets*, Washington, DC, Copyright 1990 [1994 (metric)], Figure III-17. Used by permission. The side-friction factor at 15 mph was extrapolated from values in Table III-17.

Table 4.2, also adapted from AASHTO's Green Book, presents vehicle turning radii and other characteristics relevant to the design of traffic calming measures. A horizontal curve of 43-foot radius, which will slow passenger cars to about 15 mph (as listed in table 4.1), will accommodate all but the largest trucks if the lanes are wide enough. The corresponding radius at the centerline of the street, on the order of 50 feet, is greater than the sweep radius of every design vehicle up to a WB-96 truck (not shown in the table).

The bigger problem on such tight curves is the swept path of a truck or bus due to offtracking and vehicle overhang. A single-unit truck sweeps an area over 16 feet wide on a horizontal curve of 43-foot radius.[3] Such vehicles must either be accommodated through lane widening or allowed to sweep into the opposing lane when no traffic is approaching. On low-volume residential streets, the probability of two vehicles meeting at a slow point, and one vehicle being oversized, may be low enough to permit the latter.

## Vertical Curvature versus Vehicle Speed

As with horizontal curves, vertical curves produce forces of acceleration that are uncomfortable for drivers exceeding given operating speeds. The sharper the vertical curvature at speed humps, speed tables, and other slow points, the slower motorists will travel over them. Once the desired maximum speed of a street is set, slow points are designed with enough vertical curvature to maintain something less than this speed at the points themselves, so that acceleration between slow points does not result in midpoint speeds well above the desired speed.

For horizontal curves, AASHTO has defined the maximum side-friction factor for a "tolerable degree of discomfort." For vertical curves, AASHTO does not provide a comparable definition but states that "riding is comfortable on sag vertical curves when the centrifugal acceleration does not exceed 1 ft/sec$^2$."[4] A greater degree of vertical acceleration is tolerable on crest vertical curves (rises) than on sag vertical curves (dips) because gravitational and centrifugal forces oppose one another on crests

and combine with one another on sags. But how much greater than 1 ft/sec$^2$ should be considered acceptable, particularly when some discomfort is necessary to discourage speeding? The international traffic calming literature suggests that vertical acceleration of up to 1 g, or 32 ft/sec$^2$, is tolerable for short periods, but this much force may seem excessive on its face. So the answer may lie somewhere between these extremes.[5]

The following demonstrates the potential application of physics to speed humps. In this application, the 12-foot speed hump is used as a reference point. Whatever force of centrifugal acceleration is tolerable going over a 12-foot hump at its 85th percentile speed (the speed below which 85 percent of vehicles travel) is assumed to likewise be tolerable going over other slow points at their 85th percentile speeds. Admittedly, the physics involved when a vehicle crosses a hump are being oversimplified. At higher speeds, the suspension system collapses on contact with a hump, with front wheels rising into the wheel wells while the chassis continues on a more level path. The force of impact with the hump will tend to reduce speeds; the smaller vertical displacement will tend to increase them. It would require a much more sophisticated analysis than this one to represent these high-speed effects. Here, only centrifugal force is accounted for.

The rate of centrifugal acceleration is defined as

$$A = 2.15V^2/R$$

where $A$ is acceleration (in ft/sec$^2$), $V$ is the speed of travel over a vertical curve (in miles per hour), $R$ is the radius of the curve (in feet), and the constant is a conversion factor from miles per hour to feet per second.

A 12-foot hump with a height of 3.5 inches is equivalent to an arc of a circle with a radius of 62 feet (as determined from trigonometry). This hump (or rather, its parabolic counterpart) has an 85th percentile speed of 19 mph (see chapter 5).

Plugging these values into the preceding equation, the assumed tolerable rate of centrifugal acceleration crossing a 12-foot hump is calculated to be on the order of 12.5 ft/sec$^2$. Otherwise, drivers would go faster. Substi-

**Table 4.2. Design Vehicle Characteristics.**

| Vehicle | Width (feet) | Minimum Inside Radius (feet) | Minimum Design Turning Radius (feet) | Minimum Sweep Radius (feet) | Maximum Swept Path (feet) |
|---|---|---|---|---|---|
| Passenger car | 7 | 13.8 | 24 | 25.2 | 11.9 |
| Single-unit truck | 8.5 | 27.8 | 42 | 44.2 | 16.4 |
| Semitrailer (WB-40) | 8.5 | 18.9 | 40 | 41.4 | 22.5 |

Source: Adapted from American Association of State Highway and Transportation Officials (AASHTO), *A Policy on Geometric Design of Highways and Streets*, Washington, DC, Copyright 1990 [1994 (metric)], Tables II–1 and II–2 and Figure III–24. Used by permission.

tuting this value for $A$ in the above equation and solving for $R$, the resulting formula represents an approximation of the relationship between 85th percentile travel speed and the radius of any hump of nearly circular shape:

$$R = V^2/5.81$$

where, again, $R$ is in feet and $V$ is in mph. Or equivalently:

$$V = 2.41 \ (R)^{1/2}$$

This equation, of course, applies only up to the 85th percentile speed of the street itself. As the hump levels off, and this speed is reached, further increases in vertical radii will have no effect.

What is the value of the above relationship when addressing flat-topped slow points—speed tables, raised crossings, and raised intersections? The more the profile of a hump deviates from a purely circular shape, the less applicable the above equation will be. Crossing speed is a function of the cross-sectional area of a hump relative to its length.[6] The greater the ratio of cross-sectional area to length, the lower the design speed. A parabolic hump of the same height and length as a circular hump, for example, will have a slightly lower crossing speed. The 22-foot speed table designed by Seminole County, FL, has 6-foot ramps at both ends with the same parabolic shape as the rises of a 12-foot hump; it is as if the 12-foot hump were pulled apart and a flat section inserted in between. Yet, the 85th percentile speed of the 22-foot table is about 27 mph, 8 mph higher than that of the 12-foot hump. The greater cross-sectional area of the 22-foot table relative to the 12-foot hump is spread over a much greater length.

The effective curvature of a 22-foot table appears to be somewhere between the curvature of a 12-foot hump and the curvature of a 22-foot hump with the same overall rise of 3.5 inches. If the same overall rise were distributed over 22 feet in a rounded hump, trigonometric calculations indicate the hump would have a radius of 210 feet. From the preceding formula, such a hump would have an 85th percentile speed of 35 mph. Thus, the 22-foot speed table has a design speed exactly halfway between the design speeds of the two hump profiles to which it relates—19 mph for the 12-foot hump and 35 mph for the 22-foot hump. More field testing of flat-topped measures will be necessary to validate this hypothesis.

As with horizontal curvature, an additional constraint on vertical curvature may be the presence of trucks, buses, and other large vehicles. Such vehicles tend to have stiffer suspension systems and higher centers of gravity than do passenger cars, potentially increasing the discomfort associated with abrupt changes in vertical alignment. Their longer wheelbases mean that they can straddle short humps or tables, increasing the risk of bottoming out. Such ve-hicles will have no problem as long as they go slowly. But they cannot always go slowly, especially emergency vehicles. Emergency vehicles may be as low as 7.5 inches from axle to ground, and their wheelbases may be as long as 23 feet. While there are conflicting claims about the speeds at which emergency vehicles can safely cross 12-foot humps, and crossing speeds naturally vary by type of vehicle and status (e.g., with or without patient), 10 mph is the median value from the emergency response studies summarized in chapter 7. Plugging this value into the equation for vertical acceleration, the estimated maximum tolerable acceleration for the typical emergency vehicle is on the order of 3.5 feet/sec². The assumed maximum tolerable speed at which the typical emergency vehicle can cross a vertical slow point of radius $R$ is thus given by the expression

$$V = 1.28 \ (R)^{1/2}$$

where, again, $V$ is in mph and $R$ is in feet.

For emergency vehicles, longer speed humps and tables are preferable to short ones. Specifically, a 22-foot table will typically have a comfortable crossing speed of about 14 mph, 4 mph higher than the 12-foot hump.

## Underdesigns and Overdesigns

Howard County, MD, designed a speed table that could be used on an arterial road, reasoning that if a speed table of 3- to 4-inch height was suitable for collector streets, a table with less rise might work well on an arterial street posted at 45 mph. When flatter tables were built and tested, it was found that a 1.5-inch table was undetectable at 60 mph and a 2-inch table could just barely be felt.

Another Howard County example: When a collector street outfitted with 22-foot speed tables was resurfaced with a 1.5-inch overlay, the tables became ineffective because of inadequate deflection. The county then added 1.5 inches of asphalt to the plateaus of the tables, only to find that cars were bottoming out at 15 mph. The tables were then stripped of the 1.5-inch overlay, and a 1-inch overlay was applied in its place; only then did the tables produce the desired crossing speeds.

For speed control, there must be an abrupt (but safe) change in horizontal or vertical alignment. On site visits, a few traffic calming measures were observed to cause only modest reductions in speed. This is the case with gently sloped speed tables in Orlando, FL; a raised crosswalk that is barely detectable in Bellevue; a midblock deflector island that does not compel lateral deflection in Winter Park, FL; and a roundabout that does not compel deflection in Bradenton Beach, FL (see figure 4.4).

Yet, the change in alignment should not be *too* abrupt. The site visits also provided examples of raised crossings that seemed steep, circles that seemed tight, and so forth. A few scuff marks on ramps or tire marks on curbs may be blamed on irresponsible driving. Many suggest that too much deflection was designed into slow points. Humps in Montgomery County, MD, are now limited to a 3-inch height, subject to a tolerance of 1/8 inch. Legislative intervention was prompted by the construction of humps, with a target height of 3.5 inches, sometimes ending up over 4 inches high. Likewise, Ft. Lauderdale built some 4-inch speed tables. They proved too severe for a collector street, producing approximately the same crossing speed as a 12-foot hump. Ft. Lauderdale has settled on 3.5 inches as the optimal height for a 22-foot table.

## Geometric Design Dimensions

Using the approximate mathematical relationships derived in this chapter, traffic managers can estimate proper design dimensions for some traffic calming measures. Alternatively, they can make use of geometric designs with empirically derived 85th percentile speeds. Three vertical measures (the 12-foot hump, the 14-foot hump, and the 22-foot table) and two horizontal measures (traffic circles and roundabouts) have been so widely used in the United States that there is documentation of the effectiveness of particular geometric design dimensions.

## Speed Humps and Tables

The most common traffic calming measure in the United States, and the only one for which ITE has developed a recommended practice for its design and application, is the *12-foot hump*.[7] The 12-foot hump is parabolic in shape and has an 85th percentile speed of 15 to 20 mph. Much effort is expended to replicate this precise profile (see figure 4.5). Exact hump dimensions for three different heights are shown in figure 4.6. The 4-inch height has fallen out of favor in the United States, being too harsh for most applications. The 3- and 3.5-inch profiles are still in common use.

Limitations of the 12-foot hump, discussed in chapter 3, have led to the development of other hump profiles.

**Figure 4.4. Underdesigned Measures.**

One, Portland's *14-foot hump,* has received a measure of acceptance nationally.[8] It has the same parabolic shape and same height as the 12-foot hump, but because of its greater length in the direction of travel, it produces a gentler ride and 85th percentile speed approximately 3 mph higher than the 12-foot hump (see figure 4.7).

One speed table, the *22-foot table,* has become quite popular. It is used in 11 of the 20 featured communities, and exclusively in 3 of them. Reasons for the popularity of this profile are described in chapter 3. Having the same vertical rise as the 12-foot hump over almost twice the length, and having a flat section upon which both front and rear wheels of a passenger car can momentarily rest, the 22-foot speed table produces a gentler ride than either speed hump profile. It cannot be completely straddled by most vehicles of interest, such as single-unit trucks, which makes it less likely that they will bottom out (see figure 4.8). The 85th percentile speed of this profile has been measured to range between 25 and 30 mph. In effect, it lops off the top operating speeds without greatly affecting the average driver.

There are two alternative designs for 22-foot speed tables. The original design, from Seminole County, is modeled after the 12-foot hump. Its 6-foot ramps are the same parabolic shape as the rises of a 12-foot hump; a flat

**Figure 4.5. Use of Cutout to Replicate the 12-foot Parabolic Hump Profile. (Ft. Lauderdale, FL)**

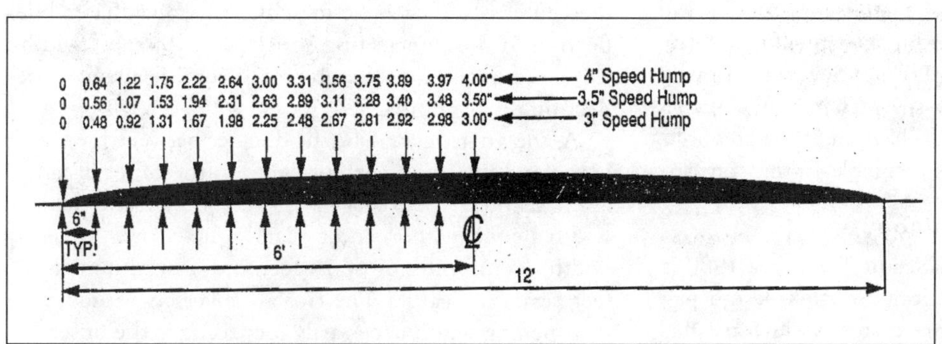


**Figure 4.6. 12-foot Speed Hump Profile.**

Source: ITE Traffic Engineering Council Speed Humps Task Force, *Guidelines for the Design and Application of Speed Humps—A Recommended Practice,* Institute of Transportation Engineers, Washington, DC, 1997, p.13.

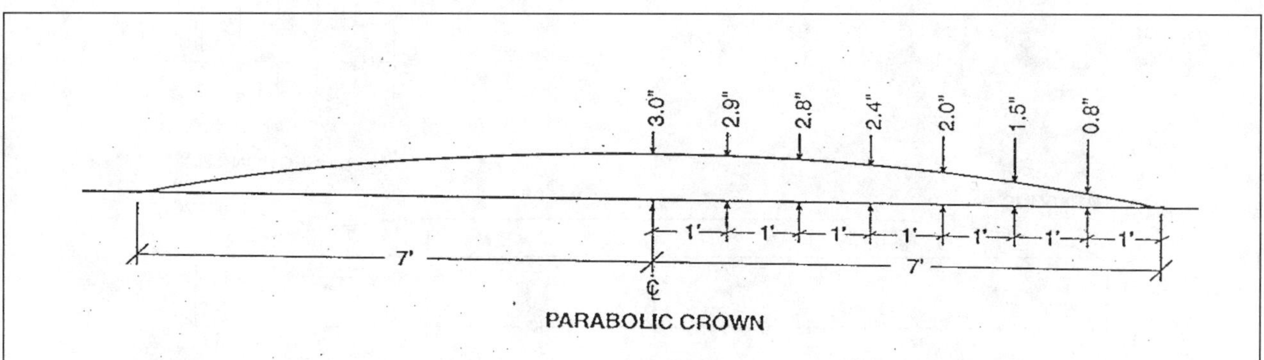


**Figure 4.7. 14-foot Speed Hump Profile. (Portland, OR)**

Source: Bureau of Traffic Management, "Traffic Manual," Portland, OR, December 1994, Chapter 11.

Figure 4.8. Bus Crossing a 22-foot Table. (Charlotte, NC)

10-foot plateau has simply been inserted between the two ramps to create a speed table (see figure 4.9). For various reasons, including aesthetics and ease of construction, Gwinnett County, GA, developed an alternative design that seems to be gaining popularity. It has straight rather than curved ramps, making it trapezoidal in shape like European and British speed tables (see figure 4.10). The Gwinnett County profile can be replicated with great consistency by laying concrete blocks laterally to form the plateau's borders, and filling in the center with asphalt (see figure 4.11). Because of its sharp change in slope at the plateau, this profile appears to have an 85th percentile speed 2 to 3 mph lower than the Seminole County profile.

## Traffic Circles and Roundabouts

A *mini-traffic circle* pioneered by Seattle, WA, circa 1980 is also built to standard specifications. Seattle's design parameters have been adopted in places such as Dayton, OH, and Madison, WI. Seattle originally designed its traffic circles so that vehicles could pass to the right of center islands when making left turns. To accommodate large vehicles, intersections had to be enlarged or center islands had to be very small. The former made circles prohibitively expensive as a result of the amount of curb work involved, whereas the latter made circles relatively ineffective in reducing speeds of passenger cars.

In response, Seattle began sizing circles to existing intersections and allowing left turns in front of center islands. Standard specifications were developed using a single-unit truck as the design vehicle. Dimensions are sufficient for such a truck to circulate halfway around the center island; larger vehicles must mount the curb on the center island to pass through the intersection. These geometrics yield an 85th percentile speed of 15 to 20 mph for passenger cars, depending on the exact geometric design. If limited to intersections with low left-turning volumes, the unconventional circulation pattern is workable.

Because circles are sized to fit intersections, they cannot have a single geometric design. Rather, standard specifications must be defined in terms of intersection geometrics. The wider the intersecting streets, the bigger the center island must be to achieve adequate lateral deflection. If the intersecting streets have different widths, the center island must be oblong to achieve adequate deflection on all approaches.

As shown in figure 4.12, the distance between the center island and the street curb projection (the offset distance) is a maximum of 5.5 feet in the Seattle standard; the lane width between the center island and corner (opening width) is a minimum of 16 feet and a maximum of 20 feet (again in Seattle). The two are inversely related, with the opening width necessarily increasing as the offset distance decreases. Applying these parameters to streets of

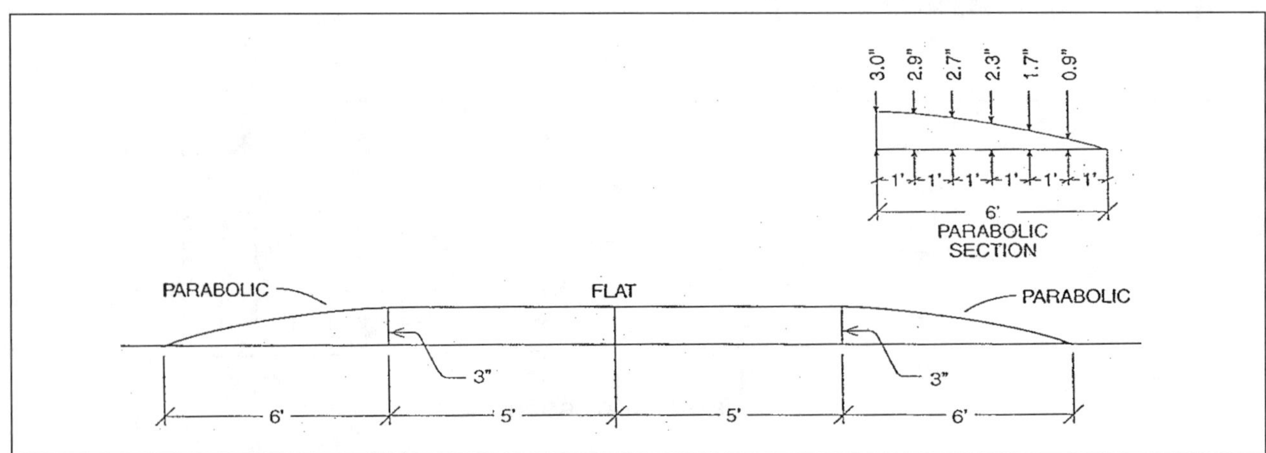


Figure 4.9. Original 22-foot Speed Table Profile. (Seminole County, FL)

Source: Bureau of Traffic Management, "Traffic Manual" Portland, OR, December 1994, Chapter 11.

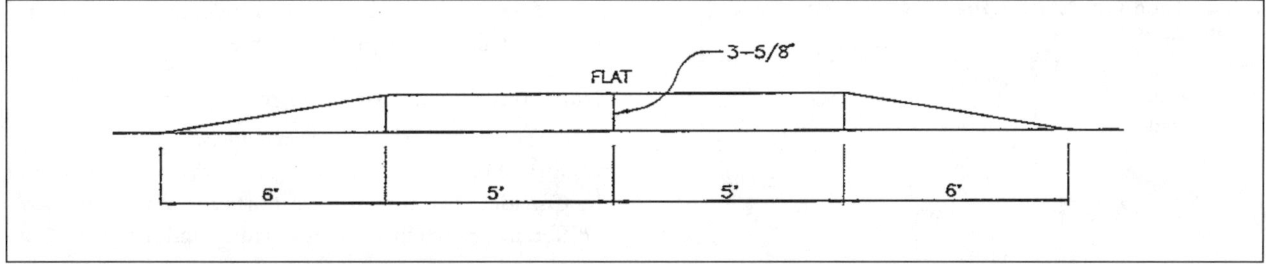


**Figure 4.10. Alternative 22-foot Speed Table Profile. (Gwinnett County, GA)**

Source: County Traffic Engineer, "Standard Plan—22' Speed Hump," Gwinnett County, GA, undated.

**Figure 4.11. Gwinnett County's Concrete Block Form—Perspective View.**

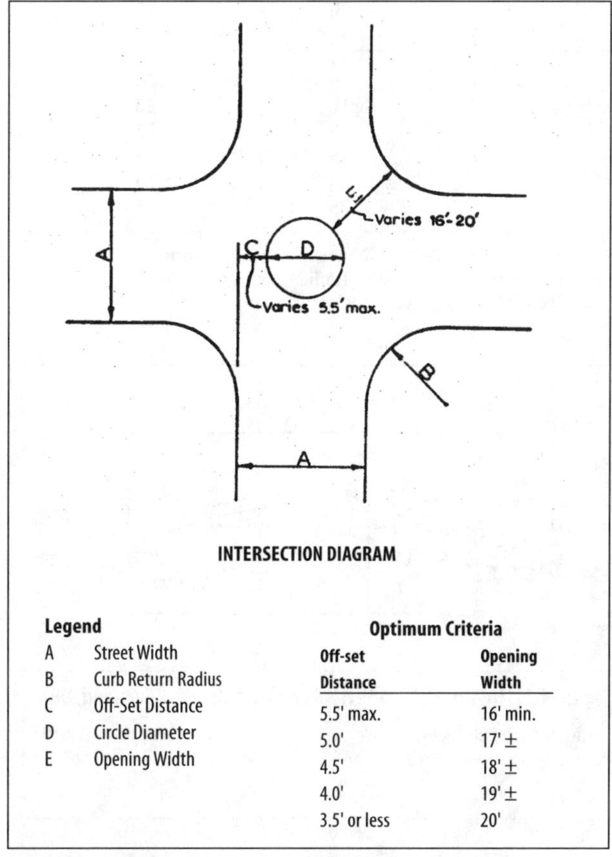


| Legend | | Optimum Criteria | |
| --- | --- | --- | --- |
| | | **Off-set** | **Opening** |
| A | Street Width | Distance | Width |
| B | Curb Return Radius | | |
| C | Off-Set Distance | 5.5' max. | 16' min. |
| D | Circle Diameter | 5.0' | 17' ± |
| E | Opening Width | 4.5' | 18' ± |
| | | 4.0' | 19' ± |
| | | 3.5' or less | 20' |

**Figure 4.12. Sample Traffic Circle Design Elements. (Seattle, WA)**

Source: City of Seattle, "Neighborhood Traffic Control Program—Citizen Requested Traffic Circle (City Funded)," Policy No. 23, Seattle, WA, 1986.

different widths and corners of different radii, circle dimensions in Seattle are as indicated in table 4.3.

Design of traffic circles has a vertical dimension as well. The pavement at intersections typically slopes away from center islands, making the islands more visible to approaching motorists and also helping with drainage. The curb on the center island is typically mountable on all but the widest streets. Mountable curbs make circles negotiable by larger vehicles, while maintaining enough lateral deflection to slow down passenger cars. A mountable curb 2 to 4 inches high is not particularly visible from the driver's angle, nor is it protective of whatever landscaping occupies the center island. Therefore, a mountable outer ring (or lip) is often coupled with a taller inner ring that makes the circle more conspicuous and protects the landscaped center. Throughout this report are photographic examples of circles designed this way. Portland's original and redesigned center islands illustrate the change in design philosophy (figures 4.13 and 4.14).

One additional horizontal measure, the *roundabout,* has been standardized through the issuance of design manuals by two State governments: Florida and Maryland (figure 4.15).[9] A national design manual is in preparation with publication of the FHWA *Roundabout Design Guide* expected in fall 1999. Readers are referred to these manuals for design guidance.

In some of the featured communities, roundabouts have been implemented on the main thoroughfares (see chapters 3 and 9). Properly designed, roundabouts force traffic to slow down as it enters an intersection. Roundabouts are often safer and more efficient than signals or all-way

| Street Width (feet) | Corner Radius (feet) | Circle Diameter (feet) |
|---|---|---|
| 24 | <12 | Reconstruct curbs |
|  | 12 | 13 |
|  | 15 | 14 |
|  | 20 | 15 |
|  | 25 | 17 |
| 30 | 10 | 19 |
|  | 12 | 20 |
|  | 15 | 20 |
|  | 20 | 22 |
|  | 25 | 24 |
| 36 | 10 | 26 |
|  | 12 | 26 |
|  | 15 | 27 |
|  | 18 | 28 |
|  | 20 | 29 |
|  | 25 | 33 |

Source: City of Seattle, "Neighborhood Traffic Control Program—Citizen Requested Traffic Circle (City Funded)," Policy No. 23, Seattle, WA, 1986.

stops when traffic volumes are moderate to heavy and flows are balanced at the cross streets.[10]

## Standard Canadian Designs

The *Canadian Guide to Neighbourhood Traffic Calming,* a product of the Transportation Association of Canada and the Canadian Institute of Transportation Engineers, takes a different approach to geometric design. Instead of attempting to relate 85th percentile speed to curvature so that professional engineers can custom-design calming measures, the Canadians have developed standard design guidelines. Their aim is to achieve a degree of uniformity throughout Canada.[11] Several standard Canadian geometric designs are reproduced in figures 4.16a through 4.16g, using metric dimensions and Canadian sign designations. In addition to these seven designs, the Canadians have standard designs for street closures, speed humps, traffic circles, and a few other measures.

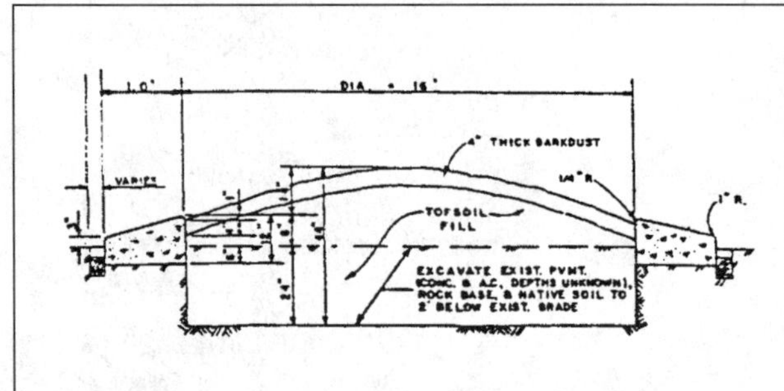

**Figure 4.13. Original Island Section and Curb Details. (Portland, OR)**

Source: Kittelson & Associates, Inc. "Peer Review Analysis—Traffic Circle Program—Portland, Oregon," 1991, p. 10.

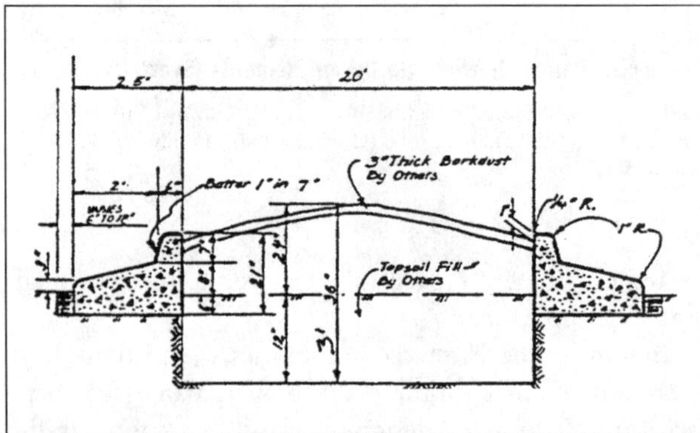

**Figure 4.14. Redesigned Island Section and Curb Details. (Portland, OR)**

Source: Kittelson & Associates, Inc. "Peer Review Analysis—Traffic Circle Program—Portland, Oregon," 1991, p. 10.

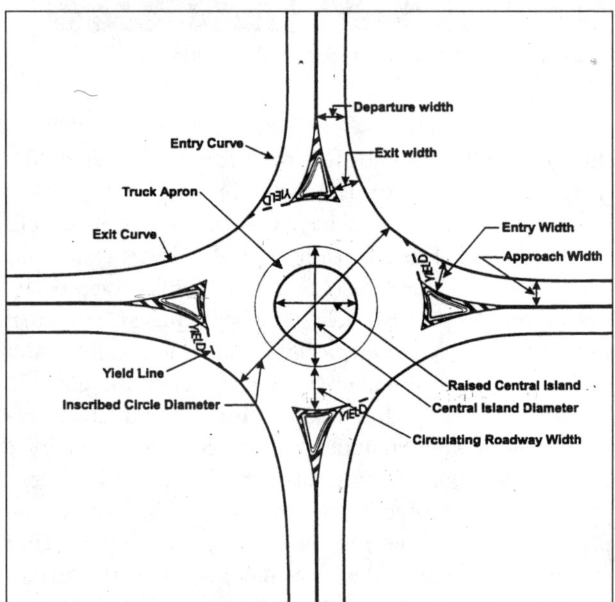


**Figure 4.15. Standard Roundabout Design Used in Florida.**

Source: Florida Department of Transportation, *Florida Roundabout Guide,* Tallahassee, FL, 1996, p. 4-2.

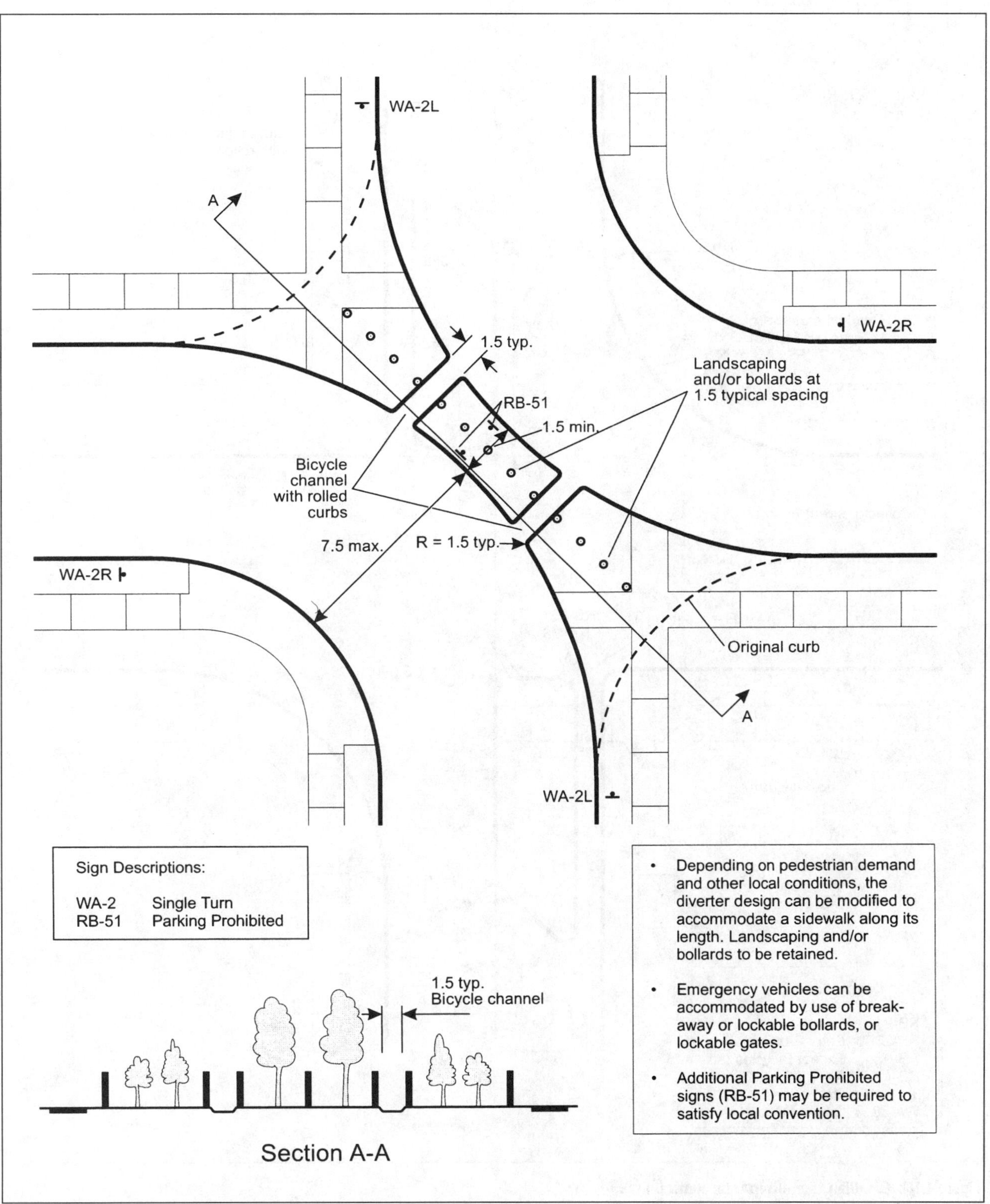


**Figure 4.16a. Canadian Diagonal Diverter (in Metric Units).**

Source: *Canadian Guide to Neighbourhood Traffic Calming,* 1998, p. 4–22. © Transportation Association of Canada. Used with permission.

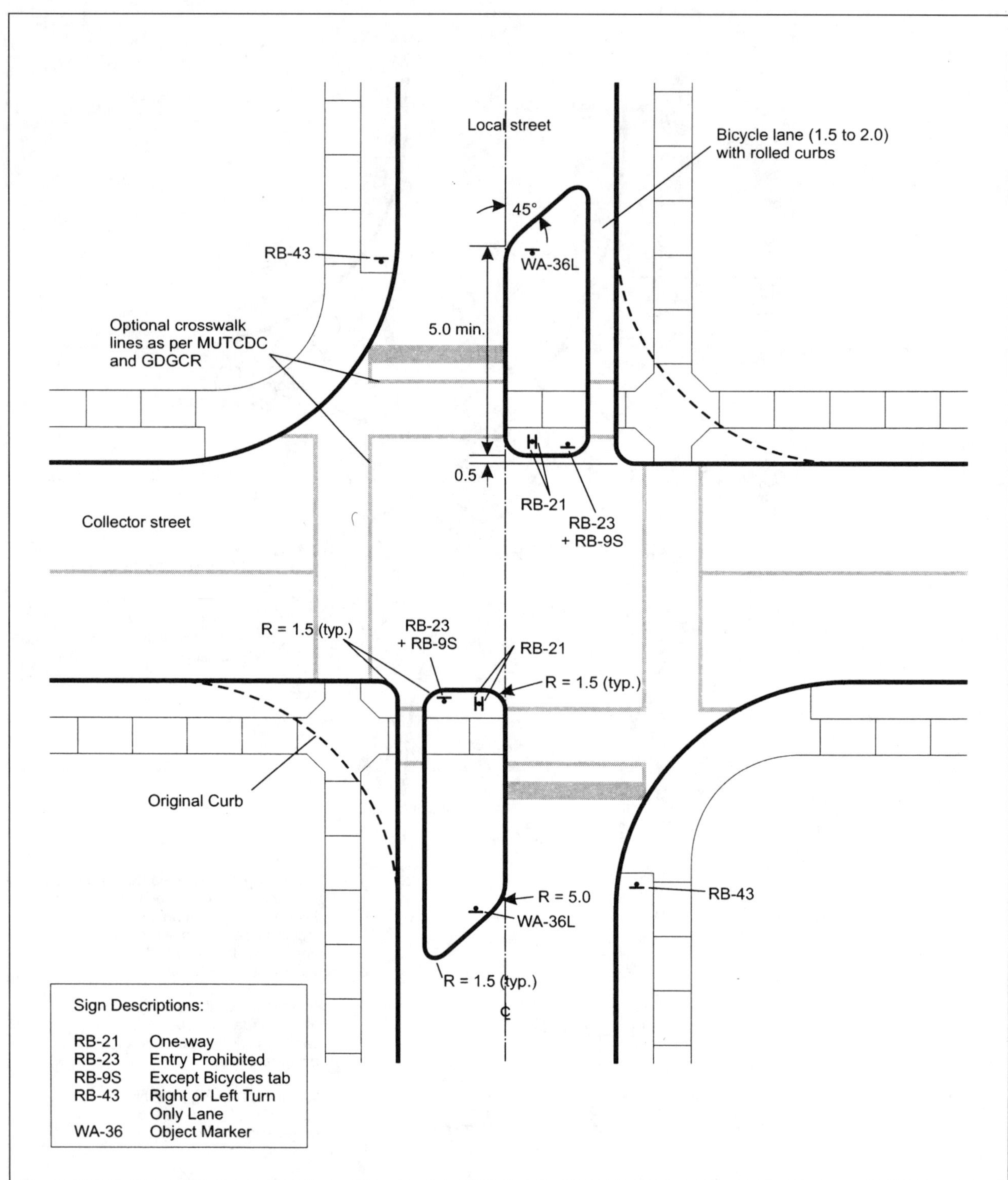


**Figure 4.16b. Canadian Semi-Diverter (in Metric Units).**

Source: *Canadian Guide to Neighbourhood Traffic Calming,* 1998, p. 4–20. © Transportation Association of Canada. Used with permission.

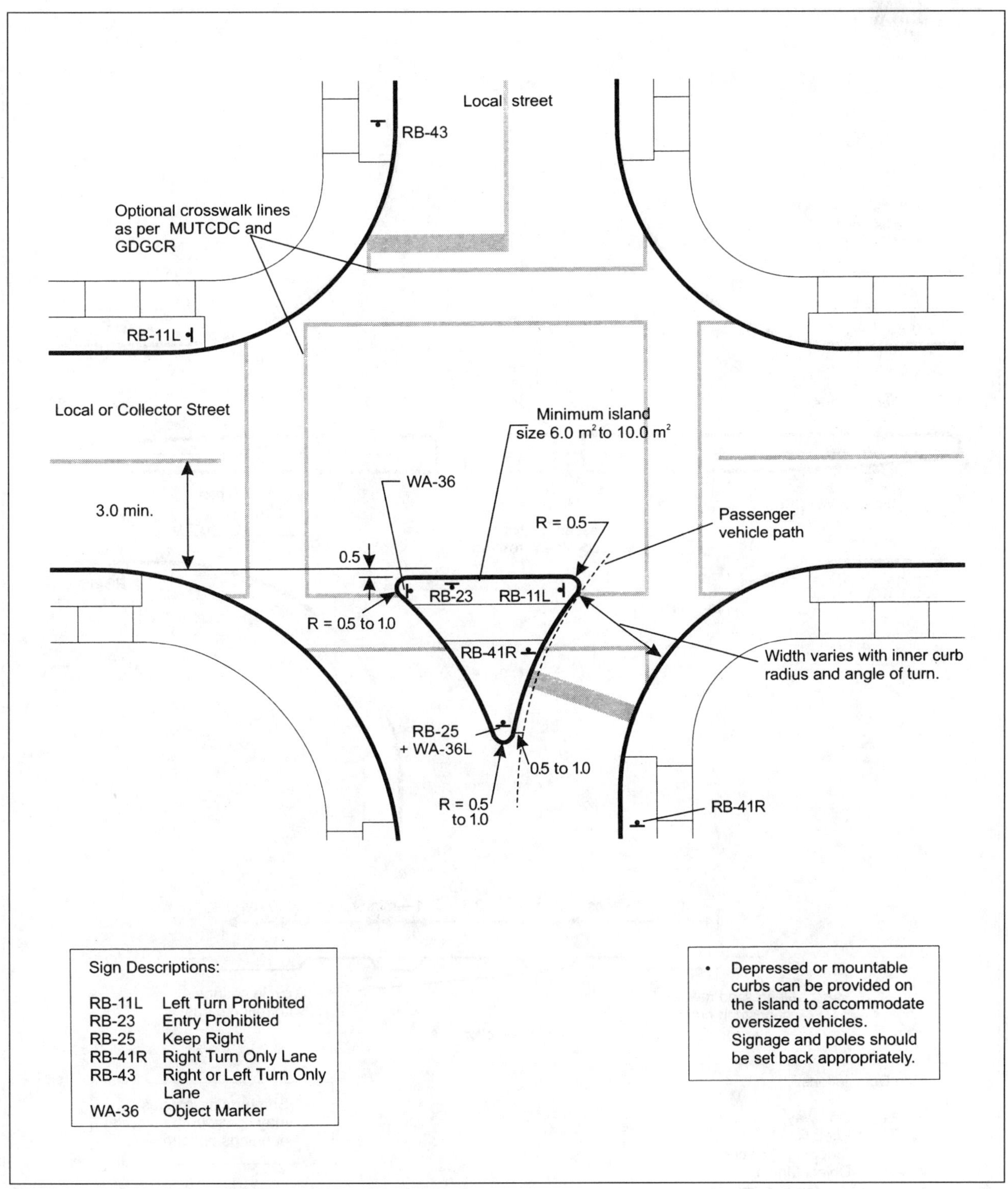


**Figure 4.16c. Canadian Forced Turn Island (in Metric Units).**

Source: *Canadian Guide to Neighbourhood Traffic Calming,* 1998, p. 4–28. © Transportation Association of Canada. Used with permission.

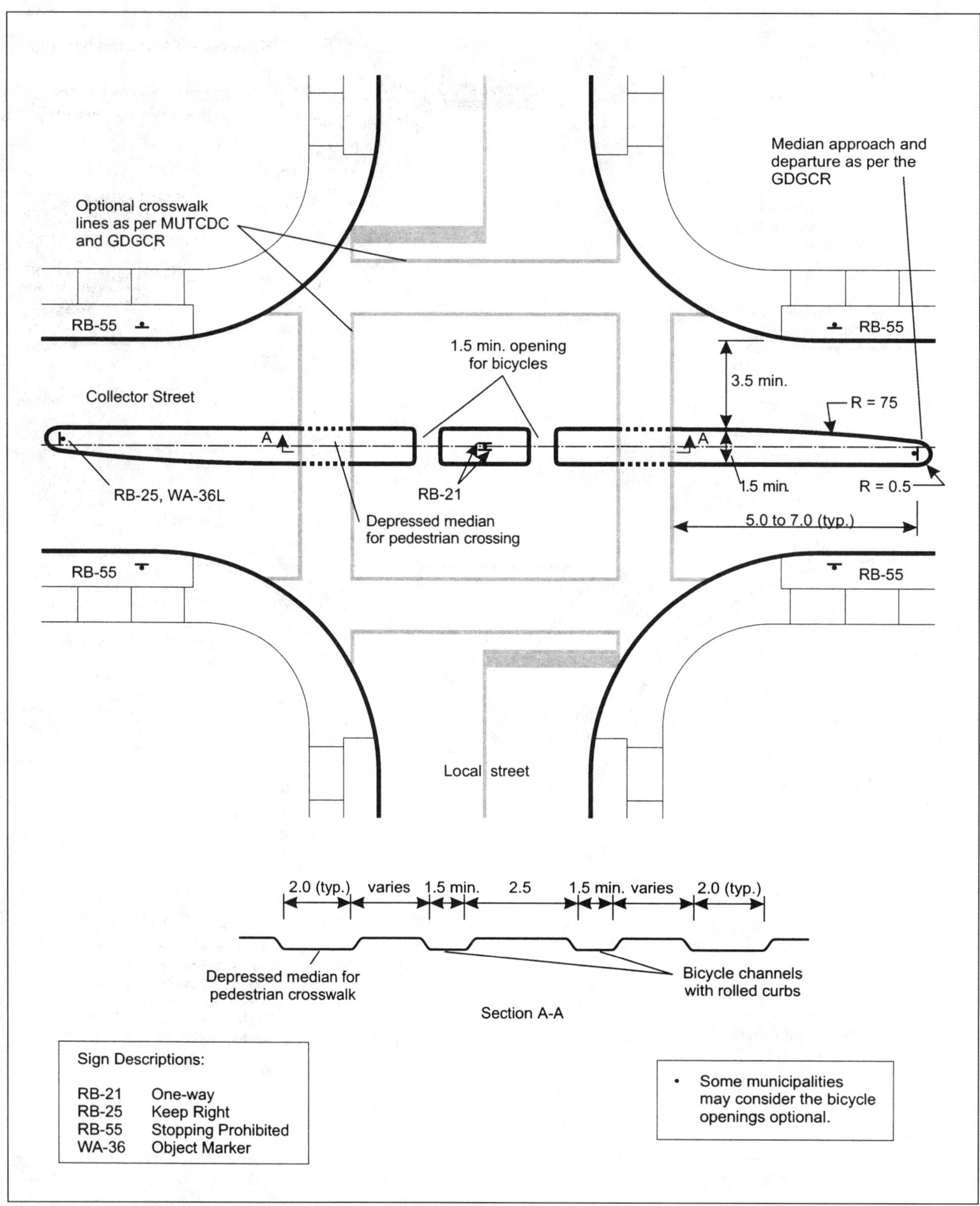



**Figure 4.16d. Canadian Median Barrier (in Metric Units).**

Source: *Canadian Guide to Neighbourhood Traffic Calming*, 1998, p. 4–27. © Transportation Association of Canada. Used with permission.

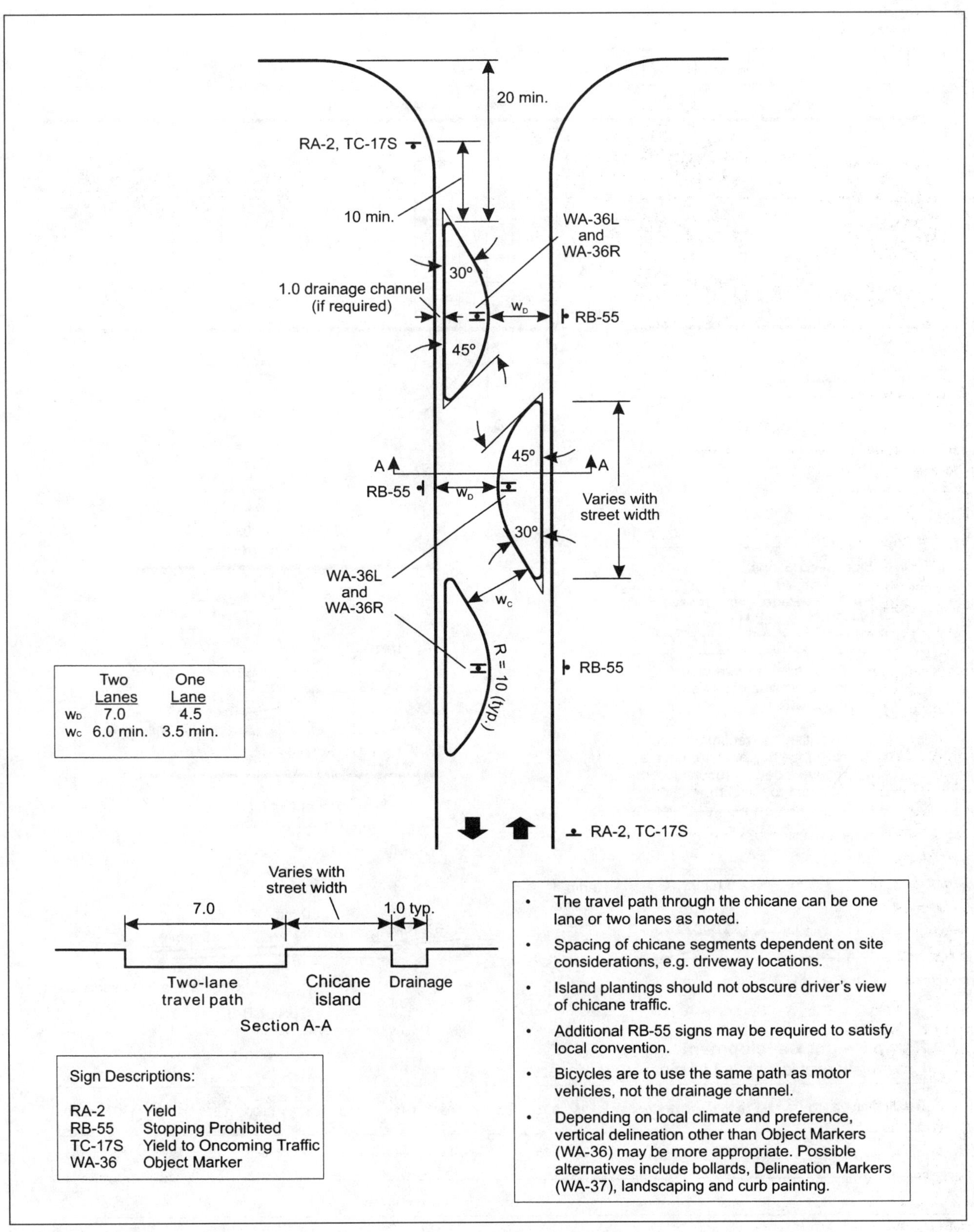


**Figure 4.16e. Canadian Chicane (in Metric Units).**

Source: *Canadian Guide to Neighbourhood Traffic Calming,* 1998, p. 4–10. © Transportation Association of Canada. Used with permission.

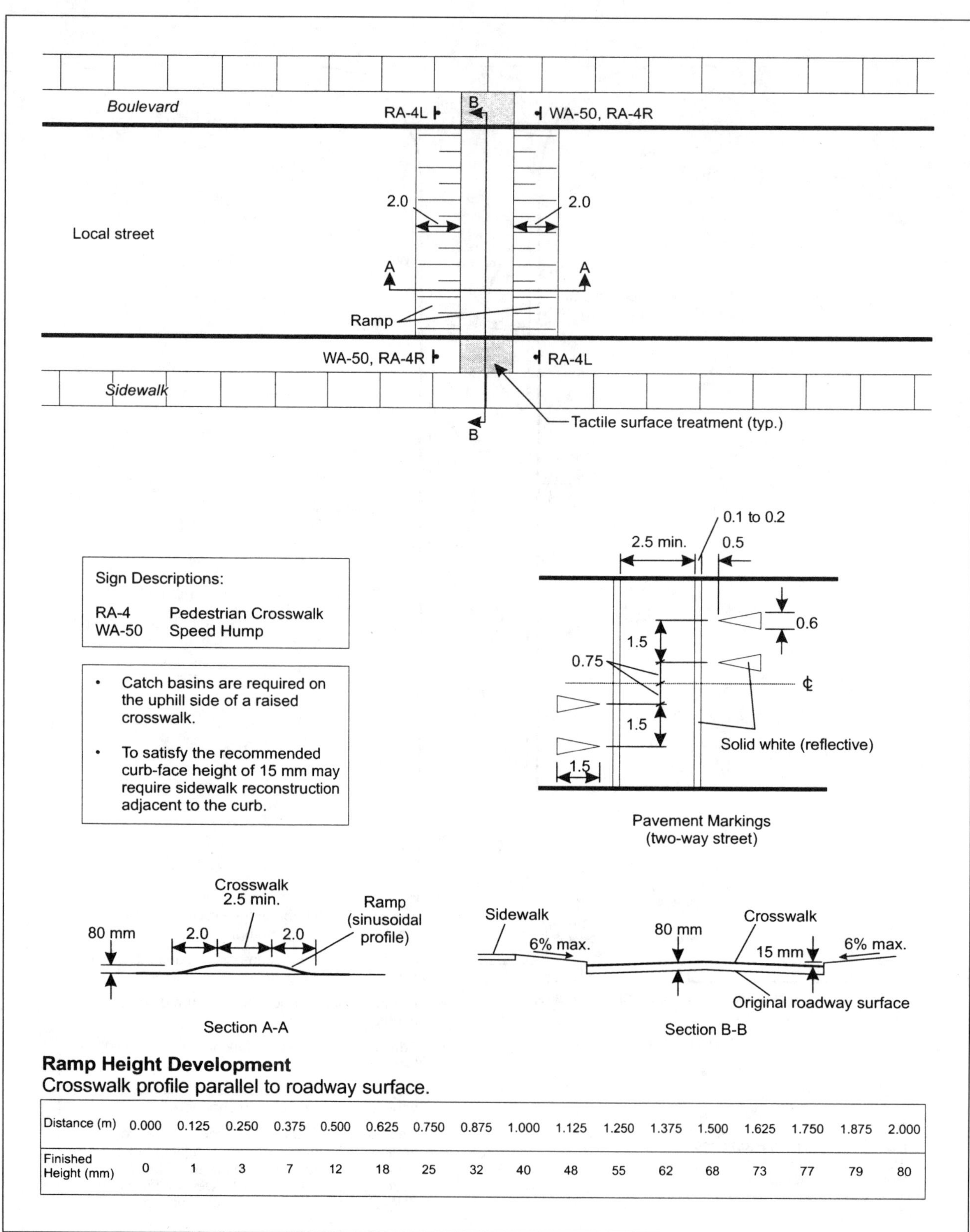


**Ramp Height Development**
Crosswalk profile parallel to roadway surface.

| Distance (m) | 0.000 | 0.125 | 0.250 | 0.375 | 0.500 | 0.625 | 0.750 | 0.875 | 1.000 | 1.125 | 1.250 | 1.375 | 1.500 | 1.625 | 1.750 | 1.875 | 2.000 |
|---|---|---|---|---|---|---|---|---|---|---|---|---|---|---|---|---|---|
| Finished Height (mm) | 0 | 1 | 3 | 7 | 12 | 18 | 25 | 32 | 40 | 48 | 55 | 62 | 68 | 73 | 77 | 79 | 80 |

**Figure 4.16f. Canadian Raised Crosswalk (in Metric Units).**

Source: *Canadian Guide to Neighbourhood Traffic Calming*, 1998, p. 4–4. © Transportation Association of Canada. Used with permission.

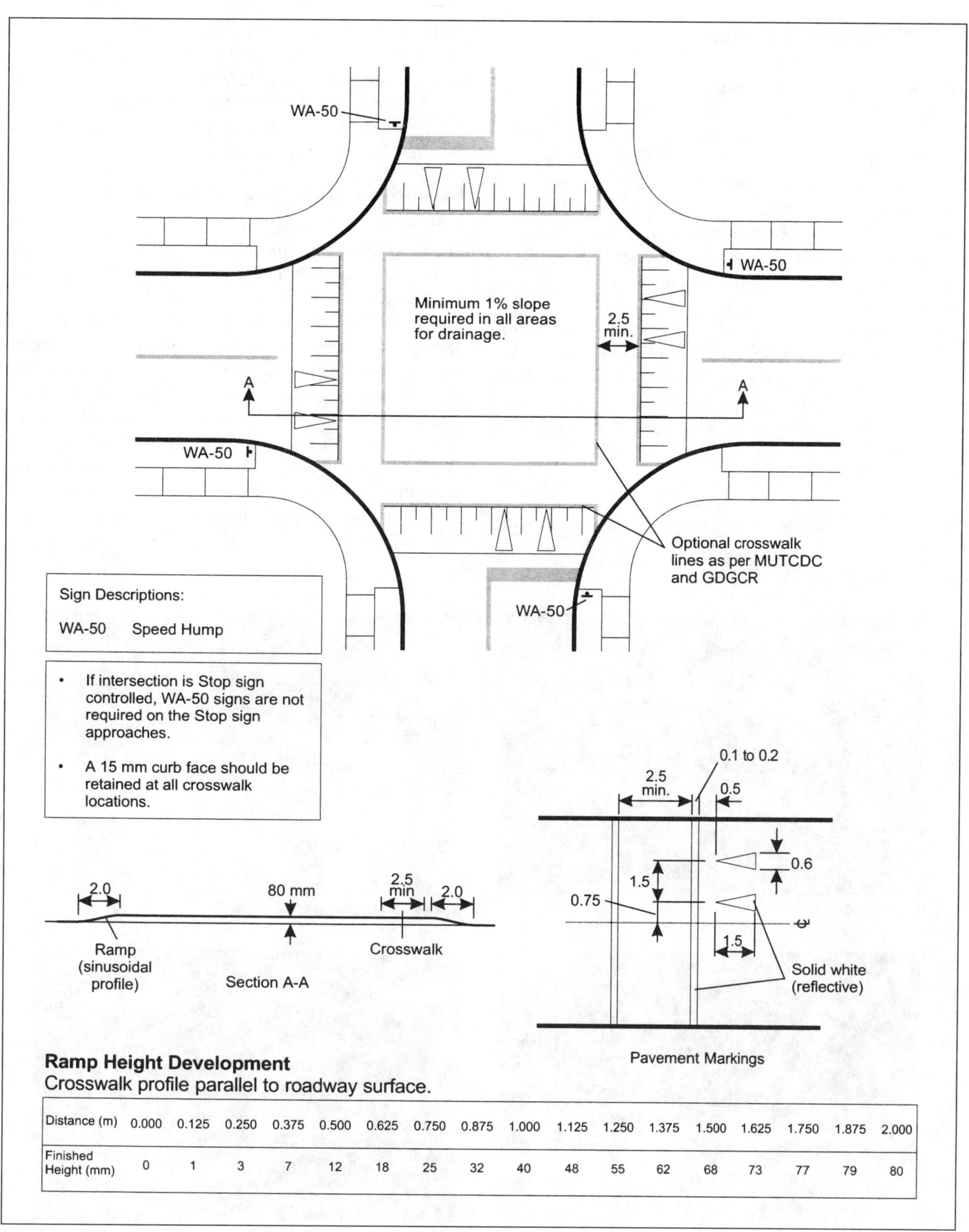


| Distance (m) | 0.000 | 0.125 | 0.250 | 0.375 | 0.500 | 0.625 | 0.750 | 0.875 | 1.000 | 1.125 | 1.250 | 1.375 | 1.500 | 1.625 | 1.750 | 1.875 | 2.000 |
|---|---|---|---|---|---|---|---|---|---|---|---|---|---|---|---|---|---|
| Finished Height (mm) | 0 | 1 | 3 | 7 | 12 | 18 | 25 | 32 | 40 | 48 | 55 | 62 | 68 | 73 | 77 | 79 | 80 |

**Figure 4.16g. Canadian Raised Intersection (in Metric Units).**

Source: *Canadian Guide to Neighbourhood Traffic Calming,* 1998, p. 4–5. © Transportation Association of Canada. Used with permission.

## Use of Temporary Measures

Aesthetics are often an important influence on the acceptance of traffic calming measures. Nowhere is the trade-off between cost and aesthetics more evident than in the use of temporary measures. Most programs install at least some measures on a temporary basis, subject to an assessment of impacts and approval by residents. Program managers have the option of installing makeshift measures (which may cost less, but may also be unaesthetic) or permanent measures (which look good, but may result in a waste of public money if ultimately removed). If they install makeshift measures, such as construction barricades to simulate traffic circles or plastic planters to simulate street closures, they run the risk of public opposition solely because of aesthetic concerns (see figure 4.17). As one traffic manager put it, "criticism of appearance becomes criticism of effectiveness."

Seattle changed its policy on temporary measures long ago. In the early years, construction barrels were used to simulate traffic circles. Now, Seattle builds permanent circles and calls them temporary until they receive resident and staff approval. West Palm Beach, FL, and Bellevue have also stopped using temporary measures because of aesthetic concerns. According to the featured communities, relatively few permanent measures installed for trial purposes have been removed.

### Exceptions to the Use of Permanent Measures

There is one obvious exception to the use of permanent measures. Complex areawide treatments involving diverters or other volume control measures have unpredictable effects on traffic volumes. Traffic diversion from one local street to another often requires fine tuning of designs, something that would be prohibitively expensive if permanent measures were installed initially. In Phoenix, AZ, it took three iterations before acceptable traffic impacts were reported in one neighborhood (see figure 4.18). In this case, residents have accepted temporary measures because the nature of the test was well publicized and examples of aesthetic permanent measures were shown to them beforehand.

Ft. Lauderdale, FL

North York, ON, Canada

Eugene, OR

Santa Barbara, CA

**Figure 4.17. Unaesthetic Temporary Measures.**

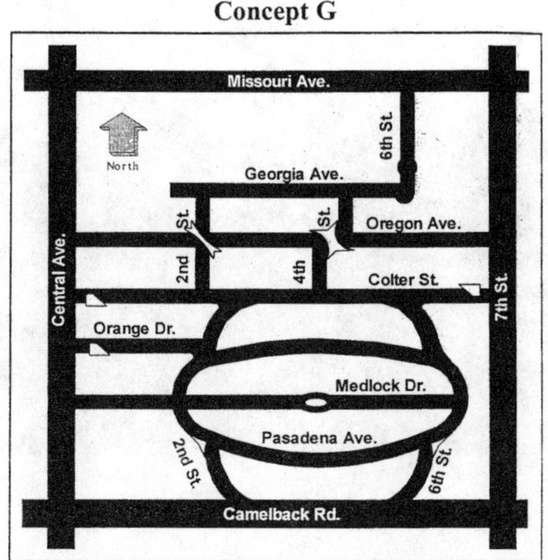


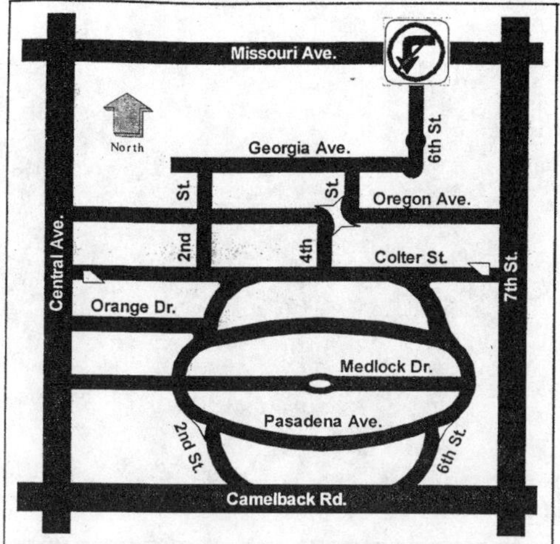


Concept J (proposed for permanent installation)

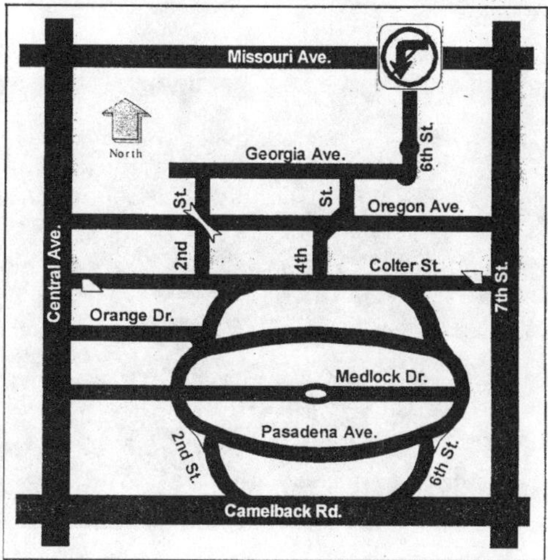


**Figure 4.18. Successive Test Treatments. (Phoenix, AZ)**

Source: City of Phoenix, "Windsor Square Neighborhood Traffic Bulletin," August 1996.

Another exception to the use of permanent measures is when a measure is first tested in an area. Even if the speed or volume impacts can be predicted from tests elsewhere, it is impossible to predict how local residents will react. Charlotte, NC, may have been only the second U.S. community, after Seattle, to test a one-lane chicane on a street with any significant traffic volume. There was a good chance that public reaction would be negative, and in fact it was. Rather than spend an estimated $20,000 or more to construct each of three permanent chicanes, Charlotte opted for plastic posts (see figure 4.19). The temporary chicanes are due to be replaced with speed tables.

## Temporary But Not Unsightly

Temporary measures will generally not be as attractive as landscaped permanent measures. But given the right materials, colors, and composition, they do not have to be unattractive. Charlotte's temporary one-lane chicane, constructed with plastic posts, is coherent enough in appearance to make effectiveness the principal issue. Planters used as temporary street closures provide a little greenery, as well as access control. Even construction barricades or barrels forming temporary circles can be inoffensive if they clearly convey their status as test installations (see figure 4.20).

## Use of Landscaping

In visual preference surveys, scenes containing landscaping and other natural elements tend to be rated highest.[12] Landscaped street edges soften the appearance of speed humps and other vertical traffic calming measures. Landscaped chicanes, center islands, and traffic circles may create distinctive and pleasing streetscapes (see figure 4.21).

**Figure 4.19. Temporary One-Lane Chicane. (Charlotte, NC)**

**Figure 4.20. Temporary Measures Less Likely to Offend.**

**Figure 4.21. Contrasting Images with and without Landscaping.**

In Howard County, the appearance of concrete-topped traffic circles has generated controversy (see figure 4.22). Landscaping could enhance appearance and might also improve the effectiveness and safety of the circles by drawing attention to them. Any vertical element—trees, shrubs, planters, bollards, signage—should draw attention to traffic calming measures.

## Landscape Maintenance

Although beneficial in other respects, landscaping creates some unique challenges in the area of maintenance. Landscaping adds a substantial increment to the cost of constructing traffic calming measures; the absence of landscaping is one of the reasons why speed humps and tables are so much cheaper than other measures (see "Cost of Traffic Calming Measures" in chapter 3). But it is not the initial construction cost that proves problematic for most

**Figure 4.22. Concrete-Topped Circle Controversial for Its Aesthetics. (Howard County, MD)**

jurisdictions. Rather it is the ongoing maintenance costs. The maintenance crews of most jurisdictions are poorly equipped to deal with small-scale landscape maintenance.

Seattle and Portland may have more landscaped traffic calming measures than any other city in the United States. Their contrasting philosophies and experiences are instructive. Seattle initially maintained the landscaping in its traffic circles. As the number of circles grew (it is now at 700), the maintenance burden became overwhelming, and Seattle began to rely on neighborhood volunteers. The city is responsible for the initial landscaping; to simplify maintenance, the city uses drought-tolerant plants. The neighborhood then, as its matching contribution, maintains and replaces landscape materials as needed (see figure 4.23).

Seattle's experience with volunteers is usually good. Occasionally, a neighborhood will renege on its agreement, and the city will threaten to pave over the center island with asphalt. This usually motivates a neighborhood to renew maintenance activities. Though the city has never had to carry out the threat, the quality of landscaping in Seattle is a bit uneven (see figure 4.24).

In contrast, Portland had initially planned to rely on citizen volunteers for maintenance of landscaping, but had second thoughts. Volunteers had not proved reliable in other city enterprises. Poorly maintained circles might reflect poorly on the city. The city may become liable for tools left in the public right-of-way, rocks placed in islands as protection for landscape materials, etc. (see figure 4.25). The city thus chose to assume complete responsibility for landscape maintenance, at an annual cost of $15,000 for all circles citywide.

Among the communities surveyed, Portland was the exception, Seattle the general rule. Landscape maintenance policies of selected programs are reported in table 4.4.

## Signing and Marking

If vehicles are driven at excessive speeds, beyond that for which the traffic calming measures are designed, the measures may pose a hazard to motorists. Government has a ministerial duty to warn motorists of any hazardous conditions that it creates or becomes aware of. The relevant legal theory is presented in chapter 6. It is this "duty to warn" that compels the judicious signing and marking of traffic calming measures.

This section applies general principles from the *Manual on Uniform Traffic Control Devices for Streets and Highways (MUTCD)* to the field of traffic calming and presents sample applications from traffic calming programs around the United States.

**Figure 4.23. Volunteer Repairing Damage Caused by Truck Traffic. (Seattle, WA)**

**Figure 4.24. Uneven Quality of Volunteer Landscaping. (Seattle, WA)**

**Figure 4.25. Rocks Placed in Islands by Volunteers.**

**Table 4.4. Landscape Maintenance Policies.**

| Community | Policy |
|---|---|
| Dayton, OH | City installs—neighborhoods maintain |
| Eugene, OR | City installs—neighborhoods originally maintain but city assumes function when volunteer efforts end |
| Gainesville, FL | City offers two options: free Xeriscape or plants of choice from city nursery—city installs—neighborhoods maintain |
| Howard County, MD | County installs and maintains |
| Montgomery County, MD | Neighborhoods choose from approved list—county installs—neighborhoods maintain |
| San Diego, CA | Neighborhoods choose landscape palette—city installs—neighborhoods maintain |
| Tallahassee, FL | Neighborhoods install and maintain—policy is being reconsidered in light of "uglies" |

Source: Interviews with staffs of traffic calming programs.

## The Case of Traffic Islands

Setting the standard for signing and marking in the United States is the *MUTCD*. Published by FHWA, "[T]he *MUTCD* is used day to day in the courts of this land to argue about the safety of particular highway locations with reference to whether appropriate traffic control devices were present or needed."[13]

The only physical features commonly used in traffic calming that are addressed specifically in the *MUTCD* are traffic islands. Islands themselves are not considered traffic control devices, but are included in the *MUTCD* to clarify signing and marking conventions. The *MUTCD* specifies: "All approach noses of islands in the line of traffic *should* be designated by an appropriate sign [such as the Keep Right (R4-7) sign]... Object markers *should* be used on island approach noses to indicate the presence of a raised curb or other obstruction. The marker *should* be used even where a sign is installed... On the approach to islands, the triangular neutral area, just in advance of the end of the island, *shall* include pavement markings [to guide vehicles in desired paths of travel along the island edge]... Landscaping, where used, *should* be carefully planned to provide unrestricted visibility for vehicle operators and pedestrians" (emphasis added in italic; commentary in brackets).[14]

Observance of all *MUTCD* guidelines for islands can create visual clutter and reduce comprehension. For this reason, it is seldom that all suggestions for *MUTCD* signs and markings are followed on traffic-calmed residential streets. Figure 4.26 shows center island narrowings in four communities. They are typical. No collisions involving these islands have been reported (perhaps, in part, because the islands are plainly delineated, each in its own way).

**Figure 4.26. Signing and Marking of Center Island Narrowings.**

## Absence of Specific *MUTCD* Guidance

Part V of the *MUTCD*—relating to traffic islands—was not designed to address traffic calming measures. In 1988, when the *MUTCD* was last updated, few North American transportation professionals had been introduced to traffic calming.

From an operational standpoint, the lack of signing and marking guidance for traffic calming measures creates two potential problems. First, it means that warnings to motorists may less often be quickly recognized for what they are. The use of a single horizontal curve sign nationwide ensures near-universal recognition. The widespread use of different traffic circle signs precludes near-universal recognition (see figure 4.27). Second, from a legal standpoint, lack of signing and marking guidance means that injured parties could possibly file tort actions, leaving expert witnesses to argue whether the signing and marking provided adequate warning.

Clearly, one alternative would be to have the *MUTCD* expanded with sensitivity to the context of traffic calming and to include traffic calming measures. The British and Australians have uniform standards for signing and marking of traffic calming measures (see figure 4.28).[15] FHWA and the National Committee on Uniform Traffic Control Devices plan to address signing and marking of traffic circles as part of an *MUTCD* rewrite. However, there are currently no plans to address humps, chokers, and other common traffic calming measures as part of the rewrite. Until the *MUTCD* is updated to include traffic calming measures, engineering judgment must prevail.

In the interim, some jurisdictions in proximate geographic areas have agreed on common signing and marking conventions. The Maryland Traffic Engineers Council has adopted standard signs for humps and circles, making recognition easier as residents travel among neighboring counties with active traffic calming programs (see figure 4.29). Other States or metropolitan areas could do the same, perhaps with State departments of transportation or metropolitan planning organizations playing a coordinating role.

Charlotte, NC

Naples, FL

Orlando, FL

Seattle, WA

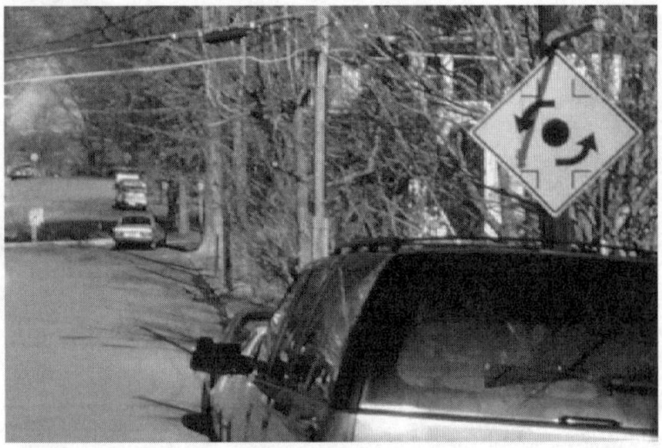

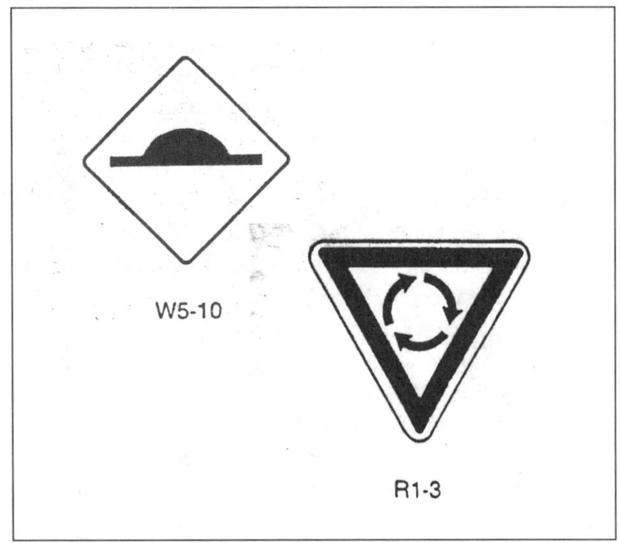

**Figure 4.27. Traffic Circle Signs in Different Communities.**

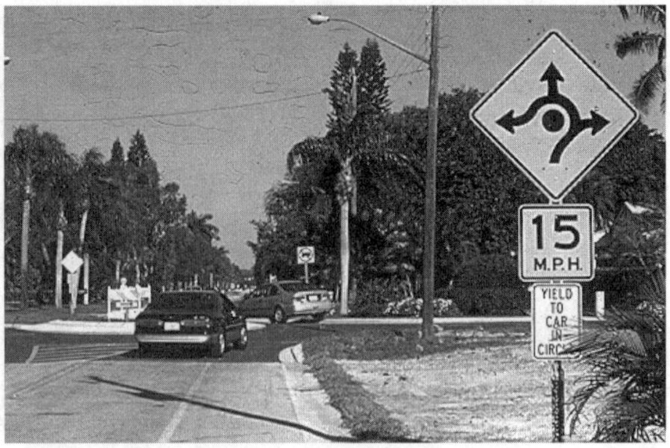

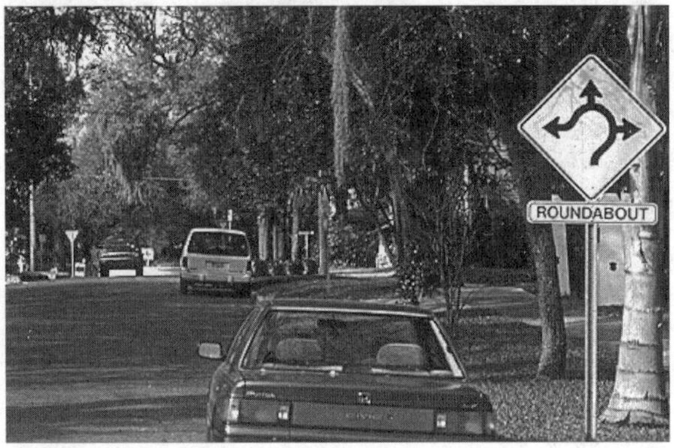

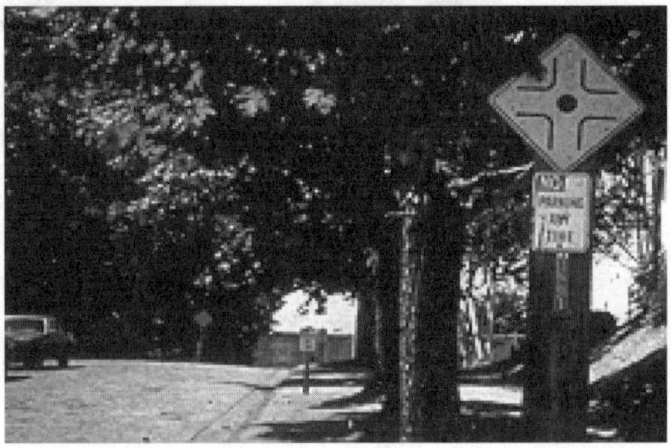

**Figure 4.28. Australian Standard Signs.**

Source: Committee MS/12, *Manual of Uniform Traffic Control Devices—Part 13: Local Area Traffic Management*, Standards Association of Australia, Sydney, NSW, Australia, 1991.

Speed Hump Sign

Traffic Circle Sign

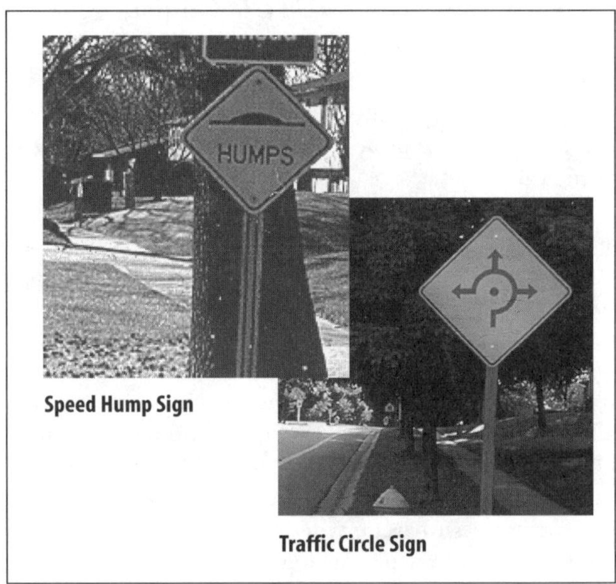

**Figure 4.29. Maryland Standard Signs.**

Another approach taken is for a locality to standardize within its own boundaries. Consider Montgomery County's dilemma over the signing and marking of traffic circles. Most circles are signed and marked as shown in the upper photograph in figure 4.30. The Fort Sumner neighborhood did not like the appearance of approach markings at the entries to traffic circles or the chevron signs on the islands themselves. When the residential street shown in the lower photograph was slurry sealed, the neighborhood and the county's sign and marking unit disagreed over the need to replace the approach markings. They also disagreed over the need for chevron signs on the island itself.

### *MUTCD* Principles Applicable to Traffic Calming Measures

While only addressing traffic islands specifically, the *MUTCD* establishes principles that may be relevant to other traffic calming measures. First, the *MUTCD* offers a degree of flexibility in the application of signs and markings. It states, for example:

**Figure 4.30. Traffic Circles in the Same Jurisdiction Signed and Marked Differently. (Montgomery County, MD)**

[E]ngineering judgment is essential to the proper use of signs, the same as with other traffic control devices. Traffic engineering studies may indicate that signs would be unnecessary at certain locations.[16]

Added flexibility is provided by the *MUTCD*'s frequent use of the term "should" rather than "shall." The term "should" denotes a recommended practice, while the term "shall" denotes a mandatory practice.

Second, the *MUTCD* urges conservative use of signage, which is consistent with the aesthetic orientation of this chapter:

Care should be taken not to install too many signs. A conservative use of regulatory and warning signs is recommended as these signs, if used to excess, tend to lose their effectiveness.[17]

More than one surveyed traffic calming program has learned through experience that excessive signage detracts from sign comprehension and street aesthetics (see figure 4.31).

Third, the *MUTCD* provides general guidance for warning signs, object markers, curb markers, lane lines, pedestrian crossings, and other traffic control devices that in some communities have been applied to traffic calming measures as well as to other geometric features. Examples include:

- Warning signs are rectangular or diamond-shaped with a yellow background and black messages.
- White lines mark the right edge of the pavement; yellow lines always separate opposing traffic and mark the left edge of the pavement on divided highways.

**Figure 4.31. Headline: "Engineers Insist It's Not A Vicious Circle."**
Source: *The Tampa Tribune*, June 7, 1996. Reprinted with permission.

- Legibility is the basic requirement of street signs. "This means high visibility, lettering or symbols of adequate size, and short legends for quick comprehension..."[18]

- Use of symbols is favored over word messages.[19] Symbol signs should be evaluated for motorist comprehension before they are approved for installation. New symbol signs not readily recognizable should be accompanied by educational plaques.

- Advance warning signs are to be placed upstream of measures wherever "high driver judgment" or "deceleration to a specific speed" is required. A one-lane choker is an example of a situation that requires high driver judgment. A 12-foot hump in a 30-mph zone is an example of a situation that requires deceleration to a specific speed of 20 mph. The *MUTCD* advance warning placement guidelines are listed in table 4.5.

Fourth, the *MUTCD* allows State and local highway agencies to develop word message signs for conditions not addressed in the *MUTCD*, provided the appropriate shape and color sign is used:

> In situations where messages are required other than those herein provided for, the signs shall be the same shape and color as standard signs of the same functional type.[20]

The ONE LANE BRIDGE sign (W5–3), for example, suggests a functionally analogous traffic calming sign: a diamond-shaped ONE LANE ROAD sign with a black legend and border on a yellow background.

## Example—Seattle's Signing and Marking Practices

Seattle's signing and marking practices appear to be generally consistent with the *MUTCD*, but at the same time sensitive to context (see figure 4.32). Seattle has a long history of traffic calming without serious legal problems (see chapter 6).

For traffic circles, yellow pavement markers are placed on the tops of island curbs and yellow diamond-shaped (Type 1) object markers are placed in landscaped areas facing all approaches. The pavement markers are retroreflective and two-sided so the entire circle is outlined at night. The object markers are positioned low enough to be visible at normal headlight angles. No special pavement markings are used except on uphill approaches where circles are not visible. There, a line of reflectorized pavement markers directs traffic to the right. Seattle subscribes to the theory that if geometric features are clearly marked and plainly visible, pavement markings are unnecessary.

For one-lane chicanes, silver pavement markers are placed on the tops of curbs, and yellow-and-black-striped (Type 3) object markers are placed in the landscaped areas to direct traffic to the left or right, as appropriate. The pavement markers are also retroreflective and two-sided so as to be visible to traffic in both directions. No special pavement markings are used.

For two-lane chokers, no signs or markers are provided on the theory that curb extensions are outside the travel lanes and parked cars jut out just as far. Indeed, wherever full-lane widths are maintained in both directions, Seattle perceives no need for special signing or marking.

**Table 4.5. Advance Warning Sign Placement Distance (number of feet upstream of condition).**

| Posted or 85th Percentile Speed (mph) | A High Judgment Needed (feet) | Deceleration Distance to Listed Advisory Speed (feet) | | |
|---|---|---|---|---|
| | | 10 mph | 20 mph | 30 mph |
| 25 | 250 | 100 | N/A | N/A |
| 30 | 325 | 150 | 100 | N/A |
| 35 | 400 | 200 | 175 | N/A |
| 40 | 475 | 275 | 250 | 175 |
| 45 | 550 | 350 | 300 | 250 |

mph = miles per hour

Source: Federal Highway Administration, *Manual on Uniform Traffic Control Devices for Streets and Highways*, Washington, DC, 1988, p. 2C–2a.

Figure 4.32. Moderate Signing and Marking Practices. (Seattle, WA)

**Half Closure. (Sacramento, CA)**

**Diagonal Diverter. (Eugene, OR)**

**Traffic Circle. (West Palm Beach, FL)**

**Traffic Circle. (Eugene, OR)**

**Figure 4.33. Use of Signs from the *Manual on Uniform Traffic Control Devices* for Traffic Calming Measures.**

For half closures, a DO NOT ENTER sign (R5-1) is placed at one end of the curb extension, and a Type 3 object marker or nothing is placed at the other end. In the case of longer one-way sections, one-sided retro-reflective pavement markers outline the curb, with the reflective side in the direction of travel.

Humps are marked with reflective thermoplastic. No object markers are used except where a telephone pole or other obstruction is situated at the roadside and drivers trying to avoid the hump might collide with it. In curbless sections, Type 3 object markers or 4 x 4 wooden posts with reflectors are sometimes placed at the roadside to keep drivers in the travel lane.

Advance warning signs are kept to a minimum. They are provided at the beginning of speed humps and one-lane chicanes only. Seattle's early one-lane chicanes had three advance warning signs—a ONE LANE ROAD sign, a Winding Road sign (W1-5), and a speed advisory sign. Newer ones have only the ONE LANE ROAD sign. The object markings on the chicanes themselves are thought to be warning enough.

## Examples of *MUTCD* Signs Used in Conjunction with Traffic Calming Measures

Figure 4.33 illustrates the use in several communities of *MUTCD* signs as part of traffic calming measures. DO NOT ENTER signs (R5-1) have been used at half closures and other traffic calming features that allow only one-way movement for short distances. Turn signs (W1-1R or W1-1L) have been applied to diagonal diverters and other traffic calming measures whose geometrics require turns to be made at less than 30 mph and less than the posted speed limit approaching the turn. The regulatory KEEP RIGHT sign (R4-7) has been applied at center islands of various lengths. The Large Arrow sign (W1-6) and the Chevron Alignment sign (W1-8) have been used on features that involve sharp changes in the direction of travel, such as diverters and certain traffic

**Speed Bumps. (Portland, OR)**

**Speed Humps. (Ft. Lauderdale, FL)**

**Road Humps. (Austin, TX)**

**Speed Tables. (Sarasota, FL)**

**Figure 4.34. Hump and Table Warning Signs.**

circles. KEEP RIGHT signs (R4-7a or R4-7b) have also been used at traffic circles where deflection is not pronounced. The Winding Road sign (W1-5) has been used for chicanes. The Reverse Turn sign (W1-3) and Reverse Curve sign (W1-4) have been applied to lateral shifts, the appropriate sign depending on the design speed of the feature (W1-3 at 30 mph or less, W1-4 at higher speeds).

Another example is the very common use of BUMP signs to warn of speed humps and speed tables (see figure 4.34). The many jurisdictions that use BUMP signs reason that (1) the BUMP sign is *MUTCD*-approved; (2) the BUMP sign is intended for use wherever, as with humps and tables, a rise is "sufficiently abrupt to...cause considerable discomfort to passengers, to cause a shifting of the cargo, or to deflect a vehicle from its true course at the normal driving speeds for the road";[21] (3) the term "bump" is universally understood, while terms like "speed table" are not; and (4) a HUMP or HUMP AHEAD sign may prove irresistible to vandals.

Arguing against the signing of humps or tables with the BUMP sign is (1) the common use of BUMP signs to warn of true speed bumps on access drives; and (2) the *MUTCD* preference for symbols over word message signs.

The Australians and Canadians have designed special symbol signs to designate speed humps and tables. While the BUMP sign is currently being used in the United States, it may not be ideal for long-term use.

## Examples of Specialty Signs

Figure 4.35 shows some specialty signs from traffic calming programs across the United States. Effective signs are legible at ordinary operating speeds, use familiar terminology, and accurately depict the geometrics. Some otherwise effective examples found in the communities surveyed, however, fail to follow certain *MUTCD* guidelines and can be misleading in some respects. Great care must be exercised in the design of specialty signs.

**Raised Intersection. (Tallahassee, FL)**

**One-Lane Chicane. (Charlotte, NC)**

**Raised Crosswalk. (Montgomery County, MD)**

**Figure 4.35. Effective Specialty Signs.**

## Signing and Marking of Humps

The signing and marking of speed humps and speed tables deserve special attention because these are the most common traffic calming measures in the United States. Signing and marking practices of different communities are summarized in table 4.6. In degree of warning provided, the extremes are Bellevue and West Palm Beach. Bellevue no longer installs reflectors on the humps themselves, but still has an advance warning sign before a series of humps, a BUMP sign next to each hump, a pavement legend in front of each hump, and reflective pavement markings on each hump. West Palm Beach has none of these. Even the humps themselves are not marked with reflective material but are painted a terra cotta color. The only reflective markings are raised pavement markers on curb extensions to the side of West Palm Beach's humps (see figure 4.36).

From table 4.6, the norm for signing and marking in the surveyed communities is an advance warning sign and reflective markings on the humps or tables themselves. Also from table 4.6, the trend is toward less extensive signing and marking. Every reference to "older humps only" represents one practice that was deemed excessive and dropped, resulting in cost savings. The combination of an advance warning sign and reflective markings attempts to satisfy general *MUTCD* requirements, except in those cases where the posted speed of the street and 85th percentile speed at humps are sufficiently different to warrant a speed advisory sign. In areas that receive significant snowfall, and perhaps those that receive torrential rain, markings may not be visible all the time. In such areas, an object marker (a small Type 2 marker or post with reflectors) to the side of each hump or table has been used to provide adequate warning. Object markers have also been used to prevent drivers from going around humps and tables on curbless street sections.

As for the marking of individual humps or tables, the most common markings in the United States are the zigzag, shark's tooth, chevron, and zebra patterns (see figure 4.37). Less common markings include the diamond, arrow, and Danish checkerboard patterns, and the Seminole County transverse marking pattern that creates the illusion of increasing speed (see chapter 5).

Aesthetics are subjective. The Danish checkerboard pattern may have a classy European look to some, and a busy baroque look to others. This report offers no insights on aesthetics. The functional considerations are manifold. First, the diamond pattern, and perhaps the shark's tooth and arrow patterns, may accentuate

**Table 4.6. Various Marking and Signing Practices for Speed Humps and Speed Tables.**

| Practice | Bellevue, WA | Eugene, OR | Gwinnett County, GA | Portland, OR | Sarasota, FL | Seattle, WA | West Palm Beach, FL |
|---|---|---|---|---|---|---|---|
| Advance warning signs* | X | X | X | X | X | X | |
| Advance speed advisory signs | X | | X | X (older humps only) | Part of advance signs | X (older humps only) | |
| Hump signs at individual humps | X | X (older humps only) | X (older humps only) | X (older humps only) | | X (older humps only) | |
| Other object markers at individual humps | | | | | Reflectorized posts serve as object markers | Only when objects placed at side to stop gutter running | Curb extensions serve as markers |
| Markings on humps themselves | X | X | X | X | X | X | Colored and textured surface serves as marking |
| Pavement legends in front of humps | X | | | X | X | | |
| Reflectors on humps | X (older humps only) | | | | | | |

Source: Interviews and site visits.
* Note: Advance warning signs may appear either just before the first hump in a series or before each individual hump.

**Bellevue, WA**

**West Palm Beach, FL**

**Figure 4.36. Extremes of Hump Signing and Marking.**

Figure 4.37. Marking Patterns.

the apparent vertical rise of the hump or table. The shark's tooth, arrow, and chevron patterns direct traffic to the right in the absence of a centerline. How important this is on streets that typically lack centerlines is unclear. The zebra pattern resembles crosswalk markings, which may be problematic if midblock pedestrian crossings are being discouraged.

As an example, Gwinnett County initially signed its 22-foot speed tables with individual ROAD HUMP signs and 15-mph speed advisories (see figure 4.38). In the next

**Figure 4.38. Evolution of Signing Practices (from top to bottom). (Gwinnett County, GA)**

iteration, SPEED HUMP signs were substituted for ROAD HUMP signs, and 20-mph speed advisories were substituted for 15-mph speed advisories (the latter being closer to the 85th percentile speed of a 22-foot trapezoidal speed table). In the final iteration, individual signs were dropped in favor of advance warning signs at the beginning of each series of tables. Gwinnett County recently switched from the zigzag to the shark's tooth pattern. This was done to enhance aesthetics and visibility; the shark's tooth pattern was considered to have one of the largest white reflective areas of any standard pattern.

Portland recently began marking all vertical measures with the chevron pattern. Previously, Portland's 14-foot humps were marked this way, but the 22-foot tables instead had Seminole County's transverse striping. Transverse stripes on the tables themselves could be hot-rolled into the asphalt for durability, but advance stripes had to be glued to the existing roadway surface and tended to ravel.

## Endnotes

1. The superelevation rate is the cross slope of a road banking into a curve. The side-friction factor is the frictional force between tires and road surface, counteracting centrifugal force, divided by the weight of the vehicle.

2. American Association of State Highway and Transportation Officials (AASHTO), *A Policy on Geometric Design of Highways and Streets,* Washington, DC, 1990, p. 187.

3. For information on track width and overhang for other design vehicles, see AASHTO, op. cit., Figure III-24.

4. AASHTO, op. cit., p. 290.

5. A. R. Hodge, *Speed Control Humps—A Trial At TRL, Project Report 32,* Transportation Research Laboratory, Crowthorne, Berkshire, England, 1993.

6. T. F. Fwa and L. S. Tan, "Geometric Characterization of Road Humps for Speed-Control Design," *Journal of Transportation Engineering,* Vol. 118, July/August 1992, pp. 593-598.

7. ITE Traffic Engineering Council Speed Humps Task Force, *Guidelines for the Design and Application of Speed Humps— A Recommended Practice,* Institute of Transportation Engineers, Washington, DC, 1997.

8. The Portland profile is being used in Eugene, OR; Kirkland, WA; Menlo Park, CA; and San Leandro, CA. For reasons, see R. E. Davis and G. Lum, "Growing Pains or Growing Calmer? Lessons Learned from a Pilot Traffic Calming Program," in *Harmonizing Transportation & Community Goals* (ITE International Conference, Monterey, CA, 1998), Institute of Transportation Engineers, Washington, DC, 1998, CD-ROM; and D. T. Smith, "End to Menlo Park's Traffic Calming Wars?" paper presented at the 67th ITE Annual Meeting, Institute of Transportation Engineers, Washington, DC, 1997.

9. Florida Department of Transportation, *Florida Roundabout Guide,* Tallahassee, FL, 1996; and State Highway Administration, *Roundabout Design Guidelines,* Maryland Department of Transportation, Annapolis, MD, 1994.

10. C. Schoon and J. van Minnen, "The Safety of Roundabouts in the Netherlands," *Traffic Engineering + Control,* Vol. 35, 1994, pp. 142–147; L. Ourston and J.G. Bared, "Roundabouts: A Direct Way to Safer Highways," *Public Roads,* Vol. 59, Autumn 1995, pp.41–49; A. Flannery and T.K. Datta, "Modern Roundabouts and Traffic Crash Experience in the United States," *Transportation Research Record 1553,* 1996, pp. 103–109; M.E. Niederhauser, B.A. Collins, and E.J. Myers, "The Use of Roundabouts: Comparison of Alternate Design Solutions," in *Compendium of Technical Papers for the 67th ITE Annual Meeting* (Boston, MA, 1997), Institute of Transportation Engineers, Washington, DC, 1997, CD-ROM; A. Flannery et al. "Safety, Delay and Capacity of Single-Lane Roundabouts in the United States," paper presented at the 77th Annual Meeting, Transportation Research Board, Washington, DC, 1998; and G. Jacquemart, *Modern Roundabout Practice in the United States,* Synthesis of Highway Practice 264, Transportation Research Board, Washington, DC, 1998, pp. 25–29.

11. Transportation Association of Canada, *Canadian Guide to Neighbourhood Traffic Calming,* Ottawa, ON, Canada, December 1998, Chapter 4.

12. T.R. Herzog, S. Kaplan, and R. Kaplan, "The Prediction of Preference for Familiar Urban Places," *Environment and Behavior,* Vol. 8, 1976, pp. 627–645; J.L. Nasar, "A Model Relating Visual Attributes in the Residential Environment to Fear of Crime," *Journal of Environmental Systems,* Vol. 11, 1981–82, pp. 247–255; T.R. Herzog, S. Kaplan, and R. Kaplan, "The Prediction of Preference for Unfamiliar Urban Places," *Population and Environment,* Vol. 5, 1982, pp. 43–59; G.S. Shaffer and L.M. Anderson, "Perceptions of the Security and Attractiveness of Urban Parking Lots," *Journal of Environmental Psychology,* Vol. 5, 1983, pp. 311–323; R.S. Ulrich, "Aesthetic and Affective Response to Natural Environment," in I. Altman and J.F. Wohlwill (eds.), *Behavior and the Natural Environment,* Plenum Press, New York, 1983, pp. 85–125; R.S. Ulrich, "Human Responses to Vegetation and Landscapes," *Landscape and Urban Planning,* Vol. 13, 1986, pp. 29–44. H.W. Schroeder, "Environment, Behavior, and Design Research on Urban Forests," in E.H. Zube and G.T. Moore (eds.), *Advances in Environment, Behavior, and Design—Volume 2,* Plenum Press, New York, 1988, pp. 87–117; T.R. Herzog, "A Cognitive Analysis of Preference for Urban Nature," *Journal of Environmental Psychology,* Vol. 9, 1989, pp. 27–43; R. Kaplan and S. Kaplan, *The Experience of Nature—A Psychological Perspective,* Cambridge University Press, New York, 1989, pp. 216–291; and A.C. Nelessen, *Visions for a New American Dream,* American Planning Association, Chicago, IL, 1994.

13. J.C. Glennon, "The *MUTCD* at Court," *1991 Compendium of Technical Papers,* Institute of Transportation Engineers, Washington, DC, 1991, pp. 160–162.

14. Federal Highway Administration (FHWA), *Manual on Uniform Traffic Control Devices for Streets and Highways,* Washington, DC, 1988, pp. 5E-1, 5F-1, 5B-2.

15. *Traffic Signs Regulations and General Directions,* Her Majesty's Stationery Office, London, England, 1993; and Committee MS/12, *Manual of Uniform Traffic Control Devices—Part 13: Local Area Traffic Management,* Standards Association of Australia, Sydney, NSW, Australia, 1991.

16. FHWA, op. cit., p. 2A-2.

17. FHWA, op. cit., p. 2A-3.

18. FHWA, op. cit., p. 2A-4.

19. FHWA, op. cit., p. 2A-6.

20. FHWA, op. cit., p. 2A-4.

21. FHWA, op. cit., p. 2C-14.

# CHAPTER 5

# Traffic Calming Impacts

This chapter describes impacts of traffic management measures of various types (not just traffic calming measures, as defined in chapter 1). To the extent possible, this chapter quantifies the impacts of different measures and estimates impact models for use by traffic managers.

The North Ida Avenue project in Portland, OR, illustrates the power of impact analysis. The first phase of the project involved 14-foot speed humps at three locations and chokers (curb extensions) at two locations. These installations were followed by the narrowing of travel lanes to make room for bicycle lanes.

As shown in figure 5.1, 85th percentile speeds (the speeds below which 85 percent of vehicles travel) declined by 4 to 7 mph at four points along the project with first phase improvements, and by another 2 to 5 mph in the second phase. This brought 85th percentile speeds down to the speed limit of 25 mph at certain locations, and close to it at others. Daily traffic volumes also dropped by an average of 130 vehicles per day (vpd), as shown in figure 5.2. Under Portland's diversion policy, traffic increases of up to 150 vpd are deemed acceptable on parallel local streets. In this case, diverted traffic was within the city's policy limits (see figure 5.3). Also, speed measurements on parallel streets showed no evidence of increased speed (a problem that often accompanies diversion).

Additional qualitative impacts of the project were reported to include (1) easier street crossings for pedestrians because of slower traffic and shorter crossing distances at curb extensions; and (2) safer bicycle operation, a result of slower traffic plus the addition of exclusive bicycle lanes.

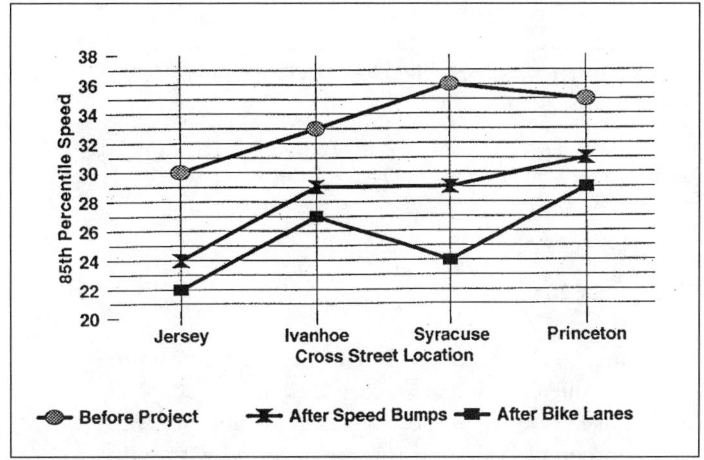


**Figure 5.1. 85th Percentile Speeds Before and After Traffic Calming on N. Ida Avenue. (Portland, OR)**

Source: Bureau of Traffic Management, "N. Ida Avenue Neighborhood Traffic Management Project—Final Report," City of Portland, OR, February 1996.

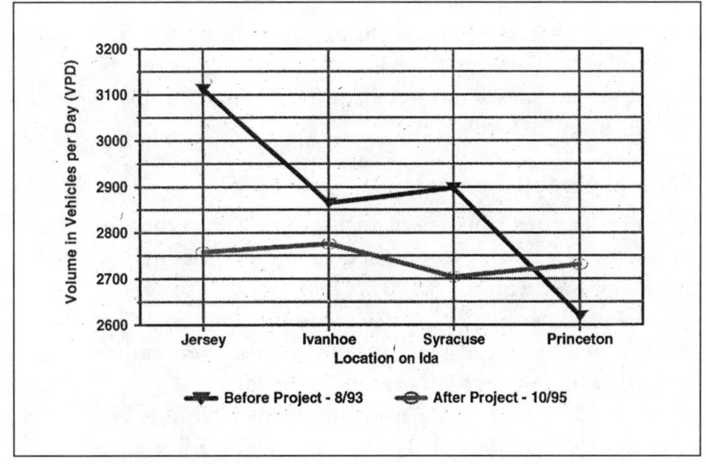


**Figure 5.2. Daily Traffic Volumes Before and After Traffic Calming on N. Ida Avenue. (Portland, OR)**

Source: Bureau of Traffic Management, "N. Ida Avenue Neighborhood Traffic Management Project—Final Report," City of Portland, OR, February 1996.

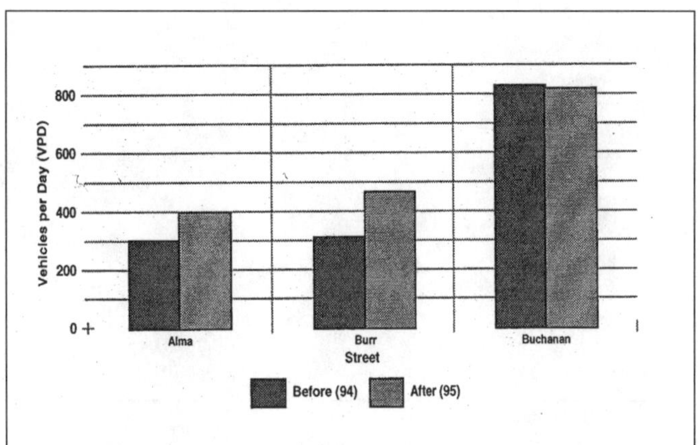

Figure 5.3. Before-and-After Traffic Volumes on Streets Parallel to N. Ida Avenue. (Portland, OR)

Source: Bureau of Traffic Management, "N. Ida Avenue Neighborhood Traffic Management Project—Final Report," City of Portland, OR, February 1996.

40 → 28 mph, 7,611 → 7,018 vpd

Figure 5.4. 12-foot Speed Humps. (Woodland Ave.—Austin, TX)

32 → 27 mph, 2,185 → 1,255 vpd

Figure 5.5. 14-foot Speed Humps. (Friendly St.—Eugene, OR)

35 → 29 mph, 2,540 → 1,942 vpd

Figure 5.6. 22-foot Speed Tables. (108th Ave. SE— Bellevue, WA)

## Traffic Speeds

Returning to the definition in chapter 1, traffic calming seeks to reduce *speeds* and *volumes* of traffic to acceptable levels. For illustrative purposes, the following pages combine photographs of traffic calming measures with traffic speeds and volumes before and after traffic calming. Some of these applications have been very effective in reducing speeds or volumes. Others have not. Impacts are highly *case-specific,* depending on the geometrics and spacing of measures, availability of alternative routes, treatment of other streets in areawide applications, and many other factors. Just how case-specific is apparent from figures 5.4 through 5.21. This section and the next attempt to generalize about impacts across installations and also to explain impacts in quantitative terms.

### Typical Speed Impacts

In traffic engineering, speed distributions are typically represented by 85th percentile speeds. It is not the highest speed any motorist travels, but is high enough to represent the probable safe end of the speed distribution. Most of the speed data available from before-and-after studies of traffic calming are 85th percentile speeds.

Before-and-after results from hundreds of studies are presented in appendix A. These individual studies have been used to generate summary statistics on speed impacts of different slow points. Three measures of impact are summarized in table 5.1—average 85th percentile speed after treatment, average absolute change in 85th percentile speed from before to after treatment, and average percentage change in 85th percentile speed from before to

37 → 35 mph, volumes not available

**Figure 5.7. Raised Intersection. (Eliots Oak Rd.—Howard County, MD)**

30 → 21 mph, volumes not available

**Figure 5.8. Raised Crosswalks/Raised Intersection/Chicane. (Berkshire St.—Cambridge, MA)**

40 → 37 mph, 13,000 → 10,300 vpd

**Figure 5.9. 22-foot Speed Tables. (Barklay Downs Dr.—Charlotte, NC)**

40 → 34 mph, 14,500 → 14,400 vpd

**Figure 5.10. 22-foot Raised Crosswalks. (Bel Pre Rd.—Montgomery County, MD)**

31 → 28 mph, 770 → 331 vpd

**Figure 5.11. One-Lane Angled Slow Point. (128th Ave. NE—Bellevue, WA)**

Speeds not available, 1,599 → 1,285 vpd

**Figure 5.12. 10-foot Diameter Traffic Circle. (NE 10th Ave.—Gainesville, FL)**

34 → 28 mph,  volumes not available

Figure 5.13. 18-foot Diameter Traffic Circle with Neckdowns. (SE 46th Way—Bellevue, WA)

Speeds not available, 2,157 → 214 vpd

Figure 5.16. Diagonal Diverter. (6th Ave.—Phoenix, AZ)

34→ 30 mph, 1,500→ 1,390 vpd

Figure 5.14. Chicanes/22-foot Speed Tables. (Huntington Pkwy.—Montgomery County, MD)

34 → 32 mph, 6,150 → 5,040 vpd

Figure 5.17. Median Chokers. (William St.—San Jose, CA)

25 → 23 mph, 561 → 583 vpd

Figure 5.15. 13-foot x 20-foot Oblong Traffic Circle. (8th St.—Charlotte, NC)

Speeds not available, 5,300 → 1,200 vpd

Figure 5.18. Diverter/Closure. (17th St.—San Jose, CA)

38 → 23 mph, 224 → 92 vpd

**Figure 5.19. Semi-Diverter. (Irving St.—Sarasota, FL)**

Speeds not available, 860 → 360 vpd

**Figure 5.20. Diagonal Diverter. (16th Ave. E—Seattle, WA)**

Speeds not available, 3,770 → 1,830 vpd

**Figure 5.21. Half Closure. (NE 103rd St.—Seattle, WA)**

after treatment. Speed humps have the greatest impact on 85th percentile speeds, reducing them by an average of more than 7 mph, or 20 percent. Raised intersections, long speed tables, and circles have the least impact.

One critical caveat: Rarely in the researched before-and-after studies is it made clear where speed measurements were taken in relation to the traffic calming measures. Occasionally a study will report "midpoint" or "midblock" speeds, but because the spacing of traffic calming measures or the length of blocks is unknown, the exact location of speed measurements is also unknown. The after speeds may be 100 feet from slow points, 200 feet, or some other distance. Obviously, where the measurement is taken has a profound effect on the result, because motorists decelerate as they approach slow points and accelerate as they leave them. Summary statistics of this sort provide, at best, ballpark estimates of impacts.

Also, the exact date of measurement is seldom known. The "before" measurement may be 1 month or 3 years before installation; the "after" measurement, 1 week or 2 years afterward. The exact time of measurement may affect results because of the natural growth of traffic and the tendency of travelers to adjust to the new measures. As for when and where measurements were taken, whatever information is available for individual studies is presented in the final column of the table in appendix A. The sheer number of studies precluded any follow-up with jurisdictions to acquire more complete information.

A final caveat: While sample sizes for some measures are large, and sample averages are thus likely to be close to true averages by virtue of the law of large numbers, sample sizes for other measures are miniscule. The sample includes 179 studies of standard 12-foot humps, but only 3 studies of raised intersections. The potential sampling error is accordingly many times greater for raised intersections than for 12-foot humps.

## Determinants of Traffic Speed

Speed impacts of traffic calming measures depend primarily on geometrics and spacing. Geometrics determine the speeds at which motorists travel through slow points. Spacing determines the extent to which motorists speed up between slow points.

The effects of geometrics are captured in figures 5.22 and 5.23, prepared by the Portland Bureau of Traffic Management. Before they were traffic calmed, streets treated with 14-foot speed humps (at a 3-inch height) had 85th percentile speeds averaging 32 mph. After traffic calming, 85th percentile speeds fell to about 21 mph at the humps

**Table 5.1. Speed Impacts Downstream of Traffic Calming Measures.**

| Sample Measure | Sample Size | 85th Percentile Speed (mph)* | | Percentage Change* |
| --- | --- | --- | --- | --- |
| | | Average After Calming | Average Change After Calming | |
| 12-foot humps | 179 | 27.4 (4.0) | -7.6 (3.5) | -22 (9) |
| 14-foot humps | 15 | 25.6 (2.1) | -7.7 (2.1) | -23 (6) |
| 22-foot tables | 58 | 30.1 (2.7) | -6.6 (3.2) | -18 (8) |
| Longer tables | 10 | 31.6 (2.8) | -3.2 (2.4) | -9 (7) |
| Raised intersections | 3 | 34.3 (6.0) | -.3 (3.8) | -1 (10) |
| Circles | 45 | 30.3 (4.4) | -3.9 (3.2) | -11 (10) |
| Narrowings | 7 | 32.3 (2.8) | -2.6 (5.5) | -4 (22) |
| One-lane slow points | 5 | 28.6 (3.1) | -4.8 (1.3) | -14 (4) |
| Half closures | 16 | 26.3 (5.2) | -6.0 (5.2) | -19 (11) |
| Diagonal diverters | 7 | 27.9 (5.2) | -1.4 (4.7) | -4 (17) |

*Measures within parentheses represent the standard deviation from the average. This table is summarized from data presented in appendix A.

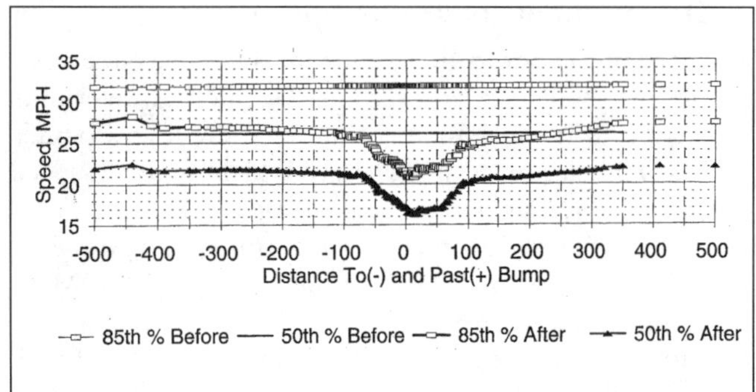


**Figure 5.22. Speed Profile for a 14-foot Hump. (Portland, OR)**

Source: Bureau of Traffic Management, City of Portland, June 1997.

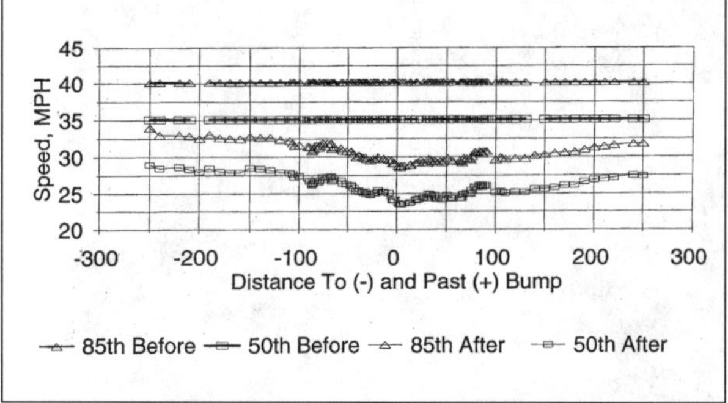


**Figure 5.23. Speed Profile for a 22-foot Table. (Portland, OR)**

Source: Bureau of Traffic Management, City of Portland, June 1997.

themselves, 26 mph at a point 100 feet upstream, and 25 mph 100 feet downstream.

In contrast, 22-foot speed tables (also with a 3-inch height), deployed on higher order streets, originally had 85th percentile speeds averaging 40 mph. After traffic calming, 85th percentile speeds fell to 27 mph at the tables themselves, 33 mph 100 feet upstream, and 30 mph 100 feet downstream. In both cases (1) the traffic speed at the hump/table was one-third lower than the original 85th percentile speed, and (2) the 100-foot upstream and downstream speeds were 3–6 mph greater than the speed at the hump/table.

### Spacing of Slow Points

The featured communities provided before-and-after speed data and separation distances between humps on 58 streets, as shown in appendix B. The data indicate that speeds increase approximately 0.5 to 1.0 mph for every 100 feet of separation for hump spacing up to 1,000 feet. Figure 5.24 shows a plot of the 85th percentile midpoint speeds after traffic calming in relation to speeds prior to treatment. The data demonstrate that even with wide spacing of slow points, speeds after traffic calming do not rise all the way to pre-calming levels.

## Traffic Volumes

The effectiveness of traffic calming measures is also judged by impacts on traffic volumes. Volume impacts are much more complex and case-specific than are speed impacts. They depend on the entire network of which a street is a part, not just on the characteristics of the street itself. The availability of alternative routes and the application of other measures in areawide schemes may have as large an impact on volumes as do the geometrics and spacing of traffic calming measures.

In particular, volume impacts depend fundamentally on the split between local and through traffic. This split also affects speeds, but to a lesser degree.[1] Traffic calming measures will not affect the amount of locally bound traffic unless they are so severe or restrictive as to "degenerate" motor vehicle trips.

What traffic calming measures may do is to reroute nonlocal traffic. Measures fall into three classes: those that *preclude* through traffic, which will be referred to as class I measures; those that *discourage* but still allow through traffic—class II measures; and those that *are neutral* with re-

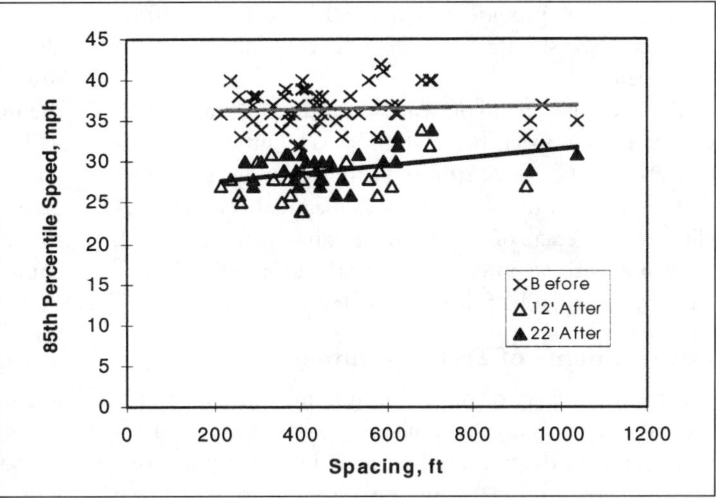



**Figure 5.24. Effect of Hump Spacing on Speeds Between Humps.**

spect to through traffic other than to slow it down—class III measures. Where individual measures fit into this scheme will, as already noted, be case-specific. It will depend on geometrics and spacing, quality of alternative routes, and other factors. Still, there may be some value in generalizing about *diversion potential*.

Portland reports more diversion with 14-foot humps than 22-foot tables, and more diversion with either than with traffic circles. San Diego, CA, and Seattle, WA, report significant diversion with standard 12-foot humps but minimal diversion with traffic circles. In terms of the three classes defined above, speed humps appear to be class II measures, discouraging but still allowing through traffic. If a good alternative route exists, humps will divert through trips in substantial numbers. Traffic circles appear to be class III measures, causing minimal diversion even where good alternative routes exist. Speed tables (22 feet and up) could fall into either class; diversion information is too limited to be sure.

### Typical Volume Impacts

Appendix A reports before-and-after study results for volumes as well as speeds. These have been used to generate summary statistics on volume impacts by type of traffic calming treatment. Two measures of impact are summarized in table 5.2—average absolute change in daily traffic after treatment, and average percentage change in daily traffic after treatment.

Note that while sample sizes for several measures are large enough to provide meaningful results, the small sample sizes for others provide only general indicators of effectiveness. Care should be taken when considering their effectiveness.

Also, results depend on where measurements are taken, with volume impacts being attenuated by intervening intersections. Data from studies in the appendices indicate that volumes in the same block as diagonal diverters decline by an average of 45 percent after installation. A block away, but with an intervening intersection, volumes decline by less than half that percentage.

## Determinants of Traffic Volumes

Clearly, the impact of traffic calming measures on traffic volumes depends on the availability and quality of alternative routes. For streets traffic calmed with volume control measures, impacts would be expected to depend on which movements are prohibited along a stretch of road or at an intersection. A full closure precludes through trips in both directions and will have the biggest impact. A half closure precludes through movement in only one direction and should have an impact about half that of a full closure (discounting trips that begin or end on the street in question—which will be unaffected). A diagonal diverter allows through movement in both directions along the street itself but precludes two out of three movements at the intersection with a cross street.

For streets traffic calmed with speed control measures, volume impacts would be expected to vary with the degree of speed reduction. Route choice depends on relative travel times, and a route that is traffic calmed becomes less attractive relative to alternate routes. How traffic calming of one roadway link affects relative travel time for an entire trip, end-to-end, is impossible to say without detailed origin-destination data. But there should be some impact on link volumes.

Examples from Bellevue illustrate the above principles. SE 63rd Street and 162nd Avenue SE were both treated with 12-foot humps (see figure 5.25). Hump spacing is comparable, and impacts on speed are nearly the same. But SE 63rd Street has no parallel route available to through traffic, and 162nd Avenue SE has a good alternate route available. Before-and-after studies show an increase in traffic on SE 63rd Street, and a sizable decrease on 162nd Avenue SE (see table 5.3).

**Table 5.2. Volume Impacts of Traffic Calming Measures.**

| Measure | Sample Size | Average Change in Volume* (vehicles per day) | Average Percentage Change in Volume* (vehicles per day) |
|---|---|---|---|
| 12-foot humps | 143 | -355 (591) | -18 (24) |
| 14-foot humps | 15 | -529 (741) | -22 (26) |
| 22-foot tables | 46 | -415 (649) | -12 (20) |
| Circles | 49 | -293 (584) | -5 (46) |
| Narrowings | 11 | -263 (2,178) | -10 (51) |
| One-lane slow points | 5 | -392 (384) | -20 (19) |
| Full closures | 19 | -671 (786) | -44 (36) |
| Half closures | 53 | -1,611 (2,444) | -42 (41) |
| Diagonal diverters | 27 | -501 (622) | -35 (46) |
| Other volume controls | 10 | -1,167 (1,781) | -31 (36) |

*Measures in parentheses represent the standard deviation from the average.

Somerset Drive in Bellevue was initially treated with 12-foot humps of 3.75-inch height spaced an average of 150 feet apart. For many residents, the humps became an annoyance as a result of their severe profiles and close spacing. Consequently, the humps were reinstalled at a height of 3 inches and an average spacing of 340 feet. When first treated, Somerset Drive saw its daily traffic volumes drop by a third, with significant diversion to parallel local streets. When the number and height of humps were reduced, daily volumes nearly returned to their pretreatment levels (see table 5.4).

## Modeling Volume Impacts

Given origin-destination data for trips on the local street network, and given estimates of link speeds after treatment, it should be possible to predict the volume impacts of traffic calming measures using a traffic assignment program that seeks the path with the minimum travel time for each trip. The fact that this has never been done (as far as can be determined) hints at the difficulty of doing so.[2]

Short of developing or testing traffic assignment software, the most that could be accomplished in this study was to estimate simple statistical models using before-and-

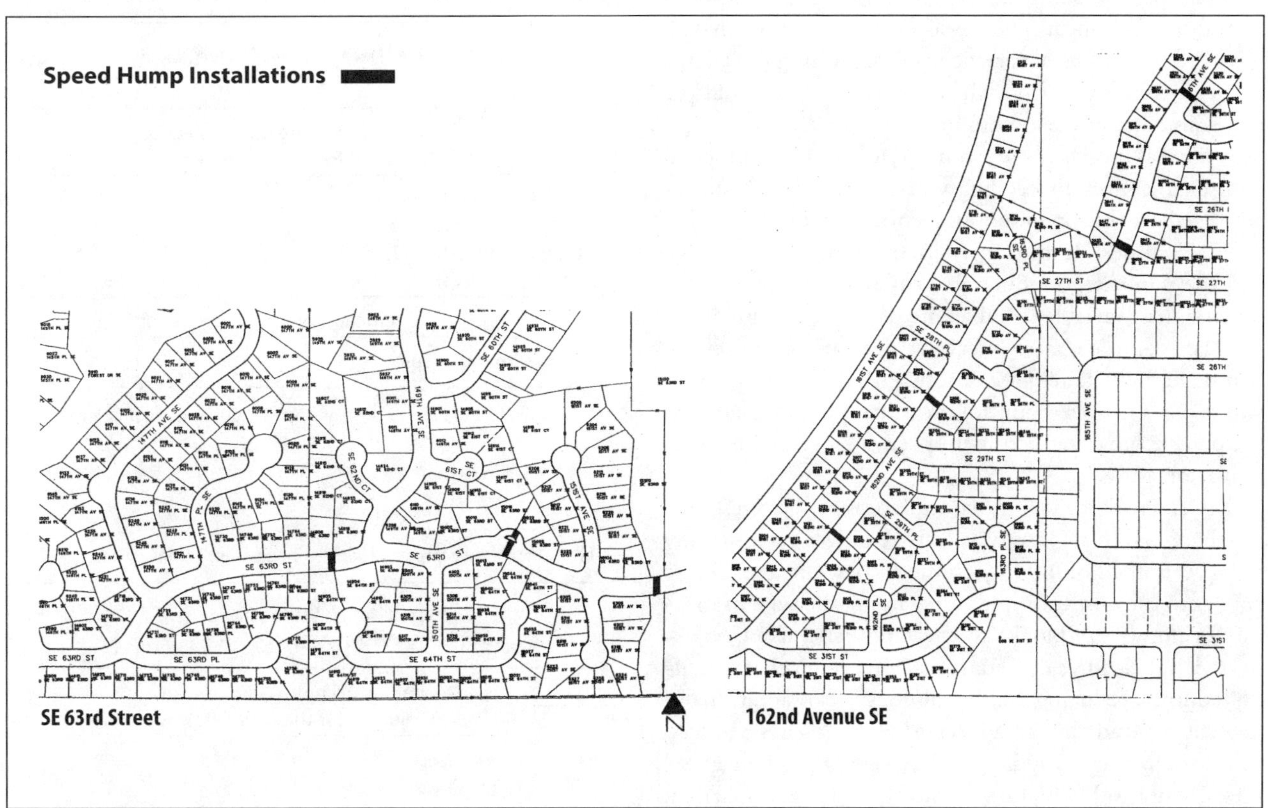


**Figure 5.25. Treated Streets without (left) and with (right) Parallel Routes. (Bellevue, WA)**

Source: City of Bellevue, Transportation Department, Bellevue, WA.

**Table 5.3. Comparable Treatments with Different Results. (Bellevue, WA)**

| Location | Measure | Speed Change (miles per hour) | Volume Change (vehicles per day) |
|---|---|---|---|
| SE 63rd Street | 12' humps spaced 500' apart (average) | 36 ➔ 25 | 2,456 ➔ 2,593 |
| 162nd Avenue SE | 12' humps spaced 580' apart (average) | 37 ➔ 27 | 1,472 ➔ 1,071 |

Source: Department of Public Works and Utilities, "Bellevue's Experience with Speed Humps as a Speed Control Device," City of Bellevue, WA, September 1989.

**Table 5.4. Speed and Volume Changes in Response to Treatments. (Somerset Drive—Bellevue, WA)**

| Treatment | Measure | Speed Change (miles per hour) | Volume Change (vehicles per day) |
|---|---|---|---|
| Initial design | 12-feet x 3-3/4-inch humps spaced 150 feet apart | 39 → 22 (midpoint) 14 (at humps) | 795 → 541 |
| Redesign | 12-feet x 3-inch humps spaced 340 feet apart | 22 → 27 (midpoint) 23 (at humps) | 541 → 746 |

Source: Department of Public Works and Utilities, "Bellevue's Experience with Speed Humps as a Speed Control Device," City of Bellevue, WA, September 1989.

after data from appendix A. A modeling technique known as multiple classification analysis (MCA) was used. MCA is related to analysis of variance, postprocessing the latter's results. It is akin to (though much tidier than) multiple regression analysis using dummy variables.[3]

Different models were estimated for volume and speed control measures, in keeping with the different theories advanced in the previous subsection, "Determinants of Traffic Volumes." In both models, the dependent variable was the percentage reduction in traffic volume and the independent variable was the type of traffic calming measure. For volume control measures, a covariate was tested, that being how many blocks from a barrier a traffic count was taken. For speed control measures, the covariate was the percentage of reduction in speed achieved with a particular measure.

MCA results for volume control measures are presented in table 5.5a. In this study, volume controls categorically reduced traffic volumes by about 39 percent. This figure applies to the entire sample, disregarding the type of measure or number of blocks away counts were taken. As expected, full closures caused the greatest reduction in traffic volumes, reducing traffic volumes by an additional 5 percent beyond the grand mean. Half closures reduced traffic volumes by an additional 3 percent beyond the grand mean, while other volume controls had less impact on volumes than the grand mean. Each additional block from a traffic calming measure lessened the impact on traffic volumes by 5 percent. Given the tremendous variation in impacts from application to application, none of the impacts just cited is statistically different.

MCA results for speed control measures are presented in table 5.5b. Speed control measures categorically reduced traffic volumes by about 15 percent. This figure applies to the entire sample, disregarding the type of measure and its impact on speed. The percentage of reduction in traffic volume is weakly related to the percentage of reduction in speed. The value of the coefficient, 0.2, implies that traffic volumes were inelastic with respect to traffic speeds. All else being equal, a 10 percent drop in speed caused a 2 percent drop in volume.

**Table 5.5a. Volume Impact Models—Volume Control Measures.**

| Grand Mean % Volume Change -39% | |
|---|---|
| **Deviations from the Grand Mean** (adjusted for the covariate) | |
| Full closures (19 cases) | -5% |
| Half closures (53 cases) | -3% |
| Diagonal diverters (27 cases) | +5% |
| Other (10 cases) | +9% |
| **Coefficient of the Covariate** | |
| Blocks from measure | +5.2% |

Significance levels: Type of measure = .71. Blocks from measure = .16.

**Table 5.5b. Volume Impact Models—Speed Control Measures.**

| Grand Mean % Volume Change −15% | |
|---|---|
| **Deviations from the Grand Mean** (adjusted for the covariate) | |
| Humps (144 cases) | -5% |
| Tables (56 cases) | +1% |
| Circles (40 cases) | +1% |
| Other (22 cases) | +6% |
| **Coefficient of the Covariate** | |
| % Speed reduction | 0.2 |

Significance levels: Type of measure = .001. Percentage speed reduction =.33.

The type of measure employed is significant, beyond whatever effect it may have on operating speed. Humps reduced traffic volumes by an additional 5 percent beyond the grand mean. This is presumably due to the rocking motion they produce at low speeds and the jarring impact they have at high speeds. Speed tables and circles, which produce less discomfort, had less effect on traffic volumes.

An example illustrates the use of the MCA models. An estimate of the volume change expected from the installation of speed humps is the grand mean (i.e., a 15 percent reducton, as listed in table 5.5b) adjusted for the type of traffic control measure (i.e., a 5 percent reduction, as listed in table 5.5b) and adjusted for the expected speed change. This last adjustment is computed by multiplying the coefficient of the covariate (i.e., 0.2, as listed in table 5.5b) by the anticipated speed change (e.g., 22 percent, as listed in table 5.1). This last adjustment (-4.4 percent) is then added to the other values (-15 percent minus 5 percent) to yield an anticipated volume reduction of nearly 25 percent.

## Collisions

Perhaps the most compelling effect of traffic calming is in the area of safety. By slowing traffic, eliminating conflicting movements, and sharpening drivers' attention, traffic calming may result in fewer collisions. And, because of lower speeds, when collisions do occur, they may be less serious. What makes positive safety impacts so important is that opposition to traffic calming is often based principally on safety concerns and concerns related to emergency response (see Chapter 7, "Emergency Response and Other Agency Concerns").

One traffic manager speculated that Seattle's success in implementing traffic calming measures over many years and with less controversy than elsewhere may be due to its public emphasis on traffic safety (see figure 5.26). Faced with budget cuts in 1996, the Seattle Trans-portation Division resumed its accident analyses and reiterated that safety was a departmental priority. Savings in property and casualty losses were estimated to be in the millions of dollars each year (see table 5.6). The traffic calming program was spared the budget ax.

It is often difficult to draw conclusive results from traffic calming accident analyses. Most safety studies of traffic calming compare before and after accident experience. Few studies take into account the influence of potential changes in accident reporting, weather conditions, and traffic diversion. Most traffic calming measures result in some reduction in traffic. Thus collisions may migrate to other streets as motorists divert to avoid traffic-calmed streets. For a comprehensive view of the safety impact, it is important to examine a wide area, including streets with and without traffic calming. The studies presented for the purposes of this report failed to do this. In addition, the before-and-after studies presented here do not control for time trends or regression to the mean or other factors that could possibly affect the validity and reliability of the results. These limitations should be kept in mind when interpreting the results reported in the following sections.

### Outside the United States

Recently, the Insurance Corporation of British Columbia published a report titled *Safety Benefits of Traffic Calming,*[4] which summarized 43 international studies. Among the 43, collision frequencies declined by anywhere from 8 to 100 percent (figure 5.27) after traffic calming measures were implemented. In none of the studies did colli-

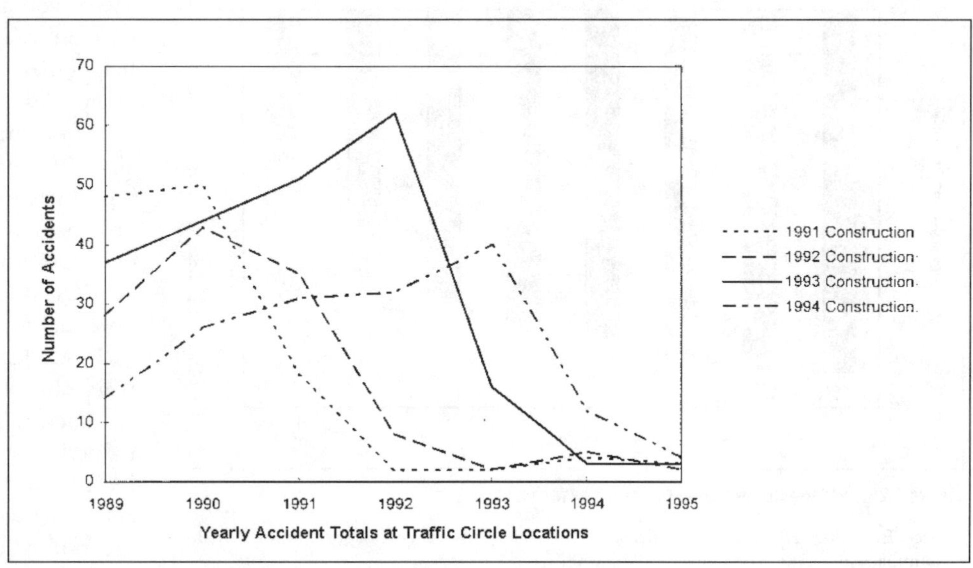


**Figure 5.26. Collision Trends by Year of Traffic Circle Construction. (Seattle, WA)**

Source: J.E. Mundell and D. Grisby, "Neighborhood Traffic Calming: Seattle's Traffic Circle Program," paper prepared for the ITE District 6 Annual Meeting, 1997.

**Table 5.6. Cost Savings Due to Accident Reduction. (Seattle, WA)**

| Type of Accident | Accidents Prevented 1991–1995 | Cost per Accident | Cost Savings 1991–1995 |
|---|---|---|---|
| Noninjury accidents | 273 | $6,500 | $1,774,500 |
| Injury accidents | 277 | $30,000 | $8,310,000 |
| All accidents | 550 | | $10,084,500 |

Source: Transportation Division, Engineering Department, City of Seattle, WA.

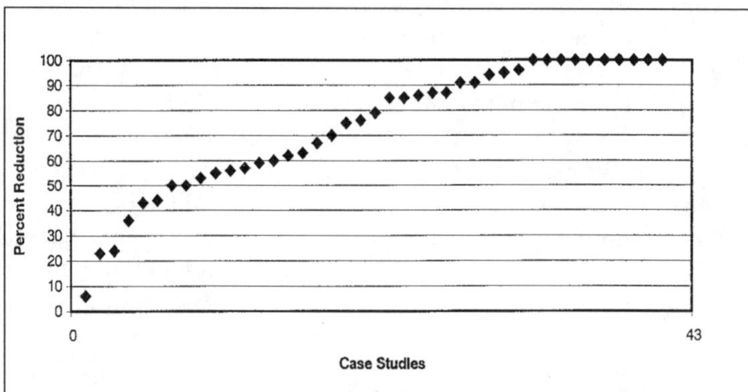

**Figure 5.27. Reduction in Collision Frequency for All Researched Case Studies.**

Source: E. Geddes et al., *Safety Benefits of Traffic Calming*, Insurance Corporation of British Columbia, Vancouver, BC, Canada, 1996, p. 36.

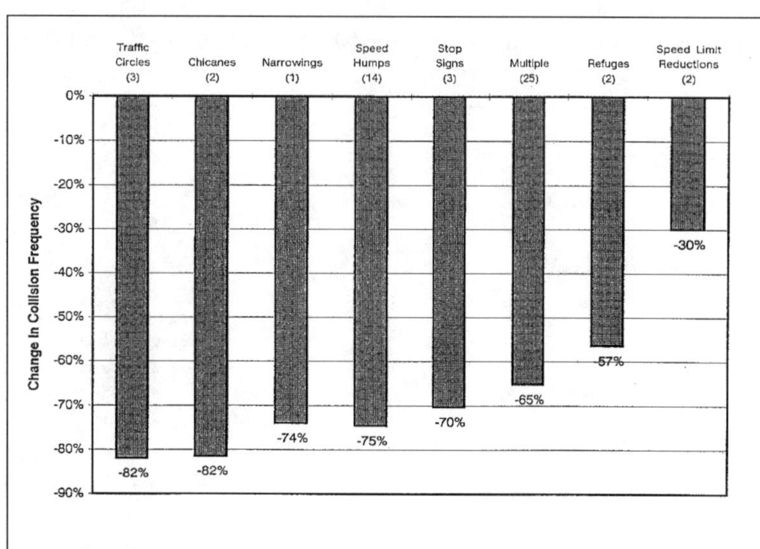

**Figure 5.28. Average Reduction in Collisions by Measure.**

Source: E. Geddes et al., *Safety Benefits of Traffic Calming*, Insurance Corporation of British Columbia, Vancouver, BC, Canada, 1996, p. 38.

sions increase with traffic calming. The conclusions reached in this survey are generally consistent with (though perhaps somewhat more positive than) many additional international studies not cited by the authors.[5]

In this particular survey, traffic circles and chicanes had the most favorable impacts on safety, reducing collision frequency by an average of 82 percent (figure 5.28). It is understandable why circles might have this effect. They are located at intersections, where a disproportionate number of traffic collisions occur. Circles not only slow traffic on the approaches, but also reduce the number of potential conflict points within the intersection from 21 to 8 (see figure 5.29).

It is harder to understand why chicanes would have such a favorable impact on safety. Perhaps it is due to the heightened attention to driving that accompanies the relatively complex maneuver of negotiating an S-curve. It was not clear from the Insurance Corporation's report whether the chicanes studied were one- or two-lane slow points. If one-lane, driver attention would be further heightened by the narrow paved width and the potential for conflict at the slow point.

In the international survey, humps were almost as effective as circles and chicanes, achieving an average collision reduction of 75 percent. This is counterintuitive. While humps slow traffic, they also create wide variations in speed within the traffic stream. Some vehicles slow down more than others, or slow down sooner than others. Variation in speed, as much as speed itself, is a cause of collisions.

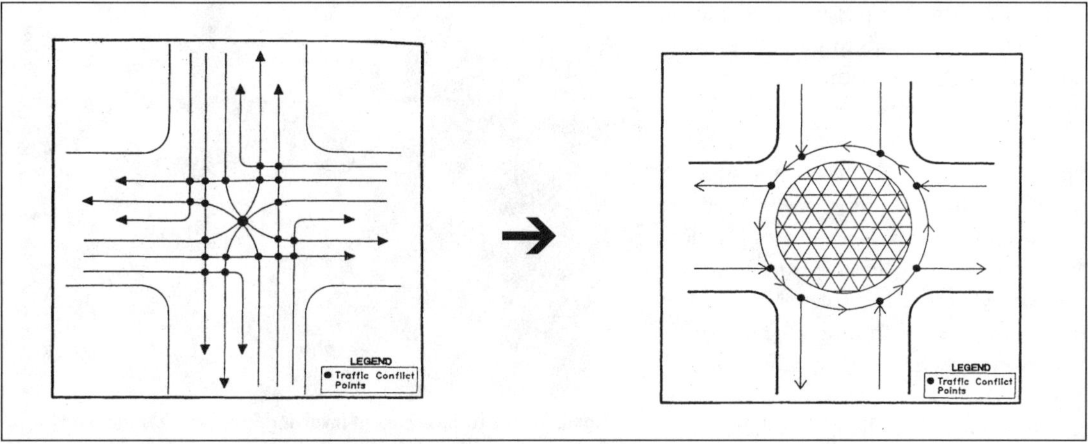

**Figure 5.29. Potential Conflicts Reduced by Traffic Circles.**

Source: H. Stein et al., "Portland's Successful Experience with Traffic Circles," in *1992 Compendium of Technical Papers*, Institute of Transportation Engineers, Washington, DC, 1992, pp. 39-44.

For safety impacts of other measures, including some that fall outside this report's definition of traffic calming, see figure 5.28. Note that physical measures outperform regulatory measures in this international survey. The reader is cautioned that the effects on numbers of collisions are in some cases based on a limited number of studies (e.g., three traffic circles, two chicanes, one narrowing).

It is interesting to note that for the Vancouver sites that were the main focus of the Insurance Corporation of British Columbia report, collisions decreased 18–60 percent with the average for all projects being 40 percent. Important details such as methods of analysis, length of before-and-after periods, and controls for trends, regression to the mean, or traffic flow variations are not provided. Most traffic calming measures result in some diversion of traffic. Thus it is likely that the reduction in volume might explain a large part of the reduction in accidents.

Most studies indicate a reduction in traffic on calmed streets. As mentioned earlier, collisions may migrate to other streets as motorists divert. One study[6] found a 72 percent reduction in injury crash rate on traffic-calmed streets in Denmark and a 96 percent increase in the injury crash rate on adjoining streets.

## Within the United States

Before-and-after studies of collisions in featured communities are summarized in appendix C. Results are less favorable than the international experience would suggest. In most cases the number of collisions went down or stayed the same, but exceptions appear frequently.

One reason for these mixed results may be due to statistics. Traffic calming in the United States is largely restricted to low-volume residential streets. Collisions oc-cur infrequently on such streets to begin with, and systematic changes in collision rates may get lost in the random variation from year to year. This limits confidence in drawing inferences about safety impacts of traffic calming.

Difference-of-means tests for paired samples were used to check for significant changes in collision frequencies after traffic calming (see table 5.7). The tests were applied to the entire sample and to subsamples of different traffic calming measures. The test was also applied to the subsample of measures for which before-and-after traffic volumes are available, adjusting collision frequencies before traffic calming for changes in traffic volumes and hence changes in exposure and collisions expected.

For the sample as a whole, collisions declined significantly. Excluding Seattle circles, which accounted for over half of the sites, collisions decreased after traffic calming but to a lesser degree. For sites that had volume data available, collisions decreased over 25 percent. But after adjusting for the reduction in traffic volumes, collisions declined only 4 percent. This highlights the importance of taking traffic diversion into account. As for individual traffic calming measures, all reduce the average number of collisions on treated streets, but only 22-foot tables and traffic circles produce differences that are statistically significant. Including Seattle data, circles are by far the best performers.

It is curious that safety impacts of traffic calming would be less favorable in the United States than elsewhere. Is it a function of roadway geometrics, driving habits, building setbacks, traffic volumes, or something else? One possible explanation is that there is less room for improvement because of the exceptional safety record of most streets in the United States. Another possible explanation is that European and British traffic calming treatments are more intensive and more integrated with their surroundings than U.S. treatments. Three illustrated volumes—one continental European, one British, and one a mix—clearly demonstrate this point.[7] Hardly a treatment pictured or described in these volumes has only one type of measure in place; most make use of two or three at a single slow point to calm traffic intensively (see figure 5.30). Reported speeds drop on average by almost 11 mph or 30 percent in the British sample, compared with under 7 mph or 20 percent for U.S. studies summarized in the appendices.

It is also curious that Seattle's experience with traffic circles is so much more favorable than elsewhere. One reason may be that Seattle selects traffic calming projects largely on the basis of collision frequency, which could bias results in a statistical sense. Another reason may be that Seattle is traffic calming low-volume residential streets that have a safety problem only because of Seattle's extensive street grid. Elsewhere, circles tend to be used at higher volume intersections that carry more through traffic. A third reason may be that Seattle data relate specifically to intersections, while other places sometime report collisions for roadway segments including the intersections. The effect of the circles would be diluted in the latter case.

**Figure 5.30. British Treatment Involving Multiple Measures (and Reducing Travel Speeds by 15 mph).**

Source: County Surveyors Society, *Traffic Calming in Practice*, Landor Publishing, Ltd., London, England, 1994, p. 108. Reprinted with permission.

## Crime

In the field of crime prevention through environmental design, two distinct theories vie for influence.[8] The *defensible space theory* emphasizes social control. Public streets and spaces should be designed to encourage natural surveillance and territorial attitudes; the more people (and

**Table 5.7. Average Annual Collision Frequencies Before and After Traffic Calming.**

| Traffic Calming Measure | Number of Sites | Average Annual Collisions | | |
|---|---|---|---|---|
| | | Before Calming | After Calming | Percentage Change |
| 12-foot humps | 50 | 2.62 | 2.29 | -13 |
| 14-foot humps | 5 | 4.36 | 2.62 | -40 |
| 22-foot tables | 8 | 6.71 | 3.66 | -45 |
| Circles (without Seattle data) | 17 | 5.89 | 4.24 | -28 |
| Circles (with Seattle data) | 130 | 2.19 | 0.64 | -71 |
| **Overall** | **193** | **2.54** | **1.24** | **-51** |
| Without Seattle data | 80 | 3.83 | 2.86 | -25 |
| Sites with volume data | 55 | 4.43 | 3.22 | -27 |
| Rate adjusted | 55 | 3.36 | 3.22 | -4 |

Source: Unpublished documents supplied by the traffic calming programs.

eyes) on the street, the better. The *opportunity theory* emphasizes access control. Public streets and spaces should be designed for difficulty of entry and escape; the fewer potential victims and offenders on the street, the better.

Traffic calming could potentially discourage crime under either theory. If calming generates street life, crime could be discouraged by social control. If it restricts access, crime could be discouraged by lack of opportunity.

The opportunity theory has dominated traffic calming initiatives to date. Street closures and diverters have been used to fight crime in Chicago, IL; Columbus, OH; Dayton, OH; Ft. Lauderdale, FL; Phoenix, AZ; and many other cities. Berkeley and San Jose, CA, installed speed humps in areas known for their drug trafficking. The idea was both to slow escape and to demonstrate the city's commitment to these areas.

What difference has traffic calming made? Chapter 1 reports on a successful intervention in a Dayton neighborhood. Massive public investments to close and beautify streets may have contributed to a 50 percent decline in violent crime and a 24 percent drop in nonviolent crime in the neighborhood. The investments seem to have helped stabilize a neighborhood that was in decline.

Less aggressive interventions, or interventions in neighborhoods that are already critically depressed, have had less impact. A longitudinal study of crime in a neighborhood in Florida showed no drop in serious crimes after streets were closed in 1988.[9] Only prowler calls and traffic incidents declined (see figures 5.31 and 5.32).

In Berkeley, drug-related crimes went down on some streets outfitted with humps, and went up dramatically on others. The random pattern caused the Police Special Enforcement Unit to conclude that "speed humps generally have no discernable impact on the amount of criminal activity on a street."[10]

Another study, of street closures in Miami and Coral Gables, FL, found no evidence of impact.[11] Comparing property crimes for 2 years before and after closures in Coral Gables, all streets seem to have benefited from a general downward trend in crime (see figure 5.33). Streets closed during the period benefited no more than nearby "control" streets that were left open. In no case was the impact of street closures on property crimes statistically significant.

Accessibility and opportunity may still matter. The Miami study showed that property crime declined with distance from a major thoroughfare (and escape route). It appears that marginal changes in accessibility, as a result of a street closure here or there, have marginal impacts.

The successful intervention in Dayton suggests

**Figure 5.31. Street Closure in the Riverside Park Neighborhood. (Ft. Lauderdale, FL)**

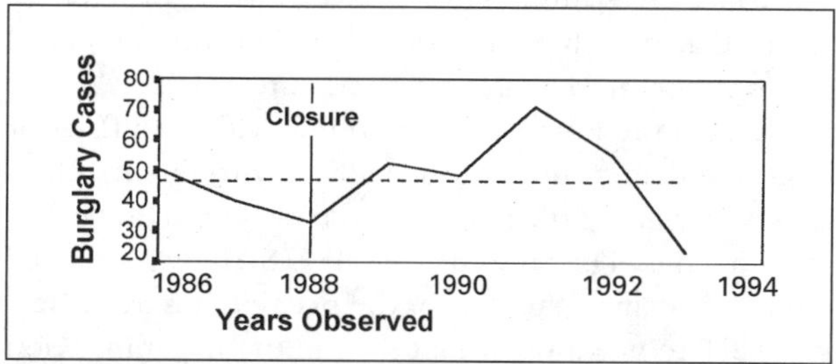


**Figure 5.32. Burglaries in the Riverside Park Neighborhood—Before and After Closures. (Ft. Lauderdale, FL)**

Source: Adapted from R. Szymanski, *Can Changing Neighborhood Traffic Circulation Patterns Reduce Crime and Improve Personal Safety? A Quantitative Analysis of One Neighborhood's Efforts*, Master's Thesis, Florida International University, Ft. Lauderdale, FL, 1994.

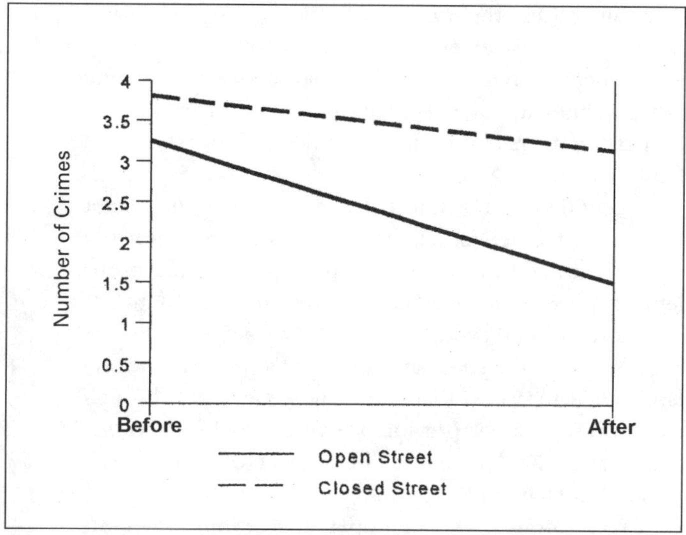


**Figure 5.33. Property Crimes Before and After Closures—Closed versus Open Streets. (Coral Gables, FL)**

Source: Unpublished study conducted by Aileen Ramirez and other students in Research Methods for Planners, Florida International University, Miami, FL, 1998.

another possibility: that the investment itself made the difference, not the change in access and opportunity. Without closing a single street, West Palm Beach is beautifying and calming its lowest income neighborhood (see chapter 1). It will be interesting to see if these efforts have the same impact as street closures did in Dayton.

## Other Quality of Life Impacts

### Street Life

European studies suggest that lower speeds and volumes after traffic calming encourage walking, bicycling, and street life.[12] A Danish before-and-after study of intercity routes that have been calmed as they go through small towns is typical (see table 5.8 and figure 5.34).

Because the Europeans calm traffic with such flare for design and in pedestrian-friendly environments, their results may have little relevance to most U.S. traffic calming programs. The only comparable U.S. study uncovered while researching the state of the practice was from Berkeley. There was a significant shift in traffic composition from motor vehicles to bicycles and pedestrians after Milvia Street was reconstructed as a "slow street" with neckdowns, chicanes, speed humps, and center islands (see table 5.9 and figure 5.35).

### Property Values

There are two theories relating traffic calming to property values. One theory is that traffic calming eliminates or lessens negative externalities of motor vehicle use. Property values rise in response. The other theory is that traffic calming stigmatizes a street, announcing to all prospective property owners that traffic is a problem. Property values fall in reaction.

Absent much empirical evidence, property values might be expected to depend on the aesthetics and functionality of measures and the severity of preexisting traffic problems. A series of overmarked and oversigned speed humps on a low-volume residential street may detract from the appearance of the street and advertise a problem. Nicely landscaped measures that eliminate some or all through traffic from a street previously overrun is likely to enhance residential amenity. The subject of aesthetics is covered in chapter 4.

Two rigorous studies of property value impacts appear in the literature. They point empirically in different directions. This is doubtless for the reason just cited—different measures were used under different conditions. One study is from Grand Rapids, MI.[13] In the aftermath of a fatal traffic crash, the Dickinson neighborhood was treated

**Table 5.8. Number of Highway Crossings Before and After Traffic Calming. (Vinderup, Denmark)**

| Pedestrians<br>Before → After | Cyclists<br>Before → After |
|---|---|
| 1,062 → 1,935 | 840 → 1,168 |

Counts were taken over 7.5 daytime hours. Source: L. Herrstedt, "Traffic Calming Design—A Speed Management Method," *Accident Analysis & Prevention*, Vol. 24, No. 1, 1992, pp. 3–16.

**Figure 5.34. Traffic-Calmed Highway. (Vinderup, Denmark)**

Source: L. Herrstedt et al., *An Improved Traffic Environment—A Catalogue of Ideas*, Danish Road Directorate, Copenhagen, Denmark, 1993, p. 119.

**Table 5.9. Afternoon Peak Hour Traffic Counts on Milvia Street Before and After Traffic Calming. (Berkeley, CA)**

| Segment | Before<br>(motor vehicles/<br>bicycles/pedestrians) | After<br>(motor vehicles/<br>bicycles/pedestrians) |
|---|---|---|
| Block #1 | 540/52/63 | 441/113/93 |
| Block #2 | 500/73/42 | 399/109/95 |

Source: M. Bouaouina and B. Robinson, "An Assessment of Neighborhood Traffic Calming—Milvia Slow Street in Berkeley, California," paper for course CP 213, University of California at Berkeley, 1990.

**Figure 5.35. Bicyclist on Traffic-Calmed Milvia Street. (Berkeley, CA)**

with diagonal diverters. The Burton Heights neighborhood, with a nearly identical street network and land-use pattern, was not treated. In the period following treatment, residential property appreciated at a much faster rate in the "calmed" Dickinson neighborhood than in Burton Heights.

The other study is from Gwinnett County, GA. Neighborhoods treated with speed tables were paired with similar neighborhoods left untreated (see figure 5.36). The rate of price appreciation was compared for home sales. For six neighborhood pairs, the neighborhoods with tables showed more appreciation. For three, they showed less. For one pair, the rate of appreciation was the same. In most cases, the differences were slight. The traffic managers were "unable to demonstrate that installing humps will affect property values in any predictable way."[14]

Beyond these two studies, only anecdotal evidence is available. In the Old Northwood neighborhood of West Palm Beach, streets were closed and traffic circles, neckdowns, and humps were installed for speed control. Home sale prices, which averaged $65,000 in 1994, have risen in only a few years to an average of $106,000.[15] In 1993, Clematis Street in downtown West Palm Beach had only 30 percent of its building space occupied; commercial space leased for $6 per square foot. Today—after the roadway was converted from one-way to two-way operation and narrowed, after a raised intersection was installed, and after the street was beautified with trees, street furniture, and ornamental sidewalks—more than 80 percent of building space is occupied, and commercial space is leasing at $30 per square foot. The West Palm Beach experience drives home the importance of aesthetics. Many successful projects to date have involved street beautification as well as traffic calming (see figure 5.37).

**Figure 5.36. Two Phases of the Same Development— One Traffic Calmed and the Other Not. (Gwinnett County, GA)**

**Figure 5.37. Traffic-Calmed Areas Experiencing Rapid Price Appreciation. (West Palm Beach, FL)**

## Noise Levels

Residents are often concerned that vertical measures—humps, tables, and especially, textured surfaces—will raise noise levels in their neighborhoods. However, experience in the surveyed communities indicates the lower speeds that result from proper design and application of traffic calming measures tend to lower noise levels. The one exception is just downstream of the measures themselves, particularly when cargo-carrying trucks make up a significant fraction of the traffic stream.

Charlotte, NC, took noise readings before and after installation of speed humps in three neighborhoods. Noise levels did not change in two, and showed a slight decrease in the third. San Jose found that average noise levels fell from 77 to 75 A-rated decibels (dBA) after speed humps were installed.

Boulder, CO, conducted what may be the most thorough evaluation of noise impacts to date, at least in the United States (see table 5.10). Traffic circles were perceptibly less noisy than untreated streets. Raised crossings also produced lower and more uniform noise levels than did untreated streets.

Interestingly, since STOP signs are viewed as a panacea for traffic problems by many citizens and elected officials, this option may be the worst from a noise standpoint. Although deceleration is relatively quiet, acceleration from rest or near rest is not. Noise levels rise until drivers shift gears, and then rise again until they shift again.

The Europeans, who have studied noise impacts of traffic calming measures far more thoroughly than have communities in the United States, have reached similar conclusions. The more speeds are reduced, the more noise levels are reduced. Simple mathematical relationships have been estimated. Noise impacts are less favorable where commercial traffic is heavy and where slow points are so far apart that traffic fully accelerates between them.[16]

What is not captured by noise studies is the occasional screeching of tires, clunking of cargo, or in a few communities, honking in protest when vertical measures are first installed. This is one advantage of horizontal measures, and one argument for raised intersections over midblock humps or tables. At least the raised intersections are not directly in front of people's houses.

### Future Research

No information on other impacts of traffic calming—for example, impact on people with disabilities, air quality, or social interactions among neighbors—was uncovered in this review of U.S. practice. Europeans have assessed some of these other impacts in their formal evaluations. These impacts are related to quality of life and should be candidates for future research in the United States.

## Impacts of Education and Enforcement

This section reviews the limited evidence available on the effectiveness of education and enforcement activities (see appendix D for individual study results). The evidence is not encouraging. Yet, these activities cannot be dismissed. There have been successes, and enforcement activities in the communities surveyed seem particularly successful on high-volume collectors and arterials, the streets that are least amenable to restrictive engineering measures.

### Neighborhood Traffic Safety Campaigns

Neighborhood traffic safety campaigns usually consist of personalized letters or general flyers that are distributed to all residents of a neighborhood and that cite statistics on speeding within the neighborhood and appeal for compliance with traffic laws (see figure 5.38). No empirical evidence was uncovered regarding the impacts of such campaigns. Among traffic managers, there is skepticism about their effectiveness.

### Radar Speed Display Units

Radar speed display units are rotated from street to street, based on citizen requests. Their purpose is to remind drivers that they are speeding, thus encouraging compliance

**Table 5.10. Traffic Noise Levels Near an Uncontrolled Intersection, 4-Way Stop, Traffic Circle, and Raised Intersection. (Boulder, CO)**

| Location | Measure | Usual Level (decibels) | Peak Level (decibels) |
| --- | --- | --- | --- |
| 17th and Balsam | None | 68–69 | 72 |
| 13th and Balsam | 4-way stop | 66–67 | 69 |
| 14th and Balsam | Traffic circle | 60–64 | 70 |
| Nicholl and Edgewood (extension of Balsam) | Raised crossing | 60–62 | 64 |

Source: City of Boulder, "Environmental Enforcement Department Sound Study," Attachment F, Study Session on the Neighborhood Traffic Mitigation Program, Boulder City Council, April 8, 1997.

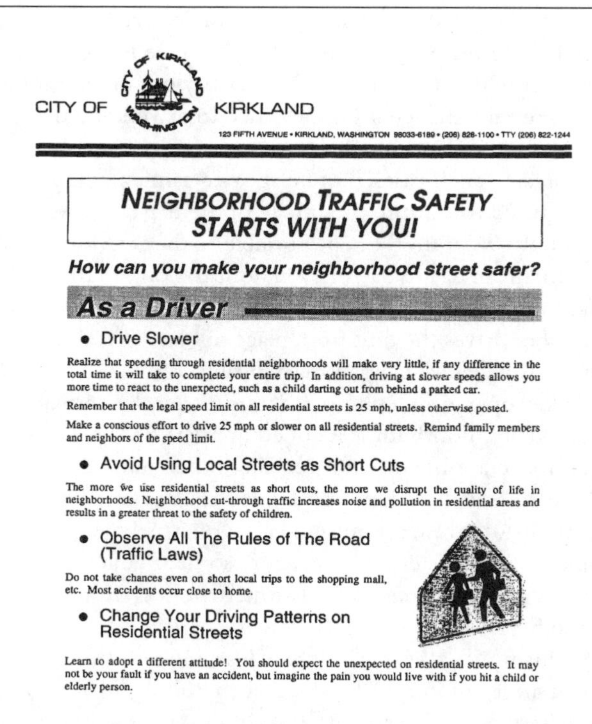


**Figure 5.38. Example of a Neighborhood Safety Flyer. (Kirkland, WA)**

**Figure 5.39. Radar Speed Trailer in the Field. (Kirkland, WA)**

with the speed limit. The most common form of radar speed display unit is a portable trailer equipped with a radar unit that detects the speed of passing vehicles and displays it on a reader board, often with a speed limit sign next to the display (see figure 5.39).

San Jose has found radar speed trailers effective only while displayed. The residual effect is negligible. Kirkland, WA, reports that radar speed trailers, while displayed, reduce speed by 25 percent.[17] In the longer term (30 days after a series of applications), speeds are reduced by 6 percent on streets with traffic volumes below 600 vehicles per day; on such streets, most traffic is local, and radar speed trailers raise residents' consciousness. On higher volume streets serving through traffic, the long-term effect of radar speed trailers has been found to be negligible.

## Neighborhood Speed Watch

In some communities, speed watch programs lend residents radar guns and have them record the speeds, makes, models, and license plate numbers of all vehicles clocked speeding through their neighborhood. The police department then sends warning letters to the owners of offending vehicles, reminding them of the posted speed limit and the neighborhood's concern for safety.

In San Jose, neighborhood speed watch was dropped for lack of resident interest. There, as elsewhere, the program was hampered by resident fear of confrontation with irate motorists and by a lack of volunteers during hours when traffic speeding is at its worst.

In Phoenix, neighborhood speed watch programs have had marginal impacts on 85th percentile speeds. Among five streets for which measurements are available, the median speed reduction was only 1 mph; one street actually experienced an increase in the 85th percentile speed (see appendix D). The traffic management team in Phoenix refers to neighborhood speed watch as their "resident calming" program, since residents seem to feel better after the experience despite lack of manifest results.

In Kirkland, WA, neighborhood speed watch proved even less effective than the radar speed trailer. Thirty days after speed monitoring, 85th percentile speeds were unchanged at two locations and had fallen by 2 mph at a third. At the third location, the drop in speed may have been due to intensive police enforcement rather than speed watch.[18]

The one reported exception to generally unimpressive results is Gwinnett County's speed watch program in which 85th percentile speeds fell from 45 to 35 mph.[19] Gwinnett County's program, now defunct, was different from others in several respects. Transportation department personnel performed the radar speed checks, avoiding the problems of resident reluctance and unreliability. Offending residents were personally visited by neighborhood committee members who appealed for cooperation. Names of offenders were published in a neighborhood newsletter, and in at least a few cases, membership in a subdivision swim and tennis club was suspended over speeding violations. The labor intensiveness of the program, not its effectiveness, was its downfall. It fell victim to budget cuts.

## Targeted Police Enforcement

Communities cannot place a police officer on every corner. In an extensive network of local streets, there are too few officers, too many corners, and too many hours in the day when speeding can occur. Limited personnel can be more cost-effectively deployed on main thoroughfares.

The best that can be offered to those living on low-volume streets is periodic daytime speed enforcement. Boulder tried targeted speed enforcement on streets that had applied for traffic calming measures but were ineligible, having been designated critical emergency response routes. In all, 38 high-enforcement zones (HEZs) were established on 30 individual streets. Results were disappointing. After enforcement, speeds were unchanged in three HEZs for which before-and-after data are available, and speeds actually went up in the fourth (see appendix D).

## Photo-Radar Speed Enforcement

Where authorized by State law, photo-radar is a new speed enforcement option. Photo-radar uses a radar unit to measure the speed of passing vehicles and a camera to take a photograph of any vehicle exceeding the speed limit (see figure 5.40). The photograph usually captures the image of a speeding vehicle with sufficient clarity to read the license plate. The owner of the vehicle is then sent a citation which he or she can either pay or contest. Some states require that citations be issued to drivers and treated as moving violations, with points assessed against drivers' licenses. In such cases, more elaborate camera equipment is required to capture the image of the driver's face.

Photo-radar units can be portable, so they can be moved around from day to day or even hour to hour. In the communities surveyed, each unit is staffed full-time. The staff member drives the unit from place to place, sets it up, and protects it against vandalism. Typically contracted out as a turnkey operation, a photo-radar unit typically costs about $4,000 per month for lease of equipment, $3,000 for program operation, and $20 per citation issued. On top of these costs is the salary of full-time staff assigned to each unit. Photo-radar emerges as a relatively expensive option, though certainly no more so than targeted speed enforcement using commissioned police officers (see table 5.11).

During its trial period, San Jose rotated one photo-radar unit among 20 local streets, resulting in relatively low levels of enforcement. Peak-hour speeds fell on 13 of 20 streets and rose slightly on 5 (see appendix D). Speeding continued to be a problem on evenings and weekends. On the positive side, speed reductions seemed to hold up over time without enforcement, and may have spilled over to nearby streets that were not treated (which is not true of engineering measures). Also, public reaction was positive because only speeders were penalized (which, again, is not true of some engineering measures).

Because it is relatively expensive to operate, photo-radar is most cost-effectively deployed on high-volume streets with speeding and collision problems. These are the streets least amenable to the use of physical measures to slow traffic. So photo-radar may be very complementary to physical measures as part of a comprehensive traffic management program.

**Figure 5.40. Photo-Radar Warning Sign Combined with a Choker. (San Jose, CA)**

**Table 5.11. Cost Comparison—Photo-Radar, Police Enforcement, and Humps. (San Jose, CA)**

| Measure | Initial Cost | Annual Cost | Annual Revenues |
|---|---|---|---|
| Photo-radar (ownership option) | $85,000 | $145,000 | $40,000 |
| Photo-radar (lease option) | 0 | $214,000 | $40,000 |
| Targeted police enforcement | $70,000 | $194,000 | $40,000 |
| Speed humps | $300,000 | $30,000 | $0 |

Source: City of San Jose, "Final Report on the Neighborhood Automated Speed Compliance Program," Report to Mayor and Council, December 12, 1997.

## Impacts of Regulatory Measures

Regulatory measures are generally perceived as less effective at calming traffic than are physical measures that by their nature are self-enforcing. Typical of attitudes among featured communities is this one from San Jose:

> The exclusive use of passive devices (signs and markings) has been proposed in lieu of the combination of both passive and active devices (physical diverters) that were used in Naglee Park. Observation of motorist behavior by city staff during the project period has confirmed our belief that fewer motorists would be discouraged without the physical diverters.[20]

Yet, like education and enforcement programs, all regulatory measures are not equally effective, and all experiences with regulatory measures are not alike (see appendix E). Regulatory measures certainly have a role in neighborhood traffic management, either as a precursor to the use of physical measures or as a complement.

### STOP Signs

The use of STOP signs at low-volume intersections strictly for traffic calming purposes is controversial. The *Manual on Uniform Traffic Control Devices for Streets and Highways (MUTCD)* states explicitly, "...STOP signs should not be used for speed control."[21] The majority of communities surveyed observe this recommendation and follow related STOP sign warrants. The communities reason that drivers will run unwarranted STOP signs or speed to make up for lost time. A minority of engineers break with the *MUTCD*.[22] They view the *MUTCD*'s warrants as too stringent for residential streets, and view STOP signs as a low-cost alternative to slow or divert traffic.

Most published studies of STOP signs show little or no midblock speed reduction and many more rolling than complete stops.[23] At the same time, cut-through traffic appears to be discouraged by STOP signs, and collisions may be less frequent and severe.[24] And, while their impact on speed is limited to the immediate vicinity of intersections, in this respect they differ only in degree from any traffic calming measure, all of which have limited areas of influence (for example, see figure 5.41).

A few featured communities have experience with unwarranted STOP signs, and this experience supplements the published literature. Unwarranted STOP signs are an integral part of neighborhood traffic management programs in at least two communities and have been tested in several others.

In one application, Seattle found that midblock speeds actually increased with unwarranted STOP signs. More typically, midblock speeds decrease but remain well above posted speed limits. Traffic calming effects were found to be very localized, extending no farther than 150 to 200 feet downstream of intersections and even shorter distances upstream.[25]

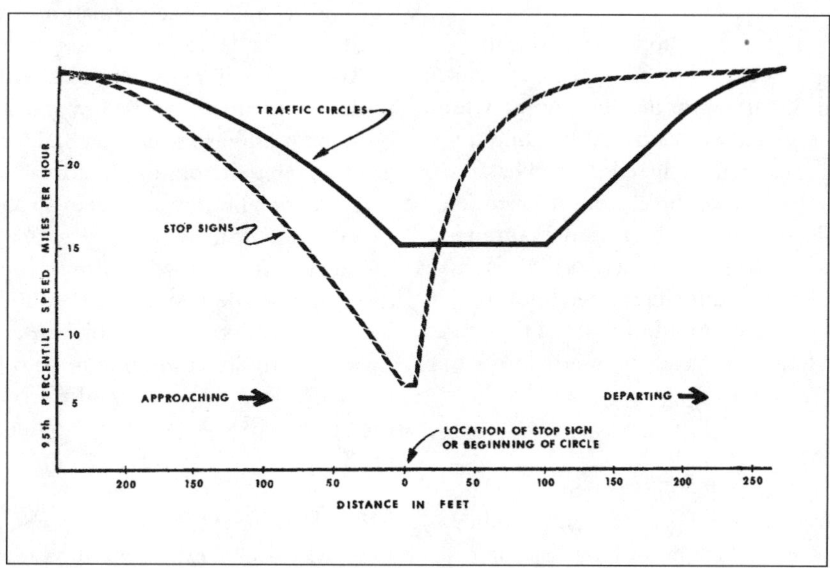


**Figure 5.41. Areas of Influence—STOP Signs versus Traffic Circles.**

Source: W. Marconi, "Speed Control Measures in Residential Areas," *Traffic Engineering*, Vol. 47, March 1977, pp. 28-30.

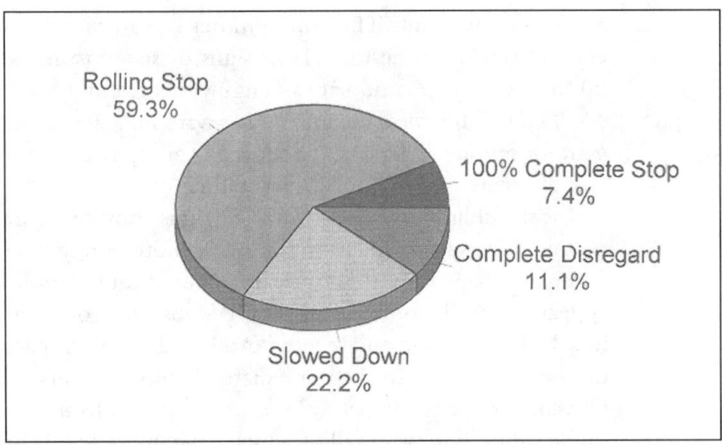


**Figure 5.42. Compliance with All-Way Stops. (Gwinnett County, GA)**

Source: Department of Transportation, "Brentford Lane—Stop Sign Compliance Study," Gwinnett County, GA, September 1997.

**Table 5.12. Performance of All-Way Stops. (Portland, OR)**

| STOP Signs | Speed | Accidents | Compliance |
|---|---|---|---|
| Warranted | reduced 2–10 mph | decrease | good |
| Unwarranted | reduced 2–10 mph | increase | poor |

Source: Citizens Advisory Committee, *Evaluation of the Neighborhood Traffic Management Program (NTMP) for Local Service Streets—Report and Recommendations*, City of Portland, OR, March 1992, p. B-4.

Full compliance with stop control is rare, but so is complete disregard. In nearly every evaluation, a majority of drivers roll slowly through unwarranted STOP signs (see figure 5.42).

Portland's assessment of all-way stops appears balanced (see table 5.12). Except for the reported increase in collisions at unwarranted STOP signs, it is consistent with most other research. Portland concluded that while unwarranted STOP signs may reduce speeds somewhat, the negative tradeoffs involved make the use of unwarranted STOP signs unwise. Even Dayton, the featured community relying most heavily on unwarranted STOP signs, has made it procedurally more difficult for neighborhoods to qualify, and has taken the extraordinary step of installing speed bumps or "jiggle bumps" at intersections to compel compliance (see figure 5.43).

## Turn Restrictions

Among featured communities, Phoenix and San Jose have made turn restrictions an integral part of their neighborhood traffic management programs. The last of the areawide plans in San Jose—for the Dry Creek Road neighborhood—relied exclusively on turn restrictions and all-way stops. Violation rates for the turn restrictions hovered around 50 percent without enforcement, but were reduced to 20 percent with active enforcement. After active enforcement ended, violation rates rose again but not to their initial levels.

Turn restrictions are popular with neighborhoods in Phoenix, being one of the few measures that cost neighborhoods nothing (see chapter 8). Despite violations, peak-hour turn restrictions in Phoenix cut peak-hour volumes on some neighborhood streets by about half, on average (see figure 5.44).

Turn restrictions appear most effective when limited to peak hours. When applied around the clock, turn restrictions are less effective (for an example, compare results for 37th Street in Phoenix to other streets with turn restrictions shown in appendix E). Communities wanting around-the-clock volume reductions would be better served by half closures.

## One-Way Streets

One-way streets can be used to restrict through traffic, either in isolated applications or in combinations that create maze-like routes through a neighborhood. Historic

Figure 5.43. Intersection Jiggle Bump. (Dayton, OH)

Figure 5.44. Effective Peak-Hour Turn Restriction Despite Violators. (Phoenix, AZ)

Figure 5.45. Restrictive Use of One-Way Streets in a Historic City. (St. Augustine, FL)

cities such as St. Augustine, FL, which need the street capacity to handle tourist traffic but wish to avoid speeding or cut-through problems, combine one-way streets in ways that force turns every block or two (see figure 5.45).

This use of one-way streets is entirely different from the pairing of one-way streets for purposes of improving traffic flow. The latter practice, common in the 1950's and now being undone in some locales as part of downtown

Figure 5.46. Short One-Way Section to Discourage Traffic Through a Neighborhood. (Minneapolis, MN)

revitalization programs, may increase traffic speeds. The return to two-way operation in such settings is a traffic calming measure discussed in chapter 9.

Several featured communities have tried restrictive one-way streets (see figure 5.46). Yet because of inconvenience to residents, enforcement concerns, and speeding problems that cannot be solved with one-way streets, most communities have made limited use of this option. Three communities—Gwinnett County, Phoenix, and Seattle—recommend that half closures be used instead of, or in addition to, restrictive one-way streets to reduce violation rates.

No before-and-after data are available from which to judge the effectiveness of restrictive one-way streets.

### "Rest on Red" and "Rest on Green"

Boulder is testing "rest on red," where all approaches to an intersection face red lights. If advance loops detect an approaching vehicle moving at or below the desired speed, and no other vehicle is being served at the cross street, the signal turns green. If speeding is detected, the green phase is not triggered until the vehicle comes to rest at the stop line.

Boulder will also be testing "rest on green" signal operation, where approaches along a main street will get a green light as long as traffic is moving at or below the desired speed and no one is waiting on the side street. Signals will switch to red if speeding is detected, thus punishing or rewarding based on compliance with speed limits.

No performance data are available as yet for "rest on green" or "rest on red."

## Impacts of Psycho-Perception Controls

A predecessor to this report, a state-of-the-art report produced for FHWA circa 1980, describes psycho-perception controls in these terms:

Another approach to the problem [of speeding] is to try to play upon ingrained driver responses to certain stimuli to induce or even trick them into a desired behavior pattern or to use materials and messages which heighten driver response.[26]

The psycho-perception controls listed in the FHWA report included transverse lines with increasingly close spacing, odd speed limit signs, unique message signs, and speed-actuated flashing warning signs. None were reported to have had much success in local street applications.

This report adds several cases to the earlier performance database (see appendix F).

## Centerline and Edgeline Striping

Painting an edgeline several feet from the pavement edge has the effect of visually narrowing the roadway. A double yellow line striped down the center of roadway might have a comparable effect, visually limiting drivers to half of the road. In theory, the perceived narrowing could cause a modest speed reduction, just as a real narrowing causes a modest speed reduction.

The theory is not borne out by empirical studies. Results from Howard County, MD, Beaverton, OR, and San Antonio, TX, suggest that vehicle operating speeds are as likely to increase as decrease with striping. One explanation is that centerlines and edgelines define the vehicle travel path more clearly, creating a gun barrel effect.

Results from the aforementioned studies could be dismissed because even with the narrowings, pavement and lane widths remained substantial. Yet, results from Orlando, FL, where travel lanes were taken down to 9 feet, showed speeds to be unaffected (see figure 5.47).[27] This psycho-perception control was not "tricking" anyone and hence was removed from both the centerline and edgelines.

One reported exception is the North Ida Avenue project in Portland (see discussion at beginning of this chapter). Whether this restriping/narrowing proved more effective because it created bicycle lanes rather than shoulders, or because it was coupled with physical measures, is an issue for further study.

## Transverse Markings

At least one study found that a pattern of transverse markings at decreasing intervals across the travel path slows traffic.[28] This pattern supposedly creates the illusion of increasing speed, thus inducing drivers to slow down. If the study is correct, the effect is substantial (see appendix F). However, independent verification of this study's findings could not be found, and it is possible that the novelty of these markings was a primary cause of the initial effectiveness.

A transverse marking pattern is part of the standard 22-foot speed table design, developed by Seminole County (see chapter 3 and figure 5.48). Motorists slow down for these tables. But it is questionable how much of the reported speed reduction is due to the tables and how much is due to the markings.

**Figure 5.47. Remnant of Visual Narrowing that Proved Ineffective. (Orlando, FL)**

**Figure 5.48. Transverse Markings on the Approach to a Speed Hump. (Seminole County, FL)**

Eugene installed a transverse marking pattern on a horizontal curve that had been the site of three run-off-the-road accidents in the year before treatment (see figure 5.49). There have been no similar accidents since then. After the treatment, the 85th percentile speed decreased by 2 mph and the top speed recorded fell by 5 mph. What is not clear from this study, nor from two earlier studies documenting the same effect, is whether transverse markings have a speed reducing effect only if placed on the approaches to sharp curves or only until the novelty wears off.[29]

**Figure 5.49. Transverse Markings on a Horizontal Curve. (Eugene, OR)**

## Small Setbacks

Trees or buildings at the street edge create a sense of enclosure. A tenet of urban design is that visual enclosure is required to transform streets into pedestrian places (see figure 5.50).

The same qualities that make enclosed street spaces comfortable for pedestrians may make them uncomfortable for speeding motorists. A 1980 FHWA study[30] correlated vehicle operating speeds with pavement width, with pavement width plus building setbacks (distance from building face to building face), and with several other variables (see figure 5.51). The strongest correlation was with pavement width plus building setbacks, indicating the importance of setbacks.

Street trees may or may not have the same effect as buildings near the street. A tree canopy by itself may not signal human presence in the same way as do doors and windows at the street edge. One featured community, Tallahassee, FL, has signed streets with tree canopies for slower speeds, but has no data on the effect of the canopies (see figure 5.52). Another, Portland, has data for a single street that is otherwise comparable along its length except for tree cover (see figure 5.53). The segments of NE 15th Avenue from Broadway to Knott and from Knott to Fremont have a mature tree canopy. The segment from Fremont to Prescott does not. The street showed no variation in speed along its length before or after speed tables were installed.

**Figure 5.50. Examples of Semi-Enclosed Street Spaces.**

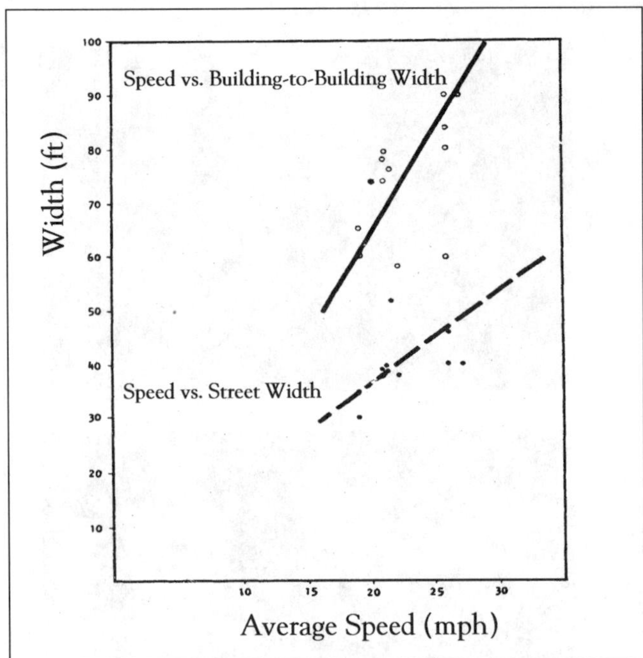


**Figure 5.51. Speed versus Pavement Width and Pavement Width Plus Setbacks.**

Source: D.T. Smith and D. Appleyard, *Improving the Residential Street Environment—Final Report,* Federal Highway Administration, Washington, DC, 1981, p. 127.

**Figure 5.52. Canopied Street Signed for Slower Speeds. (Tallahassee, FL)**

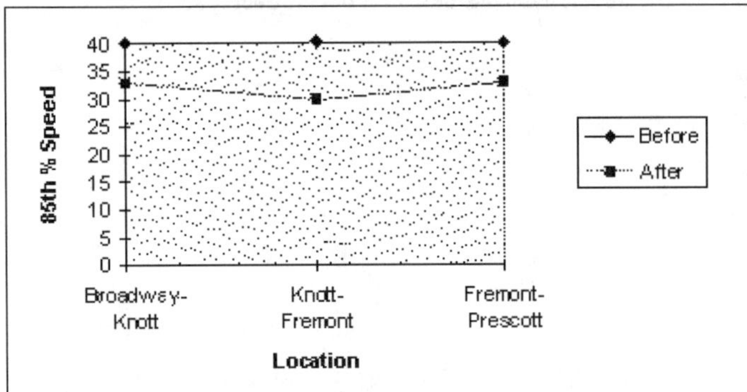


**Figure 5.53. Variation in Speed Along Street with and without Canopy. (Portland, OR)**

Source: Bureau of Traffic Management, City of Portland.



## Endnotes

1. A recent study suggests that the proportion of through traffic is a more important determinant of running speed than previously realized, even more important, for example, than street width. See J.L. Gattis and A. Watts, "Urban Street Speed Related to Width and Functional Class," *Journal of Transportation Engineering,* Vol. 125, No. 3, pp. 193–200, May-June 1999.

2. The most similar application we came across was the use of NETSIM, a widely accepted traffic simulation program, to analyze the impacts of a street closure in San Diego. NETSIM does not assign traffic to the network; it only analyzes traffic operations given assigned volumes. The program can be of assistance in predicting speeds posttreatment, but not traffic volumes.

3. For more on MCA and its advantages, see the pioneering application of MCA to trip generation by Stopher and McDonald. P.R. Stopher and K.G. McDonald, "Trip Generation by Cross-Classification: An Alternative Methodology," *Transportation Research Record 944,* 1983, pp. 84–91. Also see F.M. Andrew et al., *Multiple Classification Analysis—A Report on a Computer Program for Multiple Regression Using Categorical Predictors,* Institute for Social Research, University of Michigan, Ann Arbor, 1973.

4. E. Geddes et al., *Safety Benefits of Traffic Calming,* Insurance Corporation of British Columbia, Vancouver, BC, Canada, 1996.

5. M. Jenks, "Residential Roads Researched: Are Innovative Estates Safer?" *Architects' Journal,* Vol. 177, June 1983, pp. 46–49; Transport and Road Research Laboratory (TRRL), *Urban Safety Project—Interim Results for Area-Wide Schemes,* Digest of Research Report 154, London, England, 1988 (plus other reports in the same series); various chapters in R. Tolley, *Calming Traffic in Residential Areas,* Brefi Press, Brefi, England, 1990; H.H. Topp, "Traffic Safety, Usability, and Streetscape Effects of New Design Principles for Major Urban Roads," *Transportation,* Vol. 16, 1990, pp. 297–310; S.T. Janssen, "Road Safety in Urban Districts—Final Results of Accident Studies in the Dutch Demonstration Projects of the 1970s," *Traffic Engineering + Control,* 1991, pp. 292–296; S.J. Thompson and S. Heydon, "Improving Pedestrian Conspicuity by the Use of a Promontory," *Traffic Engineering + Control,* Vol. 32, 1991, 370–371; S.D. Challis, "North Earlham Estate, Worwich: The First UK 20 mph Zone," in *Traffic Management and Road Safety,* PTRC Education and Research Services Ltd., London, England, 1992, pp. 61–72; C. Hass-Klau et al., *Civilised Streets—A Guide to Traffic Calming, Environment & Transport Planning,* Brighton, England, 1992, pp. 71–72; R. Schnull and J. Lange, "Speed

Reduction on Through Roads in Nordrhein-Westfalen," *Accident Analysis & Prevention,* Vol. 24, 1992, pp. 67–74; W. Brilon and H. Blanke, "Extensive Traffic Calming: Results of the Accident Analyses in Six Model Towns," in *1993 Compendium of Technical Papers,* Institute of Transportation Engineers, Washington, DC, 1993, pp. 119–123; various case studies in L. Herrstedt et al., *An Improved Traffic Environment—A Catalogue of Ideas,* Danish Road Directorate, Copenhagen, Denmark, 1993; various case studies in County Surveyors Society, *Traffic Calming in Practice,* Landor Publishing, London, England, 1994; P. Hidas, K. Weerasekera, and M. Dunne, "Negative Effects of Mid-Block Speed Control Devices and Their Importance in the Overall Impact of Traffic Calming on the Environment," *Transportation Research D,* Vol. 3D, 1998, pp. 41–50; and L. Leden, P. Garder, and U. Pulkkinen, "Measuring the Safety Effect of Raised Bicycle Crossings Using a New Research Methodology," paper presented at the 77th Annual Meeting, Transportation Research Board, Washington, DC, 1998.

6. Engel and Thompson, "Safety Effects of Speed Reducing Measures," *Accident Analysis & Prevention,* Vol. 24, No. 1, 1992.

7. Hass-Klau et al., op. cit.; Herrstedt et al., op. cit.; County Surveyors Society, *Traffic Calming in Practice,* Landor Publishing, London, England, 1994.

8. The two perspectives are depicted, and the evidence is reviewed, in S.W. Greenberg and W.M. Rohe, "Neighborhood Design and Crime—A Test of Two Perspectives," *Journal of the American Planning Association,* Vol. 50, 1984, pp. 48–61; and B. Hillier, "Against Enclosure," in N. Teymur, T.A. Markus, and T. Woolley (eds.), *Rehumanizing Housing,* Butterworths, London, 1988, pp. 63–88.

9. R. Szymanski, *Can Changing Neighborhood Traffic Circulation Patterns Reduce Crime and Improve Personal Safety? A Quantitative Analysis of One Neighborhood's Efforts,* Master's Thesis, Florida International University, Ft. Lauderdale, FL, 1994.

10. Advance Planning Division, "An Evaluation of the Speed Hump Program in the City of Berkeley," Berkeley, CA, October 1997, draft, p. 33.

11. Unpublished study conducted by Aileen Ramirez and other students in Research Methods for Planners, Florida International University, Miami, FL, 1998.

12. M. Fager, "Environmental Traffic Management in Stockholm," *ITE Journal,* Vol. 54, July 1984, pp. 16–19; J.H. Kraay, "Woonerven and Other Experiments in the Netherlands," *Built Environment,* Vol. 12, 1986, pp. 20–29; W.B. Hagan and S.E. Amamoo, "Residential Street Management in South Australia," *ITE Journal,* Vol. 58, March 1988, pp. 35–41; W.S. Homburger et al., *Residential Street Design and Traffic Control,* Prentice Hall, Englewood Cliffs, NJ, 1989, pp. 79–112; B. Eubanks-Ahrens, "A Closer Look at the Users of Woonerven," in A. Vernez Moudon (ed.), *Public Streets for Public Use,* Columbia University Press, New York, NY, 1991, pp. 63–79; S.D. Challis, "North Earlham Estate, Worwich: The First UK 20 mph Zone," in *Traffic Manage-*

*ment and Road Safety,* PTRC Education and Research Services Ltd., London, England, 1992, pp. 61–72; M. Durkin and T. Pheby, "York: Aiming To Be the UK's First Traffic Calmed City," in *Traffic Management and Road Safety,* PTRC Education and Research Services Ltd., London, England, 1992, pp. 73–90; L. Herrstedt, "Traffic Calming Design— A Speed Management Method—Danish Experience on Environmentally Adapted Through Roads," *Accident Analysis & Prevention,* Vol. 24, 1992, pp. 3–16; B. Preston, "The Need for Home Zones," in *Environmental Issues,* PTRC Education and Research Services Ltd., London, England, 1993, pp. 215–226; E. Ben-Joseph, "Changing the Residential Street Scene—Adapting the Shared Street (Woonerf) Concept to the Suburban Environment," *Journal of the American Planning Association,* Vol. 61, 1995, pp. 504–515; and C.L. Hoyle, *Traffic Calming,* Planning Advisory Service Report Number 456, 1995.

13. D.G. Bagby, "The Effects of Traffic Flow on Residential Property Values," *Journal of the American Planning Association,* Vol. 46, 1980, pp. 88–94.

14. V. Edwards and W.M. Bretherton, "The Economic Impact of Speed Humps on Housing Values," in *68th Annual Meeting Compendium of Technical Papers* (Toronto, ON, Canada, 1998), Institute of Transportation Engineers, Washington, DC, 1998, CD-ROM.

15. I.M. Lockwood, "Meeting Community Objectives Through Street Design (The West Palm Beach Approach)," *Harmonizing Transportation & Community Goals* (ITE International Conference, Monterey, CA, 1998), Institute of Transportation Engineers, Washington, DC, 1998, CD-ROM.

16. Hass-Klau et al., op. cit., p. 74; Tolley, op. cit., pp. 48–54; and P. Abbott, M. Taylor, and R. Layfield, "The Effects of Traffic Calming Measures on Vehicle and Traffic Noise," *Traffic Engineering + Control,* Vol. 38, 1997, pp. 447–453.

17. T. Mazzella and D. Godfrey, "Building and Testing a Customer Responsive Neighborhood Traffic Control Program," in *1995 Compendium of Technical Papers,* Institute of Transportation Engineers, Washington, DC, 1995, pp. 75–79.

18. Ibid.

19. J.E. Womble, "Neighborhood Speed Watch: Another Weapon in the Residential Speed Control Arsenal," *ITE Journal,* Vol. 60, February 1990, pp. 16–17.

20. Department of Traffic Operations, *Naglee Park Traffic Plan— Final Project Report,* City of San Jose, CA, 1984, p. 16.

21. Federal Highway Administration, *Manual on Uniform Traffic Control Devices for Streets and Highways,* Washington, DC, 1989, p. 2B-3.

22. G.M. Ebbecke and J.J. Schuster, "Areawide Impact of Traffic Control Devices," *Transportation Research Record 644,* 1977, pp. 54–57; H.H. Bissell and L.G. Neudorff, "Criteria for Removing Traffic Signals," in *1980 Compendium of Technical Papers,* Institute of Transportation Engineers, Washington, DC, 1980, pp. 56–66; W.M. Bretherton, "Signal Warrants—Are They Doing the Job?" in *1991 Compen-*

*dium of Technical Papers,* Institute of Transportation Engineers, Washington, DC, 1991, pp. 163–167; and J.N. LaPlante and C.R. Kropidlowski, "Stop Sign Warrants: Time for Change," *ITE Journal,* Vol. 62, 1992, pp. 25–29.

23. See, for example, W. Marconi, "Speed Control Measures in Residential Areas," *Traffic Engineering,* Vol. 47, March 1977, pp. 28–30; J.M. Mounce, "Driver Compliance with Stop-Sign Control at Low-Volume Intersections," *Transportation Research Record 808,* 1981, pp. 30–37; D. Meier, "The Policy Adopted in Arlington County, Virginia, for Solving Real and Perceived Speeding Problems on Residential Streets," in *1985 Compendium of Technical Papers,* Institute of Transportation Engineers, Washington, DC, 1985, pp. 97–101; R.W. Eck and J.A. Biega, "Field Evaluation of Two-Way Versus Four-Way Stop Sign Control at Low Volume Intersections in Residential Areas," *Transportation Research Record 1160,* 1988, pp. 7–13; R.F. Beaubien, "Controlling Speeds on Residential Streets," *ITE Journal,* Vol. 59, April 1989, pp. 37–39; and P.B. Noyes, "Responding to Citizen Requests for Multiway Stops," *ITE Journal,* Vol. 64, January 1994, pp. 43–48.

24. J. Lovell and E. Hauer, "The Safety Effect of Conversion to All-Way Stop Control," *Transportation Research Record 1068,* 1986, pp. 103–107; and B.H. Cottrell, "Using All-Way Stop Control for Residential Traffic Management," paper presented at the 76th Annual Meeting, Transportation Research Board, Washington, DC, 1997.

25. One study suggests a much greater area of impact. It is atypical. A.J. Ballard, "Efforts to Control Speeds on Residential Collector Streets," in *1990 Compendium of Technical Papers,* Institute of Transportation Engineers, Washington, DC, 1990, pp. 92–95.

26. D.T. Smith and D. Appleyard, *State-of-the-Art: Residential Traffic Management,* Federal Highway Administration, Washington, DC, 1980; and D.T. Smith and D. Appleyard, *Improving the Residential Street Environment—Final Report,* Federal Highway Administration, Washington, DC, 1981, p. 26.

27. H.S. Lum, "The Use of Road Markings to Narrow Lanes for Controlling Speed in Residential Areas," *ITE Journal,* Vol. 54, June 1984, pp. 50–53.

28. G.E. Frangos, "Howard County's Speed Control in Residential Areas Utilizing Psycho-Perceptive Traffic Controls," in *1985 Compendium of Technical Papers,* Institute of Transportation Engineers, Washington, DC, 1985, pp. 87–92.

29. Two early studies that reportedly also found transverse markings to be effective in reducing speeds on curves are cited by R.A. Retting and C.M. Farmer, "Use of Pavement Markings to Reduce Excessive Traffic Speeds on Hazardous Curves," *ITE Journal,* Vol. 68, September 1998, pp. 30–34.

30. Smith and Appleyard, 1980, op. cit.

# CHAPTER 6

# Legal Authority and Liability

The issue of government liability always surfaces in discussions of traffic calming. "What if we close a street and a fire rages on?" "What if we install speed humps and a motorcyclist goes flying?"[1] Lawsuits and damage claims are not nearly the problem commonly assumed. In legal research in the literature, only two lawsuits against traffic calming programs have been successful, and one of those is currently under appeal.[2] Close to 50 cities and counties were surveyed for this report, including every major program in the United States. Many have had no legal problems at all, and the remainder have experienced more threats than legal actions. The legal maneuvering has more often involved city attorneys concerned about potential liability than private attorneys claiming actual damages.

The legal histories of the 20 featured communities are summarized in table 6.1. Where cells are blank, these communities have no experience to report.

## Chilling Effect—Gainesville, FL, Case Study

Gainesville, FL, has been spared lawsuits and damage claims, but the possibility of legal action has still had a chilling effect. Traffic circles, street closures, and semi-diverters have been installed without significant controversy. However, single-lane chokers, which may create conflicts between opposing traffic flows, and speed humps, which have been likened to inverted potholes, have been viewed differently. Worries caused these measures to be initially rejected.

Then came the election of a new city commission, and a visit by a national expert on accommodating the needs of pedestrians. The expert convinced the new commission that speed humps would fill a program gap left by circles and semi-diverters. Circles, for example, had proven ineffective in one neighborhood with many T-intersections; vehicle deflection and corresponding speed reduction are difficult to achieve at the top of the T (see figure 6.1). Humps are not so limited, and thus were chosen by the neighborhood as a replacement for the circles. Two years after its first hump was installed, Gainesville now has many more humps than circles (see figure 6.2).

## Minimizing Liability

Perception is often interpreted as reality, and the perceived threat of liability has a real impact on traffic calming practice. From the local government perspective, the legal issues surrounding traffic calming fall into three categories: *statutory authority, constitutionality,* and *tort liability.* First, the local government must have legal authority to implement

**Figure 6.1. Ineffective Traffic Circle at a T-Intersection. (Gainesville, FL)**

**Figure 6.2. New Tool in Toolbox—12-foot Speed Hump. (Gainesville, FL)**

**Table 6.1. Legal Challenges to Featured Programs.**

| Community | Legal Threats/Concerns | Lawsuits | Damage Claims |
|---|---|---|---|
| Austin, TX | | | |
| Bellevue, WA | Two threats of litigation, one from a local resident over undercarriage damage sustained on a hump and the other from a commuter complaining of humps on a through street | | |
| Berkeley, CA | Two voter initiatives to rescind citywide traffic management plan failed | Lawsuit challenging use of traffic diverters—successful but decision rendered moot when the California legislature excluded diverters from state regulation | |
| Boulder, CO | Concerns about bicyclists being "squeezed" at traffic circles | Lawsuit by motorist injured at temporary circle—dropped | |
| Charlotte, NC | | | Claim by motorist who bottomed out on a hump at high speed—denied |
| Dayton, OH | Potential liability with unwarranted 4-way stops | | 15 damage claims—denied |
| Eugene, OR | | Lawsuit by pedestrian claiming that raised cross-walk and narrowing should have been coupled with pedestrian signal—pending | Only claim passed on to Oregon Department of Transportation |
| Ft. Lauderdale, FL | Threats of litigation over street closures | Lawsuit by property owner over street closure—city excused from suit; lawsuit by cyclist injured at angle point—pending | Several claims over damage at chokers on one high-volume collector street—paid |
| Gainesville, FL | Opposition from city attorney to one-lane narrowings and speed humps—humps installed anyway after city council reversed earlier position | | |
| Gwinnett County, GA | | | |
| Howard County, MD | | | Claim by motorist who bottomed out on raised intersection—dropped |

| Community | Legal Threats/Concerns | Lawsuits | Damage Claims |
|---|---|---|---|
| Montgomery County, MD | Petition drive to ban speed humps | Lawsuit by disabled veteran alleging that speed humps violate Americans with Disabilities Act—suit dismissed because humps do not deny "meaningful access" | Two damage claims paid, one over improperly applied hump markings and the other over an injury sustained on a hump |
| Phoenix, AZ | Concern about the legality of humps on collectors—litigation threatened by residents experiencing cut-through traffic on local streets | | |
| Portland, OR | | Lawsuit by family of fatal crash victim alleging that city had not done enough to calm traffic—suit dismissed but under appeal | Many claims rejected—one paid when contractor prematurely removed an advisory sign from a traffic circle |
| San Diego, CA | | | Two claims associated with damage from humps—one paid |
| San Jose, CA | | Lawsuit by bicyclist who struck debris from damaged choker—suit dismissed because city maintenance program had no time to respond | Claim by motorist hung up on choker after illegal maneuver—denied |
| Sarasota, FL | | Lawsuit challenging humps as unapproved traffic control devices—city lost at trial court level and has appealed | Claim by motorcyclist injured on hump under construction—denied |
| Seattle, WA | Many threats of litigation over the years, often for not doing enough to calm traffic | | About two claims filed per year—only three small claims paid over 15 years—two based on inadequate signage and one on a poorly designed measure |
| Tallahassee, FL | Resident demanded written acknowledgment of city's responsibility for humps in front of resident's home | | |
| West Palm Beach, FL | | | |

Source: Interviews with staffs of traffic calming programs.

a given set of traffic calming measures on a given class of roadways. Second, the local government must respect the constitutional rights of affected landowners and travelers on the roadways. Finally, the local government must take steps to minimize the risk to travelers from the installation of such measures. These issues are introduced and discussed below.

## Rational Planning and Implementation—Bellevue, WA

Transportation professionals are accustomed to working with guidance documents. The American Association of State Highway and Transportation Officials' (AASHTO's) *A Policy on Geometric Design of Highways and Streets* (the Green Book) and the Federal Highway Administration's (FHWA's) *Manual on Uniform Traffic Control Devices for Streets and Highways (MUTCD)* have been characterized as the profession's "bibles." These universally accepted manuals take much of the risk out of roadway design. By following these manuals, the transportation professional is unlikely to end up on the losing end of a lawsuit.

Traffic calming presents a more difficult challenge because of the lack of any comparable guidance document on this subject. Traffic calming measures are not included in the geometric features section of AASHTO's Green Book, nor are they included among the traffic control devices contained in the *MUTCD*. Thus, the standard guidance documents are of limited use.

The Europeans, British, and Australians have granted their localities statutory authority to install traffic calming measures and have provided detailed guidance on how to go about it.[3] The Canadians have also developed design guidelines.[4] But in the United States, there are no authorizing laws, professional standards, or generally accepted practices. In the communities surveyed there seems to be as much support among traffic managers for flexibility as for standardization.

In the absence of standards, what is to protect U.S. traffic calming programs against legal challenges? One community's answer is: a *rational planning and implementation process* (see figure 6.3). Government's exercise of police powers, including the power to manage traffic, must not be arbitrary, capricious, or unreasonable. If it is, government may be

challenged on statutory, constitutional, and common law grounds.

Several of Bellevue's program features include:

- Identification of traffic problems based on speed measurements, traffic counts, accident analyses, and other special studies
- Consideration of alternative traffic calming measures and selection (with public input) of one capable of solving documented problems
- Prioritization of projects for funding on some objective basis
- Installation of measures on a trial basis, subject to followup performance evaluation
- Follow-up evaluation to check that measures have performed as intended, and if not, that they are modified or removed
- Thorough documentation of the entire process[5]

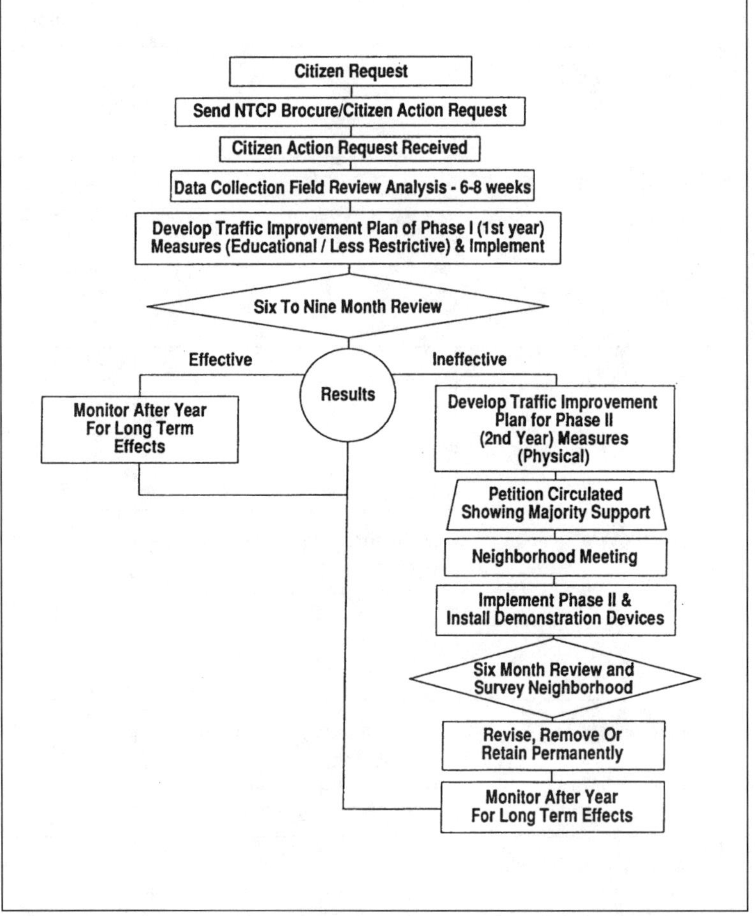


**Figure 6.3. One Rational Traffic Calming Planning and Implementation Process. (Bellevue, WA)**

Source: K.L. Gonzalez, "Neighborhood Traffic Control: Bellevue's Approach," *ITE Journal*, Vol. 63, 1993, pp. 43–45.

Traffic calming programs structured as popularity contests, relying exclusively on neighborhood petitions and financial antes to decide what gets built, are inviting litigation. Likewise, programs relying on casual observation of traffic conditions, ad hoc contacts with neighbors, and intuitive judgments are at legal risk. Examples of each can be found among the featured programs. See chapter 8 for more on programmatic options.

## Case Law—Legal Authority

While members of the public have a right to use public highways without obstruction and interruption, this right is subject to the power of local governments to impose reasonable restrictions for the protection of the public. In some States, the right of a local government to interfere with the free flow of traffic requires express statutory authority. These States have preempted the regulation and control of traffic on all highways and streets, including those under the jurisdiction of local governments. In other States, local governments' general authority to construct and maintain streets has been interpreted by courts as providing ample authority for street closures and similar actions.

### Challenge to Diverters and Half Closures—Berkeley, CA

In California, the State has preempted the entire field of traffic control. A locality has no right to interfere with the free flow of traffic unless expressly authorized by State statute. This fact led to the best known legal challenge to traffic calming, *Rumford* v. *City of Berkeley,* 31 Cal.3d 545, 645 P.2d 124. At the time of the lawsuit, Berkeley had placed large, movable concrete bollards on more than 40 streets to create full closures, diagonal diverters, and half closures (see figure 6.4). The barriers had proven effective in reducing traffic volumes and collisions. Twice, the electorate had voted down ballot measures to remove the barriers.

The California Supreme Court ruled that the diverters and half closures were traffic control devices not authorized by State law. They were not complete closures, which had been authorized under certain circumstances, nor were they signs or symbols, which had also been authorized. They were not permanent changes in curb location or median installations, which had been authorized as well. Hence the diverters and half closures were declared illegal.

Dissenting judges noted the inconsistency of banning measures that had the same effect as mandatory turn signs but were less easily disobeyed. They also noted the absurdity of banning measures that had the same effect as permanent changes in the curb line but were movable as conditions changed.

Ultimately, the matter was settled by the State legislature, which gave local governments the authority to block entry to, or exit from, any street by means of islands, curbs, traffic barriers, or roadway design features. The legislature also excluded traffic calming measures from the definition of traffic control devices and hence from State regulation. This statutory exclusion, expanded recently, applies to islands, curbs, traffic barriers, speed humps, speed bumps, or roadway design features.

### Challenge to Humps and Tables—Sarasota, FL

As traffic calming has become more common, arguments over the authority to install traffic calming measures have subsided. Thus, it came as a surprise when Sarasota was sued recently on essentially the same grounds as was Berkeley 15 years earlier (see figure 6.5). Like California, the State of Florida has preempted the field of traffic control. Cities and counties have the power to regulate traffic only

**Figure 6.4. "Temporary" Diverter Challenged in Court. (Berkeley, CA)**

**Figure 6.5. Speed Table also Challenged. (Sarasota, FL)**

by means of official traffic control devices, which must conform to the specifications of the Florida Department of Transportation (FDOT). FDOT has adopted the *MUTCD* as its official guide to traffic control devices.[6]

In *Windom* v. *City of Sarasota,* the plaintiffs claimed that speed humps and speed tables are traffic control devices not recognized by the *MUTCD* and hence illegal. In a letter to the plaintiffs, the State transportation engineer agreed. The city's response was that sovereign immunity protects the city from such claims; speed humps and speed tables are not traffic control devices but instead traffic calming measures, and the installation of such measures falls under the city's broad home rule and police powers.

In June 1998, the circuit court ruled against the city, finding that speed humps and speed tables are unauthorized traffic control devices. The city was enjoined from installing additional humps or tables, and was ordered to remove existing humps and tables. Removal, which could cost as much as a quarter million dollars, is stayed pending appeal. The State's Land Use and Transportation Study Committee has recommended legislative action to solve the problem.

## Case Law—Tort Liability

Government has a legal duty to exercise ordinary care for the safety of motorists who are themselves exercising ordinary care. If this duty is breached, and someone is injured, a tort claim for government negligence can result. In order to establish tort liability, the following elements must be proven:

- The defendant must owe a legal duty to the injured plaintiff;
- There must be a breach of duty through the failure to perform or the negligent performance of that duty;
- The breach of duty must be a proximate cause of the accident;
- The plaintiff must have suffered damages as a result of the accident.

In both case and statutory law, the distinction is made between *discretionary* functions, which are generally immune from tort claims, and *ministerial* functions, which are not. Discretionary functions involve a choice among valid alternatives. Ministerial functions involve operational decisions that leave minimal leeway for personal judgment.

The decision to spend public funds on traffic calming, to install one set of measures versus another, or to design measures for one speed versus another is discretionary. The duty to warn motorists of traffic calming measures that require slowing down, to maintain measures in a safe condition, or to construct measures per design specifications is ministerial.

### Discretion in the Choice of Measures

Under sovereign immunity, courts will not second-guess discretionary decisions by public officials if there is reasonable basis for them. A recent case involving Portland is most germane. A young woman died in a collision on a street that was traffic calmed farther downstream, but not at the accident location. While complicated by alleged drinking and reckless driving, and by the question of whether the exact measures approved by the city council had been installed, the central issue was whether the city had done enough to prevent collisions of this type. The plaintiffs claimed that a diverter should have been installed on this particular street to prevent the teenage practice of "hill jumping" (roller-coaster-like speeding in hilly terrain). Instead, following its standard planning process, the city had installed a traffic island and a couple of traffic circles many years before. The neighborhood had specifically considered and rejected a diverter. A jury found in favor of the city. The verdict is currently under appeal.

There may be one exception to government discretion in the choice of traffic calming measures. One physical measure has been found by some courts to be patently unsafe when applied to public streets. It is the speed bump, as opposed to the longer speed hump.[7] Speed bumps are abrupt features that rise and fall 3 to 4 inches over a span of 1 to 3 feet (see figure 6.6). Bumps have comfortable crossing speeds of 5 mph or less, which relegates them to

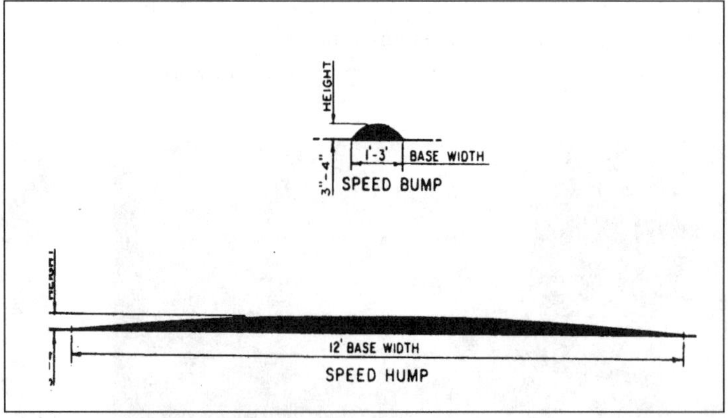


**Figure 6.6. Bump Profile versus Hump Profile.**

Source: H.S. Chadda and S.E. Cross, "Speed (Road) Bumps: Issues and Opinions," *Journal of Transportation Engineering,* Vol. 111, 1985, pp. 410-418. Reproduced with permission of the publisher.

parking lots and private driveways as opposed to public roadways with higher posted speed limits.[8]

In *Vicksburg* v. *Harrellton,* a landmark case, the Mississippi Supreme Court ruled that speed bumps constituted an inherent danger to motorists. The Connecticut courts reached the same conclusion, but had another reason for declaring them a public nuisance: Their low design speeds could so delay emergency vehicles as to cause serious injury or loss of life.[9] An occasional bump can still be found on a public roadway.

## Adequate Response to Safety Hazard— San Jose, CA

If government creates a hazardous condition, or knows of one on public property, it has a ministerial duty to either remove the hazard or warn of it. Designing a road with a sharp curve does not in itself create liability. "If, however, the governmental entity knows when it creates a curve that vehicles cannot safely negotiate the curve at speeds of more than twenty-five miles per hour, such entity must take steps to warn the public of the danger."[10]

In the featured communities examined for this report, traffic calming generally improved traffic safety. Favorable impacts are documented in chapter 5. Yet, unless measures are well marked and well signed, they can catch motorists by surprise. Likewise, unless they are well maintained, measures can deteriorate under use to the point of creating a hazard.

Diverters and chokers in one San Jose neighborhood have tight geometrics that result in an occasional large vehicle striking them while making a turn (see figure 6.7). A bicyclist was injured when she ran over debris left from one such incident. She sued. While the city had a ministerial duty to clean up the debris, it was absolved of responsibility for the bicycle accident because it happened so soon after the truck incident. The city's maintenance program was found to be adequate overall.

**Figure 6.7. Tight Geometrics at the Site of a Bicycle Accident. (San Jose, CA)**

## Case Law—Loss of Access

The takings clauses of the Federal Constitution and those of most States require that private property not be taken without just compensation. An access restriction does not effect a taking if it "substantially advance[s] legitimate State interests" and does not "deny an owner economically viable use of his land" (*Agins* v. *City of Tiburon,* 100 S.Ct. 2138, 1980). Typically, in takings litigation, the courts engage in a case-by-case inquiry in which the following factors are assessed:

- The economic impact of the regulation on the claimant
- The extent to which the regulation has interfered with investment-backed expectations
- The character of the governmental action

Businesses, in particular, rely on good access to remain viable. Thus, street closures and other access limitations can generate takings claims against a government.

### Commercial Access—Seattle, WA

There have been many lawsuits occasioned by access management projects on major roads. Projects such as the installation of medians, creation of service roads, and construction of overpasses often impact businesses at the same time that they improve traffic flow. There have also been a fair number of lawsuits occasioned by the creation of transit and pedestrian malls in which automobile access is cut off or at least limited. These are not traffic calming cases per se, but the same legal principles apply. A taking of property occurs, and businesses are entitled to just compensation, if their right of access is "substantially diminished." Generally, loss of the most convenient access or circuitry of route is not compensable where a reasonable alternative exists. Government action that diminishes traffic flow past a business is also not compensable. Only if direct access to an abutting highway is cut off entirely and no reasonable alternative route exists, is compensation required (that is assuming that under State law there is no prescriptive easement that would allow the property owner to have reasonable ingress and egress over the old roadbed).[11]

The only related traffic calming case is *Mackie* v. *Seattle,* 19 Wash. App. 464, 576 P.2d. 414. Seattle was sued over the inconvenience and potential loss of sales caused by the closure of a through street (see figure 6.8). Although the street had provided the most direct route to the business, the court found no ground for compensation since access had not been completely denied.

### Residential Access—Memphis, TN

There have been lawsuits involving the closure of neighborhood streets to outsiders through gating. If the streets

Figure 6.8. Street Closure that Prompted an Unsuccessful Lawsuit. (Seattle, WA)

Figure 6.9. One of More than 1,100 Speed Humps in Montgomery County, MD.

are public to begin with, this kind of closure is discriminatory and illegal. That is not so with a closure or access limitation that leaves a street open to everyone, but makes it more difficult for everyone to get in and out. This kind of closure—in response to traffic, crime, or some other threat to public welfare—is a legitimate use of police power, constrained only by requirements of equal protection and due process.

In *Memphis* v. *Greene,* 451 U.S. 100, the U.S. Supreme Court upheld a street closure against a civil rights challenge. A barrier was erected at the dividing line between black and white neighborhoods. The court ruled that tranquility and safety from traffic are "legitimate" interests sufficient to justify "an adverse impact on motorists who are somewhat inconvenienced by the street closing." The only injury suffered by black or white residents was that one street rather than another would have to be used for certain trips.

### Access for People with Disabilities—Montgomery County, MD

In a different kind of access-related challenge, *Slager* v. *Duncan,* a disabled veteran with a spinal injury sued Montgomery County to prevent the installation of speed humps on his street (see figure 6.9). His suit was filed under the Americans with Disabilities Act of 1990. The veteran alleged that the proliferation of humps interfered with his use of county streets because of the pain they caused him; that he spent an extra 20 minutes commuting to work just to avoid them; and that he would have no way of avoiding them if they were placed on his own residential street. The court dismissed his lawsuit, concluding that while the humps presented the man with difficulty, they did not "totally bar his use of the roads" or leave him without "meaningful access."

## Case Law—Failure to Act

This discussion ends with a new cause of legal action, alleged government negligence for failure to calm traffic on streets with excessive volumes or speeds. Seattle reports more threats of litigation for failure to act than for acting.

As already noted, the courts will not generally interfere with discretionary functions of other branches of government. Perhaps the most important discretionary function is deciding where tax dollars should be spent. Traffic calming is just one of many competing local government priorities, and within the traffic calming budget, a particular project is just one of many competing for funds. Even where a need for traffic calming can be clearly demonstrated, private parties have no direct remedy to abate public nuisances. Traffic is a public, not a private, nuisance.

### Public Nuisance—Sacramento, CA

In *Friends of H Street* v. *City of Sacramento,* 24 Cal.2d 607, residents filed a nuisance complaint to force the city to do something about freeway-level volumes and excessive speeds on their street (see figure 6.10). The relief sought was the designation of their street as a local one, with operational changes to bring volumes down to the street's "environmental capacity" (that is, down to the maximum volume consistent with a residential environment). The court ruled against the residents, holding that the routing of traffic is at the discretion of the city council, that the rerouting of traffic in this case would hurt other streets, and that the city council could not please everyone. As the court saw it: "[l]oss of peace and quiet is a fact of life which must be endured by all who live in the vicinity of freeways, highways, and city streets." While the disputed section of H Street is still not traffic calmed, a section closer to downtown—part of a complete grid—has been

Figure 6.10. Section of H Street that Is Still Not Traffic Calmed. (Sacramento, CA)

converted from one-way to two-way operation and treated with a traffic circle, center islands, and half closures. This action appears to have resulted in somewhat reduced volumes.

## Damage Claims

From table 6.1, it is apparent that damage claims filed with cities and counties are much more common than lawsuits filed with courts (as they must be, since State laws require that administrative remedies be exhausted before lawsuits are filed). But damage claims are still relatively rare, and the number of claims paid is minuscule. Given the hundreds of traffic calming measures in place for many years in featured communities, these numbers are surprisingly small.

With one of the longest running programs and the most measures in place, Seattle has the most experience with damage claims.[12] About two claims are filed on average per year. Over the past 15 years, only three claims have been paid. This is very low compared with the number of claims filed and paid in connection with, for example, potholes.

Two of the three claims paid to date involved signage. Government's ministerial duty to warn motorists of hazards was breached in both cases. In one case, an object marker on a traffic circle had been knocked down and was not replaced for lack of a spare in inventory. When an automobile ran over the center island, the undercarriage sustained $600 in damage. In another case, barricades were removed prematurely from a circle under construction. An automobile had to be realigned, at a cost of $30, after it ran over the curb and into the center island, which was as yet unfilled with dirt.

The third claim paid by Seattle involved a poorly constructed speed hump. It was paid in the early 1980's, before hump designs had been standardized in the community. A hump only slightly longer than a speed bump and about 6 inches high took the bottom out of an automobile. Damages were paid, and the offending hump was removed.

These experiences, and lawsuits and damage claims arising from street design and maintenance, have made Seattle officials sensitive to the potential for liability in its traffic calming program. While photographing traffic calming measures with the manager of the Seattle program, the author came across a choker "landscaped" with some medium-sized rocks (see figure 6.11). The rocks, placed there by neighbors responsible for landscape maintenance, were apparently intended to protect the landscaping from errant vehicles. Aware of a large damage award over rocks in a highway median, the manager declared that the "foreign objects" would be removed from the island posthaste, and they were.

Two other featured communities have had to pay multiple claims. Claims in Ft. Lauderdale, FL, have involved wheel damage sustained by cars striking chokers on a high-volume collector street. One choker posed a particular threat because it has a vertical monument on one side of the street and nothing on the other side as a result of a fronting property owner's objection (see figure 6.12). The number of claims and apparent design flaw caused the city's risk manager to take a public stand against this installation. The city traffic engineer responded by having a tree planted in the small choker island, mitigating the risk (see figure 6.13).

Montgomery County has paid two claims involving speed humps. In one case, the driver of a community college van went over a hump at a speed alleged to be too high, and a student was injured. The county agreed to pay $2,500 in medical expenses to avoid the expense of litiga-

Figure 6.11. Rocks in a Choker Island. (Seattle, WA)

**Figure 6.12. Problem Choker Prior to Improvement. (Ft. Lauderdale, FL)**

**Figure 6.13. Problem Choker After Improvement. (Ft. Lauderdale, FL)**

tion. In the other case, hump markings came off on the undercarriage of a car that had bottomed out traveling too fast. Because the hump markings had been improperly applied, the county assumed liability for $300 in damages associated with removal of tape and glue.

# Endnotes

1. A survey of 98 traffic agencies uncovered only 6 lawsuits related to traffic calming, this among agencies that collectively reported over 1,500 traffic-related lawsuits each year. These same agencies reported paying only two damage claims. R.S. McCourt, "Survey of Neighborhood Traffic Management Performance and Results," in *Harmonizing Transportation & Community Goals* (ITE International Conference, Monterey, CA, 1998), Institute of Transportation Engineers, Washington, DC, 1998. A survey of 407 urban traffic agencies found legal liability to be their greatest concern about use of speed humps. Yet, among the dozens of agencies using speed humps at that time, only one had ever paid a damage claim, and this for only $2,500. ITE Technical Council Committee 5B-15, "Road Bumps—Appropriate for Use on Public Streets," *ITE Journal,* Vol. 56, November 1986, pp. 18–21.

2. A review of case law conducted for the State of Washington came up with nothing except the Berkeley case described in this chapter. J.P. Savage, R.D. MacDonald, and J. Ewell, *A Guidebook for Residential Traffic Management,* Washington Department of Transportation, Olympia, WA, 1994.

3. Director General of Transport for South Australia, *Residential Street Management Manual,* Adelaide, 1987; AUSTROADS, *Guide to Traffic Engineering Practice—Part 10—Local Area Traffic Management,* Sydney, NSW, Australia, 1988; Main Roads Department—Western Australia, Guidelines of Local Area Traffic Management, East Perth, WA, Australia, 1990; Committee MS/12, *Manual of Uniform Traffic Control Devices—Part 13: Local Area Traffic Management,* Standards Association of Australia, Sydney, NSW, Australia, 1991; Danish Road Directorate, *Urban Traffic Areas,* Copenhagen, Denmark, 1991 (10-volume series of road standards for urban areas); Devon County Council, *Traffic Calming Guidelines,* Exeter, England, 1991; and Kent County Council, *Traffic Calming—A Code of Practice,* Maidstone, England, 1992.

4. Transportation Association of Canada, *Canadian Guide to Neighbourhood Traffic Calming,* Ottawa, ON, Canada, 1998.

5. In an early legal analysis of traffic calming, "reasonableness" in the exercise of police powers was linked to these elements:
   - Evidence of need for action—harm to residents
   - Alternative traffic control measures, attempted or considered
   - Relationship to an overall transportation plan
   - Reasonable access for emergency vehicles
   - Conduct of public hearings

   D.T. Smith and D. Appleyard, *Improving the Residential Street Environment—Final Report,* Federal Highway Administration, Washington, DC, 1981, pp. 132–133.

   A report on minimizing tort liability included these pre-accident actions:
   - Weighing of multiple objectives
   - Identification of problem areas
   - Prioritization of needs
   - Evaluation of alternatives
   - Documentation and record keeping

   R.M. Lewis, *Practical Guidelines for Minimizing Tort Liability,* National Cooperative Highway Research Program Synthesis of Highway Practice 106, Transportation Research Board, Washington, DC, 1983, pp. 11–17.

6. Federal Highway Administration, *Manual on Uniform Traffic Control Devices for Streets and Highways,* Washington, DC, 1988.

7. The distinction between humps and bumps is elaborated in H.S. Chadda and S.E. Cross, "Speed (Road) Bumps: Issues and Opinions," *Journal of Transportation Engineering,* Vol. 111, 1985, pp. 410–418.

8. Despite their low comfortable crossing speeds, bumps have less overall impact at high speeds than do humps because the vehicle suspension quickly absorbs the impact of bumps before the vehicle body has time to react. Bicycles, motorcycles, and other vehicles with rigid suspensions are more susceptible to damage and loss of control on bumps or humps.

9. A. Davis, "Speed Bumps Enjoined in Connecticut," *ITE Journal,* Vol. 50, May 1980, p. 16.

10. *Polk County* v. *Donna M. Safka,* 675 So. 2d 615.

11. Representative access control cases include: *City of Orlando* v. *Cullom,* 400 So.2d 513; *Steel* v. *Bach,* 124 Wis.2d 250, 369 N.W.2d 174; *Paradyne Corp.* v. *Florida Department of Transportation,* 528 So.2d 921; *Palm Beach County* v. *Tessler,* 538 So.2d 846, 850; *Rubano* v. *Department of Transportation,* 656 So.2d 1264; *State Department of Transportation* v. *Kreider,* 658 So.2d 548; *Brumer* v. *Los Angeles County Metropolitan Transportation Authority,* 36 Cal.App.4th 1738, 43 Cal.Rptr.2d 314; and *Pringle* v. *City of Wichita,* 22 Kan.App.2d 297, 917 P.2d 1351.

12. For descriptions of damage claims filed against other programs, see R. Ewing and C. Kooshian, "U.S. Experience with Traffic Calming," *ITE Journal,* Vol. 67, August 1997, pp. 28–33.

# CHAPTER 7

# Emergency Response and Other Agency Concerns

In 1997, the National Fire Protection Association published an article on traffic calming with an attention-getting title: "Things That Go Bump in the Night."[1] While balanced in its treatment of the subject and moderate in its tone, the article was a wake-up call to the fire chiefs of America. The message was that their vital interests are threatened by traffic calming initiatives.

Without question, a major obstacle to traffic calming in the United States is opposition from fire-rescue services. Traffic calming measures that are effective in slowing or diverting automobiles will have the same effect, or sometimes even greater effect on fire-rescue vehicles. The biggest challenge is to keep the effect on emergency response times within acceptable bounds or to find new ways of slowing and diverting other traffic without substantially impeding emergency response. As reported by the Portland, OR, Bureau of Traffic Management, this challenge will require "public policies, traffic calming practices, and emergency response strategies that strike a balance between the desire for slower and safer traffic conditions and the desire for prompt emergency response."[2]

## Varying Experiences

From a national survey conducted by traffic calming staff of Berkeley, CA, four out of five cities report "some concern" on the part of emergency services over the use of speed humps.[3] Fortunately for traffic managers wishing to implement traffic calming measures, it is a long way from "some concern" about speed humps to active opposition to all traffic calming measures.

Table 7.1 summarizes the positions taken by fire-rescue and police departments of the communities featured in this report. Police are generally supportive; fire and emergency medical staff are not. In a few places, fire officials have hardly reacted at all. In others, such as Sarasota, FL, and Seattle, WA, fire officials opposed traffic calming measures initially but after some experience took a neutral position. Finally, there are many cases of outright opposition.

## Conflict and Resolution—Portland Case Study

In six communities—Boulder, CO; Berkeley; Eugene, OR; Montgomery County, MD; Portland; and San Diego, CA—reactions of fire officials have been strong enough to precipitate moratoria on the installation of speed humps, traffic circles, and other speed control measures. In most cases, concern turned to opposition when one or both of the following conditions were met:

- Measures were installed at such a rapid rate that all local streets would soon be treated.
- Measures once limited to local streets were extended to higher order streets that served as primary emergency response routes.

Until 1995, Portland's Bureau of Traffic Management worked well with its fire bureau on the design and installation of traffic calming measures. There was frequent consultation and sensitivity to the fire bureau's 4-minute response time goal. Measures were chosen with fire-rescue vehicles in mind, as when Portland tested 12-foot, 14-foot, and 22-foot humps with fire trucks and police cars, and decided against the standard 12-foot hump based on the results.

Yet by 1995, both prerequisites for opposition to traffic calming were met. Portland's big-budget program was calming local streets at a rate of about 20 per year. Emergency services were seeing new humps everywhere and becoming concerned. Plus, starting in 1992, Portland had begun calming higher order streets under its collector recovery program, the first of its kind in the United States. The fact that only 22-foot tables, center islands, and curb extensions were placed on such streets was small consolation for the fire bureau (see figure 7.1).

In early 1996, the city council, at the fire bureau's request, imposed a partial moratorium on new speed humps and traffic circles until a new classification system of emergency routes could be devised. The resulting "response grid" took 2 years to negotiate and was only recently approved by the city council (see figure 7.2).

**Table 7.1. Emergency Service Department Positions on Traffic Calming.**

| Community | Fire and Emergency Medical Service Departments | Police Department |
| --- | --- | --- |
| Austin, TX | Escalated its opposition to traffic calming—agreed to 2 years of new hump installations | In favor of humps—receptive to other measures as yet untested |
| Bellevue, WA | Negotiating new emergency routes with limitations on measures permitted on each route—oppose use of humps and circles on slopes where emergency vehicles have trouble accelerating | Supportive generally—humps and other self-enforcing measures reduce manpower needs |
| Berkeley, CA | Forced moratorium on humps until program could be fully evaluated—evaluation ongoing—oppose diverters to lesser extent than humps | No stated position or neutral |
| Boulder, CO | Forced virtual moratorium on physical measures—opposed to humps, circles, and "anything else that is effective"—experimenting instead with emergency-response–neutral measures | No stated position or neutral |
| Charlotte, NC | Concerned about humps on collectors—fire chief publicly neutral despite opposition from firefighters | No stated position or neutral |
| Dayton, OH | Publicly neutral due to a supportive city administration—prefer circles to humps | Supportive generally—instrumental in street closures to fight crime |
| Eugene, OR | Opposed to speed humps—favored midblock deflector island over chicane on street next to fire station, and then insisted on design that rendered measure ineffective | No stated position or neutral |
| Ft. Lauderdale, FL | Opposed to humps—opposition expressed in survey letter at time of neighborhood vote on measures | In favor of humps to discourage speeding—in favor of street closures to fight crime |
| Gainesville, FL | Opposed to any measure that slows response—mollified if measures are kept off collectors and arterials | In favor of access restrictions to fight crime—opposed to measures such as semi-diverters that require police enforcement |
| Gwinnett County, GA | Publicly neutral toward 22-foot tables | In favor of tables to discourage speeding |
| Howard County, MD | Neutral as long as kept off primary response routes—lack of opposition to traffic calming may be related to use of 22-foot tables on residential collectors | In favor of humps and other self-enforcing measures to discourage speeding |
| Montgomery County, MD | Opposed to vertical measures, particularly standard 12-foot humps | In favor of humps |

| Community | Fire and Emergency Medical Service Departments | Police Department |
|---|---|---|
| Phoenix, AZ | Opposed to humps and diagonal diverters—neutral toward partial closures—cannot stop hump installations under neighborhood-initiated process | Against any measure that increases workload, particularly turn restrictions |
| Portland, OR | Previously opposed to humps and anything else that slowed response—neutral now that emergency response grid has been negotiated | In favor of circles as "DUI (driving under the influence) catchers" |
| San Diego, CA | Opposed to any physical measure on emergency response routes | Neutral |
| San Jose, CA | Neutral | No stated position or neutral |
| Sarasota, FL | Initially opposed to humps on collectors—supportive since completed emergency response study | Initially opposed to humps but now in favor of them—still opposed to one-lane chokers, which are due to be removed |
| Seattle, WA | Initially concerned about diagonal diverters and closures—neutral since these have been supplanted by other measures | No stated position or neutral |
| Tallahassee, FL | Neutral | In favor of humps to discourage speeding |
| West Palm Beach, FL | Neutral-to-supportive due to safety benefits of traffic calming | In favor of more measures to discourage speeding and more closures to fight crime—latter now precluded by city policy |

Nearly all problem local streets are once again eligible for the full array of traffic calming measures (see table 7.2). In theory, most residential collectors are also eligible again, though the fate of the Neighborhood Collector Program is uncertain. At least for the next 2 years, the city council has provided no funding for traffic calming measures because of a budget shortfall.

## Emergency Response Times

Even though the public purposes pursued by traffic and fire officials are all legitimate, the debate between proponents of traffic calming and providers of emergency services can be intense. At the height of discord in one fea-

**Figure 7.1. Traffic-Calmed Collector. (Portland, OR)**

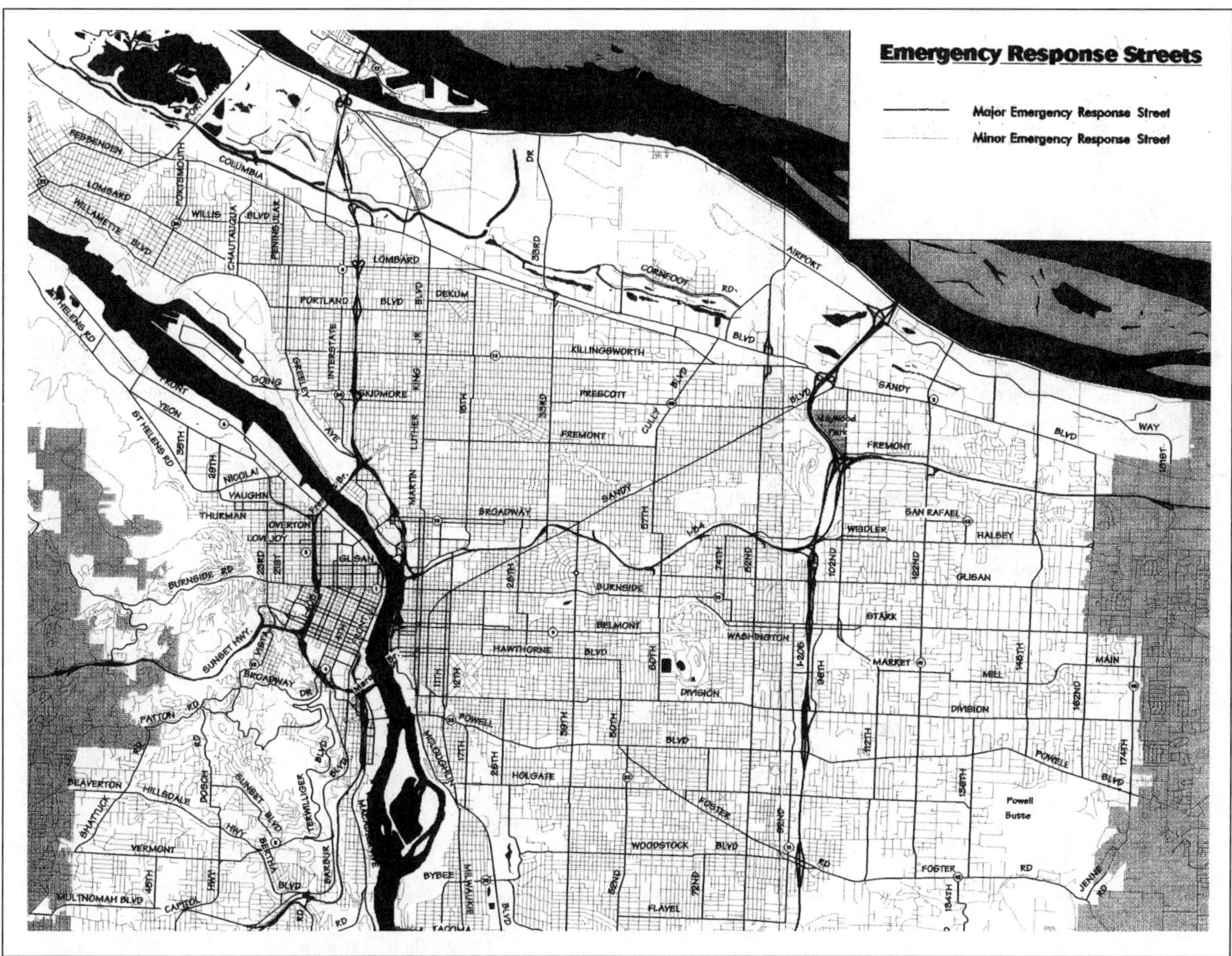


**Figure 7.2. Portland's New "Response Grid."**

Source: City of Portland, "Emergency Response Classification Study—Report and Recommendations," April 1998.

**Table 7.2. Eligibility for Traffic Calming. (Portland, OR)**

| Street Type | Ineligible | Eligible |
| --- | --- | --- |
| Problem local street segments | 5 | 775 |
| Problem collector segments | 100 | 300 |

Source: Bureau of Traffic Management, City of Portland.

tured community, the fire chief suggested, "One minute is a long time to wait when you're not breathing."

The fire chief was correct in one respect. He focused on the key issue in emergency response, time delay. This section presents the best available information on time delay associated with different measures in different applications.

## Emergency Response Tests

Several localities have performed controlled tests of speed humps, speed tables, and traffic circles to see how much delay is produced by them. Multiple runs are made with multiple vehicles driven by multiple drivers to estimate average travel times with traffic calming measures in place. These are then compared with travel times on untreated streets to obtain delay estimates. A sample test course is shown in figure 7.3.

Results of several studies are reported in table 7.3. Some tentative conclusions follow:

- Regardless of the traffic calming measure or fire-rescue vehicle, the delay per slow point is nearly always under 10 seconds. That can add up when slow points are strung along an emergency response route. Still, it is less than the 30-second delay per hump suggested by critics.[4]

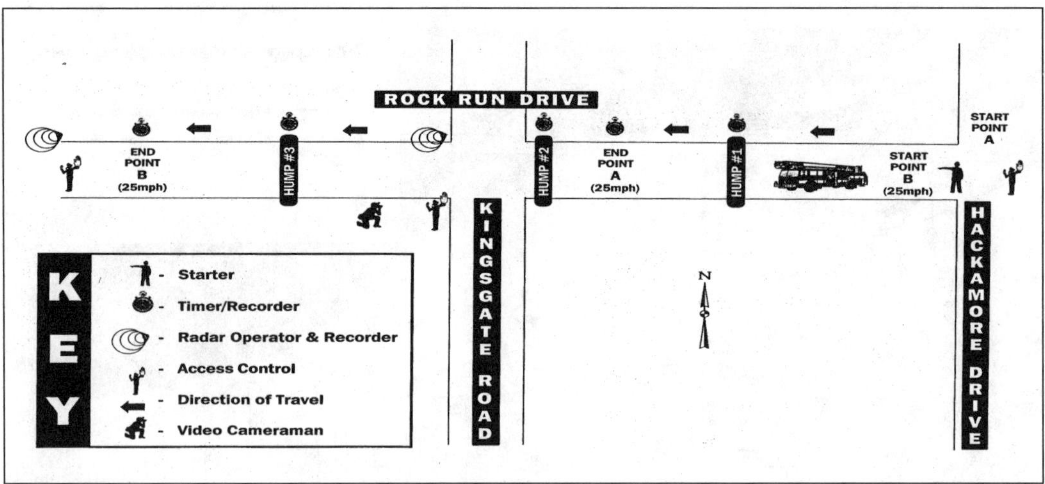


**Figure 7.3. Speed Hump Test Course. (Montgomery County, MD)**

Source: Fire and Rescue Commission, "The Effects of Speed Humps and Traffic Circles on Responding Fire–Rescue Apparatus in Montgomery County, Maryland," August 1997, Appendix F-1.

**Table 7.3. Emergency Response Time Study Results.**

| Community | Measure | Delay at Slow Point (seconds) |
|---|---|---|
| Austin, TX | 12-foot speed humps | 2.8 (fire engine)<br>3.0 (ladder truck)<br>2.3 (ambulance without patient)<br>9.7 (ambulance with patient) |
| Berkeley, CA | 12-foot speed humps | 10.7 (fire engine)<br>9.2 (ladder truck) |
| | 22-foot speed tables | 3.0 (fire engine)<br>13.5 (ladder truck) |
| Boulder, CO | 8-foot speed hump | 4.7 (fire engine) |
| | 12-foot speed hump | 2.8 (fire engine) |
| | 37-foot speed table (6-inch rise) | 3.8 (fire engine) |
| | 40-foot speed table (6-inch rise) | 3.8 (fire engine) |
| | 25-foot-diameter traffic circle | 7.5 (fire engine) |
| Montgomery County, MD | 12-foot speed humps | 2.8 (ladder truck)<br>3.8 (ambulance)<br>4.2 (fire engine)<br>7.3 (pumper truck) |
| | 18-foot-diameter traffic circle | 5.4 (ladder truck)<br>3.2 (ambulance)<br>5.0 (fire engine)<br>7.0 (pumper truck) |

continued on next page

| Community | Measure | Delay at Slow Point (seconds) |
|---|---|---|
| Portland, OR* | 14-foot speed humps | 5.2 (fire engine)<br>2.9 (custom rescue vehicle)<br>6.6 (ladder truck) |
| | 22-foot speed tables | 3.0 (fire truck)<br>0.3 (custom rescue vehicle)<br>3.0 (ladder truck) |
| | 16–24-foot oblong traffic circles | 6.1 (fire engine)<br>3.1 (custom rescue vehicle)<br>8.4 (ladder truck) |
| Sarasota, FL | 12-foot humps | 9.5 (ambulance) |

* Assumes a 35-mph response cruising speed.　　　Source: Unpublished documents supplied by the traffic calming programs.

- Traffic circles appear to create longer delays than speed humps. This fact must be weighed against the greater probability of damage to fire-rescue vehicles and injury to patients and emergency response personnel that can result from humps.

- The 22-foot speed tables appear to create shorter delays than 12-foot humps. This is as expected given the higher comfortable crossing speed of tables (for more on operating speeds, see chapter 4). Boulder's very long speed tables are the exceptions. The greater distances traveled on the longer tables more than offset the time savings resulting from higher operating speeds.[5]

- The shortest delays are experienced by ambulances without patients, the longest by ambulances with patients. When patients have already received basic life support at the scene and are receiving advanced life support en route, the latter delays may or may not be critical, depending on the medical condition being treated.

- Probably the most significant results are those for fire engines. Because all fire stations have emergency medical capabilities, fire engines are often first on the scene in medical emergencies. Their crews are trained to perform basic life support functions. Thus, the delays they experience at traffic calming measures may affect 100 percent of emergency calls.

## Response Time Goals

When considering the delay added by traffic calming measures, thought should be given to emergency response times and emergency response time goals. Any delay entails some added risk to life and property. But the risk may be acceptable as long as response time goals continue to be met. Response time goals of several featured communities are presented in table 7.4. They apparently represent acceptable levels of risk to the communities adopting them,

**Table 7.4. Emergency Response Time Goals.**

| Community | Goal (minutes) |
|---|---|
| Austin, TX | 3.5 (fire) |
| Berkeley, CA | 4 (fire)<br>5 (medical) |
| Boulder, CO | 6 (fire)<br>4 (medical) |
| Montgomery County, MD | 5 |
| Portland, OR | 4 |
| Seattle, WA | 5 |

Source: Interviews and unpublished documents.

given financial constraints and likely outcomes in life-threatening situations.[6]

Given such goals, and given realistic delay estimates, communities have an objective basis for assessing traffic calming proposals. For example, Boca Raton, FL, initially tested midblock deflector islands on NW 3rd Avenue (see figure 7.4). As an alternative, a series of speed humps was proposed to lower speeds further. Although the fire chief opposed the alternative, it appeared acceptable from an emergency response time standpoint, given a reasonable delay estimate and a goal of 60 percent of emergency responses within 5 minutes (see table 7.5).

## Strategies for Addressing Fire-Rescue Concerns

Many strategies have been used to address fire-rescue concerns about traffic calming. The featured communities have used avoidance of emergency response routes and emergency facilities, gradual escalation of traffic calming, communication, accommodating measures, redesign, innovations, and citizen support.

**Figure 7.4. Test Installations on NW 3rd Avenue. (Boca Raton, FL)**

**Table 7.5. Response Time Comparisons for NW 3rd Avenue. (Boca Raton, FL)**

| | |
|---|---|
| Original conditions | 3 mins 6 secs |
| Current conditions (circle and island) | 3 mins 30 secs |
| Expected conditions (humps) | 3 mins 48 secs |

Source: K.B. Koen, "Speed Tables – N.W. 3rd and N.W. 5th Avenue," memo from the fire chief of Boca Raton dated February 2, 1998.

## Avoidance of Emergency Response Routes

Traffic managers try to keep traffic calming measures off of emergency response routes. The challenge is twofold. First, many of the streets most in need of traffic calming make ideal emergency response routes for the same reasons they need to be calmed: higher operating speed and shortcut potential. In Boulder, 80 percent of the streets requesting traffic calming measures during 1995 were identified by the fire department as critical emergency response streets (see figure 7.5).

Second, the list of emergency response routes may prove elastic, as individual station captains contemplate every possible response route to every possible emergency. Austin, TX, had this experience. The fire department initially proposed that humps be kept off all streets with fire stations along them, then off all collectors, and finally, off all primary response routes (which included much of the city street network, according to different fire stations).

From a traffic calming perspective, the ideal hierarchy of routes would permit more traffic calming measures on secondary than primary response routes, and still more on tertiary response routes.

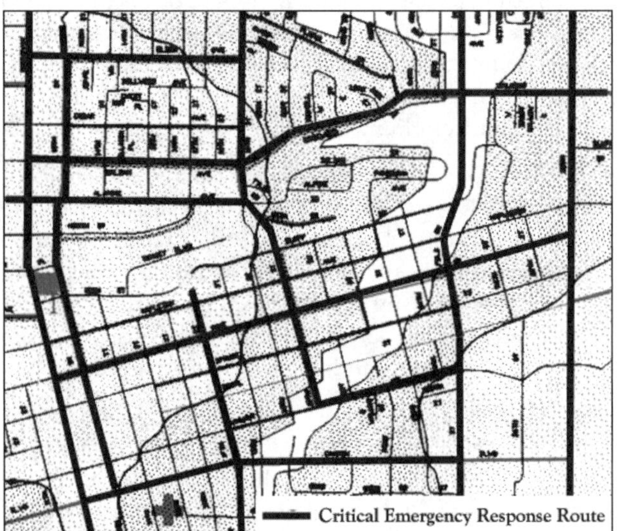


**Figure 7.5. Critical Emergency Response Routes in the Urban Core. (Boulder, CO)**

Source: City of Boulder, "NTMP/Emergency Response Map," March 8, 1997.

In the featured communities, when designation of the emergency response routes included a public input process, the implementation of traffic calming measures was helped. The outcome of the Portland process might have been much less favorable to the Bureau of Traffic Management if a citizens advisory group had not been involved. The Austin hump program might have remained in moratorium if a public focus group had not convinced the city council that emergency services should play an advisory role rather than have veto power (see figure 7.6). The Austin focus group process is described in chapter 8.

Figure 7.6. Focus Group Meeting Broadcast on Public Access TV. (Austin, TX)

## Avoidance of Emergency Response Facilities

Experience has shown that there can be negative impacts if restrictive traffic calming measures are placed on access streets to fire stations. It is one thing for fire trucks to encounter traffic calming measures periodically as they respond to emergencies. It is quite another for them to encounter measures every time they leave the station.

In Charlotte, NC, the first set of 22-foot speed tables was placed on Laurel Avenue, down the street and across a major thoroughfare from a fire station. While collector roads with higher traffic volumes have been calmed with 22-foot speed tables, no installation has generated as much controversy as that on Laurel Avenue. A fire truck drove by while a photograph (shown in figure 7.7) of a table on Laurel Avenue was being taken. The driver felt compelled to stop and announce that the speed tables were the "worst thing that ever happened" to emergency response in Charlotte.

The same cautionary note applies to hospitals. With all the controversy surrounding traffic calming in Boulder,

only two sets of measures have ever been removed. One was the series of speed tables installed on Edgewood Drive, adjacent to a regional hospital (see figure 7.8). Such a hospital generates more emergency vehicle traffic than a fire station and is likely to oppose any traffic calming efforts that emergency vehicles cannot avoid.

### Gradual Escalation of Traffic Calming Measures

Many believe that engineering measures should be used only as a last resort, after education and enforcement efforts have failed. Whether this view is reasonable, given the effectiveness of education and enforcement, is subject to debate (see Chapter 5—"Traffic Calming Impacts"). But trying more conservative approaches does help neutralize opposition.

Bellevue has managed to calm its streets, including residential collectors, with less controversy than most other places. It has done so by gradually escalating to engineering measures. Phase I involves neighborhood speed watch, a traffic safety campaign, signing, restriping, and other less restrictive measures. Phase II involves engineering measures and is undertaken only if needed. Of 20 or so locations each year participating in Phase I, only 2 or 3 graduate to Phase II.

Boulder is taking a similar tack, with some high-tech twists. More emphasis is now placed on education and enforcement in order to "provide greater balance to the program." Photo-radar is being tested. In conventional speed watch programs, the worst that can happen to speeders is to receive warning letters. With photo-radar, warning letters are replaced by speeding tickets and fines (for more on photo-radar, see chapter 5).

Also, Boulder is testing speed-sensitive traffic signals that use loops to measure speeds upstream of intersections. In the "rest on red" test, all approaches to an intersection face red lights (see figure 7.9). If advance loops

Figure 7.7. "Worst Thing that Ever Happened." (Charlotte, NC)

Figure 7.8. Former Speed Table Location on Edgewood Drive. (Boulder, CO)

**Figure 7.9. Photo-Radar and Rest-on-Red Demonstrations. (Boulder, CO)**

Source: Department of Public Works, City of Boulder, CO.

detect an approaching vehicle moving at or below the desired speed and no other vehicle is being served on the cross street, the signal turns green. If the vehicle is detected to be speeding, the green phase is not triggered until the vehicle comes to rest in the traditional fashion at the stop line. In the "rest on green" test, signals along a main street will remain green as long as traffic is moving at or below the desired speed and no one is waiting on the side streets. Signals will switch to red if speeding is detected, thus penalizing or rewarding based on compliance with speed limits.[7]

## Communication

As everyone knows, communication is the key to working out differences. Yet, emergency services are not always consulted about traffic calming plans. In one case, speed tables were installed down the street from a fire station, reportedly without prior consultation. In another case, humps were installed without warning or even adequate marking and signing. A fire-rescue vehicle was damaged and a staff member injured when the humps were encountered unexpectedly.

Among the featured programs, communication between traffic management and emergency services varies in nature and extent. In Tallahassee, FL, the fire department is simply informed of streets that will be treated. In Boulder, the fire chief exercises a virtual veto over new installations. In Austin, the fire department once had veto power but lost it when a public focus group recommended, and the city council adopted, an advisory role for the fire department.

## Use of Measures that Accommodate Fire-Rescue Vehicles

Fire-rescue units nearly always oppose volume controls that lengthen response routes. Street closures, diagonal diverters, and median barriers may have this effect. In the featured communities, fire-rescue units demonstrated less opposition to half closures, semi-diverters, and forced turn islands that permit wrong-way movements up short one-way sections.

Fire-rescue units usually oppose speed humps and other vertical measures that rattle and rock speeding vehicles. Horizontal measures such as traffic circles and chicanes are preferred (even though they appear to create slightly more delay than vertical measures). Horizontal measures force emergency vehicles to slow down, but they do so without the jostling that accompanies vertical displacement.

In the featured communities, narrowings present little problem for fire-rescue vehicles. This applies to chokers, center islands, split medians, and even neckdowns. The Boulder fire chief, who opposes speed humps and traffic circles, accepts neckdowns because his department plans emergency access routes to minimize turning movements ("they plan for straight shots").

Traffic calming measures favored by fire-rescue units are among the most expensive, involving curb work and landscaping. Thus, these measures may prove cost-effective only on emergency routes that get a lot of use.

Whatever measures are used must be designed for fire trucks. Several featured programs test designs by placing cones on the roadway and running the fire department's largest vehicle around them (see figure 7.10). Others simply work off plans using AASHTO's turning movement templates for longer vehicles.[8]

The challenge to designers is this: Geometric designs that accommodate fire trucks are oversized for automobiles. Vehicle deflection will be minimal, as will be the impact on automobile speeds. The Phoenix Fire Department's requirement that half closures be 16 feet wide, to permit turns in and out, invites violations by motorists who see an open street almost two lanes wide (see figure 7.11). Such challenges can be met with clever designs such as Portland's half closure with a bike lane (see figure 7.12).

## Redesign of Traffic Calming Measures

Another strategy is to modify traffic calming measures to better accommodate fire-rescue vehicles. Tight traffic circles, street closures, and full diverters are not favorites of emergency services. Yet each can be redesigned to be more acceptable. At the request of the fire department, Orlando changed the design of its traffic circles, lowering the lip from 4 to 2 inches for easier mounting (see figure 7.13). Dayton opted for locked gates rather than landscaped street closures to maintain emergency access to the Five Oaks neighborhood (see figure 7.14). Boulder outfitted all closures and diverters in one neighborhood with removable bollards (see figure 7.15).

Speed humps and speed tables are not favorites, either. Yet, they too can be designed to be more acceptable to fire-rescue units. Austin and Gwinnett County ran emergency vehicles over multiple hump profiles. Based on the results, these two programs now use nothing but 22-foot speed tables, the least jarring alternative tested. Eugene has placed a moratorium on 14-foot speed humps in re-

**Figure 7.10. Field Test with a Fire Truck. (Seattle, WA)**

**Figure 7.12. Half Closure that Discourages Violations. (Portland, OR)**

**Figure 7.11. Half Closure that Invites Violations. (Phoenix, AZ)**

**Figure 7.13. Traffic Circle with a 2-inch Lip to Accommodate Fire Trucks. (Orlando, FL)**

**Figure 7.14. Gated Street Closures. (Dayton, OH)**

**Figure 7.16. 46-foot (12 foot, 22 foot, 12 foot) Raised Crosswalk. (Boulder, CO)**

**Figure 7.15. Diagonal Diverter with Removable Bollards. (Boulder, CO)**

**Figure 7.17. 32-foot (6 foot, 20 foot, 6 foot) Speed Table. (Minneapolis, MN)**

sponse to fire department concerns, but continues to build longer raised crosswalks that have less effect on emergency vehicles. Boulder; Minneapolis, MN; and several other places have built speed tables or raised intersections big enough for the entire wheelbase of a fire truck to rest upon the flat section (see figures 7.16 and 7.17). These measures reduce the jolt to fire trucks even more than do the 22-foot tables.

Fire-rescue, in turn, has an obligation to keep its requests reasonable. The Public Works Department in Eugene planned to install chicanes on a short, dead-end local street leading to a high school; the purpose was to discourage speeding. After a field test showed a slight delay with the chicanes (no more than a few seconds over the entire length of this short street), the proposed chicanes were replaced with midblock deflector islands. To further accommodate the fire chief, the dimensions of the deflector islands were cut back. Note in figure 7.18 the difference between island dimensions as built versus as marked out originally.

## Traffic Calming Innovations

Austin has tested speed "cushions," dome-shaped speed humps that are narrow enough to be straddled by wide-bodied vehicles but must be mounted by passenger cars. Widely used in Europe to minimize impacts of traffic calming on transit buses and emergency vehicles, speed cushions may or may not prove as useful in the United States. Fire trucks in the United States have inner and outer wheels on the rear axles, making the inner wheels closer together than on a passenger car. The problem is illustrated by dimensional data from Austin (see table 7.6). Still, fire-rescue units in Austin favor the cushions over either 12-foot humps or 22-foot tables since their front wheels can straddle the cushions and the rear wheels need ride up on only one side. Austin has recorded very significant reductions in 85th percentile speeds (the speed below which 85 percent of vehicles travel) with speed cushions—comparable to those experienced with speed humps—and therefore plans to install the cushions permanently (see figure 7.19).

**Figure 7.18. Scaled Down Deflector Island with Reduced Effectiveness. (Eugene, OR)**

**Figure 7.19. Test of a Speed Cushion. (Austin, TX)**

**Table 7.6. Tire Spacing (inside to inside) for Different Vehicle Types (feet).**

| | |
|---|---|
| Fire engine | 5.7 (front) |
| | 4.0 (rear) |
| Ladder truck | 5.5 (front) |
| | 3.9 (rear) |
| Ambulance | 6.0 (front) |
| | 4.3 (rear) |
| Compact car | 4.3 |
| Full-size car | 4.4 |
| Minivan | 4.6 |
| Sport utility vehicle | 4.3 |

Source: Department of Public Works and Transportation, City of Austin, TX.

Portland has designed "split" or "offset" humps, which extend from curb to centerline on one side of the street and then, separated by a gap, continue on the other side (see figure 7.20). Fire trucks can weave around split humps in slalom-like fashion, while to date (seen in hours of videotape), private vehicles have shown little inclination to cross the centerline just to avoid the humps. Raised center islands and signs in advance of each hump half, plus dense centerline striping and raised pavement markers between the two halves, give the illusion of a continuous median. The original spacing of 28 feet between halves proved too narrow, and fire-rescue vehicles had to slow down to negotiate the resulting horizontal curve. But with later spacing of 50 feet between halves, even the largest fire trucks lose no more than 1 to 2 seconds. Based on Portland's success, Austin and Boulder plan to test split humps or split speed tables.

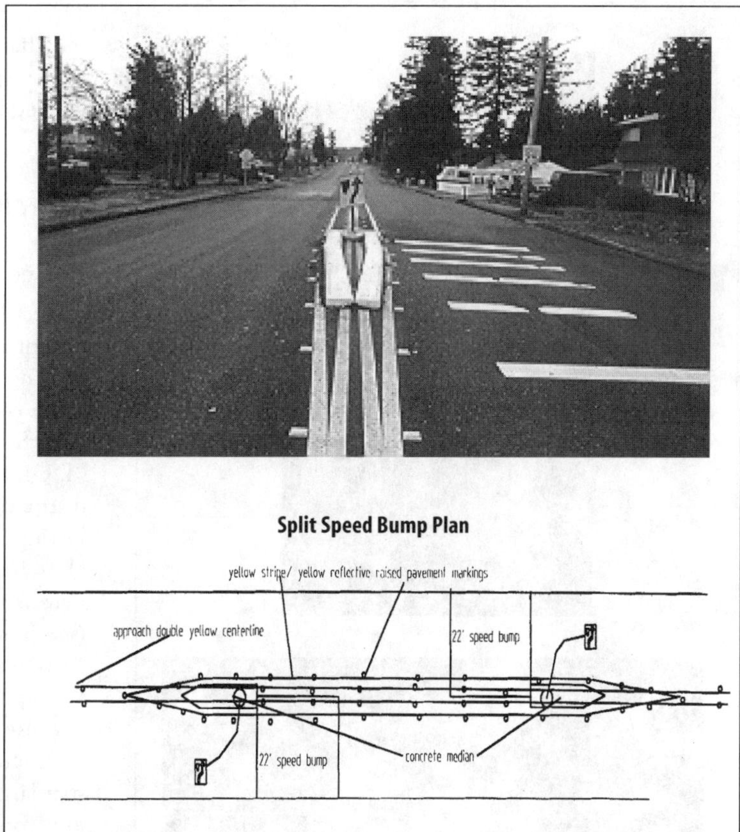


**Figure 7.20. Split Hump. (Portland, OR)**

Source: Bureau of Traffic Management, City of Portland, OR.

Coral Gables, FL, has installed motorized gates at street closures. While closed to private vehicles, these gates can be activated by emergency vehicles via radio control (see figure 7.21).

Innovations like those in Austin, Portland, and Coral Gables represent the ultimate in traffic management, as they slow or divert other traffic without substantially impeding emergency response.

## Citizen Support

The National Fire Protection Association article, "Things That Go Bump in the Night," offers a candid view about public priorities: "When given the choice between a quick response time by emergency service providers or a re-duction in the speed and volume of cars on their neighborhood streets, residents will invariably place a greater value on the latter."[9]

Beyond anecdotal evidence, a public opinion survey lent some support to the previous statement (see table 7.7). When Berkeley residents were asked if emergency response delays were reason for curtailing new speed hump installations, a majority said they were not. This survey was taken during a moratorium on new speed humps over the issue of emergency response.

With citizen support, some traffic calming plans have prevailed over opposition from fire departments. At the fire chief's insistence, Ft. Lauderdale now warns of slower response times in a survey letter sent out to residents before speed humps are installed (see figure 7.22). These surveys still garner 80 percent resident approval in some cases. The city traffic engineer speculates that "people weigh the chance of getting burned to death against the chance of being killed by a speeding car." Apparently, the latter is viewed as a bigger threat.[10]

## Other Public Agencies

### Police

Police generally support traffic calming measures for their potential to control speeding and reduce collision severity. Engineering measures are self-enforcing, which takes some of the pressure off police officers to enforce traffic laws. Some police officers fondly refer to traffic circles as "DUI (driving under the influence) catchers," because drunk drivers often sober up and head straight home after hitting the center islands (see figure 7.23). In Sarasota and elsewhere, speed humps are called "sleeping policemen" because they quietly enforce speed limits 24 hours a day (see figure 7.24).

In several featured communities—Berkeley, Dayton, Ft. Lauderdale, Gainesville, and West Palm Beach—the police also support certain measures, those restricting access, for their potential to reduce crime. Street closures are a standard strategy in the field of crime prevention through environmental design (CPTED). A most ambitious CPTED project in Dayton is described in chapter 1.

While traffic calming measures must have some effect on police response times, it does not seem to be an issue in featured communities. Use of vehicles with small wheelbases and good suspensions makes the difference. New patrol cars can maintain speeds of 25 mph over 12-foot speed humps. This is two or three times the comfortable crossing speed of many fire trucks, with their longer wheelbases, higher centers of gravity, stiffer suspensions, and hence more severe rocking motion. The advantage of

**Figure 7.21. Street Closure with a Motorized Gate. (Coral Gables, FL)**

**Table 7.7. Public Opinion on Speed Control versus Emergency Response. (Berkeley, CA)**

| Question: *Speed humps delay fire trucks and ambulances responding to emergencies. More than one minute may be added to the average response time of four minutes. Do you feel this is reason for the city to avoid adding new speed humps?* | | | |
| --- | --- | --- | --- |
| **Resident Response** | **Blocks with Humps (%)** | **Blocks without Humps (%)** | **All Blocks (%)** |
| Yes | 23 | 42 | 33 |
| No | 48 | 35 | 42 |
| Not sure | 26 | 20 | 23 |
| No response | 3 | 3 | 3 |

Source: City of Berkeley, "An Evaluation of the Speed Hump Program of the City of Berkeley," October 1997 draft, Table 1.

Excerpt from page 2 of letter:

So that an informed decision can be made by residents regarding speed hump usage in their neighborhood, the Fort Lauderdale Fire-Rescue and Building Department wants all residents to be aware of both the potential advantages and disadvantages of speed humps. Speed humps increase response times to emergencies when compared to response times with the street remaining unobstructed. Emergency vehicles must travel in the 10-15 mph range in order to safely negotiate the speed humps, as opposed to traveling at the 25 mph speed cited above for other type vehicles. The Fire-Rescue and Building Department will be evaluating the "flat-topped" trial speed hump, which is thought to be able to be traveled at higher speeds by emergency vehicles than those of the City's current design.

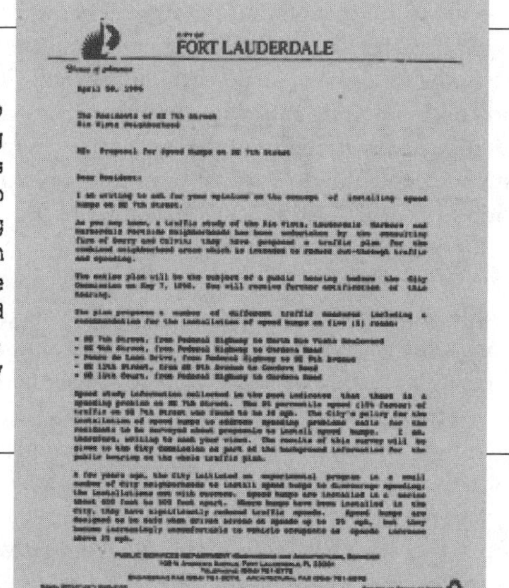

**Figure 7.22. Survey Letter Warning of Longer Response Time. (Ft. Lauderdale, FL)**

**Figure 7.23. "DUI (Driving Under the Influence) Catcher." (Portland, OR)**

**Figure 7.24. "Sleeping Policeman." (Sarasota, FL)**

small wheelbases is also realized on the tight curves of traffic circles and chicanes.

## Public Works

The issue of snow removal almost always comes up at professional sessions on traffic calming. As a theoretical concern, it looms as large as tort liability and emergency response. As a practical matter, snow removal is not reported to be much of a problem.

Most of the featured communities get little or no snow. Nationally, traffic calming programs are concentrated in the Sunbelt and Pacific Northwest, where snow is not a factor. In the featured communities experiencing significant snowfall, staff responsible for snow removal are typically housed within the same departments as traffic calming, and collegiality prevails. Humps, circles, chokers, and closures have not been reported to prevent snow removal, leave streets unsafe due to residual snow and ice, damage snowplows, or suffer serious damage themselves. But they may add to workload and expense.

Here are a few examples of how different communities handle snow removal. Dayton, which averages 28 inches of snow per year, plows residential streets only when they receive more than 3 inches of snow. This happens five or six times a year. About 90 percent of Dayton's street closures have gates that can be opened after big snowfalls. This allows operators to plow through closures rather than simply depositing snow at closures. Snowplow operators who have set routes usually know where humps are located. As a reminder, each hump is marked with an advance warning sign. Operators know to go slowly over the humps thus marked, and going slowly, ride up and over them. Snowplow blades are rubber-tipped to avoid damage to humps (see figure 7.25).

Bellevue receives about 10 inches of snow per year. Like Dayton, Bellevue assigns plow operators set routes, marks individual humps, and uses rubber-tipped snowplow blades. The task of snow clearance is complicated by the widespread use of raised pavement markers throughout Bellevue, even on humps. Rather than plow down to the surface of the roadway, operators leave an inch of snow and then apply sand to the surface. The snow/sand combination is thought to provide better traction than the thin layer of ice or snow left by conventional plowing.

Montgomery County averages just over 20 inches of snow annually, but occasionally gets pummeled, as in 1996 when 50 inches fell. Plows have rollers on their blades that cause them to rise up and over when they strike something. This system tends to scrape snow off the front of humps but to leave a wedge of snow on the back. Plows are equipped with salt applicators to deal with the latter. They often require a second application to melt this snow. Plastic posts are used to mark chokers so that plow operators know exactly where to slow down and diverge from a straight path.

Three places that experience extreme winter weather were contacted separately. Minneapolis may represent the best case among the snowbelt communities since it has a full array of traffic calming measures. Given the frequent need to remove ice under a layer of snow, the blades on Minneapolis' snowplows must be steel-tipped. They are outfitted with "shoes" (metal extensions) to protect against damage. Plows thus leave a thin layer of ice, which has to be removed with a mix of salt and sand. These plows have no problem with Minneapolis' humps or tables, which all rise 3 inches over 6 feet; blades automatically climb this gentle rise. Plows also have no problem with standard traffic circles at cross streets or with permanent chokers marked by landscaping. What creates a minor problem are traffic circles at T-intersections. Unable to plow all the way around, plows leave a windrow, which has to be removed with a front-end loader. Also creating a small problem are

**Figure 7.25. Snow Removal in One Featured Community. (Dayton, OH)**

temporary curbs used to test measures. Without landscaping, temporary curbs are occasionally struck by snowplows.

Yakima, WA, reports no special problems clearing snow off suburban streets with speed humps and tables. Downtown streets are trickier. Unlike the suburbs, where plow operators can plow snow off the edge of the street, downtown streets with curbside parking are plowed from edge to center. Snow accumulates around center islands and has to be removed with a front-end loader. Following the curve of chokers requires more time than normal plowing, but operators apparently know the curb line well enough to avoid damaging contact. However, unless center islands are marked with cones before big snow storms, operators have been known to strike and damage the islands.

In Toronto, ON, speed tables and raised intersections have ramps of 6 or 7 percent slope, which are easily negotiated by snowplows (see figure 7.26). Speed humps have sinusoidal rather than standard parabolic profiles. These too are easily negotiated. With a parabolic profile, the gradient is its steepest at the point of intersection between hump and street. With a sinusoidal profile, the gradient is zero at the point of intersection. The ride is smoother for snowplows, motorists, and bicyclists. The only problem with snow removal reported by Toronto, other than the added time required, was minor damage to a couple of traffic islands in the first winter after construction. In one respect, snow removal is actually simplified by traffic calming. As Toronto has narrowed its streets, it has widened the planting strips between streets and sidewalks, creating more storage space for snow.

Generalizing, communities have dealt with snow removal on traffic-calmed streets by marking traffic calming measures, using appropriate or specialized equipment, innovating in geometric design of measures, familiarizing personnel with snowplow routes, and in all cases, devoting more time to the task.

**Figure 7.26. Gradual Ramp on a Raised Intersection. (Toronto, ON)**

## Endnotes


1. L. McGinnis, "Things That Go Bump in the Night," *NFPA Journal,* January/February 1997, pp. 78–82.

2. Bureau of Traffic Management, *The Influence of Traffic Calming Devices on Fire Vehicle Travel Times,* City of Portland, OR, January 1996.

3. City of Berkeley, "An Evaluation of the Speed Hump Program of the City of Berkeley," October 1997 draft, page 23.

4. In both San Diego and Austin, humps were presumed to cause delays of 30 seconds per hump. Measurements in Austin put an end to that presumption.

5. Boulder's estimates of safe speeds at slow points:

    | | |
    |---|---|
    | 8' hump (3" rise) | 7 mph |
    | 12' hump (3" rise) | 9 mph |
    | 37' table (6" rise—7.5' ramps—22' flat top) | 13 mph |
    | 40' table (6" rise—9' ramps—22' flat top) | 16 mph |
    | 25' diameter circle | 13 mph |

    City of Boulder, "Fire Engine Delay Measured for Various Mitigation Devices," Attachment G, Study Session on the Neighborhood Traffic Mitigation Program, Boulder City Council, April 8, 1997.

6. As examples, a flashover fire will ordinarily occur within 6 to 10 minutes after ignition, and the chance of survival in cardiac cases declines sharply if cardiopulmonary resuscitation is not administered within 4 minutes and electric shock within 10 minutes. It is such risk assessments that underlie response time goals.

7. Boulder's rest-on-red demonstration is already underway. The idea was borrowed from Los Angeles. The rest-on-green demonstration has proven trickier to implement since there are no known precedents.

8. J.E. Leisch, *Turning Vehicle Templates—English System,* Institute of Transportation Engineers, Washington, DC, 1991.

9. McGinnis, op. cit.

10. A compendium of counter arguments in favor of humps has been assembled by Zaidel et al. Here is a sampling:

    - Humps cause no damage to police and fire vehicles if crossed at the recommended speed.
    - Humps are no worse than the off-road and on-curb maneuvering done in the course of normal duties by police and fire personnel.
    - Emergency response times are primarily determined by the adequacy of main roads, not the last short stretches in neighborhoods themselves.
    - "…life style and quality of life during normal times…cannot be overshadowed by the requirements of rare events."
    - To the extent that humps and other calming measures reduce collisions, they will reduce the need for emergency services.

    D. Zaidel, A.S. Hakkert, and A.H. Pistiner, "The Use of Road Humps for Moderating Speeds on Urban Streets," *Accident Analysis & Prevention,* Vol. 24, 1992, pp. 45–56.

# CHAPTER 8

# Warrants, Project Selection Procedures, and Public Involvement

Traffic managers in the featured communities strive for balance between "study it to death" and "get it built now," and between "respond to neighborhood wishes" and "use your best technical judgment." They also report that they attempt to be sufficiently process-oriented to avoid political and legal fallout, yet sufficiently output-oriented to satisfy constituents.

Finding a proper balance is not always easy, as Portland, OR, discovered. Through the early 1990's, Portland was at the "process" end of the process-output continuum (see figure 8.1). Portland's North Ida project, described in chapter 4, began in 1987, when residents first contacted the city. Construction was not completed until 1995, and the evaluation phase continued into 1996. The process would have taken even longer except that a test period was not required on this particular project.

The process in place at the time of the North Ida project is outlined in table 8.1. The nominal time from start to finish, if everything went right, was about 3 years.

Pressure from neighborhoods to get more traffic calming measures on the ground caused Portland to stream-line its process. In 1992, the Streamlined Speed Bump Program (or unofficially, the "buy a bump" program) was created.[1] Speed hump projects meeting strict program guidelines could be built on an expedited basis at neighbors' expense. In 1994, Portland's basic program was also restructured to be easier and faster. The old process required a petition to initiate and a neighborhood traffic committee to help with planning and implementation. The new process substituted a neighborhood survey for the petition process and replaced the traffic committee with a one-time focus group.

After 12 years of traffic calming measure implementation throughout the city, the new process produced the program's first rejection (in a ballot) of new speed tables and chokers proposed for a residential collector street. Those living on the street were generally supportive of the project, but those using the street as a through route were adamantly opposed and even resorted to threats and smear tactics. The neighborhood never assumed ownership of the process.

This loss resulted in the reinstatement of neighbor-

**Figure 8.1. Portland: Process-Oriented.**

**Table 8.1. Planning and Implementation Process. (Portland, OR)**

| Action | Time frame |
| --- | --- |
| Project requests | Ongoing |
| Preliminary review | Within 6 months of request |
| Priority ranking | July/August |
| Petition-to-study | 2 1/2 months |
| Plan development | 5 months |
| Petition-to-test/ test installation | 4 months |
| Project evaluation | 1 month |
| Ballot to install permanently | 1 1/2 months |
| Council action | 1 month |
| Design | 5 months |
| Construction | 3–4 months |
| Monitoring | Ongoing |
| Follow-up evaluation | Within 3–5 years |

Source: Bureau of Traffic Management, "Neighborhood Traffic Management for Local Service Streets," City of Portland, OR, March 1992, p. 10.

hood traffic committees and the return to more meetings. While painful, Portland's search for its equilibrium point has apparently paid off. The program has garnered a string of affirmative votes in neighborhood balloting since its one loss.

## Basic Program Options

A traffic calming program may be reactive, responding to citizen requests for action, or it may be proactive, with staff identifying problems and initiating action. A nationwide survey by researchers at the University of California at Berkeley determined that all but a "handful" of programs are reactive.[2]

A traffic calming program may make *spot* improvements, street by street, or it may plan and implement improvements on an *areawide* basis, with multiple streets treated at the same time. The same survey by the University of California at Berkeley found that almost all programs operate on a spot improvement basis.

With two choices in each of two program areas, traffic managers are faced with four distinct options (table 8.2). As far as can be determined, three of the four alternatives work well enough. Proactive/areawide treatments have theoretical advantages over the others; experience with them has been good. The fourth alternative, reactive/areawide treatment, has been less successful. The reason, it seems, is that areawide treatment involves extensive coordination and consensus-building, something unlikely to occur without proactive involvement of staff.

**Table 8.2. Alternative Program Options.**

|  | Reactive | Proactive |
|---|---|---|
| **Spot treatment** | Somewhat successful | More successful |
| **Areawide treatment** | Less successful | Most successful |

The experiences of four communities illustrate the pros and cons of different program structures.

### Reactive Spot Treatment → Proactive Areawide Treatment (Austin, TX)

In the wake of a moratorium on speed humps, Austin formed task forces to address the most thorny issues facing the city's traffic managers: traffic diversion, emergency response, funding, treatment of residential collectors, and neighborhood endorsement procedures. The primary recommendation to emerge from the process was to replace

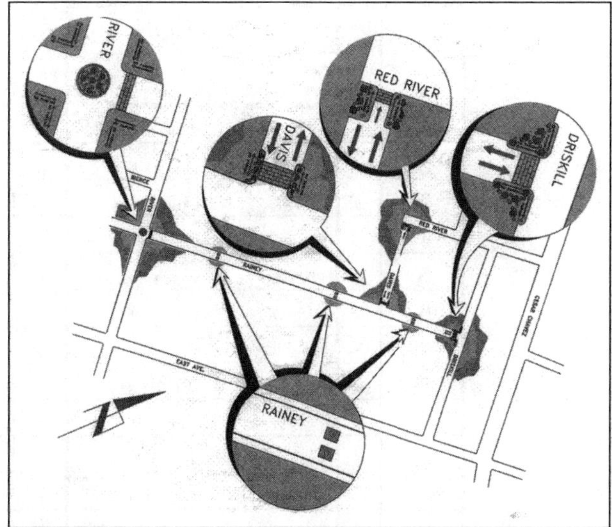


**Figure 8.2. One of the Pilot Projects Under New Areawide Policy. (Austin, TX)**

Source: Department of Public Works and Transportation, "Rainey Street Neighborhood—Pilot Project Area," Austin, TX, May 1998.

spot treatments with areawide treatments based on city priorities. The city council agreed and funded a $500,000 pilot program. Areawide plans have been formulated for five city neighborhoods (see figure 8.2), deploying such novel measures as speed cushions and split humps (see chapter 7 for definitions). Implementation began in mid-1998.

### Reactive Spot Treatment → Proactive Spot Treatment (Seattle, WA)

The original Seattle program simply responded to complaints. There was no guarantee that the most serious problems would be addressed, only those with the loudest constituencies. While still responding to neighborhood requests, for this is necessary to maintain political support and funding, the program now proactively seeks out high accident locations and gives them funding priority (see figure 8.3). Neighborhood residents are then contacted to determine levels of support for traffic calming. From this point on, the program functions conventionally. Nothing is forced upon residents. Public opinion surveys demonstrate overwhelming support for Seattle's program.

### Reactive Spot Treatment → Proactive Areawide Treatment (Sarasota, FL)

Although Sarasota still responds to resident petitions, the city favors areawide traffic calming initiated by staff. The reason: spot treatments generate opposition from residents of neighboring areas who fear that traffic problems will

| RANK | REQ NO. | AVENUE | & CROSS-STREET | YR 3+ TOTAL | NO OF YEARS | ACC/YR | MIDBLOCK XTRA PTS | POINTS | AWDT | POINTS | 85% MPH | POINTS |
|---|---|---|---|---|---|---|---|---|---|---|---|---|
| 1 | 362 | 1 AV NW | & NW 87 ST | 14 | 3 | 4.67 | | 12 | 3916 | 3 | 31.7 | 1 |
| 2 | 333 | SUNNYSIDE AV N | & N 77 ST | 9 | 3 | 3.00 | | 7 | 380 | 0 | 28.4 | 0.5 |
| 3 | 39 | 4 AV NW | & NW 127 ST | 8 | 3 | 2.67 | | 6 | 578 | 0.5 | 27.9 | 0.5 |
| 4 | 343 | 18 AV | & E PINE ST | 7 | 3 | 2.33 | | 5 | 1801 | 1.5 | 27.8 | 0.5 |
| 5 | 218 | 38 AV S | & S ALASKA ST | 5 | 3 | 1.67 | 0.5 | 4.5 | 1781 | 1.5 | 26.2 | 0.5 |
| 6 | 307 | DAYTON AV N | & N 77 ST | 6 | 3 | 2.00 | | 4 | 559 | 0.5 | 32.3 | 1.5 |
| 7 | 159 | 25 AV E | & E JOHN ST | 5 | 3 | 1.67 | | 4 | 2431 | 2 | 24.4 | 0 |
| 8 | 252 | 13 AV NW | & NW 73 ST | 5 | 3 | 1.67 | | 4 | 213 | 0 | 33.6 | 1.5 |
| 9 | 304 | FREMONT AV N | & N 76 ST | 5 | 3 | 1.67 | | 4 | 563 | 0.5 | 30.7 | 1 |
| 10 | 32 | 28 AV SW | & SW KENYON ST | 5 | 3 | 1.67 | | 4 | 503 | 0.5 | 30.2 | 1 |
| 11 | 168 | 30 AV NE | & NE 113 ST | 4 | 3 | 1.33 | | 3 | 543 | 0.5 | 35.9 | 2 |
| 12 | 283 | 28 AV NE | & NE 82 ST | 3 | 3 | 1.00 | | 2 | 1381 | 1 | 39.1 | 2.5 |

**Figure 8.3. 1998 Funding Priorities for Spot Treatments. (Seattle, WA)**

Source: Unpublished listing from the Engineering Department, City of Seattle, WA.

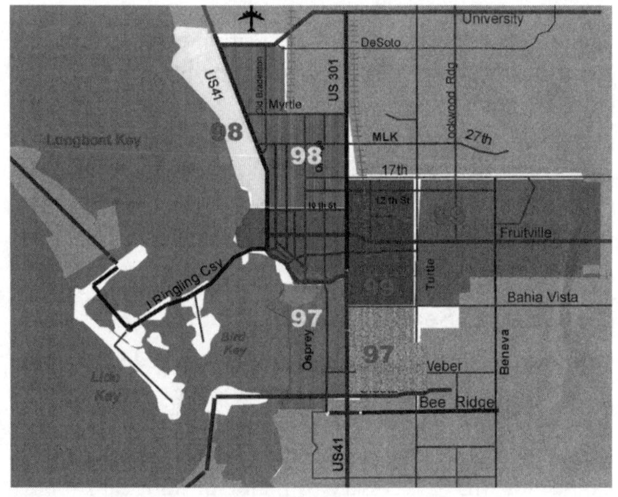


**Figure 8.4. Seven Districts Being Master Planned. (Sarasota, FL)**

Source: Engineering Department, City of Sarasota, FL.

spill over onto their streets. The city has been divided into seven sections, and a master plan is being prepared for each section in turn (see figure 8.4). Buy-in is achieved by treating traffic calming as part of a comprehensive neighborhood improvement program; creating committees to deal with each identified problem; and offering around $1 million of public funding per section to implement committee-generated plans. Traffic calming becomes part of a well-funded program of tree planting, sidewalk construction, street light installation, and other improvements.

## Reactive Areawide Treatment → Reactive Spot Treatment (San Jose, CA)

San Jose adopted its first traffic calming policy back in 1978. The policy provided for spot treatments of individual streets. In the early 1980's, San Jose developed its first areawide traffic calming plan. The experience led to adoption of a second policy, independent of the first, for neighborhood traffic management. The city's motivation was stated in the policy itself: "[L]ocalized treatments of residential traffic problems have resulted in the transfer of similar problems to adjacent streets...."[3]

The new program, with its own staff and funding, was to develop areawide plans in response to neighborhood requests. Six years and two plans later, with little interest from other neighborhoods and the city facing a fiscal crisis, the program was abolished. The two plans took longer to develop than expected and generated less neighborhood support than desired, because half the streets in a neighborhood did not want to inherit problems from the half that was traffic calmed. Despite the demise of its Neighborhood Traffic Management Program, San Jose continues to experience demand for localized traffic calming (particularly for speed humps) and continues to make spot improvements.

## Warrants and Guidelines

Beyond the choice between reactive and proactive programming, and between spot and areawide treatment, several program options are available to traffic managers. The most controversial is the decision to establish warrants for traffic calming measures. Articles have appeared advocating both in favor of and against warrants.[4]

### Two Types of Warrants

Featured programs have established two types of warrants. (As the term is used in the *Manual on Uniform Traffic Control Devices for Streets and Highways* [*MUTCD*], warrants are minimum requirements that should be met, in most cases, before a given device is installed.) Some featured programs have general warrants that apply to all traffic calming activity, in some cases even to traffic calming studies. Typical are the warrants established by Sarasota (see table 8.3). Two of five must be met before the city will even accept a petition from a neighborhood for a full-scale traffic study.

Other traffic calming programs have warrants for specific measures, particularly speed humps and speed tables. In Montgomery County, MD, three different sets of speed hump warrants, adopted sequentially, bound the typical range of requirements (see table 8.4).

To assist with the restructuring of its speed hump program, San Diego, CA, commissioned a national survey of speed hump policies. Many communities have found it convenient to standardize eligibility requirements for speed humps. They have, in effect, imposed warrants on themselves (see table 8.5).

### An Alternative to Warrants

Guidelines offer a variation to warrants. Guidelines consider the same factors as do warrants (e.g., speeds, volumes, collisions, pedestrians) when a decision is being made whether or not to traffic calm a street. However, warrants tend to have criteria with definitive thresholds (e.g., when design speed is above value A, then traffic calming measure B should be used). In contrast, guideline criteria can be more qualitative, and the preferred traffic calming measures are suggested rather than mandated.

Bellevue, WA, developed a "control matrix" for different traffic calming measures that is as complete a set of guidelines as anyone's. It is reproduced here for both its illustrative value and its content (see figure 8.5).

**Table 8.3. General Warrants. (Sarasota, FL)**

| Warrant | Major Collectors | Minor Collectors | Local Residential Streets |
|---|---|---|---|
| 1. Minimum traffic volume | >8,000 vpd or 800 vph | >4,000 vpd or 400 vph | >1,000 vpd or 100 vph |
| 2. Anticipated cut-through traffic | 50% | 40% | 25% |
| 3. 85th percentile speed | 10 mph > speed limit | 10 mph > speed limit | > speed limit |
| 4. Pedestrian crossing volume | >100 per hour | >50 per hour | >25 per hour |
| 5. Accidents per year | 6 | 6 | 3 |

vpd = vehicles per day; vph = vehicles per hour

Source: Engineering Department, City of Sarasota, FL.

**Table 8.4. Speed Hump Warrants. (Montgomery County, MD)**

| Criterion | Original | Interim | Present |
|---|---|---|---|
| Minimum volume | 60 vph | 100 vph | 100 vph |
| Minimum 85th percentile speed<br>Secondary street<br>Primary street | 31 mph<br>34 mph | 31 mph<br>31 or 36 mph<br>(depending on speed limit) | 32 mph<br>34 or 39 mph<br>(depending on speed limit) |
| Minimum length of segment | None | 1,000 feet | 1,000 feet |
| Resident concurrence | 67% | 80% on treated street | 80% on treated street<br>50% on side streets |

vph = vehicles per hour; mph = miles per hour

Source: Department of Public Works and Transportation, Montgomery County, MD.

### Table 8.5. Speed Hump Eligibility Requirements. (Survey of 42 Agencies)

| Requirement | Number of Agencies Setting Requirement | Median Value for Agencies with Requirement |
|---|---|---|
| Resident approval by petition | 30 | 67% |
| Maximum street width | 8 | 40 feet |
| Minimum traffic volume | 11 | 1,000 vehicles per day |
| Maximum traffic volume | 12 | 5,000 vehicles per day |
| Maximum grade | 12 | 6% |
| Prohibition on emergency routes | 27 | |
| Prohibition on transit routes | 7 | |

Source: Kimley–Horn and Associates, Inc., *Road Hump Evaluation Program "Final,"* Prepared for the City of San Diego, CA, 1997.

| Classification | Collector | Local Streets | | Other Considerations | | | | | | | | | | Control Device Use May be Considered |
|---|---|---|---|---|---|---|---|---|---|---|---|---|---|---|
| | | Neighborhood Collector | Local Access | | | | | | | | | | | |
| Land Use | Small Commercial Residential | Residential | Residential | Curbs & Gutters | % Grade | Curvature of Stretch | School Bus Route/Metro | Adjacent Arterials | Previous Traffic Eng. Improve. Unsuccessful | Impacts to Police/Fire | Delay Accident | Homes Front Street | Acceptable Impacts | |
| Traffic Engineering & Specialized Improvements | Yes | Yes | Yes | — | — | — | — | — | — | — | — | — | — | High Speeds |
| Police Enforcement Neighborhood Speed Watch Program | Yes | Yes | Yes | — | — | — | — | — | — | — | — | — | — | High Speeds |
| Speed Humps | No | Vol ≤3000 vpd 85% ≥35 | Vol ≥300 85% ≥35 | Yes | Not > 10% | 300— | Yes | Yes | Yes | Yes | — | Yes | Yes | High Speeds & Cut-through Volumes |
| Traffic Circles | No | Vol ≤3000 vpd 85% ≥35 | Vol ≥300 85% ≥35 | Yes | Not > 10% | — | Yes | Yes | Yes | Yes | — | Yes | Yes | Speeds or Accident History |
| Stop Signs | MUTCD | MUTCD | MUTCD | — | — | — | — | — | — | — | — | — | — | Accident History |
| Diverter | No | No | Vol ≥300 | Yes | — | — | Yes | Yes | Yes | Yes | Yes | Yes | Yes | High cut-through Volumes |
| One-Way/ Chokers | No | Vol ≥2,500 | Vol ≥300 | Yes | — | — | Yes | Yes | Yes | Yes | Yes | — | Yes | High cut-through Volumes |
| Street Closure | No | Yes, If Vol ≥6,000 Non-Local ≥20% | Yes, If Vol ≥3,000 Non-Local ≥20% | — | — | — | Yes | Yes | Yes | Yes | Yes | Yes | Yes | High cut-through Volumes |

Notes:
1. All volumes in units of typical daily traffic volumes.
2. Source for street type designation—City of Bellevue Street Classification.
3. Control devices may be considered when either the speed criteria, volume criteria or both criteria are exceeded.

*MUTCD = Manual on Uniform Traffic Control Devices for Streets and Highways;* vpd = vehicle per day

### Figure 8.5. Traffic Calming Control Matrix. (Bellevue, WA)

Source: City of Bellevue, Transportation Department, Bellevue, WA.

# Arguments For and Against Warrants

The strongest argument for warrants is standardization. Traffic control devices in the United States follow the *MUTCD*. Australians and Canadians have opted for standardization of traffic calming measures as well. Warrants may serve to insulate traffic managers from political pressure to install traffic calming measures where inappropriate. One such case, in San Diego, was described in chapter 1. As a result, San Diego is moving toward adoption of new stringent warrants for speed humps.

The strongest counterargument is that warrants stifle creativity, that every traffic calming application is unique. Warrants cannot be developed for every factor that might justify treatment (enhanced neighborhood pride, for example). Safety is one thing, and the *MUTCD* serves that purpose admirably. But livability and walkability—both valid justifications for traffic calming—are another. The city transportation planner of West Palm Beach said: "[T]raffic calming warrants relegate traffic calming to the realm of a traditional reactive program instead of allowing it to reach its full potential as a proactive approach to good street design."[5]

The debate may result in part from confusion over the nature of warrants. Warrants compel nothing. Transportation engineers always have a degree of discretion, and street improvements are always subject to availability of funds. In this sense, if speed humps were subject to warrants, traffic managers would not be required to install humps if the warrants were met, only discouraged from installing them if the warrants were not met.

The debate over warrants may also result from confusion over who would impose them on whom. *MUTCD* warrants are applied nationwide, with the Federal Highway Administration (FHWA) as their source. If a local governing body establishes warrants for a local traffic calming program, these differ little from the kind of policy guidance elected officials are supposed to give their operating staffs.

The potential downside of warrants is illustrated by two featured programs: Sarasota and Montgomery County. The warrants themselves (i.e., the criteria and standards chosen) are typical of warrants nationwide. The experiences with warrants in these programs, however, are atypical.

Warrants may fail to consider the interrelationship of streets within a network. As previously described, Sarasota's program is shifting from spot to areawide improvements. Many of the individual streets treated in Sarasota's areawide plans would not qualify under the city's general warrants for individual streets (see figure 8.6). Apparently, viewed in isolation, these streets are not problems. However, in a broader context, when other city plans were considered, these streets were in need of traffic calming.

Warrants may be used disingenuously to impair a program with stringent thresholds. Montgomery County's speed hump program has been tightened twice (as presented in table 8.4). The first tightening, in October 1997, was generally viewed as a valid midcourse adjustment. A staff analysis found that, in a sample of 32 streets treated under the original criteria, 17 would have qualified under the new criteria. However, in February 1998, the program underwent further tightening. The requirement of 50 percent approval by residents of side streets who may be inconvenienced by speed humps on the treated streets would seem difficult to meet.

## Warrants That Address Diversion

Diversion of traffic to other streets following the installation of traffic calming measures can be a positive or a negative result. A positive result involves diversion of traffic to higher order roads that are better able to handle it. Boulder, CO, describes good diversion this way: "Arterials are the most desirable facilities for through traffic. Feasible opportunities for rerouting traffic from one street to a higher classification street will be explored."[6]

| Do Not Meet Warrants for Individual Streets | | |
|---|---|---|
| **STREET** | **LOCATION** | **DESCRIPTION** |
| Alta Vista St | Pomelo Ave | Multi-Way Stop |
| Arlington St | Orange-Osprey | Speed Humps |
| Bahia Vista St | US 41-Osprey | Speed Humps |
| Flower Dr | Hillview-Harbor | Multi-Way Stop |
| Hillview St | Flower Dr | Multi-Way Stop |
| Irving St | Yale Ave | Semi-Diverter |
| Loma Linda St | Pomelo Ave | Multi-Way Stop |
| Prospect St | Pomelo Ave | Semi-Diverter |

**Figure 8.6. Public Relations Piece Announcing Deviation from Warrants. (Sarasota, FL)**

Source: South Sarasota Public Hearing, May 1995.

In Boulder, diversion that evens out traffic volumes on parallel streets at the same level in the functional hierarchy without overloading any of them is also acceptable. Boulder's description: "Traffic may be rerouted from a street of equal classification as a result of a neighborhood traffic mitigation project if the end result is more equal distribution of the traffic burden."

In the communities surveyed, an unacceptable variety of diversion sends traffic to lower order streets or overloads streets of the same order. This kind of diversion is the Achilles' heel of traffic calming. Citizens rarely turn out in protest over degradation of emergency response times since the possibility of emergencies seems remote. Outsiders inconvenienced by neighborhood traffic calming may call to complain or show up at a public hearing individually, but they rarely turn out en masse to protest a plan. Residents of nearby streets, whose quality of life may be hurt by diverted traffic, are the only ones with enough at stake to protest en masse.

Realizing this, a few communities have provided a warranty of sorts to those concerned about traffic diversion to their streets. If undesired diversion occurs, the local government will take action to mitigate the impact. Two featured communities, Boulder and Portland, have such policies.

In 1992, Portland adopted a so-called impact threshold curve that limits the amount of diversion it will accept. The curve is shown in figure 8.7. If traffic grows beyond a threshold value on any local street as a result of traffic calming measures taken on parallel streets, the city attempts to solve the problem by modifying the original design or installing traffic calming measures on the impacted street. The acceptable traffic growth threshold starts at 150 vehicles per day (vpd) for the lowest volume streets and increases to 400 vpd for streets with existing volumes of approximately 2,000 vpd. In no case may the increase on any local street exceed 400 vpd, nor may the resulting traffic volume exceed 3,000 vpd. This policy led, for example, to the replacement of 14-foot humps with 22-foot tables on a street that had diverted too much traffic. The redesign solved the diversion problem.

The Boulder policy is stricter, so strict it tends to preclude certain traffic calming measures, including speed controls that slow traffic enough to divert a little of it. The policy was adopted in response to a traffic calming plan that, in hindsight, compromised the connectivity of the street network (see figure 8.8).

The Boulder policy states that if traffic on any lower order street grows by more than 10 percent as a result of traffic mitigation, the city will "mitigate the mitigation." On a street with 200 vpd, a 10 percent increase amounts to only 20 cars per day. This threshold value lies within the daily variation of traffic volumes. Boulder staff members point to Portland's policy, which sets an absolute

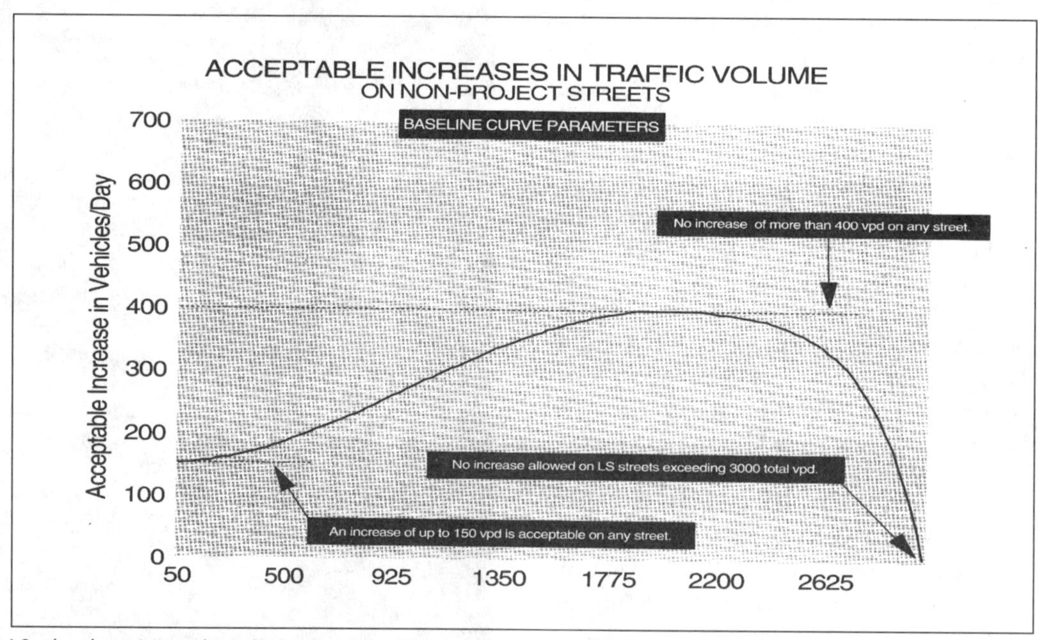


LS = local service; vpd = vehicles per day

**Figure 8.7. Impact Threshold Curve. (Portland, OR)**

Source: Bureau of Traffic Management, "Neighborhood Traffic Management for Local Service Streets," City of Portland, OR, March 1992, p. 13.

**Figure 8.8. Project that Provoked a Strict Diversion Policy. (Boulder, CO)**

**Table 8.6. Options Offered to Marine Street Residents. (Boulder, CO)**

**Narrowed List of Options**

Raised crossing and narrowing

Street closure

Raised intersection and neckdowns (with $60,000 cost borne largely by neighborhood)

Modification of Arapahoe Avenue circles

**Additional Options Offered But Initially Rejected**

Humps

Small median islands

Traffic circle

Do nothing

Other low cost solution

threshold rather than a relative one, as an alternative.

As an example of Boulder's diversion policy in action, traffic circles installed on Arapahoe Avenue may have diverted traffic to Marine Street. Four traffic counts on Marine Street showed increases of 62, 77, 0, and 40 percent over pre-calming levels. While ambiguous, the counts implied a traffic increase of more than 10 percent, triggering the mitigation policy. Residents of Marine Street were asked to vote on an array of traffic calming options for their street (see table 8.6). Ultimately, no mitigation was undertaken for lack of resident support.

## Project Priority Rating Systems

Priority rating systems differ from warrants in two respects. First, priority rating systems rank projects in order of funding priority, while warrants are used to simply qualify or disqualify projects for funding. Only if budgeted funds were just sufficient to cover all eligible projects, and no others, would priority rating systems and warrants produce the same funding outcomes. Second, priority rating systems allow tradeoffs among factors, while warrants treat qualifying factors as minimum requirements. Lower traffic speeds may balance higher traffic volumes (see figure 8.9). Some experts believe that this is the way residents perceive traffic problems. For just this reason, San Diego has considered converting two of its speed hump warrants—those relating to average daily traffic volume and 85th percentile speed (the speed below which 85 percent of the vehicles travel)—into priority rating factors. Quoting a city traffic engineer, these warrants are "screening out good candidate projects" and hence are "difficult to justify" to the public.

It is the opinion of some traffic managers that speed and volume are not substitutable for one another in some simple fashion per an economist's indifference curve. Residents may actually find an occasional speeding vehicle on their street more distressing than a steady stream of speeding vehicles that they are primed to look out for. If true, priority rating systems will not rank problem streets very accurately. This is an area for further study.

The fact that priority rating systems combine qualifying factors into one composite score makes them potentially useful for more than just setting funding priorities. They can be used in cost-sharing formulas, where lower scores translate into higher neighborhood matching requirements (see "Cost-Sharing Arrangements" in the next section). They can also be used to screen projects, much as warrants are. Boca Raton, FL, requires a minimum score in its rating system to qualify for physical traffic calming. Below the minimum, streets are only eligible for neighborhood speed awareness flyers, neighborhood speed watch, and other education and enforcement activities.

Seattle's priority rating system has been in place longer than any other, and has been adopted with minor modification by many other jurisdictions. This widely accepted model is outlined in table 8.7. Note the priority given to high-accident locations. A priority rating system simply reflects the goals of local policy makers. Seattle has made traffic safety the prime rationale for its traffic calming program, which has helped shield the program from budget cuts and emergency response controversies.

Other systems differ from Seattle's in the relative weight given to traffic volume versus speed, the volume and speed thresholds above which points are awarded, and the additional factors considered when assigning priority. Table 8.8 summarizes these differences for many systems. In

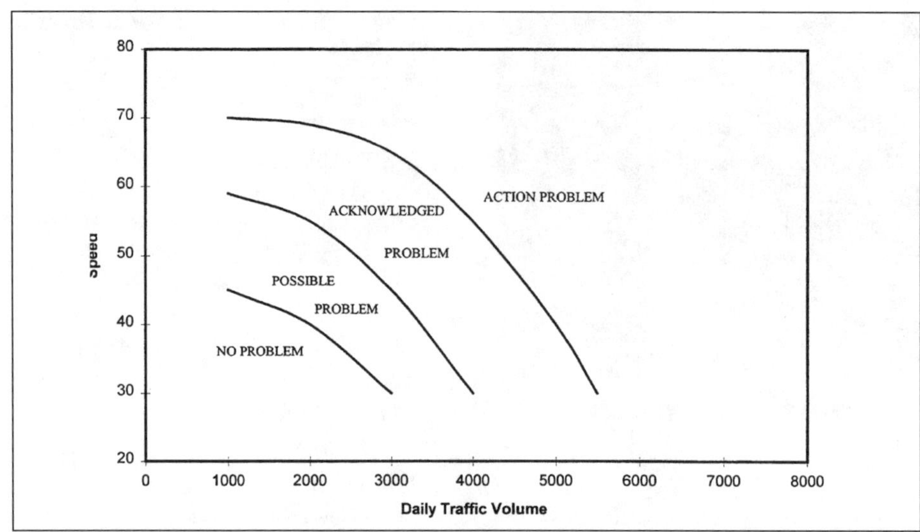


**Figure 8.9. Traffic Speed (kilometers per hour) and Volume as a Combined Problem.**

Source: A.P. O'Brien et al., "Some Australian Experiences with Warrants," *Transportation and Sustainable Communities*, (Resource Papers for 1997 ITE International Conference), Institute of Transportation Engineers, Washington, DC, 1997, pp. 71.

**Table 8.7. Details of One Priority Rating System. (Seattle's Traffic Circle Program)**

| Factor | Points |
|---|---|
| Recorded correctable accidents for past 3 years (accidents per year) | |
| 0.5–0.875 | 1 |
| 0.876–1.250 | 2 |
| 1.251–1.625 | 3 |
| 1.626–2.000 | 4 |
| 2.001–2.375 | 5 |
| 2.376–2.750 | 6 |
| If "non-correctable" accidents exceed an average of 2 per year | $^1/_2$ |
| If accidents at midblock exceed an average of 2 per year | $^1/_2$ |
| Average daily volume (vehicles per day) | |
| 500–1,100 | $^1/_2$ |
| 1,101–1,700 | 1 |
| 1,701–2,300 | 1 $^1/_2$ |
| 2,301–2,701 | 2 |
| 85th percentile speed (miles per hour) | |
| 26–29 | $^1/_2$ |
| 29.1–32 | 1 |
| 32.1–35 | 1 $^1/_2$ |
| 35.1–38 | 2 |
| 38.1–41 | 2 $^1/_2$ |
| 41.1–44 | 3 |

Source: Engineering Department, "Traffic Circles—Neighborhood Traffic Control Program," City of Seattle, WA. Undated.

**Table 8.8. Summary of Priority Rating Systems.**

| Community | Volume/Speed Tradeoff | Other Factors in Index |
|---|---|---|
| Austin, TX (humps) | 50 vph = 1 mph for volumes > 50 vph and 85th percentile speeds > 5 mph over speed limit | Speed-related accidents<br>Schools within $^1/_2$ mile<br>Pedestrian generators within 1,000 feet<br>Lack of sidewalks |
| Boca Raton, FL (local residential streets) | 200 vpd = 1 mph for volumes >500 vpd and 85th percentile speeds >25 mph | Correctable accidents |
| Berkeley, CA (humps) | 200 vpd = 1% of vehicles traveling > 30 mph for volumes > 1,000 vpd | Speed-related accidents<br>Schools/parks/institutions on block<br>Block length<br>Enforcement/education/engineering<br>Alternatives considered |
| Boulder, CO | 1,000 vpd = 1 mph for all volumes and 95th percentile, 85th percentile, or average speeds > speed limit | Gaps sufficient for street crossing<br>Residential densities<br>Pedestrian/bicyclist traffic<br>Bus stops/shops/hospitals/parks<br>Planned street improvements |
| Brookline, MA | 200 vpd = 1 mph for volumes > 500 vpd and 85th percentile speeds > 25 mph | Correctable accidents |
| Dallas, TX | 133 vpd = 1 mph for volumes > 500 vpd and 85th percentile speeds > 30 mph | Correctable accidents |
| Madison, WI | 33 vpd = 1% of vehicles traveling > speed limit for all volumes | Accidents<br>Elementary or middle schools on street<br>Pedestrian generators<br>School walk route<br>Bicycle route<br>Scheduled road reconstruction |
| Portland , OR (local streets) | 1,000 vpd = 1% of vehicles speeding for volumes > 5,000 vpd and 85th percentile speeds > 10 mph over speed limit | Elementary school zones<br>Pedestrian generators<br>Pedestrian routes<br>Bicycle routes<br>Transit routes<br>Lack of sidewalks |
| Portland, OR (humps) | 200 vpd = 1 mph for volumes > 400 vpd and 85th percentile speeds > 5 mph over speed limit | Lack of sidewalks |
| Portland , OR (neighborhood collectors) | 1,200 vpd = 1 mph for all volumes and 85th percentile speeds > 35 mph | Residential densities<br>Lack of sidewalks<br>Elementary school crossing<br>Pedestrian generators |
| Orlando, FL | 33 vpd = 1% of vehicles traveling > 30 mph for all volumes | Reported accidents<br>Schools on street<br>Other pedestrian generators<br>Designated pedestrian or bicycle routes<br>Lack of sidewalks |
| Sacramento, CA (residential streets) | 50 vpd = 1 mph for all volumes and 85th percentile speeds | Residential densities<br>Correctable accidents |
| Tallahassee, FL | 200 vpd = 1 mph for volumes > 500 vpd and 85th percentile speeds > 25 mph | Accidents<br>Schools within 1 mile<br>Pedestrian generators<br>Lack of sidewalks<br>Residential densities |

mph = miles per hour; vpd = vehicles per day; vph = vehicles per hour

Source: Unpublished documents supplied by the traffic calming programs.

Sacramento, CA, each additional mile per hour in speed is weighted the same as 50 additional vehicles per day in traffic volume. In Portland, on collector roads, an additional mile per hour is equivalent to 1,200 additional vehicles per day. That is, Portland's scoring system gives 24 times more weight to speed (relative to volume) than does Sacramento's. Generalizing the systems summarized in table 8.8, the typical system assigns points to speeds and volumes at a rate of 1 mph = 200 vpd, has thresholds of 500 vpd and 25 mph above which points start to accumulate, and also assigns points for collisions, pedestrian traffic generators, and lack of sidewalks.

The predecessor to this state-of-the-practice report, a report prepared for FHWA (1981), used experimental methods to assess acceptable speeds and volumes on residential streets.[7] A traffic speed of 15 mph proved acceptable to almost all residents, while a speed of 30 mph was unacceptable (a speed differential of 15 mph). A peak traffic volume of 1 vehicle per minute, or about 600 vpd, was generally acceptable to residents, while a peak volume of 6 vehicles per minute, or about 3,600 vpd, was generally unacceptable (a volume differential of 3,000 vpd). Thus, in terms of marginal disutility, a 1-mph increase in speed appears equivalent to a 200-vpd increase in volume (3,000 vpd/15 mph = 200 vpd/1 mph). Whether coincidental or not, the typical priority rating system conforms to its weightings for local residential streets. The volume threshold is also about right. However, the speed threshold may be a little high for a local residential street.

Higher order streets may require different weights, as in Portland. No comparable study is available.


## Public Involvement

In the years since the passage of Intermodal Surface Transportation Efficiency Act of 1991 (ISTEA), the public has become increasingly involved in transportation planning in general. Though most traffic calming is financed with local funds, and therefore falls outside ISTEA's requirements, the same emphasis (or even more) has been placed on public involvement in traffic calming programs.

Residents consider the streets they live on to be extensions of their homes. They care deeply about conditions on their streets and about government actions affecting their streets. They harbor strong opinions about the nature and extent of traffic problems, and about appropriate solutions. As has been noted in several sections of this report, it is a practical necessity to involve residents in the planning and implementation of traffic calming measures.

The relatively few traffic calming measures ever removed testify to the level of up-front public involvement that takes place in traffic calming programs (see table 8.9). Given the many reasons why traffic calming measures might fall into disfavor with residents, this record is remarkable.

Of Seattle's 600-plus traffic circles, only 2 have been taken out at the request of neighbors. Of Portland's 300-plus speed humps, just 2 sets have been removed, and 1 was replaced with speed tables. In 14 years of active programming, Bellevue has had to remove only 1 measure in response to neighborhood opposition.

### Approval Requirements

It is likely that the main reason so few measures are ever removed is the show of neighborhood support required to install measures in the first place. In most places, strong support must be demonstrated before measures are even tested. Before they are installed permanently, 50, 60, or even 70 percent of property owners and/or residents must concur.

The exceptions prove the rule. In Berkeley, a fair number of diverters and traffic circles have been removed over the long history of their program. No humps have ever been removed. One reason may be the requirement of petition signatures for speed humps, but not for other traffic calming measures.

Three issues surround public approval. One is how public support should be assessed, whether by petition, ballot, or survey. Another is what margin of public support should be required. The third is how large an area should be contacted for approval.

### Petitions Versus Ballots

Petition requirements are the most common way of establishing support. They serve as a screening mechanism for depth of commitment since residents must take the time to solicit signatures. Petition requirements are also easier to administer than are ballots or surveys.

On the negative side, signed petitions may not be the best indicator of public sentiment. Among featured communities, stories surfaced of residents feeling pressured to sign or being misled into signing by advocates of traffic calming.

It may be possible to structure petition processes so as to avoid such problems. In Gwinnett County, GA, all property owners must be given the opportunity to express their preferences. The petition itself requires the property owner to vote "yes" or "no" on the installation of humps (see figure 8.10). In Montgomery County, residents signing petitions are required to certify that they have reviewed an attached map of hump locations. The form lists neighborhood association contacts, with phone numbers, who can be called with any questions.

**Table 8.9. Removal of Traffic Calming Measures.**

| Community | Measures Removed | Reasons |
|---|---|---|
| Austin, TX | One diagonal diverter | Trial installation—cut-through traffic complained |
| Bellevue, WA | One set of humps | "Political" humps not warranted in first place |
| Berkeley, CA | Unknown number of traffic circles and diverters | Circles confusing and failed to slow traffic—diverters outgrown by neighborhoods |
| Boulder, CO | Speed tables on two streets | Emergency response concerns and resident opposition |
| Charlotte, NC | One-lane chicane, several diverters, and turn restrictions | Lack of resident support at end of trial period |
| Dayton, OH | One closure—a few speed humps | Closure left only one way into neighborhood—humps ultimately opposed by neighbors |
| Eugene, OR | None | |
| Ft. Lauderdale, FL | 5% of measures at end of trial period— mostly half closures | Half closures driven around— diverters used for drug exchanges |
| Gainesville, FL | One closure and four circles | Lack of resident support at end of trial period—circles replaced with humps |
| Gwinnett County, GA | None | |
| Howard County, MD | None | |
| Montgomery County, MD | Two sets of humps | Resident opposition developed |
| Phoenix, AZ | Several temporary diverters at end of trial period—one circle after 3 days | "Political" circle on a street with high volumes |
| Portland, OR | Two sets of humps | Ineffective trial installation—excessive diversion under Impact Threshold policy |
| San Diego, CA | Two temporary center islands<br>Two sets of humps | Plastic islands considered ugly Humps installed on collectors serving as emergency routes in violation of city's own policy |
| San Jose, CA | Many temporary measures | Plan developed by residents modified by staff—ineffective circles removed |
| Sarasota, FL | One semi-diverter | Traffic diversion to next street |
| Seattle, WA | Two traffic circles, two sets of chicanes, and two dozen temporary diverters | Inappropriate locations for circles and chicanes |
| Tallahassee, FL | One chicane | Considered ugly by neighbors |
| West Palm Beach, FL | One roundabout | Poorly designed and unwarranted |

Source: Interviews with staffs of traffic calming programs.

Even such safeguards may result in biased outcomes if residents feel pressured when approached by neighbors. One alternative is a mail-in ballot. In Dayton, OH, a petition process was generating hundreds of requests for humps. A majority of residents would casually sign petitions to install humps. Residents would wake up one morning to find humps they did not really favor. Then, a majority (including many of the same individuals) would sign petitions to remove the humps. Neighbors were unhappy, and public funds were wasted.

In response, Dayton added a balloting procedure, making it more difficult to qualify. After a petition is initially submitted, ballots are sent to all residents within the affected area. Two-thirds of all residents, not just two-thirds of all respondents, must concur before measures may be installed. By contrast, Austin has made it easier to qualify by switching from petitions to ballots. Austin had required two-thirds of residents to sign petitions. Austin now requires a simple majority of the ballots returned to be affirmative.

## Margin of Approval

Does approval by a simple majority of property owners or residents constitute adequate support for traffic calming? Or should a super-majority be required as a form of insurance? If a super-majority is required, how large should the margin be?

In San Diego's survey of 42 public agencies, the median approval requirement for speed humps was 67 percent; the range was 51 to 80 percent. Two things are apparent from the communities surveyed. Where a balloting procedure is used, judging neighborhood support is typically based on the proportion of affirmative ballots returned, not the proportion of all residents responding in the affirmative. Also, the required proportion is typically well in excess of 50 percent.

In the first test of Austin's new procedure, about a quarter of the ballots were returned, and two-thirds of respondents agreed to a neighborhood pilot project. If this response rate is typical, Dayton's requirement is clearly stringent, and Austin's may be lax (at least for permanent installations). Under Dayton's requirement, even unanimous approval by respondents would have failed to qualify the neighborhood for traffic calming. On the other hand, under Austin's new requirement, a mere 12 percent of all residents were allowed to decide for the rest, a prescription for disaster. Viewing respondents as a random sample of the entire neighborhood, super-majority support of respondents is likely necessary to have any confidence that the neighborhood as a whole is supportive. Sampling theory can be used to determine the necessary percentage support for any given sample size and any given confidence level.[8]

The higher the required approval margin, the more demand for traffic calming may be suppressed. In a community with excess demand, far beyond the supply of traffic calming funds, it is tempting to create administrative hurdles that disqualify competitors. One traffic manager spoke of curtailing 90 percent of the demand for traffic calming funds by making the process difficult; a 70 percent approval requirement is part of his process. The problem with raising administrative hurdles is that it decreases the ability to ensure the selection of the most worthy projects.

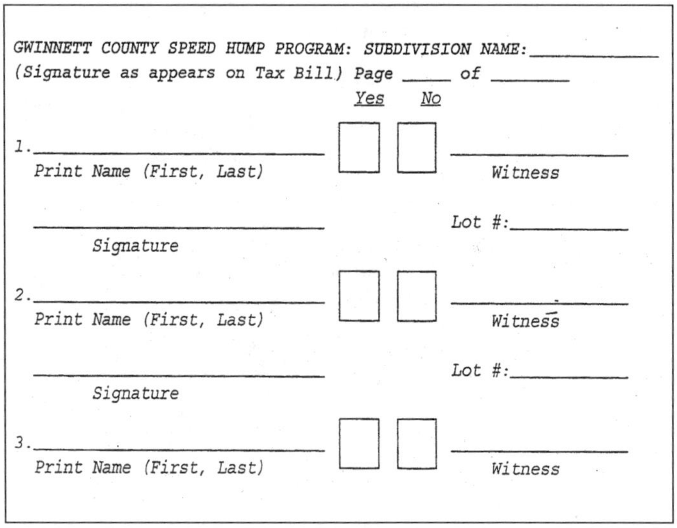
GWINNETT COUNTY SPEED HUMP PROGRAM: SUBDIVISION NAME:____________
(Signature as appears on Tax Bill) Page _____ of _______

Yes No

1. ______________________________ ☐ ☐ ______________
Print Name (First, Last) Witness

______________________________ Lot #:__________
Signature

2. ______________________________ ☐ ☐ ______________
Print Name (First, Last) Witness

______________________________ Lot #:__________
Signature

3. ______________________________ ☐ ☐ ______________
Print Name (First, Last) Witness

**Figure 8.10. Speed Hump Petition Offering a Choice. (Gwinnett County, GA)**

## Extent of Area Polled

Support for traffic calming measures is typically greatest on the streets being treated; support turns to opposition as polling moves to nearby streets that may be adversely impacted by diverted traffic. This phenomenon is illustrated by survey results from San Diego, where the issue was whether to retain traffic circles on Crest Way (see table 8.10).

One way to account for diversion is directly, by setting limits on diverted traffic, monitoring traffic levels, and taking remedial actions if limits are exceeded (see "Warrants That Address Diversion"). Another, indirect, way is to apply approval requirements to a larger area, not just to the particular street being treated. Several featured communities do so in cases where diversion is likely.

**Table 8.10. Survey Response to Question, "Should the traffic circles remain?"**

| Survey Respondents | "Yes" | "No" |
|---|---|---|
| Residents living on Crest Way | 83% | 17% |
| Residents living on adjacent streets | 33% | 67% |

Source: City of San Diego, CA, Unpublished memo to the Transportation and Land Use Committee, October 9, 1991, Attachment 2.

In Seattle, the petition area for speed control measures is one block in each direction from a measure. The petition area for traffic diverters (i.e., volume control measures) is the "impacted area" as defined by staff. While 60 percent written support of residents is required for both types of measures, approval is harder to secure for traffic diverters with large impacted areas.

In Phoenix, the petition area for speed humps and traffic circles is the street itself and, at staff discretion, parallel streets. The petition area is expanded to include the entire quarter section (0.25 square mile) around diagonal diverters, semi-diverters, and half closures. Again, although 70 percent approval is required in all cases, the requirement is harder to meet for volume control measures.

Other variations on this theme are found in Dayton, Ft. Lauderdale, and San Diego.

## Cost–Sharing Arrangements

Willingness to directly participate in the funding of traffic calming measures may be the ultimate test of public support. However, there is debate over the appropriate level of cost sharing, whether the level should vary with circumstances, and what circumstances are relevant.

At one extreme, Bellevue is opposed to cost sharing and has actually declined neighborhood offers to pay for traffic calming measures in return for expedited installation. For Bellevue, it is a matter of fairness. If traffic calming is a basic neighborhood right, then ability to pay should not be a decisive factor.

At the other extreme is Phoenix, which at one time had no public funding for traffic calming and still has limited public funds. Phoenix has found that residents are quick to spend available public funds, but must truly value traffic calming measures before they will spend their own money.

Many featured programs offer cost-sharing options. A few programs have sought to further local policies and priorities by placing neighborhoods' share of costs on sliding scales (see table 8.11). In addition to the bases for cost sharing shown in the table, Boulder has considered raising the neighborhood's share where local traffic rather than through traffic is creating a problem. Charlotte has debated a higher neighborhood share for "stable" than for "fragile" neighborhoods.

## Collaborative Planning Processes

Approval requirements and cost sharing are valuable tools for assessing public support for traffic calming measures. But several communities have found that public involvement should be more than an up-or-down vote on a staff-formulated plan. The plan is likely to be better, and to be more favorably received, if those most affected have a say in its formulation.

There are many ways of engaging the public in what were once viewed as purely technical matters, best left to experts. They are described in *Public Involvement Techniques for Transportation Decision-Making,* a how-to guide available from FHWA and the Federal Transit Administration.[9] Beyond the traditional techniques, such as public hearings, opinion polls, and citizen advisory committees, new techniques have been developed to

**Table 8.11. Creative Cost-Sharing Formulas.**

| Location | Neighborhood Share | Basis for Neighborhood Share |
|---|---|---|
| Austin, TX | 0–100% (sliding scale, based on point score) | Priority rating of project (discontinued) |
| Boca Raton, FL | 0% and up | Incremental cost of more elaborate measures |
| Boulder, CO | 50% (high priority)<br>100% (low priority) | Priority rating of project |
| Charlotte, NC | 0% and up | Incremental cost of more elaborate measures |

Source: Unpublished documents supplied by traffic calming programs.

help citizens visualize design alternatives and participate constructively in the design process. These new techniques have been put to good use in traffic calming projects:

- Guided tours of traffic calming sites
- Computer imaging (see figure 8.11)
- Visual preference surveys (see figure 8.12)
- Design charrettes (see figure 8.13)
- Focus groups (see figure 8.14)
- Neighborhood traffic committees[10]

This is not to suggest that design decisions be turned over to residents, only that residents be fully involved. Several featured communities have had bad experiences with delegated decision making. Honoring a pledge by the mayor, planning for traffic calming in one neighborhood in San Jose was turned over to a project steering committee. Implementation followed planning, and 2,500 enraged telephone calls followed implementation. The citizen-generated plan was soon replaced by a plan developed by staff, and the complaints ceased.

Likewise, a street closure in Austin was turned over to an upper-income neighborhood, which proceeded to design and build a full closure in the form of a wall. Amazingly, the full closure was not even left open to pedestrians and bicyclists. This is in contrast to street closures in places like Boulder, which while controversial for their impacts on traffic, at least remain permeable to pedestrians, bicyclists, and even emergency vehicles. Contrast figure 8.15 with figure 8.8 shown previously.

**Figure 8.11. Computer Simulation Showing One Possible Treatment of a High-Volume Intersection.**

Source: Author's study for the Alton Road Homeowners' Association, Miami Beach, FL.

Photo Credit: Susan Van Wagoner. Printed with permission of the Route 50 Corridor Coalition.

**Figure 8.13. Design Charrette Used to Develop the Plan for Rural Route 50. (Loudoun County, VA)**

**Lowest Rated Image (average score = 3.0)**

**Highest Rated Image (average score = 6.4)**

**Figure 8.12. Visual Preferences of Residents Shown Alternatives for Calming a Major Collector (on a scale of 1 to 7).**

Source: Author's study for the Ardens, DE.

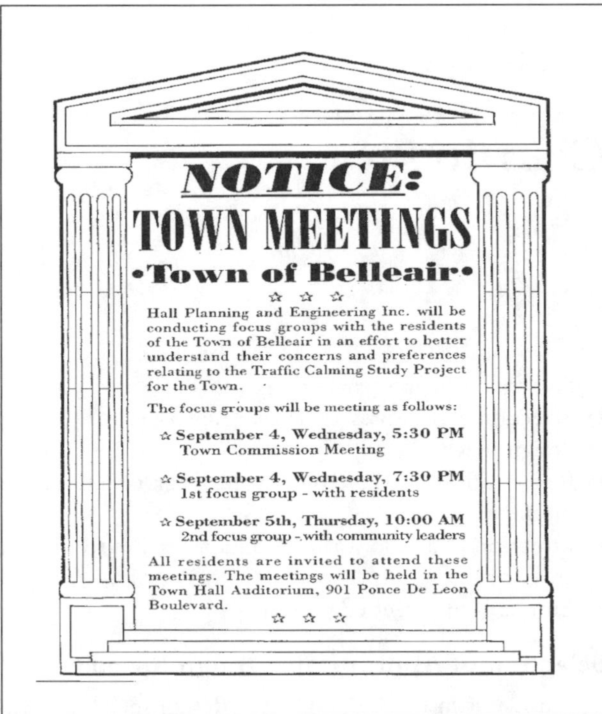


**Figure 8.14. Announcement of Focus Groups for a Citywide Traffic Calming Project. (Belleair, FL)**

**Figure 8.15. Impenetrable Street Closure. (Austin, TX)**

## Endnotes


1. Portland and several other places call their speed humps by the name "bumps."

2. A. Weinstein and E. Deakin, "A Survey of Traffic Calming Programs in the United States," paper presented at the ITE International Conference in Monterey, CA, Institute of Transportation Engineers, Washington, DC, 1998.

3. City of San Jose, "Council Policy—Neighborhood Traffic Management Programs," approved on August 4, 1997.

4. J.P. Perone, "Developing and Implementing Traffic Calming Warrants," *1996 Compendium of Technical Papers,* Institute of Transportation Engineers, Washington, DC, 1996, pp. 351–353; B.D. Kanely, "Neighborhood Traffic Calming—Do We Need Warrants?" *Transportation and Sustainable Communities: Challenge and Opportunities for the Transportation Professional,* Resource Papers for the 1997 ITE International Conference, Institute of Transportation Engineers, Washington, DC, 1997, pp. 60–64; I.M. Lockwood, "Do We Need Traffic Calming Warrants?" *Transportation and Sustainable Communities: Challenge and Opportunities for the Transportation Professional,* Resource Papers for the 1997 ITE International Conference, Institute of Transportation Engineers, Washington, DC, 1997, pp. 55–59; A.P. O'Brien, "The Need for Warrants—The Australian Experience," *Transportation and Sustainable Communities: Challenge and Opportunities for the Transportation Professional,* Resource Papers for the 1997 ITE International Conference, Institute of Transportation Engineers, Washington, DC, 1997, pp. 65–82; and A. O'Brien, R. Brindle, and R. Fairlie, "Some Australian Experiences with Warrants," *1997 Compendium of Technical Papers for the 67th ITE Annual Meeting,* (Boston, MA, 1997), Institute of Transportation Engineers, Washington, DC, 1997, CD-ROM.

5. Lockwood, op. cit.

6. City of Boulder, "Neighborhood Traffic Mitigation Program—A Status Report," City Council Study Session, April 8, 1997, p. 4.

7. D.T. Smith and D. Appleyard, "Studies of Speed and Volume on Residential Streets," *Improving the Residential Street Environment—Final Report,* Federal Highway Administration, Washington, DC, 1981, pp. 113–130.

8. See, for example, L.M. Rea and R.A. Parker, *Designing and Conducting Survey Research,* Jossey-Bass, San Francisco, CA, 1992, pp. 107–124.

9. *Public Involvement Techniques for Transportation Decision-Making,* prepared by Howard/Stein-Hudson Associates and Parsons, Brinckerhoff, Quade, & Douglas, Administration, Washington, DC, 1996.

10. A particularly readable source is C.N. Moore, *Participation Tools for Better Land-Use Planning,* Center for Livable Communities, Local Government Commission, Sacramento, CA, 1995.

# CHAPTER 9

# Beyond Residential Traffic Calming

The traffic calming applications described in previous chapters of this report were, for the most part, found on local or neighborhood collector streets with primarily residential frontage. This chapter addresses the many issues associated with traffic calming on higher order streets.

Most communities have arterials or collectors with fronting residences.[1] They may be rural highways passing through small towns or neighborhood streets at the end of tributary networks. Whether by design or as a result of growth, thousands of vehicles per day race past homes, schools, and parks, spurring residents to call for traffic calming to restore the quality of life. In many communities, their request is rejected with the rationale that traffic calming is not appropriate on higher order streets.

The result: Even though traffic may be calmed within neighborhoods, pedestrian life may end at the neighborhood borders. One writer has argued, "Making 99 percent of a journey safe and convenient by foot or bike is futile if the remaining one percent contains a dangerous road crossing."[2] Higher order roads are the locations of many more traffic accidents than are local streets.[3] Some feel that traffic calming can offer an improvement in safety and quality of life on such streets. Others disagree. The following examples show some ways traffic calming has been tried on higher order roads.

## European Experience

Calming of major roads has been common in Europe for over a decade. During this time many of the associated problems have been addressed as the process has been institutionalized. As practice in the United States is still in its formative stages, this state-of-the-practice report looks overseas for experience.

Case studies of contemporary European traffic calming are available in a number of published volumes.[4] A sample of rural and suburban through roads, as well as some high-volume city streets, are profiled, and the following provisions are highlighted:

- Selection of appropriate design speeds
- Selection of measures and spacing appropriate to higher design speeds
- Reallocation of right-of-way in favor of alternative modes
- Provision of ample warning on approaches to calmed areas
- Emphasis on street edge treatments

## Selection of Appropriate Design Speeds

In Europe, as in the United States, design speeds are determined in part by the functional class of roadways. Functional classification schemes attempt to strike a balance between mobility and other objectives such as compatibility with abutting land uses, economic development, and bicycle/pedestrian friendliness. For minor streets, mobility is secondary, and the other objectives are primary. For major streets, the reverse is true.[5]

The street hierarchy in Devon County, England, illustrates this shifting balance. Three classes of urban streets are defined, with design speeds ranging from under 20 mph for pedestrian-oriented streets to 30 mph for main access and through routes (see table 9.1). At the lower end of the hierarchy, physical measures must be used to enforce the speed limit. At the upper end, there is no such requirement. Yet, in its design speed of only 30 mph and in its special accommodation of "vulnerable road users" (pedestrians and bicyclists), the upper end in England is clearly different from the upper end of the U.S. road hierarchy.

In Europe, as in the United States, design speeds are also determined by the setting, whether urban or rural. In Great Britain, highways through rural villages are calmed to an average speed of 35 mph; main roads through urban town centers are calmed to an average speed of 21 mph.[6] In contrast, traffic-calmed highways through villages in Nordrhein-Westfalen, Germany, have 85th percentile speeds (the speeds below which 85 percent of vehicles travel) as high as 43 mph.[7]

When high design speeds are chosen, it may be at the expense of other objectives, including safety and

| Class | Speed |
|---|---|
| *Living areas*—walking, cycling, and other living functions have priority over motor vehicles—speed limits self-enforced by physical measures | Below 20 mph—pedestrian zones and shared surface streets<br>20 mph—residential streets, local and collector streets without through traffic |
| *Mixed priority areas*—priority is shared between living and traffic functions—including sections of through routes—speed limits preferably self-enforcing | 20 or 30 mph |
| *Traffic areas*—major access and through routes—speed limits not necessarily self-enforcing—traffic function takes priority but vulnerable road users must be protected | 30 mph |

mph = miles per hour

Source: Devon County Council, *Traffic Calming Guidelines,* Devon County, Exeter, England, 1991, p. 12.

walkability. In a Danish test, collision rates remained high on an intercity route calmed to 50 kph (31 mph) as it passed through a small town, whereas collisions were halved on intercity routes calmed to 40 kph (25 mph) through comparable towns.[8] Typical European design speeds, which reflect an attempt to balance mobility and other objectives, are presented in table 9.2.

## Selection of Measures and Spacing

Once design speeds are chosen, traffic calming measures and spacing appropriate to higher design speeds can be selected. Selection and spacing guidelines for achieving speeds up to 37 mph are available from several European sources.[9]

Danish guidelines are reproduced in table 9.3. At design speeds of 60 kph (37 mph) or more, only prewarnings, gateways, and lateral shifts (staggerings) are recommended. At 50 kph (31 mph), other two-lane measures are permitted, including narrowings and raised areas. At 40 kph (25 mph) or less, even one-lane slow points are allowed. Note that the Danish guidelines also consider the traffic volume and functional class of a roadway.

In addition to general application guidelines, geometric guidelines are available from European sources. As indicated in table 9.4, the Danes consider 6.5-meter humps suitable for 40-kph (25 mph) applications. Such humps are roughly equivalent to 22-foot speed tables in the United States. For 50-kph (31 mph) applications, the length of circular humps in Denmark is 9.5 meters (31 feet). No common humps or tables in the United States are this long or have this high a crossing speed. Comparable geometric guidelines are available for European speed tables and lateral shifts.

The other variable influencing design speed is the spacing of slow points. Once again, the Danes provide guidance (see table 9.5). For 40-kph (25 mph) midpoint speeds,

**Table 9.2. Typical European Design Speeds.**

- 15 kph (9 mph) on "woonerven" and other shared surface streets
- 30 kph (19 mph) on "stille veje" and other quiet streets
- 50 kph (31 mph) on traffic-calmed urban arterials
- 40–50 kph (25–31 mph) on intercity routes as they pass through rural villages

slow points are typically spaced no more than 100 meters apart (roughly 325 feet). For 50-kph (31 mph) midpoint speeds, the spacing increases to 150 meters (500 feet).

Examples of traffic calming applications on higher order roads are shown in figures 9.1 and 9.2. Figure 9.1 is an intercity route through a small village; figure 9.2 is a main road through a town center. Both applications feature lateral shifts, the workhorse of traffic calming on higher order roads in Europe. The figure 9.2 application also incorporates a gently sloped, raised crosswalk. In keeping with their different treatments and settings, the two roads have average speeds after traffic calming of 35 and 20 mph, respectively. They carry 13,500 and 16,500 vehicles per day, volumes that are well in excess of most traffic calming applications in the United States.

## Reallocation of Right-of-Way in Favor of Alternative Modes

On higher order roads, European traffic calming schemes often avoid the use of deflection to control speeds. Instead, speed control is achieved by reallocating space within the right-of-way to give motor vehicles lower priority and alternative modes higher priority. Typically one or more travel lanes are dropped to make room for bike lanes, widened sidewalks, or on-street parking. Sometimes travel

**Table 9.3. Appropriate Measures by Functional Class, Design Speed, and Traffic Volume—Danish Guidelines.**

| Main Type | | Road Class | | Desired Speed (km/h) | | | Annual Day Traffic (ADT) | |
|---|---|---|---|---|---|---|---|---|
| | | Traffic Road | Local Road | ≥60 | 50 | ≤40 | >3000 | ≤3000 |
| 1 | Pre-warnings | x | x | x | x | x | x | x |
| 2 | Gates | x | x | x | x | x | x | x |
| 3 | 2-lane raised areas | x | x | | x | x | x | x |
| 4 | 2-lane humps | x | x | | x | x | x | x |
| 5 | Staggerings | x | x | x | x | x | x | x |
| 6 | Staggerings with raised area | x | x | | x | x | x | x |
| 7 | 2-lane narrowings from road centre | x | x | | x | x | x | x |
| 8 | 2-lane narrowings from roadside | x | x | | x | x | x | x |
| 9 | Narrowings to 1 lane | (x) | x | | | x | | x |
| 10 | Narrowings to 1 lane with raised area | (x) | x | | | x | | x |
| 11 | Narrowings to 1 lane with humps | (x) | x | | | x | | x |
| 12 | Staggerings with narrowing to 1 lane | (x) | x | | | x | | x |
| 13 | Staggerings with narrowing to 1 lane and raised area | (x) | x | | | x | | x |
| 14 | Staggerings with narrowing to 1 lane and humps | (x) | x | | | x | | x |

(x): To be used only in special cases

km/h = kilometers per hour

Source: Vejdirektoratet—Vejregeludvalget, *Urban Traffic Areas—Part 7, Speed Reducers*, Danish Vejdirektoratet—Vejregeludvalget, June 1991, p. 22.

**Table 9.4. Radii and Chord Length of Circular Humps in Denmark.**

| Desired Speed (kph) | Radius (m) | Chord Length (m) | Bus Speed Over Hump (kph) |
|---|---|---|---|
| 20 | 11 | 3.0 | 5 |
| 25 | 15 | 3.5 | 10 |
| 30 | 20 | 4.0 | 15 |
| 35 | 31 | 5.0 | 20 |
| 40 | 53 | 6.5 | 25 |
| 45 | 80 | 8.0 | 30 |
| 50 | 113 | 9.5 | 35 |

kph = kilometers per hour; m = meters

Source: Vejdirektoratet—Vejregeludvalget, *Urban Traffic Areas—Part 7, Speed Reducers*, Danish Vejdirektoratet—Vejregeludvalget, June 1991, p. 30.

| Desired Speed (kph) | Distance Between Slow Points (m) |
| --- | --- |
| 50 | 150 |
| 40 | 100 |
| 30 | 75 |
| 10–20 | 25 (maximum 50) |

kph = kilometers per hour; m = meters

Source: Danish Road Directorate, Copenhagen, Denmark, 1998.

**Figure 9.1. Intercity Route Through a Small Village.**

Source: County Surveyors Society, *Traffic Calming in Practice,* Landor Publishing Ltd., London, England, 1994, p. 88.

**Figure 9.2. Main Road Through a Town Center.**

Source: County Surveyors Society, *Traffic Calming in Practice,* Landor Publishing Ltd., London, England, 1994, p. 38.

lanes are also narrowed. In the process, the character of a road changes in ways that presumably cause motorists to drive more slowly and with greater alertness to potential conflicts. The effects are more psychological (not physical as with vertical and horizontal deflection) because the motorist perceives that the road no longer belongs exclusively to motor vehicles.

Reallocation of right-of-way is also combined with deflection in many European traffic calming schemes. The effects are meant to be physical as well as psychological.

Examples of right-of-way reallocation are shown in figures 9.3 and 9.4, the first without deflection, the second with deflection. The treatment in figure 9.3 was prompted by a high collision rate. The highway was narrowed down to one travel lane in each direction. Cross-sectional width was reallocated to refuge islands, a striped

**Figure 9.3. Reallocation of Right-of-Way without Deflection.**

Source: County Surveyors Society, *Traffic Calming in Practice,* Landor Publishing Ltd., London, England, 1994, p. 84.

**Figure 9.4. Reallocation of Right-of-Way with Deflection.**

Source: L. Herrstedt et al., *An Improved Traffic Environment—A Catalogue of Ideas,* Danish Road Directorate, Copenhagen, Denmark, 1993, p. 122.

median, and bicycle lanes in both directions. Average speed fell from 60 mph before treatment to 53 mph after treatment.

The treatment in figure 9.4 was prompted by speeding on an intercity route through a small town. The speeding was a result of excessive roadway width and a straight alignment. The road was reconstructed with center islands, curb extensions, and bicycle lanes along the entire stretch. Not only was cross-sectional width reallocated, but lateral deflection was introduced. Average speed fell from 60 kph (37 mph) before treatment to 50 kph (31 mph) after treatment.

## Provision of Ample Pre-Warning

Gateways and other pre-warnings are used to send visual cues that speeds should be reduced. They are especially important at the edges of built-up areas, where transitions from highway speeds to town speeds are desired. Europeans have found that as the roadway environment becomes integrated into the built environment of the town, speeds are lowered. The lower speeds are then maintained via traffic calming measures.

Contemporary Danish examples almost all include pre-warnings of some type. They take the form of structures, rough roadway surfaces, dramatic signage, or other tools that will get the motorist's attention. The gateway in figure 9.5 has several pre-warnings: two steel towers, plantings, and a narrowing of the roadway. The strong vertical elements are important in the horizontal environment of the open road. Europeans even use literal gateways—old stone and masonry gates—to mark the beginning of traffic-calmed areas (see figure 9.6).

Danish experience suggests that gateways must be distinctive to be effective. Lampposts or trees alone have little speed-reducing effect. Center islands are believed to enhance the effectiveness of a standard gateway through a "plug in the hole" effect.

Rumble strips, not well-regarded in the United States because of noise impacts, are often used in European pre-warning schemes. They may be fine as warning devices if distant from houses and stores. Note that rumble strips are not considered to be traffic calming measures themselves and have modest effects on travel speeds. But they can effectively warn of traffic calming measures ahead (see figure 9.7).

Roundabouts sometimes serve as gateways. With landscaped center islands, possibly containing sculptures or monuments, they can serve as psychological and physical dividers between rural and urban sections. Figure 9.8 shows a roundabout at the town border of Chantepie, France. The roundabout not only warns traffic of upcoming development, but also forces traffic to slow down as it rounds the intersection.

**Figure 9.5. Danish Gateway.**

Source: L. Herrstedt et al., *An Improved Traffic Environment—A Catalogue of Ideas*, Danish Road Directorate, Copenhagen, Denmark, 1993, p. 121.

**Figure 9.6. Old Town Gate in France.**

Source: L. Herrstedt et al., *An Improved Traffic Environment—A Catalogue of Ideas*, Danish Road Directorate, Copenhagen, Denmark, 1993, p. 144.

**Figure 9.7. "Jiggle Bars" on an Approach to Town.**

Source: County Surveyors Society, *Traffic Calming in Practice*, Landor Publishing Ltd., London, England, 1994, pp. 96-97.

**Figure 9.8. Roundabout on an Approach to Town.**

Source: L. Herrstedt et al., *An Improved Traffic Environment—A Catalogue of Ideas*, Danish Road Directorate, Copenhagen, Denmark, 1993, p. 140.

### Emphasis on Street Edge Treatments

Supporting environmental measures are particularly important on higher order roadways, where some engineering measures may not be appropriate. Environmental measures are designed to create a pleasant and safe environment for pedestrians and a calm driving environment for motorists. Many European applications adhere to the principle that a combination of traffic calming and environmental measures is more effective in lowering speeds than either is alone.

Trees and other plantings are used to change the character of a street, potentially improving both the appearance and the microclimate. They can absorb noise and dust, and provide shade. Trees can also reduce the optical width of a street.

Small building setbacks can create the impression of an outdoor room (see figure 9.9). Street furniture can improve both the functional and aesthetic qualities of a street. It can encourage the use of public space by pedestrians.

**Figure 9.9. "Outdoor Room" Effect on an Intercity Route.**

Source: L. Herrstedt et al., *An Improved Traffic Environment—A Catalogue of Ideas*, Danish Road Directorate, Copenhagen, Denmark, 1993, pp. 116-119.

Objects such as phone booths, bollards, planters, and lightposts can also serve as vertical elements adjacent to the street, reducing its apparent width.

## U.S. Experience

Many of the communities featured in this report have implemented measures to calm traffic on high-volume streets, typically neighborhood collectors. Other communities have made it a policy not to do so. Of those that tried, most were successful in achieving reductions of speeds on the streets in question. Some faced opposition from commuters, emergency services, or other levels of government. Traffic calming is most controversial when applied to major streets with high volumes of through traffic. Most motorists seem to understand that local streets are access-oriented; by the same token, they expect higher order streets to provide a high level of mobility for through traffic.

The sections that follow describe experiences in U.S. communities. Some have been successful and others not.

### Boulevard—Hollywood, FL

Hollywood is bisected by Hollywood Boulevard, a five-lane arterial connecting two freeways. Although some blocks have always had street-oriented storefronts, the fast traffic and forbidding streetscapes discouraged potential customers. Reducing the arterial to two lanes through downtown, with widened sidewalks, a planted median, and angle parking, created a pedestrian-friendly zone that is credited by the community with reversing the economic decline of downtown (see figure 9.10).

### Neighborhood Collector—Beaverton, OR

Residential streets designed as neighborhood collectors can end up carrying volumes unsuitable for fronting residential uses. Beaverton, when faced with such a situation, considered three alternatives: closure, calming, or widening. On one such street, the choice was calming.

Calming had been attempted in Beaverton before, with treatments that were characterized as unattractive. Public backlash forced the removal of the treatments in 1985. But by 1997, although traffic volumes had grown to 14,000 vehicles per day in places, Beaverton went ahead with a well-conceived calming plan, based on a European design. The plan included entrance treatments, landscaping, lane narrowing, and speed tables (see figure 9.11). Curb extensions were added on sections with lower volumes. The community has embraced this plan, and speeds have come down and stayed down.

**Figure 9.10. Three Different Blocks Along the Same Street. (Hollywood, FL)**

**Figure 9.11. Speed Table with Curb Extensions on a Neighborhood Collector. (Beaverton, OR)**

## Major Collector—Columbia, MD

The planned community of Columbia is laid out as a series of neighborhoods and activity centers served by a curvilinear roadway network. High traffic speeds on the connecting streets pose a danger at intersections and reduce the walkability of the community. The traffic calming solution on one street uses warning signs and speed humps to slow motorists entering the area (see figure 9.12). Placed further down the street are a choker, circles, and speed tables. Slow points are spaced to keep speeds from creeping up too far.

## Neighborhood Collector Program— Portland, OR

A traffic calming program for local streets has been active in Portland since 1984. In 1993, the city expanded its program to include some higher order streets. The program was at first ambitiously named the "Arterial Traffic Calming Program." The name was soon changed. The program actually targeted only streets designated as neighborhood collectors, the lowest level of arterial roadway having at least 75 percent residential frontage (see figure 9.13).

Central to the program is a policy that no collector street project divert more than 150 vehicles per day to a parallel local street. Neckdowns, center islands, split medians, and 22-foot speed tables qualify for use on neighborhood collectors. Traffic circles and 14-foot humps do not. Prioritization of neighborhood collector street projects is based on staff evaluation rather than neighborhood requests.

Eleven collector streets, with volumes up to 7,600 vehicles per day, were calmed under this program, by all accounts successfully. In 1997, concerns from emergency services about the proliferation of traffic calming measures on emergency response routes prompted a moratorium on new applications. When the moratorium ended, program funding was zeroed out of the budget. Only in early 1999 was the program started up again.

## Effective and Ineffective Examples— Ft. Lauderdale, FL

Ft. Lauderdale successfully revitalized its downtown entertainment district by allowing on-street parking during evenings and weekends on Las Olas Boulevard (see figure 9.14). The city had tried to revive the economy in the 1980's through streetscape improvements, but two lanes in each direction were still filled with high-

**Figure 9.12. Series of Calming Measures on a Major Collector. (Columbia, MD)**

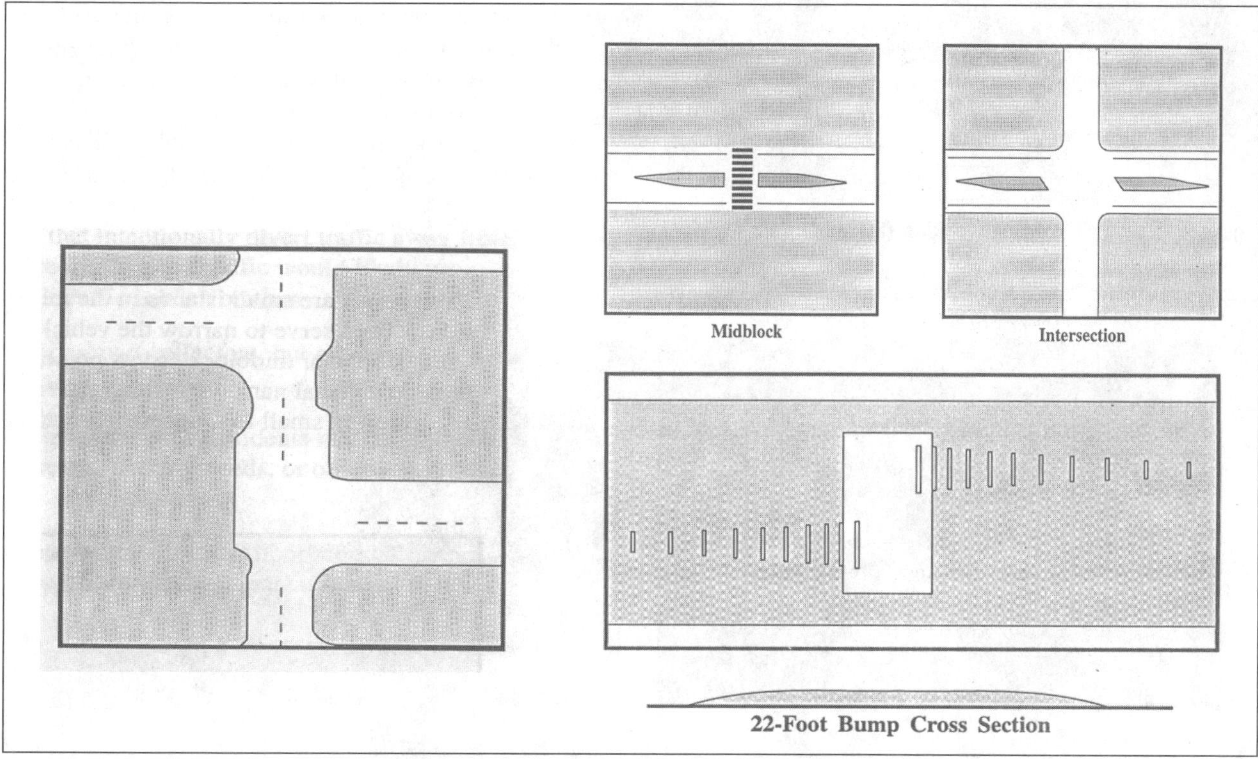



**Figure 9.13. Eligible Measures Under the Neighborhood Collector Program. (Portland, OR)**

Source: City of Portland, "Neighborhood Collector Street Projects," undated.

speed traffic. Narrowing to two lanes was proposed but rejected due to fear of diversion. Only in 1993, after a design charrette endorsed on-street parking, was the evening and weekend program tested. Pedestrian activity and nightlife picked up within weeks. The street is now a major activity generator.

In another example, a neighborhood collector was calmed with one-lane twisted chokers (see figure 9.15). Temporary designs were installed, which was fortunate as it turned out. Traffic volumes on the collector were high enough to create constant conflicts at the choke points. Drivers were never sure whether to stop or try to beat the opposing traffic through the device. The test was terminated, and speed tables were installed in place of the chokers.

### Calming or Potholes?—Tallahassee, FL

Monroe Street is a State route that cuts through historic downtown Tallahassee and passes the State capitol. A plan

**Figure 9.14. Off-Peak Curbside Parking. (Ft. Lauderdale, FL)**

to narrow the lanes to 11 feet was rejected by the Florida Department of Transportation. Instead, four intersections were outfitted with nubs and brick crosswalks. The signals were timed to slow traffic. When the crosswalks were first built, the concrete headers were badly installed in some instances, creating de facto speed bumps. This did, in fact, slow traffic. It also led a local newspaper columnist to write that simply leaving potholes in the street would be cheaper than traffic calming and just as effective. Reconstruction followed (see figure 9.16).

## Alternatives for High-Volume Streets

Other measures that are not strictly classified as traffic calming (based on the definition followed in this report) have been considered for higher volume streets. Roundabouts are a form of intersection control that can have many impacts in addition to traffic calming. Conversion of streets from one-way to two-way operation is sometimes part of downtown revitalization projects, in part for traffic calming effects.

### Roundabouts

At a modern roundabout, traffic must wait for a gap in the traffic flow before entering the intersection. Traffic must also deflect from a straight travel path to avoid the splitter island on the approach and the circle in the center. It is the deflection-at-entry primarily and the yield-at-entry secondarily that qualify roundabouts as traffic calming measures for this discussion.

Roundabouts perform best when traffic volumes are moderate and balanced (see British guidelines in figure

**Figure 9.15. Temporary One-Lane Choker and Speed Table that Replaced it. (Ft. Lauderdale, FL)**

**Figure 9.16. Crosswalk Reconstructed to Be Less Bump-Like. (Tallahassee, FL)**

9.17).[10] Under these conditions, roundabouts potentially have several advantages over other forms of intersection control:

- Safety—Roundabouts eliminate many of the conflict points present in a standard intersection and allow traffic to share space rather than take turns.

- Increased vehicular capacity—Roundabouts can provide as much as 30 percent greater capacity for motor vehicles than comparable signal systems. (It should be noted that this is not a benefit for pedestrians and bicyclists.)

- Reduced delay—Roundabouts can produce less delay than alternative forms of control at intersections with moderate-to-high traffic volumes (see figure 9.18).

- Reduced fuel consumption and improved air quality—Roundabouts can save fuel by eliminating the rapid acceleration and deceleration characteristic of signalized or sign-controlled intersections.

- Cost—Capital costs (exclusive of right-of-way costs) are often less than for signalized intersections, as are operation and maintenance costs.

- Aesthetics—Landscaped islands can visually break up bleak expanses of pavement and close vistas.

- Other features—Easy U-turns, reduced noise pollution, traffic calming.

The first modern U.S. roundabout was built in Nevada circa 1990. Roundabouts were built in California, Colorado, Florida, Maryland, and Vermont soon thereafter.[11] High-capacity roundabouts are now even being deployed at the intersections of local streets with freeway entry/exit ramps, as an alternative to traffic signals (see figure 9.19).

In order to be safe and effective, roundabouts must be properly designed. Roundabout guidelines have been published by road authorities in Europe, Australia, and two U.S. States, as well as by private consultants (see figure 9.20). The following design principles are taken from the *Florida Roundabout Guide:*[12]

- Vehicles entering a roundabout are required to yield to vehicles within the circulating roadway.

- The circulating vehicles are not subjected to any other right-of-way conflicts, and weaving is kept to a minimum.

- The speed at which a vehicle is able to negotiate the circulating roadway is controlled by the location of the center island with respect to the alignment of the right entry curb.

- No parking is allowed on the circulating roadway.

- No pedestrian activities take place on the center island. Pedestrians are not intended to cross the circulating roadway.

- All vehicles circulate counterclockwise, passing to the right of the center island.

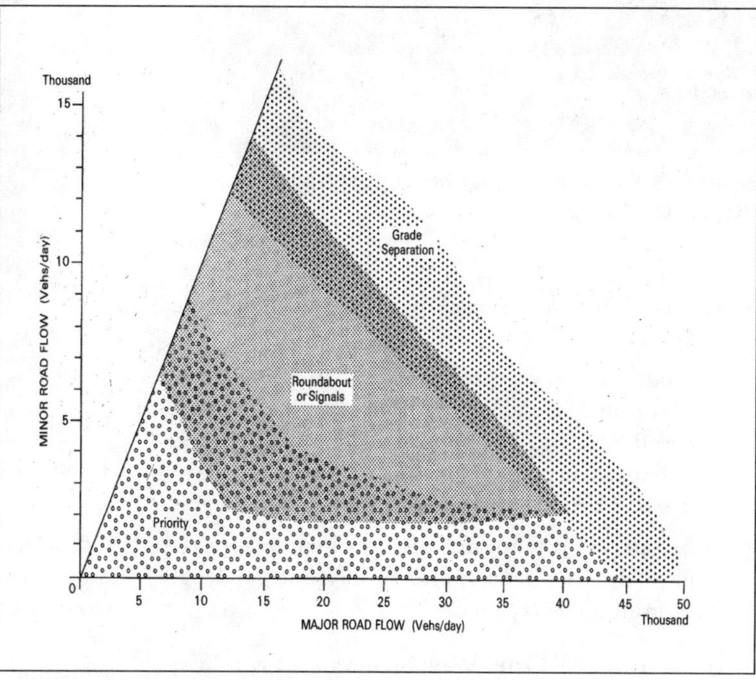


**Figure 9.17. British Guidelines for Roundabout Use.**

Source: Institution of Highways and Transportation, *Roads and Traffic in Urban Areas,* Her Majesty's Stationery Office, London, England, 1987, p. 328. Crown copyright is reproduced with the permission of the Controller of Her Majesty's Stationery Office.

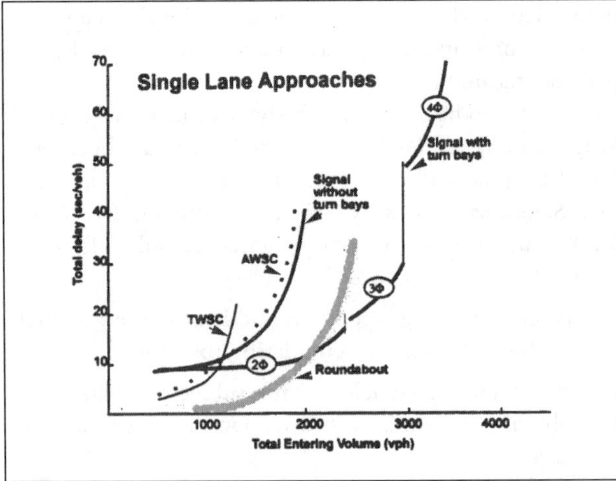


TWSC = Two-way stop control; AWSC = All-way stop control

**Figure 9.18. Delay with Roundabouts, Signals, Two-Way Stops, and All-Way Stops.**

Source: Florida Department of Transportation, *Florida Roundabout Guide*, Tallahassee, 1996, p. 3-8.

**Figure 9.19. High-Capacity Interchange Roundabout. (Howard County, MD)**

- Roundabouts are designed to accommodate specified design vehicles.

- Roundabouts have raised splitter islands. Splitter islands are an essential safety feature, necessary to separate traffic moving in opposite directions and to provide refuge for pedestrians. They are also an integral part of the deflection scheme.

- When pedestrian crossings are provided on approach roads, they are placed approximately one car-length back from the entry point.[13]

### Conversions of One-Way Streets to Two-Way Operation

In the 1950's and 1960's, many two-way streets within downtowns were converted to one-way operation to pro-

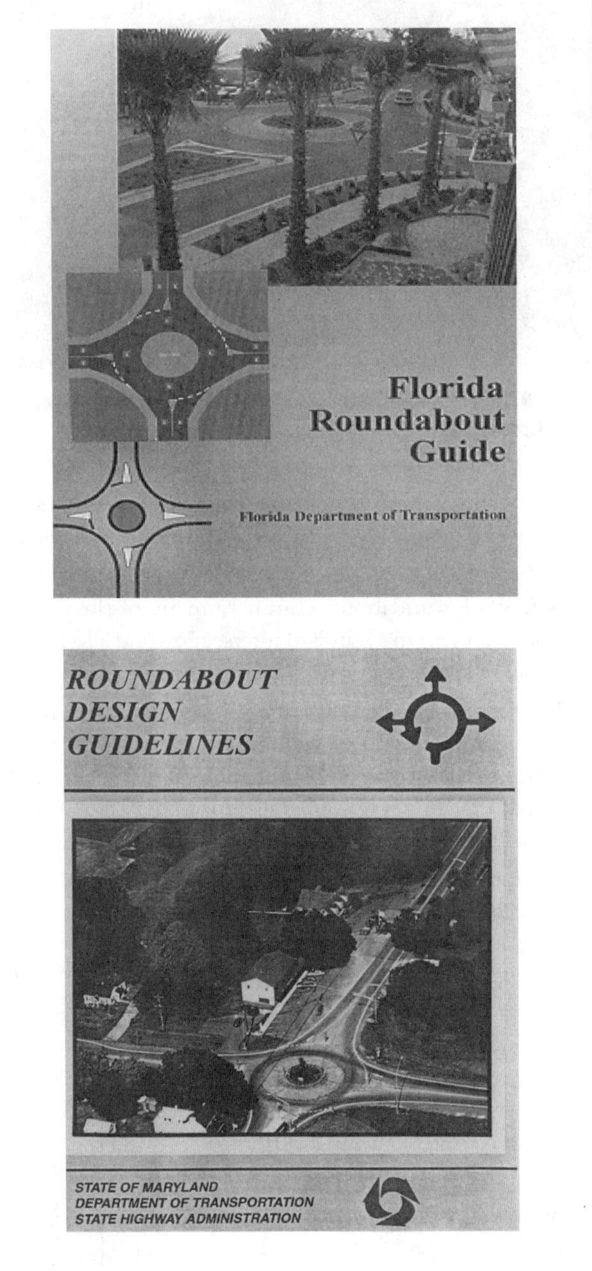


**Figure 9.20. State Guidance on Roundabouts.**

vide faster entry, exit, and through travel for growing suburban populations. In the past decade, many downtown streets have been converted back to two-way operation, often with the reintroduction of on-street parking and widening of sidewalks.

A recent survey identified many Florida cities and towns that have already converted one-way streets, or plan to convert one-way streets, back to two-way operation as part of downtown or main street improvement programs. They include Coral Gables, DeLand, Ft. Myers, Ft. Pierce, Gainesville, Lakeland, Orlando, Sarasota, and West Palm Beach. Some one-way streets in Denver, CO, and Sacramento, CA, have been converted specifically as part of traffic calming initiatives (see figure 9.21).[14]

**Figure 9.21. Commuter Route Converted Back to Two-Way Operation—and Traffic Calmed at the Same Time. (Sacramento, CA)**

## Endnotes


1. A study of San Francisco found 80 miles of residential streets carrying more than 10,000 vehicles per day. W.S. Homburger et al., *Residential Street Design and Traffic Control,* Prentice Hall, Englewood Cliffs, NJ, 1989, p. 49. A German article states that one-quarter of the urban population lives on major roads. H. H. Topp, "Traffic Safety, Usability and Streetscape Effects of New Design Principles for Major Urban Roads," *Transportation,* Vol. 16, 1990, p. 297.

2. R. Tolley, *Calming Traffic in Residential Areas,* Brefi Press, Brefi, England, 1990, p. 73.

3. R.F. Beaubien, "Does Traffic Calming Make Streets Safer?" in *Harmonizing Transportation and Community Goals* (ITE International Conference, Monterey, CA, 1998), Institute of Transportation Engineers, Washington, DC, 1998, CD-ROM.

4. L. Herrstedt et al., *An Improved Traffic Environment—A Catalogue of Ideas,* Danish Road Directorate, Copenhagen, Denmark, 1993, offers 33 examples not only from Denmark but also from France and Germany. County Surveyors Society, *Traffic Calming in Practice,* Landor Publishing Ltd., London, England, 1994, provides 85 case studies, all from Great Britain.

5. A. Clarke and M.J. Dornfeld, *National Bicycling and Walking Study: Case Study No. 19, Traffic Calming, Auto-Restricted Zones and Other Traffic Management Techniques: Their Effects on Bicycling and Pedestrians,* Federal Highway Administration, Washington, DC, 1994.

6. County Surveyors Society, op. cit., pp. 26–28.

7. R. Schnull and J. Lange, "Speed Reduction on Through Roads in Nordrhein-Westfalen," *Accident Analysis & Prevention,* Vol. 24, 1992, pp. 67–74.

8. Herrstedt et al., op. cit., p.13.

9. Herrstedt et al., op. cit.; and Vejdirektoratet-Vejregeludvalget, *Urban Traffic Areas—Part 7,* Speed Reducers, Danish Vejdirektoratet-Vejregeludvalget, June 1991.

10. The advantages of roundabouts come from many sources: ITE Technical Council Committee 5B-17, *Use of Roundabouts,* Institute of Transportation Engineers, Washington, DC, 1992; W.F. Savage and K. Al-Sahili, "Traffic Circles: A Viable Form of Intersection Control?" *ITE Journal,* Vol. 64, September 1994, pp. 40–45; L. Ourston, "Nonconforming Traffic Circle Becomes Modern Roundabout," *1994 Compendium of Technical Papers,* Institute of Transportation Engineers, Washington, DC, 1994, pp. 275–278; M.A. Rahman and T. Hicks, "A Critical Look at Roundabouts," *1994 Compendium of Technical Papers,* Institute of Transportation Engineers, Washington DC, 1994, pp. 260–264; A. Flannery and T.K. Datta, "Modern Roundabouts and Traffic Crash Experience in the United States," *Transportation Research Record 1553,* 1996, pp. 103–109; and G. Jacquemart et al., *Modern Roundabout Practice in the United States,* NCHRP Synthesis of Highway Practice 264, Transportation Research Board, Washington, DC, 1998.

11. For more detailed information on design, operation, and issues related to pedestrians and bicyclists: G. Jacquemart, *Modern Roundabout Practice in the United States,* Synthesis of Highway Practice 264, Transportation Research Board, Washington, DC, 1998.

12. State Highway Administration, *Roundabout Design Guidelines,* Maryland Department of Transportation, Annapolis, MD, 1994; and Florida Department of Transportation, *Florida Roundabout Guide,* Tallahassee, FL, 1996.

13. Roundabout design should consider the needs of people with disabilities, particularly those who have visual impairments.

14. R.F. Dorroh and R.A. Kochevar, "One-Way Conversions for Calming Denver's Streets," in *Moving Forward in a Scaled-Back World,* (Resource Papers for the 1996 ITE International Conference, Dana Point, CA), Institute of Transportation Engineers, Washington, DC, 1996, pp. 109–113; and S.J. Brown and S. Fitzsimons, "Calming the Community (Traffic Calming in Downtown Sacramento)," paper presented at the ITE International Conference in Monterey, CA, Institute of Transportation Engineers, Washington, DC, 1998.

# CHAPTER 10

# Traffic Calming in New Developments

Contemporary suburbs might appear to be traffic calmed from the outset, because the tree-like structure of suburban networks keeps through traffic off local access streets. Yet, as noted in "From Volume to Speed Controls" in chapter 3, this does not prevent speeding on longer cul-de-sacs or on residential subcollectors and collectors leading from those cul-de-sacs to the regional road network.

The problem is exemplified by the acclaimed Laguna West development, outside Sacramento, CA (see figure 10.1). Residents living on the many short cul-de-sacs are protected from speeding and cut-through traffic (see figure 10.2). Those living on the through streets are not so fortunate (see figure 10.3). The traffic problems are so serious on the axial roads to the town center that they have been walled off from some of the abutting residences, a practice that runs counter to the New Urbanist philosophy.[1]

Relatively little has been written about traffic calming in new developments, and experience is limited, too. The first section of this chapter reviews efforts of featured communities to calm traffic in new developments and identifies regulatory mechanisms that have been used to influence development decisions.

The second section outlines street network design principles from the State of Florida's *Best Development Practices*.[2] The principles are intended to produce a roadway network within which traffic is dispersed and slowed naturally (i.e., without the need of physical traffic calming measures). The result is potentially narrower street cross sections and shorter access trips to the regional road network, leaving drivers less inclined to speed.

The third section presents alternative street geometric standards developed for the Wilmington Area Planning Council in Delaware. These standards offer a traffic calming alternative to the more conventional standards of the American Association of State Highway and Transportation Officials (AASHTO).

**Figure 10.2. Short Cul-de-Sac Protected from Traffic. (Laguna West, CA)**

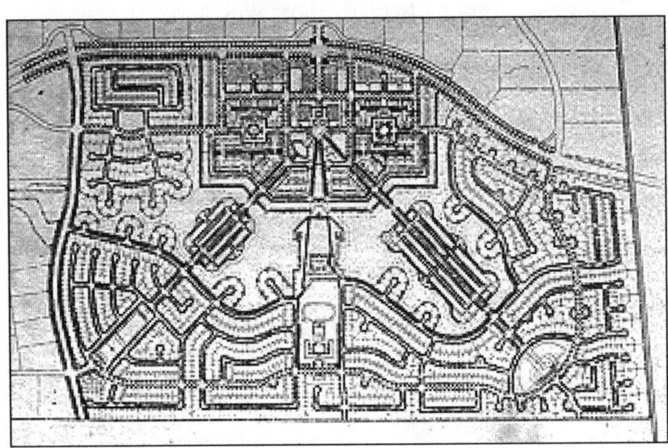

**Figure 10.1. New Urbanist Network. (Laguna West, CA)**

**Figure 10.3. Axial Road with a Traffic Problem. (Laguna West, CA)**

## Regulations of Featured Communities

Perhaps because they spend so much time on retrofits, the featured communities are more sensitive than most to the need to calm traffic in new developments. Table 10.1 summarizes their efforts in new developments to date. Communities not listed are largely built-out. Following the table, a few exemplary efforts are highlighted.

## Subdivision Regulations—Phoenix, AZ

Phoenix has adopted policies to discourage cut-through traffic in new developments. These policies are administered through the subdivision process. The ordinance states:

> Local streets should be discontinuous and generally should be interrupted with jogs and offsets. Four-way intersections should be avoided.[3]

**Table 10.1. Efforts to Calm Traffic in New Developments in Featured Communities.**

| Community | Measures |
|---|---|
| Austin, TX | Code requires neighborhood traffic analyses where commercial developments have direct access to residential streets; mitigation is required if more than 300 vehicles are added to daily volumes—one large residential development will include traffic calming measures as a result of a design charrette |
| Bellevue, WA | Heightened awareness by design engineers—in one case, curb extensions required at a connection to new development |
| Berkeley, CA | In three cases, calming measures were required as conditions of development approval—an office developer paid for reconstruction of an entire street as a "slow street" |
| Boulder, CO | Reduced street standards |
| Charlotte, NC | During subdivision review, T-intersections and circuitous routes are suggested to avoid cut-through traffic on local streets—in one case, a closure was allowed at interface with new development |
| Eugene, OR | Code provides for narrow streets, alternating parking, etc.—subdivision plans are reviewed for speeding and cut-through traffic problems |
| Gainesville, FL | In several cases, developers have been encouraged to install and pay for traffic circles—done voluntarily because circles were popular |
| Gwinnett County, GA | Developers occasionally have been advised to install humps voluntarily—county code may be amended to make humps mandatory |
| Howard County, MD | New subdivision road standards are proposed to calm traffic naturally—narrowing streets, adding roundabouts at intersections, and requiring slow points at regular intervals |
| Montgomery County, MD | New town will be test case—raised crossings, humps, chokers, and neckdowns are to be required |
| Phoenix, AZ | Subdivision regulations and design review standards discourage cut-through traffic—guidance to developers contained in *Calming Phoenix Traffic** |
| San Diego, CA | During development review, staff refers to *Transit-Oriented Development Design Guidelines*** |
| San Jose, CA | During site plan review, developers are asked to address potential for cut-through traffic—traffic study is required if more than 100 vehicles per peak hour will result from the development |
| Seattle, WA | In one redevelopment project, circles required to prevent speeding when grid reestablished |
| Tallahassee, FL | Comprehensive plan is being amended to encourage traffic calming in new developments—in one case, unspecified measures are required at intervals of 400 to 600 feet |
| West Palm Beach, FL | Large infill project was required to construct narrow streets with on-street parking, neckdowns, raised intersections, and raised crosswalks |

*City of Phoenix Traffic Calming Committee, January 1997. **Calthorpe Associates, City of San Diego, CA, 1992.

Source: Interviews with traffic calming staffs; supplemental documents supplied.

A policy supplement goes on to state:

> Local streets should not exceed 600–900 feet in length. They may, however, extend to $^1/_4$ mile if the street is curved (100–200 foot radius) for an adequate length (minimum curve length equals the curve radius) and the cut-through traffic potential is minimal.[4]

## Transit-Oriented Development Manual— San Diego, CA

When reviewing development proposals, San Diego now refers to a manual prepared by a leading New Urbanist, Peter Calthorpe. Calthorpe's transit-oriented development guidelines are 1 of about 50 sets nationally that are intended to make land development more friendly to pedestrians and transit users.[5] While Calthorpe's guidelines focus on land use mix, density, urban design, and pedestrian amenities, they offer general guidance related to street width, connectivity, and edge treatments (see figure 10.4).

## New Street Standards—Howard County, MD

New subdivision street standards were recently adopted by the Howard County Council. They were adopted over the objections of the county department of education, which worried about schoolbus operation on narrow streets. It was pointed out that schoolbuses already travel up narrow driveways to pick up special education students and travel on narrow streets in older subdivisions.

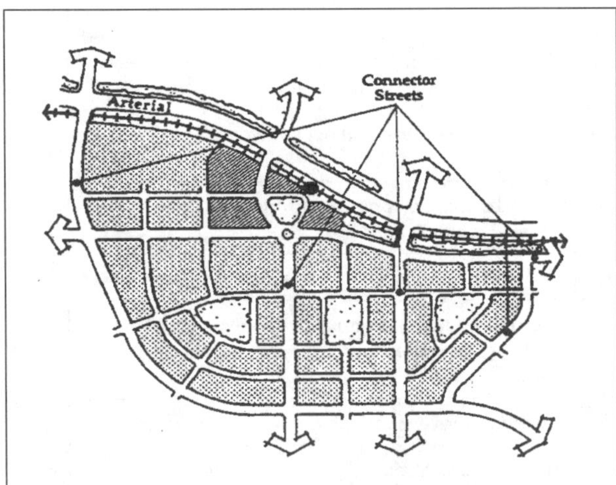


**Figure 10.4. Collectors Should be Designed as "Connectors." (San Diego, CA)**

Source: Calthorpe Associates, *Transit-Oriented Development Design Guidelines*, City of San Diego, CA, 1992, p. 63.

The code reads:

> It is the intent of these road standards to design roadways that do not encourage speeding. Typical past practices that encouraged long tangent sections of road, long sweeping curves and wide pavement only serve to invite speeding.[6]

The new standards narrow streets, require roundabouts at higher volume, four-legged intersections, and provide for sharp bends and other "slow points" at regular intervals (see figure 10.5). While the new standards may reduce speeds, it is not clear that they improve safety for motorists or bicyclists.

## Local Street Plan—Eugene, OR

In an effort to reduce reliance on the automobile, Eugene adopted the *Eugene Local Street Plan*. The plan requires interconnectedness of local streets and replaces the city's old hierarchy of wide streets with a new hierarchy of narrower streets, starting with access lanes 21 feet wide (see figure 10.6) and moving up to medium-volume residential streets 27–34 feet wide. The plan contains an entire section on traffic calming. One of the principles articulated in that section is particularly germane: "A successful [street] design will result in traffic calming and reduce the need for future installation of traffic calming measures."[7]

In addition to guidance on street network design and street geometrics, the plan specifies which traffic calming measures are appropriate as design features of new subdivision streets as well as add-ons to existing local streets (see table 10.2).

The Eugene plan was implemented in 1996 through changes in the city code. City staff reviews subdivision plans for street connectivity, bicycle and pedestrian access, and block and cul-de-sac length. Traffic calming measures may be required. In one recent case, a developer whose property is adjacent to a new public school was required to put in raised crosswalks along the main access route. A raised crosswalk can be seen, with the school in the distance, in figure 10.7.

## Street Network Design—The Florida Principles

The previous section identifies some of the regulatory mechanisms that may be used to implement traffic calming policies and standards for new developments. This section and the next summarize policies and standards that are being used to encourage development practices that produce or enable calmed streets. This section covers principles of street network design. The next focuses on geometric details of traffic-calmed streets.

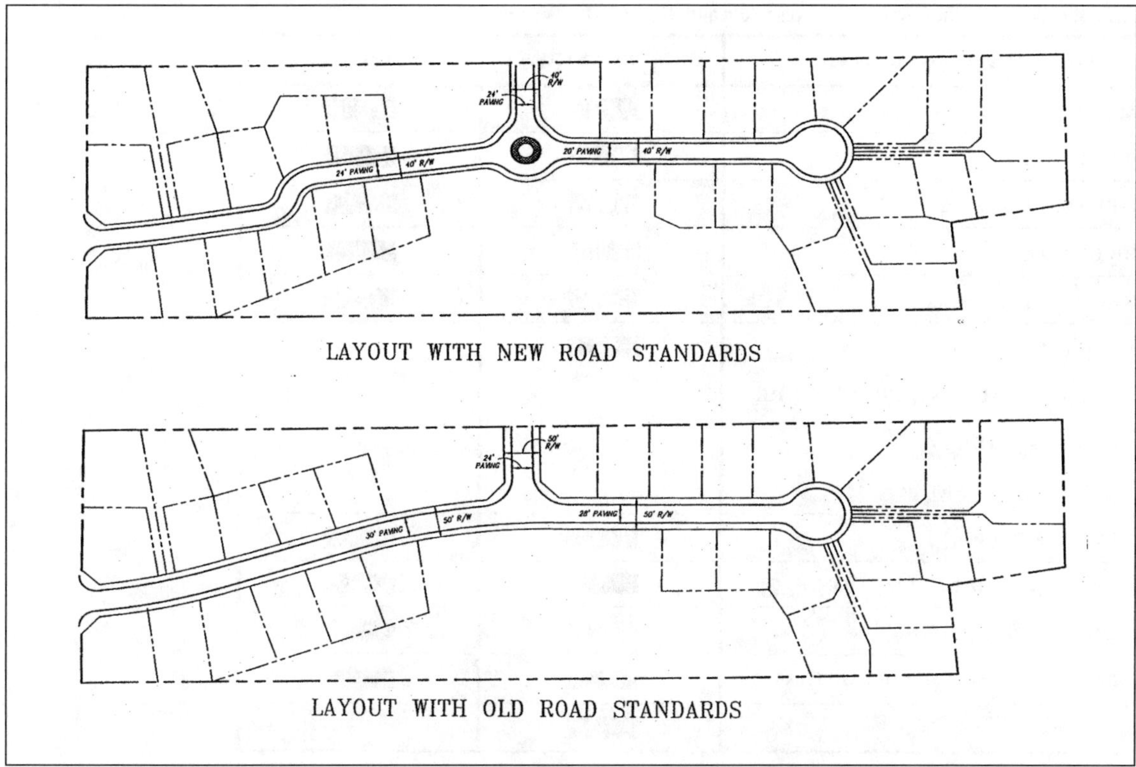



**Figure 10.5. Subdivision Street Design Under Old and New Standards. (Howard County, MD)**

Source: Howard County, MD, "Revised Subdivision Road Standards," undated, selected sections from chapter 2.

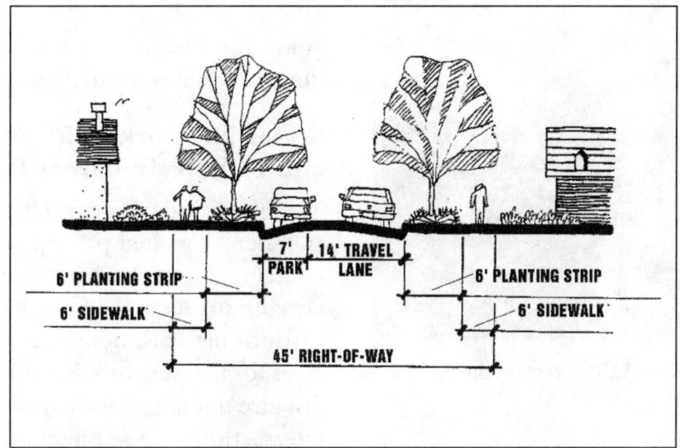



**Figure 10.6. Low-Volume Residential Street. (Eugene, OR)**

Source: City of Eugene, *Eugene Local Street Plan*, 1996, p. 71.

**Table 10.2. Application of Traffic Calming Measures to Old and New Streets. (Eugene, OR)**

| TRAFFIC CALMING DEVICE | EXISTING STREET | NEW STREET |
|---|:---:|:---:|
| TRAFFIC CIRCLES | ■ | ■ |
| SPEED HUMPS | ■ | ■ * |
| RAISED CROSSWALKS | ■ | ■ |
| CURB EXTENSIONS | ■ | ■ |
| CHICANES | ■ | ■ |
| TRAFFIC DIVERTERS | ■ | |
|     FULL DIVERTER - STREET CLOSURE | | |
|     HALF DIVERTER | | |
|     DIAGONAL DIVERTER | | |
| MEDIAN BARRIERS | ■ | ■ |
| FORCED TURN CHANNELIZATION | ■ | ■ |
| PARKING BAYS | ■ | ■ |
| PAVEMENT SURFACE MODIFICATION | ■ | ■ |
| SPEED ACTUATED SIGNING | ■ | |

*New speed humps are to be installed only at the direction of the City Traffic Engineer.*

Source: City of Eugene, *Eugene Local Street Plan*, 1996, p. 71.

**Figure 10.7. Raised Crosswalk Providing Safer Access to School. (Eugene, OR)**

Florida's state planning agency included a set of traffic calming guidelines in its comprehensive land development guide, *Best Development Practices.*[8] The examples in this section are taken from that guide.

## Street Networks with Multiple Connections and Relatively Direct Routes

The traditional urban grid has short blocks, straight streets, and a crosshatched pattern (see figure 10.8). The typical contemporary suburban street network has large blocks, curving streets, and a branching pattern (see figure 10.9).

Both network designs have advantages and disadvantages for the purposes of traffic calming. Traditional grids disperse traffic rather than concentrating it at a handful of intersections. They offer more direct routes and hence generate fewer vehicle-miles of travel than do contemporary networks.[9] They encourage walking and biking with their direct routing and their options to travel along high-volume streets.[10] The most pedestrian-oriented cities in the world are those with the densest, web-like street networks.[11]

On the other hand, contemporary networks have some obvious advantages over grids. By keeping through traffic

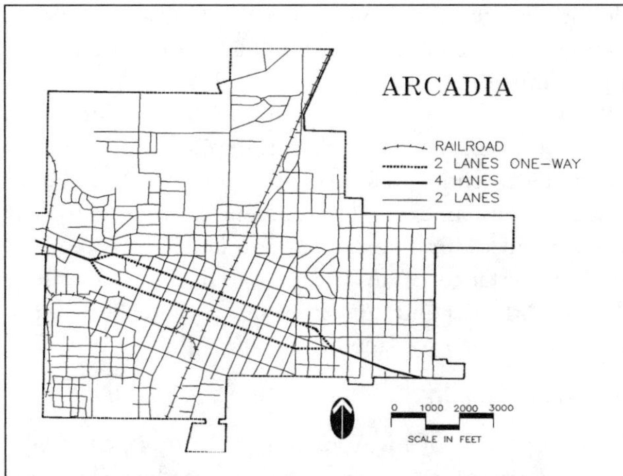

Figure 10.8. Traditional Urban Grid. (Arcadia, FL)

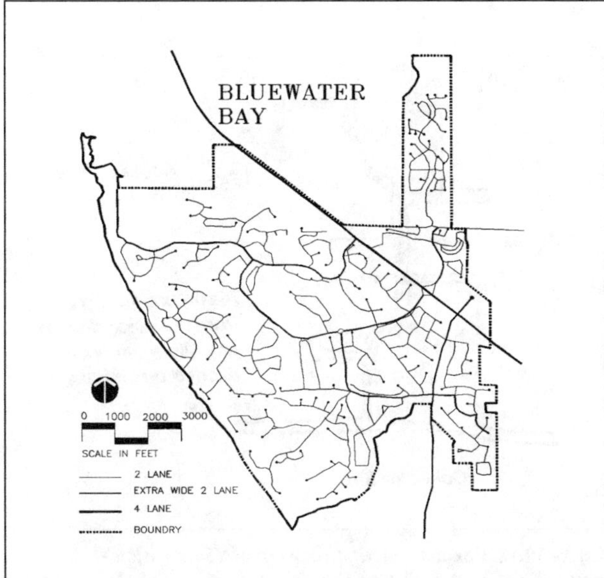

Figure 10.9. Contemporary Suburban Network. (Bluewater Bay, FL)

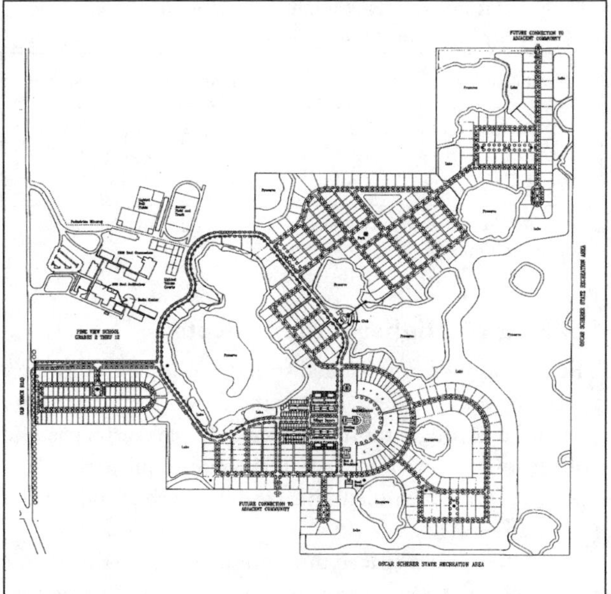

Figure 10.10. Hybrid Network. (Sarasota, FL)

out of neighborhoods, contemporary networks keep neighborhood street traffic volumes and accident rates down and, usually, property values up.[12] They may also discourage crime by making entry and escape relatively difficult for would-be offenders.[13] Cul-de-sacs, the ultimate in disconnected streets, have even lower volumes, encourage more casual interaction among neighbors, and often command a premium in real estate markets.[14]

Hybrid networks (see figure 10.10) have been developed in an attempt to garner the advantages of both traditional and contemporary residential street networks (i.e., combining the mobility of the traditional grid and the safety, security, and topographic sensitivity of the contem-

porary network). Short, curved stretches that follow the lay of the land or contribute to good urban design are used, as are short loops and cul-de-sacs, as long as they leave the higher order street network intact (i.e., arterials, collectors).

Short stretches ending in T-intersections have been shown to be particularly effective in reducing speeds and accidents.[15] Even cul-de-sacs are typically kept short, in part to discourage speeding. National authorities disagree on maximum cul-de-sac lengths, with recommendations ranging from 400 to 1,500 feet.[16] If traffic calming is a primary object, the lower end of the range is preferable.

There are various ways to measure the extent to which this practice is followed. From the literature on networks, a simple measure of connectivity is the number of street links divided by the number of nodes or link ends (including cul-de-sac heads).[17] The more links there are relative to nodes, the more connectivity within the network. It should be noted that this discussion does not consider bike/pedestrian paths and nodes as measures of connectivity.

This index of connectivity has been computed for several traditional towns and contemporary developments in Florida (see table 10.3). Note in the table the relatively lower level of connectivity found in contemporary street networks. Apalachicola and Arcadia (with near-gridirons) have the highest indices. Bluewater Bay and Haile Plantation (designed around cul-de-sacs) have the lowest indices.

**Table 10.3. Network Connectivity Indices for Traditional Towns and Contemporary Developments in Florida.**

| Traditional Towns | | Contemporary Developments | |
|---|---|---|---|
| Apalachicola | 1.69 | Bluewater Bay | 1.19 |
| Arcadia | 1.69 | Haile Plantation | 1.19 |
| Dade City | 1.49 | Hunter's Creek | 1.23 |

Source: R. Ewing, *Best Development Practices,* American Planning Association, Chicago, 1996, p. 57.

## Spacing of Higher Order Streets

The shift away from gridded streets in the contemporary street network is often accompanied by a loss of capacity to handle through traffic. Spaced far apart, arterials and collectors generate long access trips and require multilane cross sections to handle traffic from their catchment areas (see figure 10.11).

Calls for closely spaced through streets come from three sources. First, transit operators advocate closely spaced arterials and collectors.[18] If transit users are to have an easy walk to transit lines, the streets with service are preferably not spaced too far apart. Second, New Urbanists advocate dense networks of through streets. Their goal is to disperse traffic and avoid the need for multilane roads.[19] Third, a group of experts, primarily Australians, advocates that access trips to a higher order street be no more than a minute or two at restrained speeds (see figure 10.12).[20] If access trips are much longer, motorists may be tempted to speed through neighborhoods.

Considering all factors, half-mile spacing of higher order streets (i.e., collectors and above) has been used by communities as a reasonable target for suburban network

density. For curvilinear networks, the equivalent network density is 4.0 centerline miles (of higher order streets) per square mile of land area.

The street networks of traditional towns meet, or at least approach, this network density. Contemporary developments tend to fall short (see table 10.4). At build-out in a contemporary development, most residents will live beyond a 1-minute driving time and beyond practical walking distance of an arterial or collector (see figure 10.13). Arterials and collectors may eventually need to be four- or even six-laned to handle traffic.

## Narrow Streets

"The tendency of many communities to equate wider streets with better streets and to design traffic and parking lanes as if the street were a 'microfreeway' is a highly questionable practice." These words come from the American

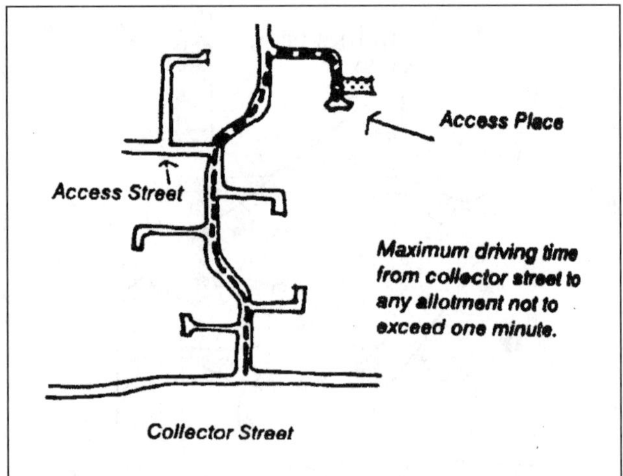


**Figure 10.12. Maximum Driving Time Out of a Subdivision— 1 Minute (Australian Model Code).**

Source: Model Code Task Force, *Australian Model Code for Residential Development,* Australian Government Publishing Service, Canberra, ACT, Australia, 1990, p. 48.

| Traditional Towns | | Contemporary Developments | |
|---|---|---|---|
| Apalachicola | 3.19 miles | Bluewater Bay | 2.20 miles |
| Arcadia | 4.15 miles | Haile Plantation | 2.64 miles |
| Dade City | 4.14 miles | Hunter's Creek | 2.25 miles |

**Table 10.4. Street Network Densities for Traditional Towns and Contemporary Developments in Florida. (miles of higher order streets per square mile of land area)**

Source: R. Ewing, *Best Development Practices,* American Planning Association, Chicago, 1996, p. 60.

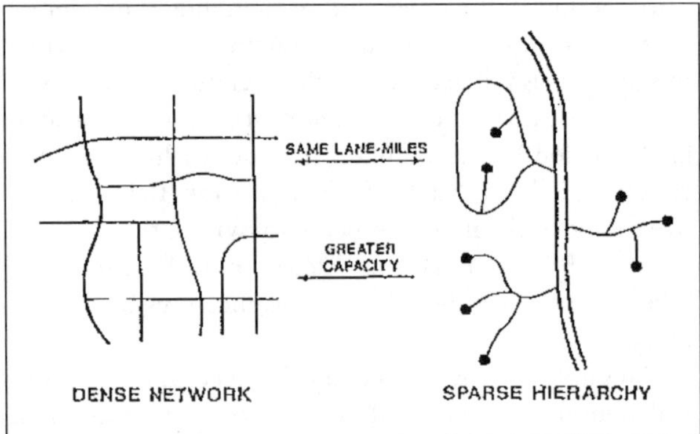


**Figure 10.11. Narrower Cross Sections and More Capacity with a Dense Street Network.**

Source: W. Kulash, "Neotraditional Town Design—Will the Traffic Work?" Workshop on Neotraditional Town Planning, American Institute of Certified Planners, Washington, DC, 1991.

Society of Civil Engineers, the National Association of Home Builders, and the Urban Land Institute.[21] There is growing sentiment that many local streets, and even some collector streets, are overdesigned, at substantial cost to society.

Relative to wide streets, narrow streets may calm traffic. Vehicle operating speeds decline somewhat as individual lanes and street sections are narrowed (but only to a point).[22] Drivers also seem to behave less aggressively on narrow streets, running fewer traffic signals, for example.[23] Further, one study reports higher pedestrian volumes on narrow streets than on wide streets.[24] More elderly users, more people out walking pets, and more pedestrians crossing back and forth all attest to a level of comfort with traffic on narrow streets that is missing on wide ones. However, all other things being equal, bicyclists may prefer a wide street to a narrow street that has speeds 10 mph slower.[25]

Why, then, do streets continue to be designed with such wide cross sections? Part of the reason is the lack of adequate route connectivity and density in contemporary networks. Beyond that, design typically strives to accommodate the worst case—the occasional service vehicle, emergency vehicle, or parked car on an access street.[26]

Many communities have reached the conclusion that it would be acceptable to design local streets for the everyday case (i.e., actual needs and intended use, rather than with blind adherence to agency design standards).[27] Communities that have opted for narrow streets report that they perform well.[28] Localities around the United States are amending their ordinances to permit narrower local streets than would have been imaginable a few years ago.[29]

## Subdivision Street Standards—The WILMAPCO Alternative

Lessons from *Best Development Practices* and a companion document, *Pedestrian- and Transit-Friendly Design,* have been combined into a single set of subdivision standards for the Wilmington Area Planning Council (WILMAPCO). They have been adopted by Middletown, DE, and Chesapeake City, MD, and are currently under review by the Delaware Department of Transportation (DelDOT) for possible statewide adoption.

The sample design standards for residential streets are set forth in table 10.5 for local streets and in table 10.6 for collectors. They illustrate how traffic calming principles can be incorporated into planning/design criteria. Three key policy decisions shape these standards and cause them to deviate in places from conventional standards:

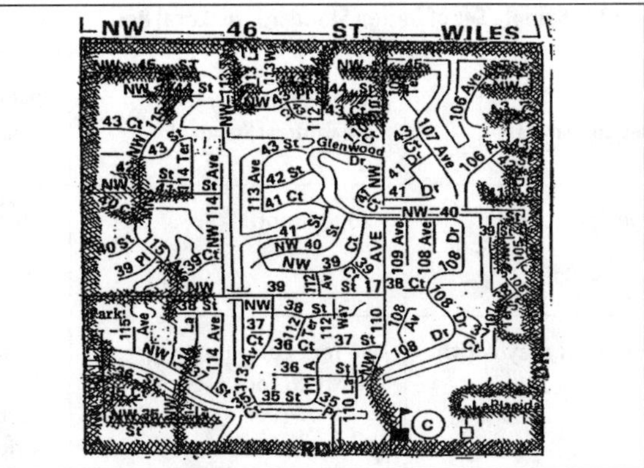

Figure 10.13. Poor Access With 1-Mile  Superblocks (shaded areas within 1/4 mile of through streets).

- The choice of design speeds: 20 mph for local streets and 25 mph for residential collectors
- The choice of design vehicle: a 266-inch wheelbase schoolbus, the largest vehicle to use subdivision streets routinely
- The priority given to pedestrians over motor vehicles

The far-right columns in tables 10.5 and 10.6 indicate *how* and *why* the proposed DelDOT standards deviate from AASHTO guidelines.[30] The streets to which they apply are subdivision streets at the bottom of the functional hierarchy, not streets that will typically be on either Federal or State highway systems. Unless a design exception is granted by FHWA, roads on the National Highway System (NHS) are subject to AASHTO guidelines, which have been adopted as national standards. Unless design exceptions are granted by State departments of transportation, non-NHS roads on State systems are usually subject to State standards not too different from AASHTO's. But off the Federal and State systems, local governments usually have a degree of design flexibility.

In one respect, the proposed standards may appear to encourage speeding. When the decision was made to recommend local streets as narrow as 18 feet and residential collectors as narrow as 22 feet, it had implications for curb return radii at corners. To accommodate the design vehicle, corners need to be rounded off more than otherwise ideal for traffic calming and pedestrianization. But after considering that most street crossings by pedestrians in subdivisions are probably at midblock anyway, the many advantages of narrow streets (e.g., human-scale streetscapes, cost savings to homeowners, reduced runoff) were deemed to outweigh the advantages of sharp corners. If a single-unit truck is adopted as the design vehicle instead of a large schoolbus, corner radii can be reduced by 10 to 15 feet.

**Table 10.5. Sample Set of Design Standards for Local Residential Streets.**

| Design Feature | AASHTO Local Urban Street Standard | DelDOT Proposed Local Street Standard | Rationale Given for DelDOT Proposed Standard |
| --- | --- | --- | --- |
| Design speed | 20–30 mph | 20 mph | Less than AASHTO guideline—20 mph is safe for pedestrians and is acceptable to most residents—30 mph is not |
| Right-of-way width | 50 feet common (with 26-foot section) | 41 feet (18-foot roadway + 6-inch curbs + 5-foot planting strips + 5-foot sidewalks + 1-foot offsets from backs of sidewalks) | Less than AASHTO guideline—41-foot right-of-way width is consistent with individual cross-sectional elements |
| Pavement width | 26 feet typical (less when right-of-way is severely limited) | 18 feet (9-foot travel lane + 7-foot parking lane on one side + 1-foot offsets to curb faces) | Less than AASHTO guideline—one clear travel lane is sufficient on streets carrying fewer than 500 vpd—on-street parking on only one side is sufficient in modern subdivisions with ample off-street parking—the recommendation provides for the narrowest possible pavement width in order to cut infrastructure cost, reduce runoff, and create human-scale streetscapes |
| Travel lane width | 9–12 feet (9 feet where right-of-way severely limited, 11 feet preferred) | 9 feet (plus 1-foot offset to curb —whether right-of-way is limited or not) | Equals AASHTO minimum—9-foot travel lane width is consistent with proposed design speed |
| Parking lane width | 7-foot minimum (may include gutter pan) | 7 feet (plus 1-foot offset) | Equals AASHTO minimum—7-foot parking lane width is sufficient when occupied by a parked car, and when unoccupied, leaves the minimum clear width to discourage speeding |
| Pavement edge treatment | Normally 4-inch to 9-inch vertical curb (1-foot offset required with curb of 6 inches or more) | 6-inch or 8-inch vertical curb | Greater than AASHTO guideline—higher curb discourages parking on planting strips and enhances pedestrian comfort and safety |
| Horizontal curve radius (measured at centerline of street) | 100-foot minimum (less with super-elevation—as large as possible preferred) | 90-foot minimum when curve is unsigned—45-foot minimum when curve is signed as a traffic calming measure | Less than AASHTO guideline—assuming a side-friction factor of 0.30 (AASHTO's own value) and no superelevation, a 90-foot curve radius corresponds to a turning speed of just over 20 mph—a 45-foot radius corresponds to a turning speed of 15 mph, 5 mph under the speed limit and appropriate as a traffic calming measure—a 45-foot radius is sufficient for the design vehicle to make a turn at a crawl speed without encroaching on the opposing lane |

**Table 10.5. Sample Set of Design Standards for Local Residential Streets (continued).**

| Design Feature | AASHTO Local Urban Street Standard | DelDOT Proposed Local Street Standard | Rationale Given for Proposed DelDOT Standard |
|---|---|---|---|
| Vertical curve length | 60-foot minimum at a design speed of 20 mph (or for larger grade changes, see AASHTO figures III-41 for crest curves and III-43 for sag curves) | Same as AASHTO when curve is unsigned—when a short vertical curve is signed and marked as a traffic calming measure, AASHTO minimum is waived | Proposed standard simply exempts traffic calming measures from minimum vertical curve requirements |
| Sidewalks | On both sides of streets used for access to schools, parks, etc.—on at least one side of all other local streets | On both sides of streets at densities of 2-plus units per acre—on one side of streets at densities of 1–2 units per acre | Sidewalks represent a small cost increment that is justified at all but the lowest residential densities—proposed standards are similar to those promoted by the Federal Highway Administration and Institute of Transportation Engineers |
| Sidewalk width | 4-foot minimum | 5 feet with planting strip 8 feet without planting strip | Greater than AASHTO guideline—5-foot sidewalk width is comfortable for pedestrians walking in pairs and occasionally passing other pedestrians—the extra 3 feet provides a small buffer from traffic when no planting strip is provided |
| Planting strip width | 2-foot minimum (12 feet desirable) | 5-foot minimum | Greater than AASHTO guideline—5-foot planting strip is a normal minimum for street trees and provides an adequate buffer for pedestrians on low-speed streets |
| Tree/Obstacle clearance | 1.5-foot minimum with vertical curb | 2.5 feet with vertical curb (from curb to centerline of tree) | 2.5 feet places street trees along centerline of planting strip—provides for about 1.5-foot clearance when trees mature |
| Corner radius | 15-foot minimum (25 feet desirable) | 25 feet (local-local) 30 feet (local-collector with parking lane) 40 feet (local-collector without parking lane) | Equal or greater than AASHTO guideline—recommended curb radii are sufficient for a large schoolbus to make turns if allowed to encroach on opposing lanes of minor streets—the low traffic volumes on minor streets (less than 50 vehicles per hour during peak period) make encroachment a low-risk event |
| Alleys | Alleys allowed (right-of-way widths of 16–20 feet) | Alleys recommended with lots less than 50 feet wide—alleys should have 12-foot paved width, 20-foot right-of-way | Alleys are encouraged to create streetscapes unbroken by driveways—recommended alley width provides for landscaping on either side so alleyway "reads" like a narrow street |

**Table 10.5. Sample Set of Design Standards for Local Residential Streets (continued).**

| Design Feature | AASHTO Local Urban Street Standard | DelDOT Proposed Local Street Standard | Rationale Given for DelDOT Proposed Standard |
|---|---|---|---|
| Traffic calming measures | None specified | Full array of horizontal and vertical measures allowed, consistent with 20-mph design speed | Traffic calming may be required in order to maintain 20-mph operating speeds |
| Spacing of slow points | None specified | 200 to 300 feet between traffic calming measures, T-intersections, or other | Slow points must be closely spaced to maintain 20-mph operating slow points |
| All-way STOPS | References *MUTCD* | Generally inappropriate as a method of speed control at low-volume intersections | Equal to *MUTCD* warrants |

AASHTO = American Association of State Highway and Transportation Officials; DelDOT = Delaware Department of Transportation
*MUTCD = Manual on Uniform Traffic Devices for Streets and Highways*

Source: R. Ewing (in cooperation with RK & K Consulting Engineers, Baltimore, MD, and LDR International, Inc., Columbia, MD), 1998.

**Table 10.6. Sample Set of Design Standards for Residential Collector Streets.**

| Design Feature | AASHTO Urban Collector Street Standard | DelDOT Proposed Collector Street Standard | Rationale Given for DelDOT Proposed Standard |
|---|---|---|---|
| Design speed | 30 mph or higher | 25 mph | Less than AASHTO guideline— 25 mph is safer for pedestrians and more acceptable to residents than is 30 mph |
| Right-of-way width | 40 to 60 feet | 53 or 61 or 69 feet (20-foot roadway + 6-inch curbs + 10-foot planting strips +5-foot sidewalks + 1-foot offsets from backs of sidewalks— parking may be on neither side, one side, or both sides) | Greater than AASHTO guideline—extra right-of-way width provides for planting strips wide enough to buffer pedestrians and residents from higher speeds and volumes of traffic on collectors |
| Pavement width | 28-foot minimum with one parking lane (if practical, build four lanes and use the extra two for parking until needed) | 22 or 29 or 36 feet (10-foot travel lanes in both directions, 7-foot parking lanes, and 1-foot offsets to curb faces) | Varies depending on the number of parking lanes provided—the recommended standard provides for the narrowest possible roadway width in order to cut infrastruc-ture cost, reduce runoff, and create human-scale streetscapes—two different cross-sections are envisioned, appropriate to different residential densities with different demands for on-street parking |
| Travel lane width | 10 to 12 feet (10 feet where right-of-way imposes severe limitations) | 10 feet (plus 1-foot offset to curb) | Equal to AASHTO minimum—10-foot travel lane width is consistent with proposed design speed |
| Parking lane width | 7 to 10 feet (may include gutter pan) | 7 feet (plus 1-foot offset) | Equal to AASHTO minimum—7-foot parking lane width is sufficient when occupied by a parked car, and when unoccupied, leaves the minimum clear width to discourage speeding |
| Pavement edge treatment | 6-inch vertical curb with1- to 2-foot offset (except on low-volume streets, where lower curb is sufficient) | 8-inch vertical curb | Greater than AASHTO guideline— higher curb discourages parking on planting strips and enhances pedestrian comfort and safety |
| Medians or center islands | On multilane roads whenever practical | On all multilane roads | A median or center island provides refuge for pedestrians, reducing crossing delay and enhancing pedestrian safety—medians or islands are particularly important in suburban areas where long blocks encourage midblock crossings |

**Table 10.6. Sample Set of Design Standards for Residential Collector Streets (continued).**

| Design Feature | AASHTO Urban Collector Street Standard | DelDOT Proposed Collector Street Standard | Rationale Given for Proposed Standard |
|---|---|---|---|
| Median/Island width | 2 to 6 feet when raised | 4-foot minimum— 6 feet preferable Always raised | Greater than AASHTO minimum— recommended median/island width can be landscaped and is consistent with *MUTCD* |
| Horizontal curve radius (measured at centerline of street) | Not specified | 170-foot minimum when curve is unsigned— 90-foot minimum when curve is signed as a traffic calming measure | No AASHTO guideline—assuming a side-friction factor of 0.25 (AASHTO's own value) and no superelevation, a 170-foot curve radius corresponds to a turning speed of slightly more than 25 mph— a 90-foot radius corresponds to a turning speed of 20 mph, 5 mph under the speed limit and appropriate as a traffic calming measure |
| Vertical curve length | 75-foot minimum at a design speed of 25 mph (or for larger grade changes, see AASHTO figures III-41 for crest curves and III-43 for sag curves) | Same as AASHTO when curve is unsigned— when a short vertical curve is signed and marked as a traffic calming measure, AASHTO minimum is waived | Proposed standard simply exempts traffic calming measures from minimum vertical curve requirements |
| Sidewalks | Both sides of roads used for access to schools, parks, etc.— elsewhere on at least one side | Both sides | Sidewalks represent a small cost increment that is justified on all residential collectors—proposed standards are consistent with those promoted by the Federal Highway Administration and Institute of Transportation Engineers |
| Sidewalk width | 4-foot minimum | 5 feet with planting strip 8 feet without planting strip | Greater than AASHTO guideline—5-foot sidewalk width is comfortable for pedestrians walking in pairs and occasionally passing other pedestrians—the extra 3 feet provides a small buffer from traffic when no planting strip is provided |
| Planting strip width | 3 to 6 feet (deduced from border width requirements) | 10-foot minimum | Greater than AASHTO guideline— 10-foot planting strip provides an adequate buffer for pedestrians and residents along collector streets with higher traffic speeds and volumes—residential collectors should have residences fronting on them, not backing up to them in reverse lotting arrangements—a 10-foot-plus planting strip increases the setback of houses from the street, thus mitigating traffic impacts |

**Table 10.6. Sample Set of Design Standards for Residential Collector Streets (continued).**

| Design Features | AASHTO Urban Collector Street Standard | DelDOT Proposed Collector Street Standard | Rationale Given for DelDOT Proposed Standard |
|---|---|---|---|
| Tree/Obstacle clearance | 1.5-foot minimum with vertical curb (2 feet desirable with parking lane to avoid interference with car doors) | 5 feet with vertical curb (from curb to centerline of tree) | Greater than AASHTO minimum—5 feet places street trees along centerline of planting strip—provides for about 3–4 feet of clearance when trees mature |
| Street tree location | Preferably outside sidewalk | Preferably between street and sidewalk | Street trees between street and sidewalk enclose street space, possibly calming traffic—they also provide pedestrians with a buffer from traffic and protection from the weather |
| Corner radius | 10–15 feet with curbside parking 30 feet without curbside parking | 30 feet (local-collector with parking lane) 25 feet (collector-collector with parking lanes) 40 feet (local-collector without parking lane) 50 feet (collector-collector without parking lanes) | Equal to or greater than AASHTO guideline—recommended curb radii are sufficient for a large school bus to make a turn without encroaching on opposing lanes of collector streets—encroachment would occur on local streets |
| Traffic calming measures | None specified | Full array of horizontal and vertical measures allowed, consistent with 25-mph design speed, except where emergency response considerations impose limitations | Traffic calming measures may be required in order to maintain 25-mph operating speeds |
| Spacing of slow points | None specified | 300 to 400 feet between traffic calming measures, STOP signs, or other slow points | Slow points must be closely spaced to maintain 25-mph operating speed |
| All-way STOPS | References *MUTCD* | Unwarranted STOP signs permitted when engineering study shows unusually high cut-through traffic volume or accident rate | *MUTCD* warrants are too stringent for residential collectors—all-way STOPS can reduce cut-through traffic and accidents |

AASHTO = American Association of State Highway and Transportation Officials; DelDOT = Delaware Department of Transportation; *MUTCD = Manual on Uniform Traffic Control Devices for Streets and Highways*

Source: R. Ewing (in cooperation with RK & K Consulting Engineers, Baltimore, MD, and LDR International, Inc., Columbia, MD), 1998.

# Endnotes


1. New Urbanism is a development strategy that seeks to integrate life components—home life, work, school, shops, businesses, recreation facilities—in compact, walkable, mixed-use neighborhoods linked by transit. The approach arose in North America in the 1980's as an alternative to the low-density, suburban sprawl typical of development during the 1960's and 1970's. Initially called "neo-traditional planning" because it was based on development patterns used prior to World War II, New Urbanist designs promote lower use of automobiles, land, and natural resources. Information is available from Congress for the New Urbanism, 5 Third Street, Suite 500A, San Francisco, CA 94103 (http://www.cnu.org).

2. R. Ewing, *Best Development Practices—Doing the Right Thing and Making Money at the Same Time,* American Planning Association (in cooperation with the Urban Land Institute), 1996, pp. 53–93.

3. City of Phoenix, Subdivision Ordinance, Section 32–26 (f).

4. City of Phoenix, Subdivision Policy, Paragraph 2.2.

5. Calthorpe Associates, *Transit-Oriented Development Design Guidelines,* City of San Diego, CA, 1992. The many other transit-oriented development manuals fall into two categories. Some are *land planning/urban design manuals* with a transit orientation. Others are *transit facility design manuals* with implications for urban design. The former emphasize the needs of transit users accessing the system, the latter, the needs of the transit operator running the system. R. Cervero, "Design Guidelines as a Tool to Promote Transit-Supportive Development," *Transit-Supportive Development in the United States: Experiences and Prospects, Technology Sharing Program,* U.S. Department of Transportation, Washington, DC, 1993, pp. 27–40; and D. Everett, T. Herrero, and R. Ewing, *Transit-Oriented Development Guidelines: Review of Literature,* background paper prepared for the Florida Department of Transportation, Tallahassee, FL, 1995.

6. Howard County Revised Subdivision Road Standards, Section 2.14.

7. City of Eugene, *Eugene Local Street Plan,* 1996, p. 59.

8. Ewing, 1996, op. cit.

9. F.A. Curtis, L. Neilsen, and A. Bjornsor, "Impact of Residential Street Design on Fuel Consumption," *Journal of Urban Planning and Development,* Vol. 110, 1984, pp. 1–8; M.G. McNally, "Regional Impacts of Neotraditional Neighborhood Development," in *1993 Compendium of Technical Papers,* Institute of Transportation Engineers, Washington, DC, 1993, pp. 463–467; and M.G. McNally and S. Ryan, "Comparative Assessment of Travel Characteristics for Neotraditional Designs," *Transportation Research Record 1400,* 1993, pp. 67–77.

10. Grids also offer less tangible benefits: what urban designers refer to as "contextual continuity" and "legibility," which are thought to be important to pedestrians.

11. Short blocks make trips feel shorter to pedestrians because progress is judged against the milestones of intersections. San Francisco has 300 intersections per square mile; Santa Monica, 180; and Irvine, 15. The walkability of these places, by all accounts, is in the same rank order. See A.B. Jacobs, "City Streets and Their Contexts," in *A Decade Reviewed—Commitment Renewed,* 10th Annual Pedestrian Conference, Boulder, CO, 1989, pp. 41–61.

12. H. Marks, "Subdividing for Traffic Safety," *Traffic Quarterly,* Vol. 11, 1957, pp. 308–325; M.A. Wallen, "Landscaped Structures for Traffic Control," *Traffic Engineering,* Vol. 31, January 1961, pp. 18–22; P.C. Box, "Accident Characteristics of Non-Arterial Streets," *Traffic Digest and Review,* March 1964, pp. 12, 17–19; G.T. Bennett and J. Marland, *Road Accidents in Traditionally Designed Residential Estates,* Supplementary Report 394, Transportation Road Research Laboratory, Crowthorne, England, 1978; D.G. Bagby, "The Effects of Traffic Flow on Residential Property Values," *Journal of the American Planning Association,* Vol. 46, 1980, pp. 88–94; and U. Henning-Hager, "Urban Development and Road Safety," *Accident Analysis & Prevention,* Vol. 18, 1986, pp. 135–145. For general perspectives, see R. Brindle, "Residential Area Planning for Pedestrian Safety," Joint ARRB/DOT Pedestrian Conference, Australian Road Research Board, VIC, Australia, 1978; J.H. Kraay, M.P.M. Mathijssen, and F.C.M. Wegman, *Toward Safer Residential Areas,* Institute of Road Safety Research SWOV/Ministry of Transport, Leidschendam, Switzerland, 1985; and S.O. Gunnarsson, "Urban Traffic Network Design—A Spatial Approach," in *Effecting Change Step-by-Step, Proceedings of the 9th Annual Pedestrian Conference,* Boulder, CO, 1988, pp. 199–218.

13. C. Bevis and J.B. Nutter, *Changing Street Layouts to Reduce Residential Burglary,* Governor's Commission on Crime Prevention and Control, St. Paul, MN, 1977; F.J. Fowler, *Reducing Residential Crime and Fear: The Hartford Neighborhood Crime Prevention Program—Executive Summary,* U.S. Department of Justice, Washington, DC, 1979, pp. 10–11, 26–41; O. Newman, *Community of Interest,* Anchor Press, Garden City, NY, 1980, pp. 137–143; S.W. Greenberg, W.M. Rohe, and J.R. Williams, "Safety in Urban Neighborhoods: A Comparison of Physical Characteristics and Informal Territorial Control in High and Low Crime Neighborhoods," *Population and Environment,* Vol. 5, 1982, pp. 141–165; B. Poyner, *Design Against Crime—Beyond Defensible Space,* Butterworths, New York, NY, 1983, pp. 15–27; S.W. Greenberg and W.M. Rohe, "Neighborhood Design and Crime—A Test of Two Perspectives," *Journal of the American Planning Association,* Vol. 50, 1984, pp. 48–61; R.B. Taylor, S.A. Schumaker, and S.D. Gottfredson, "Neighborhood—Level Link Between Physical Features and Local Sentiments: Deterioration, Fear of Crime, and Confidence," *Journal of Architectural and Planning Research,* Vol. 2,

1985, pp. 261–275; P. Stollard, *Crime Prevention Through Housing Design,* E&F N Spon, London, England, 1991, pp. 68–70; R. Tell, "Fighting Crime: An Architectural Approach," *Journal of Housing,* Vol. 47, 1990, pp. 207–212; T.D. Crowe, *Crime Prevention Through Environmental Design—Applications of Architectural Design and Space Management Concepts,* Butterworth-Heinemann, Boston, MA, 1991, p. 161; and O. Newman, "Defensible Space—A New Physical Planning Tool for Urban Revitalization," *Journal of the American Planning Association,* Vol. 61, 1995, pp. 149–155.

14. J.B. Lansing, R.W. Marans, and R.B. Zehner, *Planned Residential Environments,* Survey Research Center, University of Michigan, Ann Arbor, MI, 1970, pp. 114–115; C. Zerner, "The Street Hearth of Play," *Landscape,* Vol. 22, 1977, pp. 19–30; G.T. Bennett and J. Marland, *Road Accidents in Traditionally Designed Residential Estates,* Supplementary Report 394, Transportation Road Research Laboratory, Crowthorne, England, 1978; D. Appleyard, *Livable Streets,* University of California Press, Berkeley, 1981, p. 133; and U. Henning-Hager, "Urban Development and Road Safety," *Accident Analysis & Prevention,* Vol. 18, 1986, pp. 135–145.

15. P.R. Staffeld, "Accidents Related to Access Points and Advertising Signs in Study," *Traffic Quarterly,* Vol. 7, 1953, pp. 59–74; H. Marks, "Subdividing for Traffic Safety," *Traffic Quarterly,* Vol. 11, 1957, pp. 308–325; M.A. Wallen, "Landscaped Structures for Traffic Control," *Traffic Engineering,* Vol. 31, January 1961, pp. 18–22; P.C. Box, "Accident Characteristics of Non-Arterial Streets," *Traffic Digest and Review,* March 1964, pp. 12, 17–19; G.T. Bennett and J. Marland, *Road Accidents in Traditionally Designed Residential Estates,* Supplementary Report 394, Transportation Road Research Laboratory, Crowthorne, England, 1978; N.A. David and J.R. Norman, *Motor Vehicle Accidents in Relation to Geometric and Traffic Features of Highway Intersections, Volume II,* Federal Highway Administration, Washington, DC, 1975, pp. 51–54; and G.F. Hagenauer et al., "Intersections," in *Synthesis of Safety Research Related to Traffic Control and Roadway Elements, Volume 1,* Federal Highway Administration, Washington, DC, 1982, pp. 5-1 through 5-21.

16. For a review of recommendations from the national literature and of various rationales for limiting the lengths of cul-de-sacs, see Bucks County Planning Commission, *Performance Streets—A Concept and Model Standards for Residential Streets,* Doylestown, PA, 1980, pp. 12–13. Also see Residential Streets Task Force, *Residential Streets,* American Society of Civil Engineers/National Association of Home Builders/Urban Land Institute, Washington, DC, 1990, pp. 54–55; and ITE Technical Council Committee 5A–25A, *Guidelines for Residential Subdivision Street Design—A Recommended Practice,* Institute of Transportation Engineers, Washington, DC, 1993, p. 9.

17. There is no shortage of network performance measures in the literature. See P. Haggett and R.J. Chorley, *Network Analysis in Geography,* St. Martin Press, New York, NY, 1969, pp. 1–35, 57–105, 118–130; E.J. Taaffe and H.L. Gauthier, *Geography of Transportation,* Prentice-Hall, Englewood Cliffs, NJ, 1973, pp. 100–115; H.R. Kirby, "Accessibility Indices for Abstract Road Networks," *Regional Studies,* Vol. 10, 1976, pp. 479–482; W.R. Blunden and J.A. Black, *The Land-Use/Transport System,* Pergamon Press, New York, NY, 1984, pp. 141–144; K.G. Zografos and R.G. Crowley, "Low-Volume Roadway Network Improvements and the Accessibility of Public Facilities in Rural Areas," *Transportation Research Record 1106,* 1987, pp. 26–33; and C.J. Khisty, M.Y. Rahi, and C.S. Hsu, "Morphological Modeling of the City and Its Transportation System: A Preliminary Investigation," *Transportation Research Record 1237,* 1989, pp. 18–28.

18. Municipality of Metropolitan Seattle, *Encouraging Public Transportation through Effective Land Use Actions,* Seattle, WA, 1987, p. 44; Ontario Ministry of Transportation, *Transit-Supportive Land Use Planning Guidelines,* Toronto, ON, Canada, 1992, pp. 45–46; Alameda-Contra Costa Transit District, *Guide for Including Public Transit in Land Use Planning,* Oakland, CA, 1983, p. 20; Snohomish County Transportation Authority, *A Guide to Land Use and Public Transportation,* Technology Sharing Program, U.S. Department of Transportation, Washington, DC, 1989, pp. 7-6 and 7-7; W. Bowes, M. Gravel, and G. Noxon, *Guide to Transit Considerations in the Subdivision Design and Approval Process,* Transportation Association of Canada, Ottawa, ON, Canada, 1991, p. A-8; and Denver Regional Council of Governments, *Suburban Mobility Design Manual,* Denver, CO, 1993, p. 26.

19. W. Kulash, "Neotraditional Town Design—Will the Traffic Work?" Session Notes—AICP Workshop on Neotraditional Town Planning, American Institute of Certified Planners, Washington, DC, 1991; J.R. Stone and C.A. Johnson, "Neo-Traditional Neighborhoods: A Solution to Traffic Congestion?" in R.E. Paaswell et al. (eds.), *Proceedings of the Site Impact and Assessment Conference,* American Society of Civil Engineers, New York, NY, 1992, pp. 72–76; and M.J. Wells, "Neo-Traditional Neighborhood Developments: You Can Go Home Again," unpublished paper available from the author, Wells & Associates, Inc., Arlington, VA, 1993.

20. C. Stapleton, *Planning and Road Design for New Residential Sub-Divisions—Guidelines,* Director General of Transport for South Australia, Adelaide, SA, Australia, 1988, p. 29; Model Code Task Force, *Australian Model Code for Residential Development,* Department of Health, Housing and Community Services, Commonwealth of Australia, Canberra, ACT, Australia, 1990, pp. 48–51; Main Roads Department, *Guidelines for Local Area Traffic Management,* East Perth, WA, Australia, 1990, p. 92; and Department of Planning and Housing, *Victorian Code for Residential Development—Subdivision and Single Dwellings,* State Government of Victoria, Melbourne, VIC, Australia, 1992, pp. 37–41. Also see Residential Streets Task Force, *Residential Streets,* American Society of Civil Engineers/National Association of Home Builders/Urban Land Institute, Washington, DC, 1990, p. 27.

21. Residential Streets Task Force, op. cit., p. 37.

22. How much effect lane and street width have on running speeds is debatable, but the weight of evidence indicates that they have some effect. O.T. Farouki and W.J. Nixon, "The Effect of Width of Suburban Roads on the Mean Free Speed of Cars," *Traffic Engineering + Control,* Vol. 17, 1976, pp. 518–519; C.L. Heimbach, P.D. Cribbins, and M.S. Chang, "Some Partial Consequences of Reduced Traffic Lane Widths on Urban Arterials," *Transportation Research Record 923,* 1983, pp. 69–72; H.S. Lum, "The Use of Road Markings to Narrow Lanes for Controlling Speed in Residential Areas," *ITE Journal,* Vol. 54, June 1984, pp. 50–53; J.E. Clark, "High Speeds and Volumes on Residential Streets: An Analysis of Physical Street Characteristics as Causes in Sacramento, California," in *1985 Compendium of Technical Papers,* Institute of Transportation Engineers, Washington, DC, 1985, pp. 93–96; D.W. Harwood, *Effective Utilization of Street Width on Urban Arterials—Appendix A,* National Cooperative Highway Research Program Report 330, Transportation Research Board, Washington, DC, 1990, pp. 127–137; and S.A. Ardekani, J.C. Williams, and C.S. Bhat, "The Influence of Urban Network Features on the Quality of Traffic Service," *Transportation Research Record 1358,* 1992, pp. 6–12.

23. R.K. Untermann, "Street Design—Reassessing the Function, Safety and Comfort of Streets for Pedestrians," in *The Road Less Traveled: Getting There by Other Means,* 11th International Pedestrian Conference, Boulder, CO, 1990, pp. 19–26.

24. See R. Ewing, "Roadway Levels of Service in an Era of Growth Management," *Transportation Research Record 1364,* 1992, pp. 63–70; and R. Ewing, "Residential Street Design: Do the British and Australians Know Something We Americans Don't?" *Transportation Research Record 1455,* 1994, pp. 42–49.

25. Ibid.

26. D.L. Harkey, D.W. Reinfurt, M. Knuinan, J.R. Stewart, and A. Sorton, *Development of the Bicycle Compatibility Index: A Level of Service Concept,* Final Report, Publication No. FHWA-RD-98-072, Federal Highway Administration, Washington, DC, December, 1998.

27. For concurring opinions from three countries, see Residential Streets Task Force, op. cit., p. 49; J. Noble and A. Smith, *Residential Roads and Footpaths—Layout Considerations—Design Bulletin 32,* Her Majesty's Stationery Office, London, England, 1992, p. 63; and AUSTROADS, *Guide to Traffic Engineering Practice—Local Area Traffic Management,* Sydney, NSW, Australia, 1988, p. 19.

28. D. Bassert, "Street Standards Survey Finds Narrower Streets Perform Well," *Land Development,* Vol. 1, December 1988, pp. 6–7.

29. L. Paretchan, "Skinny Streets for Residential Neighborhoods," *Alternative Transportation: Planning, Design, Issues, Solutions,* 14th International Pedestrian Conference, Boulder, CO, 1993, pp. 41–44; J.M. Fernandez, "Boulder Brings Back the Neighborhood Street," *Planning,* Vol. 60, June 1994, pp. 21–26; and J. West and A. Lowe, "Integration of Transportation and Land Use Planning through Residential Street Design," *ITE Journal,* Vol. 67, August 1997, pp. 48–51.

30. American Association of State Highway and Transportation Officials, *A Policy on Geometric Design of Highways and Streets,* Washington, DC, 1990 [1994 (metric)].

# Selected References


Abbott, P., M. Taylor, and R. Layfield, "The Effects of Traffic Calming Measures on Vehicle and Traffic Noise," *Traffic Engineering + Control,* Vol. 38, 1997, pp. 447–453.

Appleyard, D., *Livable Streets,* University of California Press, Berkeley, CA, 1981.

Aspelin, K., "Recruiting Private Help for a Public Demonstration Project: Taking the 'Hump' Out of Traffic Calming," in *Harmonizing Transportation & Community Goals* (ITE International Conference, Monterey, CA, 1998), Institute of Transportation Engineers, Washington, DC, 1998, CD-ROM.

Atkins, C., and M. Coleman, "The Influence of Traffic Calming on Emergency Response Times," *ITE Journal,* Vol. 67, August 1997, pp. 42–46.

AUSTROADS, *Guide to Traffic Engineering Practice— Part 10—Local Area Traffic Management,* Sydney, NSW, Australia, 1988.

Ballard, A.J., "Efforts to Control Speeds on Residential Collector Streets," in *1990 Compendium of Technical Papers, 69th Annual Meeting,* Institute of Transportation Engineers, Washington, DC, 1990, pp. 92–95.

Bared, J., "Roundabouts—Improving Road Safety and Increasing Capacity," *TR News,* No. 191, July–August 1997, pp. 13–15, 27.

Beaubien, R.F., "Controlling Speeds on Residential Streets," *ITE Journal,* Vol. 59, April 1989, pp. 37–39.

Beaubien, R.F., "Does Traffic Calming Make Streets Safer?" in *Harmonizing Transportation & Community Goals* (ITE International Conference, Monterey, CA, 1998), Institute of Transportation Engineers, Washington, DC, 1998, CD-ROM.

Ben-Joseph, E., "Changing the Residential Street Scene: Adapting the Shared Street (Woonerf) Concept to the Suburban Environment," *Journal of the American Planning Association,* Vol. 61, 1995, pp. 504–515.

Ben-Joseph, E., "Traffic Calming and the Neotraditional Street," in *Transportation and Sustainable Communities* (Resource Papers for the 1997 ITE International Conference, Tampa, FL), Institute of Transportation Engineers, Washington, DC, 1997, pp. 47–52.

Bosselmann, P., "Redesigning American Residential Streets," *Built Environment,* Vol. 12, 1986, pp. 98–106.

Bowers, P.H., "Environmental Traffic Restraint: German Approaches to Traffic Management by Design," *Built Environment,* Vol. 12, 1986, pp. 60–73.

Braaksma, J.P., "A Community Based Process for Traffic Calming," paper presented at the 76th Annual Meeting, Transportation Research Board, Washington, DC, 1997.

Brennan, D.T., "The Evaluation of Residential Traffic Calming: A New Multi-Criteria Approach," *Traffic Engineering + Control,* Vol. 35, January 1994, pp. 19–24.

Bretherton, W.M., "Neighborhood Traffic Management Program," in *1992 Compendium of Technical Papers,* Institute of Transportation Engineers, Washington, DC, 1992, pp. 398–401.

Brilon, W., and H. Blanke, "Extensive Traffic Calming: Results of the Accident Analyses in Six Model Towns," in *1993 Compendium of Technical Papers,* Institute of Transportation Engineers, Washington, DC, 1993, pp. 119–123.

Brindle, R., "Local Street Speed Management in Australia: Is It 'Traffic Calming'?" *Accident Analysis & Prevention,* Vol. 24, 1992, pp. 29–38.

Brindle, R., *Living with Traffic,* ARRB Special Report 53, ARRB, Transport Research Ltd., VIC, Australia, 1996.

Brindle, R., "Traffic Calming in Australia—More Than Neighborhood Traffic Management," *ITE Journal,* Vol. 67, July 1997, pp. 26–31.

Brown, S.J., and S. Fitzsimons, "Calming the Community: Traffic Calming in Downtown Sacramento," paper presented at the ITE International Conference in Monterey, CA, Institute of Transportation Engineers, Washington, DC, 1998.

Buchanan, C., *Traffic in Towns: A Study of the Long Term Problems of Traffic in Urban Areas,* Her Majesty's Stationery Office, London, England, 1963.

Burchfield, R.M., "Traffic Calming Collector Streets: Portland's Experience," in *1995 Compendium of Technical Papers,* Institute of Transportation Engineers, Washington, DC, 1995, pp. 67–69.

Castellone, A.J., and M.M. Hasan, "Neighborhood Traffic Management: Dade County Florida's Street Closure Experience," paper presented at the ITE International Conference in Monterey, CA, Institute of Transportation Engineers, Washington, DC, 1998.

Chadda, H.S., and S.E. Cross, "Speed (Road) Bumps: Issues and Opinions," *Journal of Transportation Engineering,* Vol. 111, 1985, pp. 410–418.

Challis, S.D., "North Earlham Estate, Worwich: The First UK 20 mph Zone," in *Traffic Management and Road Safety,* PTRC Education and Research Services Ltd., London, England, 1992, pp. 61–72.

Chartier, G., and Diane G. Erickson, "Canada's Guide to Neighbourhood Traffic Calming—ITE/TAC Project 208," in *Compendium of Technical Papers for the 67th ITE Annual Meeting* (Boston, MA, 1997), Institute of Transportation Engineers, Washington, DC, 1997, CD-ROM.

Citizens Against Route Twenty (CART), *The Solution to Route 20 and a New Vision for Brisbane,* available from Sensible Transportation Options for People, Tigard, OR, 1989.

Citizens Against Route Twenty (CART), *Traffic Calming,* available from Sensible Transportation Options for People, Tigard, OR, 1989.

Clarke, A., and M.J. Dornfeld, *National Bicycling and Walking Study: Case Study No. 19, Traffic Calming, Auto-Restricted Zones and Other Traffic Management Techniques: Their Effects on Bicycling and Pedestrians,* Federal Highway Administration, Washington, DC, 1994.

Clement, J.P., "Speed Humps and the Thousand Oaks Experience," *ITE Journal,* Vol. 53, January 1983, pp. 35–39.

Committee MS/12, *Manual of Uniform Traffic Control Devices—Part 13: Local Area Traffic Management,* Standards Association of Australia, Sydney, NSW, Australia, 1991.

County Surveyors Society, *Traffic Calming in Practice,* Landor Publishing, London, England, 1994.

Craus, J., et al., "Geometric Aspects of Traffic Calming in Shared Streets," in *1993 Compendium of Technical Papers,* Institute of Transportation Engineers, Washington, DC, 1993, pp. 1–5.

Daff, M.R., and I.D.K. Siggins, "On Road Trials of Some New Types of Slow Points," *Proceedings, Australian Road Research Board,* Vol. 11, 1982, pp. 214–237.

Dallam, L.N., "Environmental Capacity of Neighborhood Streets," in *Compendium of Technical Papers for the 66th ITE Annual Meeting,* Institute of Transportation Engineers, Washington, DC, 1996, pp. 422–423.

Datta, S., and T.K. Datta, "Humps—A Speed Reduction Strategy in Local Streets," in *Transportation and Sustainable Communities* (Resource Papers for the 1997 ITE International Conference, Tampa, FL), Institute of Transportation Engineers, Washington, DC, 1997, pp. 91–95.

Davis, R.E., and G. Lum, "Growing Pains or Growing Calmer? Lessons Learned from a Pilot Traffic Calming Program," in *Harmonizing Transportation & Community Goals* (ITE International Conference, Monterey, CA, 1998), Institute of Transportation Engineers, Washington, DC, 1998, CD-ROM.

DeRobertis, M., and A. Wachtel, "Traffic Calming: Do's and Don'ts to Encourage Bicycling," in *Compendium of Technical Papers for the 66th ITE Annual Meeting,* Institute of Transportation Engineers, Washington, DC, 1996, pp. 498–503.

Devon County Council, *Traffic Calming Guidelines,* Exeter, England, 1991.

de Wit, I.T., "Dutch Experiences with Speed Control Humps," in *63rd Annual Meeting Compendium of Technical Papers,* Institute of Transportation Engineers, Washington, DC, 1993, pp. 6–10.

Dorroh, R.F., and R.A. Kochevar, "One-Way Conversions for Calming Denver's Streets," in *Moving Forward in a Scaled-Back World* (Resource Papers for the 1996 ITE International Conference, Dana Point, CA), Institute of Transportation Engineers, Washington, DC, 1996, pp. 109–113.

Drdul, R., and M. Skene, "Traffic Calming Do's and Don'ts," in *64th Annual Meeting Compendium of Technical Papers,* Institute of Transportation Engineers, Washington, DC, 1994, pp. 491–495.

Durkin, M., and T. Pheby, "York: Aiming To Be the UK's First Traffic Calmed City," in *Traffic Management and Road Safety,* PTRC Education and Research Services Ltd., London, England, 1992, pp. 73–90.

Eubanks-Ahrens, B., "A Closer Look at the Users of Woonerven," in A. Vernez Moudon (ed.), *Public Streets for Public Use,* Columbia University Press, New York, NY, 1991, pp. 63–79.

Ewing, R., "Residential Street Design: Do the British and Australians Know Something We Americans Don't?" *Transportation Research Record 1455,* 1994, pp. 42–49.

Ewing, R., *Best Development Practices—Doing the Right Thing and Making Money at the Same Time,* American Planning Association (in cooperation with the Urban Land Institute), Chicago, IL, 1996, pp. 53–93.

Ewing, R., and C. Kooshian, "U.S. Experience with Traffic Calming," *ITE Journal,* Vol. 67, August 1997, pp. 28–33.

Fager, M., "Environmental Traffic Management in Stockholm," *ITE Journal,* Vol. 54, July 1984, pp. 16–19.

Federal Highway Administration, *Flexibility in Highway Design,* Washington, DC, 1997.

Flannery, A., and T.K. Datta, "Modern Roundabouts and Traffic Crash Experience in the United States," *Transportation Research Record 1553,* 1996, pp. 103–109.

Flannery, A., et al., "Safety, Delay and Capacity of Single-Lane Roundabouts in the United States," paper presented at the 77th Annual Meeting, Transportation Research Board, Washington, DC, 1998.

Frisbie, M.S., "The Power of 'Proactivity' in Phoenix Neighborhoods," in *1995 Compendium of Technical Papers,* Institute of Transportation Engineers, Washington, DC, 1995, pp. 278–280.

Fwa, T.F., and C.Y. Liaw, "Rational Approach for Geometric Design of Speed-Control Road Humps," *Transportation Research Record 1356,* 1992, pp. 66–72.

Fwa, T.F., and L.S. Tan, "Geometric Characterization of Road Humps for Speed-Control Design," *Journal of Transportation Engineering,* Vol. 118, July/August 1992, pp. 593–598.

Geddes, E., et al., *Safety Benefits of Traffic Calming,* Insurance Corporation of British Columbia, Vancouver, BC, Canada, 1996.

Gonzalez, K.L., "Neighborhood Traffic Control: Bellevue's Approach," *ITE Journal,* Vol. 63, 1993, pp. 43–45.

Gorman, M.N., M. Moussavi, and P.T. McCoy, "Evaluation of Speed Hump Program in the City of Omaha," *ITE Journal,* Vol. 59, June 1989, pp. 28–32.

Grava, S., "Traffic Calming: Can It Be Done in America?" *Transportation Quarterly,* Vol. 47, 1993, pp. 483–505.

Guzda, M.K., *Slow Down, You're Going Too Fast!—The Community Guide to Traffic Calming,* Public Technology, Inc., Washington, DC, 1998.

Hagan, W.B., and S.E. Amamoo, "Residential Street Management in South Australia," *ITE Journal,* Vol. 58, March 1988, pp. 35–41.

Halbert, G., et al., "Implementation of a Residential Traffic Control Program in the City of San Diego," in *Environment—Changing Our Transportation Priorities* (Resource Papers for the 1994 ITE International Conference, La Jolla, CA) Institute of Transportation Engineers, Washington, DC, 1994, pp. 265–271.

Halperin, K., and R. Huston, "A Verkehrsberuhigung Design for an American Road," *ITE Journal,* Vol. 64, April 1994, pp. 28–34.

Hanks, J.R., "Traffic Calming," *ITE Journal,* Vol. 67, July 1997, p. 21.

Harkey, D.L., D.W. Reinfurt, M. Knuinan, J.R. Stewart, and A. Sorton, *Development of the Bicycle Compatibility Index: A Level of Service Concept,* Final Report, Publication No. FHWA-RD-98-072, Federal Highway Administration, Washington, DC, December, 1998.

Hass-Klau, C., "Environmental Traffic Management in Britain—Does It Exist?" *Built Environment,* Vol. 12, 1986, pp. 7–19.

Hass-Klau, C., et al., *Civilised Streets—A Guide to Traffic Calming, Environment & Transport Planning,* Brighton, England, 1992.

Hass-Klau, C., "Impact of Pedestrianization and Traffic Calming on Retailing: A Review of the Evidence from Germany and the UK," *Transport Policy,* Vol. 1, October 1993, pp. 21–31.

Hassett, R.L., and M.L. Haywood-Spells, "Neighborhood Traffic Management: Albuquerque's Experience So Far," in *Compendium of Technical Papers for the 66th ITE Annual Meeting* (Minneapolis, MN), Institute of Transportation Engineers, Washington, DC, 1996, pp. 429–432.

Herrstedt, L., "Traffic Calming Design: A Speed Management Method—Danish Experience on Environmentally Adapted Through Roads," *Accident Analysis & Prevention,* Vol. 24, 1992, pp. 3–16.

Herrstedt, L., et al., *An Improved Traffic Environment— A Catalogue of Ideas,* Danish Road Directorate, Copenhagen, Denmark, 1993.

Hidas, P., K. Weerasekera, and M. Dunne, "Negative Effects of Mid-Block Speed Control Devices and Their Importance in the Overall Impact of Traffic Calming on the Environment," *Transportation Research D,* Vol. 3D, 1998, pp. 41–50.

Homburger, W.S., et al., *Residential Street Design and Traffic Control,* Prentice Hall, Englewood Cliffs, NJ, 1989, pp. 79–112.

Hoyle, C.L., *Traffic Calming,* Planning Advisory Service Report Number 456, American Planning Association, Chicago, IL, 1995.

Hoyle, C.L., and R. Ewing, "Traffic Calming for New Residential Streets Enhances Housing Value," *Land Development,* Vol. 9, Fall 1996, pp. 7–11.

Institution of Highways and Transportation, *Roads and Traffic in Urban Areas,* Her Majesty's Stationery Office, London, England, 1987.

ITE Technical Council Committee 5B-15, "Road Bumps—Appropriate for Use on Public Streets," *ITE Journal,* Vol. 56, November 1986, pp. 18–21.

ITE Traffic Engineering Council Speed Humps Task Force, *Guidelines for the Design and Application of Speed Humps—A Recommended Practice,* Institute of Transportation Engineers, Washington, DC, 1997.

Jacquemart, G., *Modern Roundabout Practice in the United States,* Synthesis of Highway Practice 264, Transportation Research Board, Washington, DC, 1998.

Janssen, S.T., "Road Safety in Urban Districts: Final Results of Accident Studies in the Dutch Demonstration Projects of the 1970s," *Traffic Engineering + Control,* Vol. 32, 1991, pp. 292–296.

Jarvis, J.R., and G. Giummarra, "Humps for Use on Bus Routes," *Road & Transport Research,* Vol. 1, December 1992, pp. 32–47.

Jenks, M., "Residential Roads Researched: Are Innovative Estates Safer?" *Architects' Journal,* Vol. 177, June 1983, pp. 46–49.

Jepsen, S.R., "The American Woonerf: Boulder's Experience," in *1985 Compendium of Technical Papers,* Institute of Transportation Engineers, Washington, DC, 1985, pp. 102–107.

Kallberg, V., et al., "Recommendations for Speed Management on European Roads," paper presented at the 78th Annual Meeting, Transportation Research Board, Washington, DC, 1999.

Kanely, B.D., "Neighborhood Traffic Calming—
Do We Need Warrants?" in *Transportation and Sustainable
Communities* (Resource Papers for the 1997 ITE
International Conference, Tampa, FL), Institute of
Transportation Engineers, Washington, DC, 1997,
pp. 60–64.

Kanely, B.D., and B.E. Ferris, "Traffic Diverters for
Residential Traffic Control—The Gainesville Experience," in *1985 Compendium of Technical Papers,* Institute
of Transportation Engineers, Washington, DC, 1985,
pp. 72–76.

Kant, E.J., and R.D. Muller, "Neighborhood Traffic
Management: Development and Implementation—One
County's Experience," in *Transportation and Sustainable
Communities* (Resource Papers for the 1997 ITE
International Conference, Tampa, FL), Institute of
Transportation Engineers, Washington, DC, 1997,
pp. 21–24.

Kanz, A.C., and W.A. Keim, "Residential Traffic Control
in Montgomery County, Maryland," in *1979 Compendium of Technical Papers,* Institute of Transportation
Engineers, Washington, DC, 1979, pp. 148–151.

Keller, H.H., "Environmental Traffic Restraints on
Major Roads in the Federal Republic of Germany,"
*Built Environment,* Vol. 12, 1986, pp. 44–57.

Keller, H.H., "Urban and Transport Planning Concepts
to Revitalise Two Medium-Sized Town Centres in West
Germany," in *New Life for City Centres: Planning,
Transport, and Conservation in British and German Cities,*
Anglo-German Foundation for the Study of Industrial
Society, London, England, 1988, pp. 179–185.

Keller, H.H., "Three Generations of Traffic Calming in
the Federal Republic of Germany," *Environmental Issues,*
PTRC Education and Research Services, Sussex,
England, 1989, pp. 15–31.

Kemper, B.K., and P.M. Fernandez, "Neighborhood
Traffic Control Measures," in *Design and Safety of
Pedestrian Facilities,* Institute of Transportation Engineers,
Washington, DC, 1994, pp. 48–53.

Kent County Council, *Traffic Calming: A Code of Practice,*
Maidstone, England, 1992.

Kjemtrup, K., and L. Herrstedt, "Speed Management
and Traffic Calming in Europe: A Historical View,"
*Accident Analysis & Prevention,* Vol. 24, 1992, pp. 57–65.

Klaeboe, R., "Measuring the Environmental Impact of
Road Traffic in Town Areas," in *Environmental Issues,*
PTRC Education and Research Services Ltd., London,
England, 1992, pp. 81–88.

Klik, M., and A. Faghri, "A Comparative Evaluation of
Speed Humps and Deviations," *Transportation Quarterly,*
Vol. 47, 1993, pp. 457–469.

Knack, R., "Drive Nicely: Looking for Ways to Beat
Road Rage? Try Traffic Calming," *Planning,* Vol. 64,
December 1998, pp. 12–15.

Kraay, J.H., "Woonerven and Other Experiments in
the Netherlands," *Built Environment,* Vol. 12, 1986,
pp. 20–29.

Kraay, J.H., M.P.M. Mathijssen, and F.C.M. Wegman,
*Toward Safer Residential Areas,* Institute of Road Safety
Research SWOV/Ministry of Transport, Leidschendam,
Switzerland, 1985, pp. 30–39.

Leden, L., P. Garder, and U. Pulkkinen, "Measuring the
Safety Effect of Raised Bicycle Crossings Using a New
Research Methodology," paper presented at the 77th
Annual Meeting, Transportation Research Board,
Washington, DC, 1998.

Leonard, J.D., and W.J. Davis, "Urban Traffic Calming
Treatments: Performance Measures and Design Con-
formance," *ITE Journal,* Vol. 67, August 1997, pp. 34–40.

Lewis, D., "The Do's and Don'ts of Traffic Calming,"
*Traffic Safety,* Vol. 98, March/April 1998, pp. 14–17.

Litman, T., *Evaluating Traffic Calming Benefits, Costs and
Equity Impacts,* Victoria Transport Policy Institute,
Victoria, BC, Canada, 1997.

Lockwood, I.M., "Do We Need Traffic Calming
Warrants?" in *Transportation and Sustainable Communities*
(Resource Papers for the 1997 ITE International
Conference, Tampa, FL), Institute of Transportation
Engineers, Washington, DC, 1997, pp. 55–59.

Lockwood, I.M., "ITE Traffic Calming Definition," *ITE
Journal,* Vol. 67, July 1997, pp. 22–24.

Lockwood, I.M., "Meeting Community Objectives Through Street Design (The West Palm Beach Approach)," paper presented at the ITE International Conference in Monterey, CA, Institute of Transportation Engineers, Washington, DC, 1998.

Marconi, W., "Speed Control Measures in Residential Areas," *Traffic Engineering,* Vol. 47, March 1977, pp. 28–30.

Marks, H., "Traffic Capacity," *Traffic Circulation Planning for Communities,* Gruen Associates, Los Angeles, 1974, pp. 223–231.

Marstrand, J., et al., *Urban Traffic Areas—Part 7: Speed Reducers,* Vejdirektoratet—Vejregeludvalget, The Netherlands, 1991.

Mazzella, T., and D. Godfrey, "Building and Testing a Customer Responsive Neighborhood Traffic Control Program," in *1995 Compendium of Technical Papers,* Institute of Transportation Engineers, Washington, DC, 1995, pp. 75–79.

McCann, H., L. Troxell, and G. King, "Managing Traffic in Residential Areas," *Transportation Research Record 1021,* 1985, pp. 20–24.

McCourt, R.S., "Neighborhood Traffic Management Survey," *Compendium of Technical Papers for the 66th ITE Annual Meeting,* Institute of Transportation Engineers, Washington, DC, 1996, pp. 280–282.

McCourt, R.S., "Survey of Neighborhood Traffic Management Performance and Results," in *Harmonizing Transportation & Community Goals* (ITE International Conference, Monterey, CA, 1998), Institute of Transportation Engineers, Washington, DC, 1998, CD-ROM.

McGinnis, L., "Things That Go Bump in the Night: How Do Speed Humps Affect Fire Department Response Times," *NFPA Journal,* Vol. 91, January/ February 1997, pp. 78–82.

Meier, D., "The Policy Adopted in Arlington County, Virginia, for Solving Real and Perceived Speeding Problems on Residential Streets," in *1985 Compendium of Technical Papers,* Institute of Transportation Engineers, Washington, DC, 1985, pp. 97–101.

Meyers, D., "Bringing It All Together: Meshing Higher Densities, Transit Facilities, and Traffic Calming in Older Neighborhood Business Districts," in *Harmonizing Transportation & Community Goals* (ITE International Conference, Monterey, CA, 1998), Institute of Transportation Engineers, Washington, DC, 1998, CD-ROM.

Mohle, H., "Sunnyvale's Approach to the Old Challenge of Neighborhood Traffic Calming," paper presented at the 67th ITE Annual Meeting, Boston, MA, Institute of Transportation Engineers, Washington, DC, 1997.

Monheim, H., "Area-Wide Traffic Restraint: A Concept for Better Urban Transport," *Built Environment,* Vol. 12, 1986, pp. 74–82.

Mounce, J.M., "Driver Compliance with Stop-Sign Control at Low-Volume Intersections," *Transportation Research Record 808,* 1981, pp. 30–37.

Mulder, K., "Split Speed Bump," in *Harmonizing Transportation & Community Goals* (ITE International Conference, Monterey, CA, 1998), Institute of Transportation Engineers, Washington, DC, 1998, CD-ROM.

Nicodemus, D.A., "Safe and Effective Roadway Humps —The Seminole County Profile," in *1991 Compendium of Technical Papers,* Institute of Transportation Engineers, Washington, DC, 1991, pp. 102–105.

Niederhauser, M.E., B.A. Collins, and E.J. Myers, "The Use of Roundabouts: Comparison of Alternate Design Solutions," in *Compendium of Technical Papers for the 67th ITE Annual Meeting* (Boston, MA, 1997), Institute of Transportation Engineers, Washington, DC, 1997, CD-ROM.

Nielsen, O.H., and J. Rassen, "Environmental Traffic Management in Odense, Denmark," *Built Environment,* Vol. 12, 1986, pp. 83–97.

Nitzel, J.J., F.G. Schattner, and J.P. Mick, "Residential Traffic Control Policies and Measures," in *1988 Compendium of Technical Papers,* Institute of Transportation Engineers, Washington, DC, 1988, pp. 217–223.

Noble, J., and A. Smith, *Residential Roads and Footpaths— Layout Considerations—Design Bulletin 32,* Her Majesty's Stationery Office, London, England, 1992.

Noyes, P.B., and W.C. Fox, "Neighborhood Traffic Management: Process and Results," in *Harmonizing Transportation & Community Goals* (ITE International Conference, Monterey, CA, 1998), Institute of Transportation Engineers, Washington, DC, 1998, CD-ROM.

O'Brien, A.P., "Traffic Calming: Ideas Into Practice," in *1993 Compendium of Technical Papers,* Institute of Transportation Engineers, Washington, DC, 1993, pp. 129–134.

O'Brien, A.P., "The Need for Warrants—The Australian Experience," in *Transportation and Sustainable Communities* (Resource Papers for the 1997 ITE International Conference, Tampa, FL), Institute of Transportation Engineers, Washington, DC, 1997, pp. 65–82.

O'Brien, A.P., R. Brindle, and R. Fairlie, "Some Australian Experiences with Warrants," *Compendium of Technical Papers for the 67th ITE Annual Meeting* (Boston, MA, 1997), Institute of Transportation Engineers, Washington, DC, 1997, CD-ROM.

Ochia, K., "Calming Urban Street Crime through Traffic Calming: Program Development and Implementation," *Compendium of Technical Papers for the 66th ITE Annual Meeting* (Minneapolis, MN, 1996), Institute of Transportation Engineers, Washington, DC, 1996, pp. 424–428.

Ontario Traffic Conference, *Traffic Calming,* Toronto, ON, Canada, 1995.

Ourston, L., and J.G. Bared, "Roundabouts: A Direct Way to Safer Highways," *Public Roads,* Vol. 59, Autumn 1995, pp. 41–49.

Perone, J.P., "Developing and Implementing Traffic Calming Warrants," in *Compendium of Technical Papers for the 66th ITE Annual Meeting* (Minneapolis, MN, 1996), Institute of Transportation Engineers, Washington, DC, 1996, pp. 351–353.

Perone, J.P., "Traffic Calming: The Local Area Traffic Management (LATM) Approach," *Moving Forward in a Scaled-Back World* (Resource Papers for the 1996 ITE International Conference, Dana Point, CA), Institute of Transportation Engineers, Washington, DC, 1996, pp. 215–222.

Pharaoh, T.M., and J.R. Russell, "Traffic Calming Policy and Performance: The Netherlands, Denmark and Germany," *Town Planning Review,* Vol. 62, 1991, pp. 79–105.

Poe, C.M., and J.M. Mason, "Geometric Design Guidelines to Achieve Desired Operating Speed on Urban Streets," in *1995 Compendium of Technical Papers,* Institute of Transportation Engineers, Washington, DC, 1995, pp. 70–74.

Preston, B., "The Need for Home Zones," in *Environmental Issues,* PTRC Education and Research Services Ltd., London, England, 1993, pp. 215–226.

Proctor, S., "Accident Reduction Through Area-Wide Traffic Schemes," *Traffic Engineering + Control,* No. 12, 1991, pp. 566–573.

Pucher, J., and S. Clorer, "Taming the Automobile in Germany," *Transportation Quarterly,* Vol. 46, 1992, pp. 383–395.

Residential Area Speed Control Ad-Hoc Committee, *Speed Control in Residential Areas,* Michigan Office of Highway Safety Planning, 1998.

Ribbens, H., and G. Schermers, "Traffic Calming as a Means for Promoting Pedestrian Safety in Urban Areas in South Africa," paper presented at the 76th Annual Meeting, Transportation Research Board, Washington, DC, 1997.

Savage, J.P., R.D. MacDonald, and J. Ewell, *A Guidebook for Residential Traffic Management,* Washington Department of Transportation, Olympia, WA, 1994.

Schlabbach, K., "Traffic Calming in Europe," *ITE Journal,* Vol. 67, July 1997, pp. 38–40.

Schnull, R., and J. Lange, "Speed Reduction on Through Roads in Nordrhein-Westfalen," *Accident Analysis & Prevention,* Vol. 24, 1992, pp. 67–74.

Schoon, C., and J. van Minnen, "The Safety of Roundabouts in the Netherlands," *Traffic Engineering + Control,* Vol. 35, 1994, pp. 142–147.

Secunda, S., et al., "Creating Places II: Traffic Calming," in *Getting Back to Place—Using Streets to Rebuild Community,* Project for Public Spaces, New York, NY, pp. 24–34.

Skene, M., et al., "Developing a Canadian Guide to Traffic Calming," *ITE Journal,* Vol. 67, July 1997, pp. 34–36.

Smith, D.T., "End to Menlo Park's Traffic Calming Wars?" paper presented at the 67th ITE, Boston, Annual Meeting, Boston, MA, Institute of Transportation Engineers, Washington, DC, 1997.

Smith, D.T., and D. Appleyard, *Improving the Residential Street Environment—Final Report,* Federal Highway Administration, Washington, DC, 1981.

Smith, D.T., and D. Appleyard, *State-of-the-Art: Residential Traffic Management,* Federal Highway Administration, Washington, DC, 1980.

Spitz, S., "How Much Traffic Is Too Much (Traffic)," *ITE Journal,* Vol. 52, May 1982, pp. 44–45.

Stein, H., et al., "Portland's Successful Experience with Traffic Circles," in *1992 Compendium of Technical Papers,* Institute of Transportation Engineers, Washington, DC, 1992, pp. 39–44.

Sumner, R., and C. Baguley, *Speed Control Humps on Residential Roads,* Transport and Road Research Lab, Crowthorne, England, 1979, pp. 3–10.

Swartz, R.D., "Mitigating Through Traffic in Residential Areas: Issues and Perspectives," *Transportation Quarterly,* Vol. 39, pp. 467–481.

Taylor, D., and M. Tight, "Public Attitudes and Consultation in Traffic Calming Schemes," *Transport Policy,* Vol. 4, 1997, pp. 171–182.

TEST, *Quality Streets: How Traditional Urban Centres Benefit from Traffic-Calming,* study prepared for the Greater London Council, London, England, 1988, pp. 1–20.

Tolley, R., *Calming Traffic in Residential Areas,* Brefi Press, Brefi, England, 1990.

Topp, H.H., "Traffic Safety, Usability, and Streetscape Effects of New Design Principles for Major Urban Roads," *Transportation,* Vol. 16, 1990, pp. 297–310.

Ullman, G.L., "Neighborhood Speed Control—U.S. Practices," in *1996 Compendium of Technical Papers,* Institute of Transportation Engineers, Washington, DC, 1996, pp. 111–115.

Underwood, R.T., "Neighbourhood Traffic Management—An Australian Perspective," in *1993 Compendium of Technical Papers,* Institute of Transportation Engineers, Washington, DC, 1993, pp. 124–128.

Wallwork, M.J., "Traffic Calming," *Traffic Safety Toolbox,* Institute of Transportation Engineers, Washington, DC, 1993, pp. 235–245.

Walter, C.E., "Suburban Residential Traffic Calming," *ITE Journal,* Vol. 65, 1995, pp. 44–48.

Weinstein, A., and E. Deakin, "A Survey of Traffic Calming Programs in the United States," paper presented at the ITE International Conference in Monterey, CA, Institute of Transportation Engineers, Washington, DC, 1998.

Weinstein, A., and E. Deakin, "How Local Jurisdictions in the United States Finance Traffic Calming," paper presented at the 78th Annual Meeting, Transportation Research Board, Washington, DC, 1999.

Welke, R.C., and S.R. Navid, "Residential Traffic Control Initiatives," in *1988 Compendium of Technical Papers,* Institute of Transportation Engineers, Washington, DC, 1988, pp. 92–95.

Whitelegg, J., "The Principle of Environmental Traffic Management," *The Greening of Urban Transport: Planning for Walking and Cycling in Western Cities,* Belhaven Press, London, England, 1990.

Zaidel, D., A.S. Hakkert, and A.H. Pistiner, "The Use of Road Humps for Moderating Speeds on Urban Streets," *Accident Analysis & Prevention,* Vol. 24, 1992, pp. 45–56.

Zegeer, C.V., et al., *FHWA Study Tour for Pedestrian and Bicyclist Safety in England, Germany, and The Netherlands,* Federal Highway Administration, Washington, DC, 1994, pp. 38–41, 55–57, 69–73, and 81.

Zein, S.R., "Safety Benefits of Traffic Calming," paper presented at the 76th Annual Meeting, Transportation Research Board, Washington, DC, 1997.

# Speed and Volume Data Before and After Traffic Calming

| Community/Location | Measure | 85th Percentile Speed (mph) | | | Volumes (vehicles/day) | | | Comments |
|---|---|---|---|---|---|---|---|---|
| | | Before | After | % Change | Before | After | % Change | |
| **Austin, TX** | | | | | | | | |
| Richcreek Rd | 12' humps | 37 | 30 | -19 | 503 | 543 | 8 | Average or sum of two directions - speed data collected between humps - in most cases, before data 3 to 9 weeks before installation - after data collected from 2 weeks to 24 months after installation |
| Pasadena Dr | 12' humps | 36 | 31 | -14 | 523 | 535 | 20 | |
| Aspen Creek Pkwy | 12' humps | 38 | 26 | -32 | 561 | 388 | -31 | |
| Woodland Ave | 12' humps | 40 | 28 | -30 | 7,611 | 7,018 | -8 | |
| Roundup Tr | 12' humps | 39 | 31 | -22 | 734 | 469 | -36 | |
| Cedar St | 22' tables | 35 | 28 | -20 | 468 | 383 | -18 | |
| Broad Oaks Dr | 22' tables | 40 | 31 | -23 | 357 | 290 | -19 | |
| Sunstrip Dr | 22' tables | 37 | 28 | -24 | 932 | 952 | 2 | |
| Rockpoint Dr | 22' tables | 36 | 30 | -17 | 421 | 460 | 9 | |
| Pack Saddle Pass | Diagonal diverter | N/A | | | 3,600 | 1,400 | -61 | Data collected two blocks away - temporary diverter removed - traffic diverted to neighboring streets |
| Frontier Trail | Diagonal diverter | N/A | | | 800 | 500 | -38 | Data collected one block away |
| Morrow St | Forced turn island and turn restriction | N/A | | | 8,420 | 3,763 | -55 | Data collected four blocks away - Blocks westbound movement on Morrow St at Lamar Blvd |
| Davis St | Half closure | 25 | 23 | -8 | 2,233 | 568 | -75 | Data collected same block as half closure |
| Rainey St (70 blk) | Circle | 33 | 35 | 6 | 389 | 269 | -31 | Part of neighborhood traffic calming treatment involving half closures, speed cushions, traffic circle, and neckdowns (temporary installations) |
| Rainey St (80 blk) | Speed cushions | 35 | 28 | -20 | 3,323 | 2,321 | -30 | |
| Rainey St (90 blk) | Speed cushions and neckdown | 28 | 22 | -21 | 835 | 1,869 | 124 | |
| River St (600 blk) | Circle | N/A | | | 610 | 590 | -3 | |
| River St (700 blk) | Circle | 26 | 27 | 4 | 3,152 | 2,033 | -36 | |

Note. In Appendix A, the 20 communities featured in this report are listed first, alphabetically. Data for several other communities follow.

| Community/Location | Measure | 85th Percentile Speed (mph) | | | Volumes (vehicles/day) | | | Comments |
|---|---|---|---|---|---|---|---|---|
| | | Before | After | % Change | Before | After | % Change | |
| **Bellevue, WA** | | | | | | | | |
| Somerset Dr | 12' humps | 39 | 27 | -31 | 795 | 746 | -6 | Between humps - only alternate route consists of circuitous local streets - speeds at humps = 12–15 mph at 4" humps; 23–26 mph at 3" humps that replaced 4" humps |
| Highland Dr | 12' humps | 36 | 25 | -31 | 1,702 | 1,934 | 14 | No parallel route available - after measurement soon after installation |
| 128th Ave NE (S of NE 2nd ) | 12' humps | 33 | 27 | -18 | 1,305 | 1,022 | -22 | |
| 162nd Ave SE | 12' humps | 37 | 27 | -27 | 1,472 | 1,071 | -27 | Good alternate route on parallel collector (161st Ave SE) - after measurement soon after installation - also report 2 years after |
| SE 63rd St | 12' humps with chokers | 36 | 25 | -31 | 2,456 | 2,593 | 6 | No parallel route available (Forest Dr would seem to provide good alternate) - also report speeds at humps |
| NE 39th St | 12' humps with chokers | 39 | 25 | -35 | 3,685 | 2,931 | -20 | Good alternate route available on collector road (NE Northrup Way) - also report speeds at humps |
| 108th St SE (location A) | 22' tables | 35 | 29 | -17 | 2,540 | 1,942 | -24 | Speeds measured between tables - good alternate routes available on collector roads (Bellevue Way and 112th Ave, SE) |
| 108th St SE (location B) | 22' tables | 34 | 31 | -9 | 2,223 | 1,809 | -19 | |
| 108th St SE (location C) | 22' tables | 35 | 31 | -11 | 2,346 | 1,885 | -20 | |
| 128th Ave NE (N of NE 5th St) | Half closure | N/A | | | 770 | 442 | -43 | Data collected same block 20% violation rate |
| 128th Ave NE (N of NE 5th St) | One-lane angled choker | 31 | 28 | -10 | 770 | 331 | -57 | Replaced half closure that was frequently violated |
| SE 46th Way | Circle with neckdowns | 34 | 28 | -18 | N/A | | | |
| **Berkeley, CA** | | | | | | | | |
| Acton St | 12' humps | 29 | 22 | -24 | N/A | | | Also report speeds at humps and range of speeds between and at humps - smaller range of speeds after than before installation |
| Berkeley Way | 12' humps | 31 | 22 | -29 | N/A | | | |
| Bonar St | 12' humps | 32 | 21 | -34 | N/A | | | |
| Capistrano Ave | 12' humps | 32 | 24 | -25 | N/A | | | |
| Catalina Ave | 12' humps | 25 | 22 | -12 | N/A | | | |
| Cornell Ave | 12' humps | 30 | 25 | -17 | N/A | | | |
| Curtis St | 12' humps | 34 | 28 | -18 | N/A | | | |
| El Camino Real St | 12' humps | 28 | 23 | -18 | N/A | | | |

| Community/Location | Measure | 85th Percentile Speed (mph) | | | Volumes (vehicles/day) | | | Comments |
|---|---|---|---|---|---|---|---|---|
| | | Before | After | % Change | Before | After | % Change | |
| **Berkeley, CA** (continued) | | | | | | | | |
| Masonic St | 12' humps | 30 | 24 | -20 | N/A | | | Also report speeds at humps and range of speeds between and at humps - smaller range of speeds after than before installation |
| Oxford St | 12' humps | 33 | 26 | -21 | N/A | | | |
| Peralta Ave | 12' humps | 36 | 25 | -31 | N/A | | | |
| Tacoma Ave | 12' humps | 33 | 27 | -18 | N/A | | | |
| Tyler Ave | 12' humps | 26 | 20 | -23 | N/A | | | |
| Santa Fe Ave | 22' tables | 31 | 25 | -19 | N/A | | | |
| Derby St | 12' humps | 31 | 22 | -29 | 3,600 | 1,800 | -50 | Significant diversion to other residential streets |
| **Boulder, CO** | | | | | | | | |
| Mapleton Ave | 12' humps | 28 | 25 | -11 | 1,710 | 1,490 | -13 | |
| North St | 12' humps | 33 | 25 | -24 | 1,050 | 760 | -28 | |
| Floral Dr | 12' humps | 31 | 25 | -19 | 900 | 670 | -26 | |
| Moorhead Ave (3100 blk) | 46' tables | 34 | 31 | -9 | 4,590 | 4,460 | -3 | Five tables removed due to emergency response concerns |
| Moorhead Ave (4300 blk) | 46' tables | 34 | 31 | -9 | 2,810 | 2,620 | -7 | |
| Edgewood Dr | 46' tables | 36 | 28 | -22 | 11,140 | 9,690 | -13 | Modest diversion to neighboring streets - two tables removed due to emergency concerns |
| 55th St | 46' tables and raised intersection | 42 | 37 | -12 | 12,400 | 9,400 | -24 | September 1995 before - September 1997 after |
| N 9th St | Circle | 33 | 23 | -30 | 3,360 | 1,970 | -41 | Midblock speeds |
| Arapahoe Ave | Circle | 33 | 28 | -15 | 2,010 | 1,940 | -3 | |
| Balsam Ave | Circle | 38 | 25 | -34 | 10,910 | 8,280 | -24 | Significant diversion to neighboring streets but no increase in speeds |
| Pine St | Circle | 33 | 31 | -6 | 8,660 | 7,280 | -16 | |
| **Charlotte, NC** | | | | | | | | |
| Barklay Downs Dr | 22' tables | 40 | 37 | -8 | 13,000 | 10,300 | -21 | 85th percentile speeds averaged for two directions |
| Carolyn Dr | 22' tables | 40 | 31 | -23 | 600 | 500 | -17 | |
| Dalecrest Dr | 22' tables | 38 | 34 | -11 | 3,000 | 2,500 | -17 | |
| Lancer Dr | 22' tables | 31 | 30 | -3 | 1,600 | 1,400 | -13 | |
| Laurel Ave | 22' tables | 33 | 28 | -15 | 5,000 | 4,700 | -6 | |
| Marlbrook Dr | 22' tables | 37 | 32 | -14 | 3,800 | 4,000 | 5 | |
| Park Crossing Dr | 22' tables | 41 | 37 | -10 | 2,700 | 2,000 | -26 | |
| Tipperary Pl | 22' tables | 34 | 34 | 0 | 5,200 | 4,400 | -15 | |

| Community/Location | Measure | 85th Percentile Speed (mph) | | | Volumes (vehicles/day) | | | Comments |
|---|---|---|---|---|---|---|---|---|
| | | Before | After | % Change | Before | After | % Change | |
| **Charlotte, NC** (continued) | | | | | | | | |
| Westfield Rd | 22' tables | 32 | 27 | -16 | 1,000 | 900 | -10 | 85th percentile speeds averaged for two directions |
| Sherwood Ave (S of Queens Rd W) | One-lane chicane | 37 | 31 | -16 | 3,200 | 2,400 | -25 | |
| Eighth St | Circle | 25 | 23 | -8 | 561 | 583 | 4 | |
| **Dayton, OH** | | Part of neighborhood-wide plan involving humps, street closures, and all-way stops | | | | | | |
| Five Oaks Ave (between Bellevue Ave and closure) | Closure | N/A | | | 1,340 | 53 | -96 | Same block as closure - one block from another closure |
| Five Oaks Ave (between Richmond and Old Orchard Ave) | 12' humps | 34 | 25 | -26 | N/A | | | Closure at one end and stop sign at other closure |
| Grafton Ave (between Kenilworth Ave and closure) | Closure | N/A | | | 947 | 768 | -19 | Same block as closure - two blocks from another closure |
| Grafton Ave (between Neal Ave and closure) | Closure | N/A | | | 1,525 | 130 | -91 | Same block as closure - one block from another closure |
| Harvard Blvd | 12' humps | N/A | | | 864 | 1,906 | 121 | |
| Homewood Ave (between Old Orchard Ave and Forest Ave) | 12' humps | 32 | 32 | 0 | 2,351 | 1,269 | -46 | Two blocks from closure |
| Homewood Ave (between Rockwood and Old Orchard Ave) | Closure | N/A | | | 1,815 | 641 | -65 | One block from closure |
| Kenilworth Ave (between Redfern Ave and closure) | Closure | N/A | | | 1,076 | 95 | -91 | Same block as closure - one block from another |
| Kenilworth Ave (between Grafton Ave and Old Orchard Ave) | Closure | N/A | | | 656 | 333 | -49 | One block from closure |
| Kenwood Ave | Closure | N/A | | | 477 | 644 | 35 | One block from closure |
| Richmond Ave (between Harvard Blvd and Manhattan Ave) | 12' humps | N/A | | | 2,428 | 2,433 | 0 | One block from closure |
| Richmond Ave (between North Ave and Neal Ave) | Closure | N/A | | | 1,901 | 1,171 | -38 | One block from closure |
| **Eugene, OR** | | | | | | | | |
| Friendly St (N of 26th Ave) | 14' humps | 34 | 27 | -21 | 3,995 | 2,340 | -41 | 1996 before, 1998 after - 1/3 of the volume reduction diverted to parallel residential street |
| Friendly St (S of 21st Ave) | 14' humps | 32 | 27 | -16 | 2,185 | 1,255 | -43 | |

| Community/Location | Measure | 85th Percentile Speed (mph) | | | Volumes (vehicles/day) | | | Comments |
|---|---|---|---|---|---|---|---|---|
| | | Before | After | % Change | Before | After | % Change | |
| **Ft. Lauderdale, FL** | | | | | | | | |
| NE 14th Ave | 12' humps | 35 | 25 | -29 | 3,000 | 2,100 | -30 | Some diversion to NE 15th Ave - a parallel route |
| SE 7th St | 22' tables | 36 | 32 | -11 | N/A | | | Average of 85th percentile bi-directional speeds - part of a neighborhood-wide treatment involving one-lane angled chokers and speed tables |
| SE 9th St | 22' tables | 36 | 31 | -14 | N/A | | | |
| SE 11th St | 22' tables | 38 | 29 | -24 | N/A | | | |
| SE 11th Ct (E of SE 9th Ave) | 22' tables | 37 | 33 | -11 | N/A | | | |
| SE 11th Ct (W of SE 9th Ave) | 22' tables | 36 | 31 | -14 | N/A | | | |
| Cordova Rd (S of SE 12th St) | One-lane angled chokers | 34 | 31 | -9 | 4,192 | 4,278 | 2 | Measurement taken 3 months after installation midway (300') from chokers - later replaced by speed humps |
| Cordova Rd (N of SE 11th St) | One-lane angled chokers | 35 | 30 | -14 | 2,606 | 2,548 | -2 | |
| **Gainesville, FL** | | | | | | | | |
| NW 26th Tr | Circle | 38 | 36 | -5 | 2,024 | 1,959 | -3 | |
| NW 22nd St (1800 blk) | Circle | 35 | 31 | -11 | 1,507 | 1,417 | -6 | |
| NW 22nd St (2100 blk) | Circle | 39 | 34 | -13 | 970 | 825 | -15 | |
| NE 10th Ave | Circle | N/A | | | 1,599 | 1,285 | -20 | Report cut-through volumes |
| NW 19th St | Circle | 39 | 34 | -13 | 2,837 | 2,752 | -3 | 47% cut-through before - 38+% after |
| NW 14th Ave | Circle | 34 | 30 | -12 | 1,409 | 1,093 | -22 | |
| 30th Ave (1200 blk) | Half closure one block away | 36 | 29 | -19 | 1,056 | 362 | -66 | Part of neighborhood-wide treatment involving half closures and an all-way stop - treatment redesigned after test |
| 30th Ave (1100 blk) | Half closure same block | N/A | | | 923 | 170 | -82 | |
| 30th Ave (600 blk) | Half closure two blocks away | N/A | | | 929 | 382 | -59 | |
| 31st Ave (1200 blk) | Half closure one block away | 35 | 28 | -20 | 816 | 312 | -62 | |
| 31st Ave (1100 blk) | Half closure same block | N/A | | | 803 | 180 | -78 | |
| 31st Ave (600 blk) | Half closure two blocks away | N/A | | | 896 | 698 | -22 | |
| NW 31st Tr | Half closure same block | N/A | | | 621 | 536 | -14 | 67% cut-through - volumes should have declined more |
| NW 7th Ave | Closure same block | N/A | | | 425 | 160 | -62 | Report cut-through volumes |

| Community/Location | Measure | 85th Percentile Speed (mph) | | | Volumes (vehicles/day) | | | Comments |
|---|---|---|---|---|---|---|---|---|
| | | Before | After | % Change | Before | After | % Change | |
| **Gwinnett County, GA** | | | | | | | | |
| Winn Dr (W of Gloster Rd) | 4' humps, 22' tables | 39 | 30 | -23 | N/A | | | 4" high - experimental installation - later removed |
| Winn Dr (W of Adams Mill Dr) | 4' humps | 44 | 25 | -43 | N/A | | | |
| Rocky Rd | 22' tables | 36 | 30 | -17 | 466 | 428 | -8 | |
| Wakefield St | 22' tables | 38 | 29 | -24 | 718 | 658 | -8 | |
| Gwinn Oaks Dr | 22' tables | 35 | 26 | -26 | N/A | | | |
| Simpson Mill Ln | 22' tables | 36 | 30 | -17 | 798 | 522 | -35 | |
| Deshong Dr | 22' tables | 38 | 30 | -21 | 1,130 | 856 | -24 | |
| Oak Leaf Tr | 22' tables | 37 | 27 | -27 | 704 | 364 | -48 | |
| Trotters Ridge | 22' tables | 40 | 34 | -15 | 362 | 458 | 27 | |
| Valley Rd | 22' tables | 38 | 26 | -32 | 198 | 242 | 22 | |
| Grandeus Ln | 22' tables | 38 | 30 | -21 | 880 | 775 | -12 | |
| Rocky Hill Dr | 22' tables | 47 | 33 | -30 | 800 | 421 | -47 | |
| Rosedale Rd | 22' tables | 38 | 29 | -24 | 858 | 695 | -19 | |
| Hillcrest Dr | 22' tables | 37 | 30 | -19 | 2,102 | 2,061 | -2 | |
| Waterford Park Dr | 22' tables | 38 | 28 | -26 | 599 | 743 | 24 | |
| Jane Rd | 22' tables | 36 | 28 | -22 | 711 | 536 | -25 | |
| Fitzpatrick Way | 22' tables | 39 | 30 | -23 | 1,136 | 992 | -13 | |
| Weston Dr | 22' tables | 37 | 27 | -27 | 747 | 791 | 6 | |
| Clearwater Dr | 22' tables | 41 | 30 | -27 | 780 | 751 | -4 | |
| **Howard County, MD** | | | | | | | | |
| Baltimore Ave | 12' humps | 38 | 28 | -26 | N/A | | | Report speed at humps |
| Dogwood Dr | 12' humps | 40 | 28 | -30 | N/A | | | Report 24% drop in volume |
| Shaker Dr | 22' tables | 43 | 29 | -33 | N/A | | | |
| Eliots Oak Rd (S of Celestial) | 22' tables | 38 | 32 | -16 | N/A | | | Part of areawide treatment using tables and a raised intersection |
| Eliots Oak Rd (S of Evangeline) | 22' tables | 35 | 28 | -20 | 4,560 | 3,710 | -19 | |
| Eliots Oak Rd (S of Fall River Row) | 22' tables | 35 | 35 | 0 | 7,480 | 6,660 | -11 | |
| Eliots Oak Rd (S of Hesperus Dr) | Raised intersection | 37 | 35 | -5 | 4,060 | 3,860 | -5 | |
| Hesperus Dr (S of Windmill Ln) | 22' tables | 36 | 31 | -11 | 2,380 | 1,855 | -22 | |
| Hesperus Dr (S of Open Window) | 22' tables | 37 | 33 | -11 | 2,460 | 1,960 | -20 | |
| Durham Rd W (E of Dover Ct) | 22' tables | 36 | 32 | -11 | 1,635 | 1,070 | -35 | |
| Durham Rd W (N of Castle Moore) | 22' tables | 36 | 28 | -22 | N/A | | | |

| Community/Location | Measure | 85th Percentile Speed (mph) | | | Volumes (vehicles/day) | | | Comments |
|---|---|---|---|---|---|---|---|---|
| | | Before | After | % Change | Before | After | % Change | |
| **Howard County, MD** (continued) | | | | | | | | |
| Country Ln | 22' tables | 36 | 30 | -17 | N/A | | | Part of areawide treatment using tables and a raised intersection |
| Michaels Way (W of Ramblewood) | 22' tables | 39 | 33 | -15 | N/A | | | |
| Michaels Way (W of Greenway Dr) | 22' tables | 35 | 32 | -9 | N/A | | | |
| Joey Dr | 22' tables | 35 | 35 | 0 | N/A | | | |
| Hearthstone Rd (S of Crabapple) | 22' tables | 38 | 33 | -13 | N/A | | | |
| Hearthstone Rd (S of Joey Dr) | Raised intersection | 36 | 40 | 11 | N/A | | | |
| Greenway Dr (S of St. Johns Lane) | 22' tables | 40 | 36 | -10 | N/A | | | |
| Greenway Dr (S of Joey Dr) | 22' tables | 40 | 35 | -13 | N/A | | | |
| N Chatham Rd | 22' tables | 40 | 32 | -20 | N/A | | | |
| Rockburn Dr | Circle | 35 | 30 | -14 | 1,592 | 1,428 | -10 | At T-intersections - extreme deflection in one direction and no deflection in other - treatment using circles and a center island narrowing |
| Shaker Dr (E of Roveout Ln) | Circle | 38 | 36 | -5 | N/A | | | Part of a section-long treatment involving circles, tables, and a choker |
| Shaker Dr (E of Wayover Ln) | Circle | 37 | 35 | -5 | N/A | | | |
| **Montgomery County, MD** (Volumes are based on hourly counts, assuming a peak-to-daily ratio of 0.10.) | | | | | | | | |
| Notley Rd | 12' humps | 39 | 32 | -18 | 1,420 | 900 | -37 | Speed measurement not taken immediately after installation |
| Aberdeen Rd | 12' humps | 36 | 27 | -25 | 1,350 | 760 | -44 | |
| Durbin Rd | 12' humps | 33 | 25 | -24 | 810 | 500 | -38 | |
| Shorefield Rd | 12' humps | 35 | 29 | -17 | 1,240 | 1,530 | 23 | |
| Counselman Rd | 12' humps | 34 | 31 | -9 | 970 | 560 | -42 | |
| Westbard Ave | 12' humps | 35 | 28 | -20 | 990 | 920 | -7 | |
| Thayer Ave | 12' humps | 35 | 29 | -17 | 860 | 780 | -9 | |
| Burdette Rd | 12' humps | 40 | 34 | -15 | 1,330 | 1,110 | -17 | |
| Great Oak Rd | 12' humps | 37 | 32 | -14 | 410 | 320 | -22 | |
| McKnew Rd | 12' humps | 39 | 29 | -26 | 850 | 1,090 | 28 | |
| Rock Run Dr | 12' humps | 38 | 29 | -24 | 350 | 290 | -17 | |
| Lilly Stone Dr | 12' humps | 36 | 29 | -19 | 1,130 | 700 | -38 | |
| Fraley Farm Rd | 12' humps | 39 | 30 | -23 | 730 | 770 | 5 | |
| Northwest Dr | 12' humps | 34 | 30 | -12 | 1,140 | 320 | -72 | |
| Stapleford Hall Dr | 12' humps | 39 | 31 | -21 | 1,090 | 860 | -21 | |
| Cherry Grove Dr | 12' humps | 38 | 33 | -13 | 980 | 870 | -11 | |

| Community/Location | Measure | 85th Percentile Speed (mph) | | | Volumes (vehicles/day) | | | Comments |
|---|---|---|---|---|---|---|---|---|
| | | Before | After | % Change | Before | After | % Change | |
| **Montgomery County, MD** (continued) | | | | | | | | |
| Briardale Rd | 12' humps | 36 | 30 | -17 | 950 | 840 | -12 | Speed measurement not taken immediately after installation |
| Democracy Ln | 12' humps | 39 | 31 | -21 | 990 | 680 | -31 | |
| George Washington Dr | 12' humps | 36 | 30 | -17 | 710 | 800 | 13 | |
| Mill Creek Dr | 12' humps | 32 | 29 | -9 | 800 | 430 | -46 | |
| Wayfarer Rd | 12' humps | 38 | 27 | -29 | 1,120 | 540 | -52 | |
| Hermitage Rd | 12' humps | 40 | 28 | -30 | 630 | 410 | -35 | |
| Overlea Dr | 12' humps | 43 | 37 | -14 | 1,020 | 450 | -56 | |
| Venice Dr | 12' humps | 38 | 29 | -24 | 1,190 | 750 | -37 | |
| Wilmett Rd | 12' humps and 22' tables | 32 | 29 | -9 | 730 | 540 | -26 | |
| Beech Ave | 12' humps and 22' tables | 34 | 31 | -9 | 1,310 | 1,560 | 19 | |
| Galway Dr | 22' tables | 36 | 30 | -17 | 2,070 | 1,230 | -41 | |
| Bel Pre Rd | 22' tables | 40 | 34 | -15 | 14,500 | 14,400 | -1 | |
| Schuylkill Rd | 22' tables | 37 | 29 | -22 | 1,420 | 2,080 | 46 | |
| Morningwood Dr | 22' tables | 33 | 32 | -3 | 1,210 | 880 | -27 | |
| Brickyard Rd | Circle | 48 | 43 | -10 | 2,110 | 1,290 | -39 | |
| Notley Rd | Circles | 47 | 39 | -17 | 1,500 | 2,140 | 43 | |
| Cherry Valley Dr | Circle | 42 | 39 | -7 | 890 | 450 | -49 | |
| Dorset Ave | Half closure | N/A | | | 1,100 | 575 | -48 | |
| Brookside Dr | Half closure | N/A | | | 1,350 | 650 | -52 | |
| Kennedy Dr | Half closure | N/A | | | 450 | 250 | -44 | |
| Woodlawn Ave | Half closure | N/A | | | 250 | 100 | -60 | |
| Sugarbush Ln | Humps, circle, chokers, and center islands | 37 | 30 | -19 | 810 | 720 | -11 | |
| Huntington Pkwy | Chicanes and humps | 34 | 30 | -12 | 1,500 | 1,390 | -7 | |
| **Omaha, NE** | | | | | | | | |
| 33rd St | 12' humps | 36 | 32 | -11 | N/A | | | 2/84 before - 12/86 after |
| 50th St | 12' humps | 36 | 36 | 0 | N/A | | | 11/83 before - 1/84 after |
| 55th St (between Pine and Hickory) | 12' humps | 34 | 32 | -6 | N/A | | | 9/83 before - 12/86 after |
| 55th St (between Hickory and Walnut) | 12' humps | 36 | 34 | -6 | N/A | | | 12/82 before - 9/83 after |
| 56th St | 12' humps | 35 | 33 | -6 | N/A | | | 4/85 before - 1/87 after |
| 76th St (between Burt and Webster) | 12' humps | 39 | 33 | -15 | N/A | | | 3/85 before - 12/86 after |

| Community/Location | Measure | 85th Percentile Speed (mph) | | | Volumes (vehicles/day) | | | Comments |
|---|---|---|---|---|---|---|---|---|
| | | Before | After | % Change | Before | After | % Change | |
| **Omaha, NE** (continued) | | | | | | | | |
| 76th St (between Burt and Izard St) | 12' humps | 36 | 33 | -8 | N/A | | | 4/85 before - 12/86 after |
| 126th St | 12' humps | 37 | 36 | -3 | N/A | | | 9/83 before - 1/84 after |
| Nina St | 12' humps | 45 | 34 | -24 | N/A | | | 11/83 before - 11/86 after |
| Parkview Dr (between Grand Ave and Saratoga St) | 12' humps | 37 | 35 | -5 | N/A | | | 10/82 before - 11/82 after |
| Parkview Dr (at Larimore Ave) | 12' humps | 37 | 27 | -27 | N/A | | | 10/82 before -11/82 after |
| Parkview Dr (between Sahler and Sprague Sts) | 12' humps | 36 | 36 | 0 | N/A | | | 10/83 before - 12/86 after |
| Redick Ave | 12' humps | 39 | 37 | -5 | N/A | | | 2/85 before - 12/86 after |
| **Phoenix, AZ** | | * Mean speeds | | | | | | |
| Via Estrella | Diagonal diverter | N/A | | | 1,625 | 1,148 | -29 | One block away - part of neighborhood-wide treatment |
| Meadowbrook Ave (W of 14th Pl) | Diagonal diverter | 36 | 29 | -19 | 1,354 | 177 | -87 | Same block; spot treatment |
| Meadowbrook Ave (E of 13th Pl) | Diagonal diverter | 35 | 34 | -3 | 1,569 | 574 | -63 | |
| Edgemont Ave | Half closure | N/A | | | 2,238 | 718 | -68 | Same block - separate eastbound & westbound counts (eastbound down slightly) |
| 20th Ave | Half closure | N/A | | | 770 | 168 | -78 | Same block |
| Culver St | Half closure | N/A | | | 206 | 133 | -35 | Same block - built with freeway mitigation money |
| Vogel Ave | Diagonal diverter three blocks away | 26 | 23 | -12 | 2,057 | 325 | -84 | Part of neighborhood-wide treatment using a diagonal diverter and a half closure |
| 6th Ave | Diagonal diverter same block | N/A | | | 2,157 | 214 | -90 | |
| Oregon Ave (E of Central Ave) | Diagonal diverter | 25* | 18 | -28 | 521 | 353 | -32 | Part of Windsor Square Neighborhood Plan G using diagonal diverters and half closures - data collected same block as closures |
| Oregon Ave (W of 7th St) | Diagonal diverter | 26* | 24 | -8 | 598 | 224 | -63 | |
| Colter St (E of Central Ave) | Half closures at both end | 27* | 19 | -30 | 879 | 328 | -63 | |
| Colter St (W of 7th St) | Half closures at both ends | 29* | 22 | -24 | 1,233 | 533 | -57 | |
| Orange Dr | Half closure | 25* | 18 | -28 | 220 | 151 | -31 | |

| Community/Location | Measure | 85th Percentile Speed (mph) | | | Volumes (vehicles/day) | | | Comments |
|---|---|---|---|---|---|---|---|---|
| | | Before | After | % Change | Before | After | % Change | |
| **Phoenix, AZ** (continued) | | * Mean speeds | | | | | | |
| Oregon Ave (E of Central Ave) | Diagonal diverter one block away | 25* | 30 | 20 | 474 | 474 | 0 | Part of Windsor Square Neighborhood Plan I using a diagonal diverter, half closures, and a turn restriction |
| Oregon Ave (W of 7th St) | Diagonal diverter same block | 26* | 30 | 15 | 522 | 425 | -19 | |
| Colter St (E of Central Ave) | Half closures at both ends | 27* | 21 | -22 | 776 | 314 | -60 | |
| Colter St (W of 7th St) | Half closures at both ends | 29* | 19 | -34 | 1,048 | 474 | -55 | |
| Orangewood Ave | Circle | 38 | 37 | -3 | 892 | 834 | -7 | Temporary circle removed and replaced with 4-way stop |
| Clarendon Ave | 12' humps | 29* | 20 | -31 | 1,150 | 680 | -41 | Six humps spaced an average of 375' apart; 10/97 - 4/98 |
| Belmont Ave | 12' hump | N/A | | | 699 | 596 | -15 | Single hump in spot treatment |
| **Portland, OR** | | | | | | | | |
| 30th Ave | Median barrier | N/A | | | 330 | 430 | 30 | Two blocks away |
| 28th Ave | Forced turn island | N/A | | | 2,010 | 600 | -70 | One block away |
| 27th Ave | Half closure | N/A | | | 280 | 500 | 79 | One block from |
| 26th Ave | Half closure | N/A | | | 300 | 310 | 3 | One block away |
| 25th Ave | Half closure | N/A | | | 180 | 390 | 117 | One block away |
| Weidler St | Half closure | N/A | | | 680 | 220 | -68 | Same block |
| Halsey St | Closure | N/A | | | 820 | 500 | -39 | Three blocks away |
| SE Harold St | 22' tables plus neckdowns | 38 | 32 | -16 | 4,200 | 2,600 | -38 | Neckdowns at five intersections |
| NW Cornell Rd | 22' tables + center island narrowing | 36 | 30 | -17 | 6,500 | 6,400 | -2 | |
| NE 15th Ave | 22' tables + center island narrowing | 38 | 28 | -26 | 8,440 | 6,780 | -20 | |
| SE 76th Ave | 14' humps | 34 | 27 | -21 | 3,637 | 2,591 | -29 | |
| SE 119th Ave | 14' humps | 36 | 26 | -28 | 1,292 | 930 | -28 | |
| SE 67th Ave | 14' humps | 29 | 24 | -17 | 1,240 | 1,480 | 19 | |
| N Bryant St | 14' humps | 32 | 24 | -25 | 940 | 750 | -20 | |
| SE 52nd Ave | 14' humps | 33 | 30 | -9 | 1,020 | 357 | -65 | |
| NE 87th Ave | 14' humps | 37 | 28 | -24 | 765 | 504 | -34 | Speeds averaged over several locations |
| N Macrum Ave | 14' humps | 33 | 23 | -30 | 480 | 370 | -23 | |
| NE Pacific St | 14' humps | 34 | 24 | -29 | 600 | 600 | 0 | |
| NE 108th Ave | 14' humps | 32 | 23 | -28 | 770 | 700 | -9 | |
| SE 55th Ave | 14' humps | 32 | 23 | -28 | 2,300 | 1,900 | -17 | |

| Community/Location | Measure | 85th Percentile Speed (mph) | | | Volumes (vehicles/day) | | | Comments |
|---|---|---|---|---|---|---|---|---|
| | | Before | After | % Change | Before | After | % Change | |
| **Portland, OR** (continued) | | | | | | | | |
| SW Boones Ferry Rd | 14' humps | 32 | 25 | -22 | 4,000 | 1,500 | -62 | |
| N Smith St | Neckdowns, center island narrowings, and bike lanes | 39 | 37 | -5 | 4,000 | 3,500 | -13 | Previous reduction in speed limit had no effect |
| N Ida Ave | 14' humps, choker, neckdown, and bike lanes | 34 | 26 | -24 | 2,870 | 2,740 | -5 | Speeds averaged over several locations |
| NE 7th Ave | Circles | 38 | 32 | -16 | 6,500 | 5,500 | -15 | |
| SE Clinton St (#1) | Circles | 37 | 33 | -11 | 2,400 | 2,000 | -17 | |
| SE Clinton St (#2) | Circles | 36 | 32 | -11 | 1,200 | 680 | -43 | |
| NE Holman St | Circles | 33 | 33 | 0 | 1,400 | 1,100 | -21 | |
| NE 21st Ave | Circles | 34 | 30 | -12 | 5,600 | 5,600 | 0 | |
| NE 24th Ave | Circles | 36 | 29 | -19 | 3,500 | 3,200 | -9 | |
| NW 25th Ave | Circles | 33 | 28 | -15 | 7,800 | 6,500 | -17 | |
| NW Raleigh St | Circles | 30 | 26 | -13 | 2,100 | 1,500 | -29 | |
| NE Multnomah St and Imperial Ave | Circle | 29 | 27 | -7 | 550 | 500 | -9 | Midblock speeds |
| NE 37th Ave and Thompson St | Circle | 33 | 27 | -18 | 2,000 | 1,700 | -15 | Midblock speeds |
| SE Lincoln St and SE 58th Ave | Circle | 34 | 31 | -9 | 3,400 | 2,800 | -18 | Midblock speeds |
| NE 47th Ave and Brazee St | Circle | 34 | 28 | -18 | 3,700 | 3,000 | -19 | Midblock speeds |
| SE Market St | 22' split tables (28' offset) | 37 | 26 | -30 | N/A | | | Speed measured between halves of split tables |
| SE 17th Ave | 22' split tables (50' offset) | 38 | 32 | -16 | 6,900 | 4,800 | -30 | |
| **Sacramento, CA**  (Part of an areawide treatment involving half closures, circles, neckdowns, and split medians) | | | | | | | | |
| C St  (E of 22nd St) | Split median | 38 | 33 | -13 | 2,700 | 5,400 | 100 | |
| C St  (W of 21st St) | Neckdown | 20 | 29 | 45 | 2,800 | 5,660 | 102 | |
| D St  (E of 25th St) | Circle | N/A | | | 490 | 1,850 | 278 | |
| E St  (E of 28th St) | Half closure | N/A | | | 5,630 | 8,860 | 57 | One block away |
| E St  (E of 25th St) | Circle | N/A | | | 7,660 | 2,140 | -72 | Two blocks from half closure |
| E St  (W of 23rd St) | Split median | N/A | | | 6,400 | 2,450 | -62 | Two blocks from half closure |
| E St  (W of 20th St) | Half closure | N/A | | | 5,830 | 3,760 | -36 | One block away |
| F St  (E of 28th St) | Neckdown | 37 | 33 | -11 | 4,700 | 4,660 | -1 | Four blocks from half closure |
| F St  (E of 25th St) | Half closure | N/A | | | 4,740 | 4,410 | -7 | One block away |
| F St  (W of 23rd St) | Split median | 39 | 32 | -18 | 4,240 | 4,590 | 8 | |
| F St  (W of 20th St) | Half closure | N/A | | | 4,970 | 2,680 | -46 | Three blocks away |

| Community/Location | Measure | 85th Percentile Speed (mph) | | | Volumes (vehicles/day) | | | Comments |
|---|---|---|---|---|---|---|---|---|
| | | Before | After | % Change | Before | After | % Change | |
| **Sacramento, CA** (continued) | | | | | | | | |
| F St  (W of 16th St) | Half closure | 29 | 32 | 10 | 5,510 | 4,080 | -26 | One block away |
| G St  (E of 28th St) | Half closure and split median | 38 | 30 | -21 | 10,320 | 1,120 | -89 | Same block |
| G St  (E of 27th St) | Half closure/split medians (both ends) | 40 | 29 | -27 | 10,160 | 2,120 | -79 | One block away |
| G St  (E of 25th St) | Half closure | N/A | | | 9,800 | 3,730 | -62 | Three blocks away |
| G St  (W of 23rd St) | Split median | 41 | 34 | -17 | 9,250 | 4,010 | -57 | |
| G St  (W of 20th St) | Half closure | N/A | | | 9,260 | 3,280 | -65 | Same block |
| G St  (W of 17th St) | Neckdown | 29 | 28 | -3 | 8,110 | 5,100 | -37 | Three blocks from half closure |
| H St  (E of 28th St) | Half closure | 36 | 27 | -25 | 9,540 | 9,180 | -4 | Two blocks away |
| H St  (E of 25th St) | Split medians (both ends) | N/A | | | 8,780 | 3,450 | -61 | One block from half closure |
| H St  (W of 23rd St) | Circle | 39 | 34 | -13 | 8,460 | 3,760 | -56 | Four blocks from half closure |
| H St  (W of 20th St) | Half closure | N/A | | | 7,610 | 3,030 | -60 | Three blocks away |
| H St  (W of 17th St) | Half closure | 35 | 28 | -20 | 8,400 | 730 | -91 | Same block |
| I St  (E of 27th St) | Split medians | N/A | | | 2,400 | 3,300 | 38 | Both ends |
| I St  (E of 25th St) | Circles | 25 | 31 | 24 | N/A | | | |
| **San Diego, CA** | | | | | | | | |
| Marlborough Dr | Center island narrowing | 33 | 29 | -12 | 3,500 | 2,800 | -20 | |
| Armour St | 12' humps | N/A | | | 525 | 350 | -33 | Part of neighborhood treatment using humps on five streets - two experienced reduced traffic volumes, three increases - overall, traffic fell from 3,295 to 2,850 vehicles per day |
| Caledonia St | 12' humps | N/A | | | 215 | 240 | 12 | |
| Dellwood St | 12' humps | N/A | | | 1,065 | 1,260 | 18 | |
| Kirkcaldy Dr | 12' humps | N/A | | | 1,350 | 820 | -39 | |
| Lochlomond St | 12' humps | N/A | | | 140 | 180 | 29 | |
| Aquarius Dr | 12' humps and turn restrictions | 38 | 25 | -34 | 5,939 | 3,254 | -45 | Humps may be removed due to traffic diversion to local streets - prompted moratorium |
| Avenida Del Gato | 12' humps | 38 | 25 | -34 | 2,956 | 1,248 | -58 | |
| Bootes St | 12' humps | 36 | 30 | -17 | 5,714 | 4,659 | -18 | |
| Capicorn Way (Camino Ruiz and Orion Way) | 12' humps | 34 | 25 | -26 | 6,866 | 6,864 | 0 | No good alternate route |
| Capicorn Way (between Orion Way and Black Mountain Rd) | 12' humps | 36 | 25 | -31 | 11,544 | 11,043 | -4 | No good alternate route |
| Libra Dr | 12' humps | 38 | 27 | -29 | 5,578 | 2,656 | -52 | |

| Community/Location | Measure | 85th Percentile Speed (mph) | | | Volumes (vehicles/day) | | | Comments |
|---|---|---|---|---|---|---|---|---|
| | | Before | After | % Change | Before | After | % Change | |
| **San Diego, CA** (continued) | | | | | | | | |
| Twain Ave/50th St | 12' humps | 38 | 26 | -32 | 3,700 | 1,310 | -65 | Diversion to local streets - replaced with all-way stops |
| Linda Rosa | 12' humps | N/A | | | 3,600 | 1,700 | -53 | Removed due to diversion to local streets |
| **San Jose, CA** | | | | | | | | |
| San Fernando St | Half closure and forced turn island | N/A | | | 3,870 | 2,570 | -34 | Part of a neighborhood-wide treatment using diverters, median chokers, and all-way stops |
| San Carlos St | Median chokers | N/A | | | 2,150 | 2,160 | 0 | |
| William St | Median chokers | 34 | 32 | -6 | 6,150 | 5,040 | -18 | |
| 17th St | Diverter/closure | N/A | | | 5,300 | 1,200 | -77 | |
| Dana Ave | Median choker and 3-way stop | N/A | | | 5,290 | 4,140 | -22 | Part of a neighborhood-wide treatment using chokers, circles, a closure, 3- and 4-way stops, and turn restrictions |
| Hanchett Ave | Median barrier | N/A | | | 2,770 | 1,490 | -46 | |
| Martin Ave (E of Park Ave) | Circle and 4-way stop | N/A | | | 800 | 800 | 0 | |
| Martin Ave (W of Alameda ) | Median choker and circle | N/A | | | 850 | 880 | 4 | |
| Shasta Ave | Median choker | N/A | | | 7,220 | 6,210 | -14 | |
| Cinderella Ln | 12' humps | 32 | 22 | -31 | N/A | | | |
| El Cajon Dr | 12' humps | 36 | 26 | -28 | N/A | | | |
| Miami Dr | 12' humps | 33 | 20 | -39 | N/A | | | |
| **Sarasota, FL** | | | | | | | | |
| Bahia Vista St. | 12' humps | N/A | | | 4,780 | 3,256 | -32 | Spot treatments |
| Prospect St | 12' humps | 29 | 21 | -27 | 521 | 316 | -39 | Spot treatments |
| Arlington St | 12' humps | 33 | 25 | -24 | 502 | 422 | -16 | Spot treatments |
| Waldemere St | 12' humps | 34 | 25 | -26 | 640 | 579 | -10 | Spot treatments |
| Floyd St | 12' humps | 31 | 24 | -22 | 525 | 428 | -18 | Spot treatments |
| McClellan Pk | 22' tables | 42 | 25 | -41 | 9,147 | 7,216 | -21 | Spot treatments |
| N. Adams Dr | 12' humps | 35 | 28 | -20 | 1,312 | 647 | -51 | Spot treatments |
| N. Washington Dr | 12' humps | 30 | 25 | -17 | 3,891 | 1,473 | -62 | Spot treatments |
| Irving St | Semi-diverter | 38 | 23 | -39 | 224 | 92 | -59 | Spot treatments same block |
| **Seattle, WA** | | | | | | | | |
| E. Prospect St | Diagonal diverter | N/A | | | 970 | 270 | -72 | Subarea treatment with circles same block |
| E. Prospect St | Diagonal diverter | N/A | | | 1,000 | 140 | -86 | Two blocks away |
| 16th Ave E | Diagonal diverter | N/A | | | 860 | 360 | -58 | Same block |
| 16th Ave E | Diagonal diverter | N/A | | | 360 | 310 | -14 | One block away |

| Community/Location | Measure | 85th Percentile Speed (mph) | | | Volumes (vehicles/day) | | | Comments |
|---|---|---|---|---|---|---|---|---|
| | | Before | After | % Change | Before | After | % Change | |
| **Seattle, WA** (continued) | | | | | | | | |
| E. Highland St | Diagonal diverter | N/A | | | 840 | 390 | -54 | Two blocks away |
| E. Highland St | Diagonal diverter | N/A | | | 500 | 180 | -64 | Same block |
| 18th Ave E | Diagonal diverter | N/A | | | 500 | 280 | -44 | One block away |
| 18th Ave E | Diagonal diverter | N/A | | | 530 | 320 | -40 | Same block |
| 17th Ave E (N of E. Aloha St) | Half closure | N/A | | | 560 | 380 | -32 | Same block |
| 17th Ave E (S of E. Galer St) | Half closure | N/A | | | 290 | 200 | -31 | Same block |
| Fairview Ave E | Closure | 16 | 13 | -19 | 1,980 | 850 | -57 | Temporary closure removed - same block |
| Fairview Ave E | Closure | 20 | 17 | -15 | 1,540 | 1,080 | -30 | Temporary closure removed - two blocks away |
| 28th Ave E | Closure | N/A | | | 4,490 | 1,250 | -72 | Four blocks away - temporary closure made permanent - combined with turn restrictions |
| NE 98th St | Half closure same block | N/A | | | 1,030 | 390 | -62 | Neighborhood-wide treatment across from Northgate Mall |
| NE 98th St | Half closure | N/A | | | 1,000 | 650 | -35 | One block away |
| NE 100th St | Half closure | N/A | | | 660 | 390 | -41 | Same block |
| NE 100th St | Half closure | N/A | | | 320 | 470 | 47 | One block away |
| NE 102nd St | Closure | N/A | | | 490 | 140 | -71 | Same block |
| NE 102nd St | Closure | N/A | | | 360 | 400 | 11 | One block away |
| NE 103rd St | Half closure | N/A | | | 3,770 | 1,830 | -51 | Same block |
| NE 103rd St | Half closure | N/A | | | 570 | 260 | -54 | One block away |
| E. Republican St (E of 15th Ave) | Diagonal diverter | N/A | | | 1,576 | 1,248 | -21 | Part of subarea treatment one block away |
| E. Republican St (W of 19th Ave) | Diagonal diverter | N/A | | | 881 | 377 | -57 | One block away |
| 17th Ave E | Diagonal diverter | N/A | | | 255 | 488 | 91 | Two blocks away |
| 17th Ave E | Diagonal diverter | N/A | | | 554 | 542 | -2 | One block away |
| E. Mercer St | Closure | N/A | | | 898 | 894 | 0 | Two blocks away |
| E. Mercer St | Closure | N/A | | | 467 | 312 | -33 | One block away |
| E. Harrison St | Star diverter | N/A | | | 1,135 | 1,113 | -2 | Same block |
| 16th Ave E | Star diverter | N/A | | | 1,112 | 1,090 | -2 | Same block |
| E. Roy St | Star diverter | N/A | | | 422 | 310 | -27 | Same block |
| 18th Ave E | Star diverter | N/A | | | 611 | 581 | -5 | Same block |

| Community/Location | Measure | 85th Percentile Speed (mph) | | | Volumes (vehicles/day) | | | Comments |
|---|---|---|---|---|---|---|---|---|
| | | Before | After | % Change | Before | After | % Change | |
| **Seattle, WA** (continued) | | | | | | | | |
| E. Jefferson (E of 28th Ave) | Diagonal diverter | N/A | | | 430 | 417 | -3 | Part of subarea treatment using two diagonal diverters and four traffic circles - data collected one block away (illustrates the odd results one can get with an areawide treatment) |
| E. Jefferson (W of 32nd Ave) | Diagonal diverter | N/A | | | 165 | 186 | 13 | |
| 30th Ave | Diagonal diverter | N/A | | | 500 | 279 | -44 | |
| E. Adler St | Diagonal diverter same block | N/A | | | 80 | 150 | 88 | |
| NW 55th St | One-lane chicane | 31 | 27 | -13 | 1,900 | 1,300 | -32 | Speed outside chicane; 85th percentile inside = 19 mph |
| NW 56th St | One-lane chicane | 30 | 24 | -20 | 1,380 | 790 | -43 | Speed outside chicane; 85th percentile inside = 20 mph |
| NW 52nd St | Circle | N/A | | | 330 | 380 | 15 | Neighborhood treatment one block away |
| Palmer Dr NW | Half closure | N/A | | | 300 | 150 | -50 | Same block |
| **Tucson, AZ** | | | | | | | | |
| San Carlos Rd (#1) | 12' humps | 34 | 28 | -18 | 381 | 354 | -7 | Measurements at midblock locations |
| San Carlos Rd (#2) | 12' humps | 40 | 26 | -35 | 278 | 195 | -30 | |
| San Carlos Rd (#3) | 12' humps | 30 | 26 | -13 | 48 | 46 | -4 | |
| Gollob Rd | 12' humps | 39 | 27 | -31 | 1,237 | 1,001 | -19 | |
| Vista Del Rio | 12' humps | N/A | | | 2,071 | 1,954 | -6 | |
| Desert Arbors St | 12' humps | 39 | 29 | -26 | N/A | | | |
| Pantano Rd | 12' humps | 39 | 33 | -15 | 883 | 876 | -1 | |
| Camino-Miramonte (#1) | 12' humps | 33 | 21 | -36 | 1,032 | 899 | -13 | |
| Camino-Miramonte (#2) | 12' humps | 30 | 23 | -23 | 475 | 511 | 8 | |
| Sahuara Ave (N of Grant) | 12' humps | 45 | 29 | -36 | 2,550 | 1,882 | -26 | |
| Copper St | 12' humps | 30 | 29 | -3 | 615 | 700 | 14 | |
| Water St | 12' humps | 35 | 24 | -31 | 891 | 756 | -15 | |
| Chantilly Dr | 12' humps | 32 | 26 | -19 | 1,172 | 1,130 | -4 | |
| North St | 12' humps | 33 | 24 | -27 | 600 | 525 | -13 | |
| Cottonwood Ln | 12' humps | 35 | 23 | -34 | 550 | 654 | 19 | |
| Wilshire Dr (N) | 12' humps | 30 | 27 | -10 | 796 | 649 | -18 | |
| Wilshire Dr (S) | 12' humps | 36 | 23 | -36 | 327 | 254 | -22 | |
| Golob/Fifth St (#1) | 12' humps | 35 | 27 | -23 | 1,273 | 1,544 | 21 | |
| Golob/Fifth St (#2) | 12' humps | 36 | 25 | -31 | 1,136 | 968 | -15 | |
| Boojum St | 12' humps | 26 | 20 | -23 | 367 | 171 | -53 | |

| Community/Location | Measure | 85th Percentile Speed (mph) | | | Volumes (vehicles/day) | | | Comments |
|---|---|---|---|---|---|---|---|---|
| | | Before | After | % Change | Before | After | % Change | |
| **Tucson, AZ** (continued) | | | | | | | | |
| Alamo Pl | 12' humps | 35 | 28 | -20 | 783 | 435 | -44 | Measurements at midblock locations |
| Jones Blvd | 12' humps | 36 | 25 | -31 | 1,972 | 1,687 | -14 | |
| Avenita Ricardo Small | 12' humps | 36 | 27 | -25 | 899 | 504 | -44 | |
| Hampton St | 12' humps | 35 | 22 | -37 | 343 | 224 | -35 | |
| Pima St | 12' humps | 37 | 27 | -27 | 1,859 | 1,648 | -11 | |
| Fremming Ave | 12' humps | 32 | 27 | -16 | 843 | 750 | -11 | |
| Koralee/Langley/Cooper (#1) | 12' humps | 33 | 24 | -27 | 1,886 | 1,686 | -11 | |
| Koralee/Langley/Cooper (#2) | 12' humps | 30 | 22 | -27 | 1,075 | 548 | -49 | |
| Sahuara Ave (between Pima & Grant) | 12' humps | 39 | 28 | -28 | 1,021 | 838 | -18 | |
| Calle Mecedora | 12' humps | 33 | 27 | -18 | 604 | 758 | 26 | |
| 18th St | 12' humps | 37 | 28 | -24 | 859 | 829 | -4 | |
| La Jolla Circle | 12' humps | 33 | 28 | -15 | 960 | 829 | -14 | |
| W Fort Lowell Rd | 12' humps | 36 | 27 | -25 | 1,314 | 1,009 | -23 | |
| Emily Dr | 12' humps | 32 | 25 | -22 | 1,459 | 1,165 | -20 | |
| Stella Rd | 12' humps | 32 | 25 | -22 | 638 | 514 | -19 | |
| Giovanna Dr | 12' humps | 27 | 25 | -7 | 572 | 496 | -13 | |
| Langley Ave-Kingston Dr (#1) | 12' humps | 33 | 24 | -27 | 1,668 | 1,554 | -7 | |
| Langley Ave-Kingston Dr (#2) | 12' humps | 30 | 27 | -10 | 2,008 | 1,876 | -7 | |
| Langley Ave-Kingston Dr (#3) | 12' humps | 30 | 21 | -30 | 926 | 996 | 8 | |
| Terra Del Sol (#1) | 12' humps | 36 | 27 | -25 | 1,132 | 936 | -17 | |
| Terra Del Sol (#2) | 12' humps | 31 | 27 | -13 | 1,693 | 1,277 | -25 | |
| Terra Del Sol (#3) | 12' humps | 35 | 26 | -26 | 1,498 | 1,489 | -1 | |
| Terra Del Sol (#4) | 12' humps | 32 | 23 | -28 | 932 | 1,039 | 12 | |
| Grady Ave | 12' humps | 40 | 29 | -27 | 2,969 | 2,239 | -25 | |
| Campbell Ave (between 31st and 34th) | 12' humps | 38 | 24 | -37 | 4,208 | 2,577 | -39 | |
| E 7th St | 12' humps | 33 | 19 | -42 | 485 | 494 | 2 | |
| Dogwood Ave | 12' humps | 32 | 20 | -38 | 1,369 | 620 | -55 | |
| Whittier St | 12' humps | 26 | 27 | 4 | 731 | 725 | -1 | |
| Van Buren Ave | 12' humps | 33 | 27 | -18 | 891 | 823 | -8 | |
| Rosemont West (#1) | 12' humps | 32 | 21 | -34 | 325 | 340 | 5 | |
| Rosemont West (#2) | 12' humps | 34 | 27 | -21 | 895 | 760 | -15 | |

| Community/Location | Measure | 85th Percentile Speed (mph) | | | Volumes (vehicles/day) | | | Comments |
|---|---|---|---|---|---|---|---|---|
| | | Before | After | % Change | Before | After | % Change | |
| **Tucson, AZ** (continued) | | | | | | | | |
| Seneca St | 12' humps | 32 | 27 | -16 | 821 | 879 | 7 | |
| Copper St | 12' humps | 32 | 27 | -16 | 399 | 290 | -27 | |
| San Fernando Ave | 12' humps | 28 | 20 | -29 | 274 | 175 | -36 | |
| Corona Rd | 12' humps | 32 | 27 | -17 | 1,619 | 976 | -40 | |
| Eric St | 12' humps | 31 | 27 | -16 | 1,524 | 1,078 | -29 | |
| Jessica Ave | 12' humps | 31 | 23 | -26 | 1,022 | 883 | -14 | |
| Calle Altar | 12' humps | N/A | | | 522 | 511 | -2 | |
| Fontana Ave (#1) | Circle | 35 | 27 | -23 | 2,211 | 1,837 | -17 | |
| Fontana Ave (#2) | Circle | 30 | 27 | -10 | 1,168 | 1,193 | 2 | |
| Estrella Ave (#1) | Circle | 33 | 25 | -24 | 861 | 817 | -5 | |
| Estrella Ave (#2) | Circle | 27 | 27 | 0 | 546 | 604 | 11 | |
| Blacklidge Dr (#1) | Circle | 35 | 32 | -9 | 1,069 | 865 | -19 | |
| Blacklidge Dr (#2) | Circles | 33 | 32 | -3 | 1,070 | 882 | -18 | |
| Kelso St (#1) | Circles | 29 | 27 | -7 | 706 | 605 | -14 | |
| Kelso St (#2) | Circles | 32 | 29 | -9 | 884 | 972 | 10 | |
| Cooper St | Circle | 30 | 26 | -13 | 343 | 551 | 61 | |
| Longfellow St | Circle | 33 | 28 | -15 | 240 | 278 | 16 | |
| Elm St | Raised crosswalk, chokers, and center islands | N/A | | | 4,258 | 4,535 | 7 | |
| Camino del Norte (#1) | Circles | N/A | | | 717 | 668 | -7 | |
| Camino del Norte (#2) | 12' humps and circles | N/A | | | 750 | 546 | -27 | |
| **Beaverton, OR** | | | | | | | | |
| SW 155th Ave (S of SW Nightingale Ct) | 12' humps 22' table | 37 | 27 | -27 | | | | Also had center islands |
| SW 155th Ave (N of Sexton Mountain Dr) | 30' speed hump, raised intersections | 40 | 34 | -15 | | | | Also had curb extensions and center islands |
| Hart Rd (at 142nd Ave) | 22' speed tables with chokers | 33 | 28 | -15 | | | | |
| Hart Rd (at Hart Pl) | 22' speed tables with chokers | 32 | 29 | -9 | | | | |
| Hart Rd (W of 130th Ave) | 22' speed tables with chokers | 34 | 30 | -12 | | | | |
| **Boca Raton, FL** | | | | | | | | |
| NW 3rd Ave | Circle and midblock deflector islands | 39 | 34 | -13 | 1,850 | 1,300 | -30 | Part of temporary neighborhood treatment also involving humps |

| Community/Location | Measure | 85th Percentile Speed (mph) | | | Volumes (vehicles/day) | | | Comments |
|---|---|---|---|---|---|---|---|---|
| | | Before | After | % Change | Before | After | % Change | |
| **Boca Raton, FL** (continued) | | | | | | | | |
| NW 3rd Ave (N of Spanish River) | 12' humps | 39 | 35 | -10 | 1,850 | 1,300 | -30 | Part of permanent neighborhood treatment involving humps, circles, and center islands |
| NW 3rd Ave (S of Yamato Rd) | 12' humps | N/A | | | 1,500 | 1,350 | -10 | |
| NW 5th Ave | 12' humps | 34 | 31 | -9 | 1,300 | 750 | -42 | |
| NW 4th Ave | Half closure | N/A | | | 1,800 | 300 | -83 | |
| NW 45th St | Circle | N/A | | | 600 | 600 | 0 | |
| **Cambridge, MA** | | | | | | | | |
| Berkshire St | Raised intersection, raised crosswalk, chicane, and neckdowns | 30 | 21 | -30 | N/A | | | Also report speed at slow points - part of subarea treatment involving two intersecting streets |
| **Kirkland, WA** | | | | | | | | |
| 126th Ave NE | 12' humps | 34 | 26 | -24 | 950 | 845 | -11 | |
| NE 112th St (W of 132nd Ave) | 12' humps | 32 | 24 | -25 | 440 | 436 | -1 | |
| NE 113th St | 12' humps | 34 | 24 | -30 | 1,500 | 1,200 | -20 | |
| NE 104th St | 12' humps | 35 | 27 | -23 | 1,200 | 600 | -50 | |
| 111th Ave NE | 12' humps | 33 | 24 | -27 | 770 | 714 | -7 | |
| Slater St | 12' humps | 32 | 25 | -22 | 300 | 314 | 5 | |
| 128th Ave NE | 14' humps | 35 | 28 | -20 | 1,400 | 1,313 | -6 | |
| NE 90th St | 14' humps | 34 | 25 | -26 | 423 | 528 | 25 | |
| NE 112th St (E of 112th Ave) | 22' tables | 35 | 27 | -23 | 2,117 | 2,007 | -5 | |
| NE 73rd St | Circles | 33 | 27 | -18 | 400 | 275 | -31 | |
| **Las Vegas, NV*** | | | | | | | | |
| Langtry Dr | 12' humps | 29 | 23 | -21 | 238 | 191 | -20% | |
| Clarice Ave | 12' humps | 38 | 26 | -32 | 3,047 | 3,316 | 9% | |
| Campbell Dr | 12' humps | N/A | | | 4,521 | 2,283 | -50% | |
| Bonanza Rd | 12' humps | 34 | 27 | -21 | 3,006 | 3,150 | 5% | |
| Avalon Ave | 12' humps | 38 | 22 | -42 | 3,455 | 2,040 | -41% | |
| Pyramid Dr | 12' humps | 29 | 23 | -21 | N/A | | | |
| **Minneapolis, MN** | | | | | | | | |
| Douglas Ave | 32' tables | 33 | 29 | -12 | 2,886 | 3,476 | 20 | Between Fremont and Girard |
| Douglas Ave | 32' tables | 31 | 31 | 0 | 1,283 | 1,960 | 53 | Between James and Knox |
| Vincent Ave (S and W 43rd St) | Circle | N/A | | | 2,722 | 2,245 | -18 | |

* S. Datta and T.K. Datta, "Humps—A Speed Reduction Strategy in Local Streets," in *Transportation and Sustainable Communities* (Resource Papers for the 1997 ITE International Conference, Tampa, FL), Institute of Transportation Engineers, Washington, DC, 1997, pp. 91–95.

| Community/Location | Measure | 85th Percentile Speed (mph) | | | Volumes (vehicles/day) | | | Comments |
|---|---|---|---|---|---|---|---|---|
| | | Before | After | % Change | Before | After | % Change | |
| **Naples, FL** | | | | | | | | |
| 7th Ave N | Circles | 33 | 26 | -21 | N/A | | | 30% initial volume reduction considered unrepresentative of long-term impact |
| **Orlando, FL** | | | | | | | | |
| Briarcliff Dr (E of Delaney Ave) | 107' table | 36 | 36 | 0 | 9,901 | 4,250 | -57 | Part of street-long treatment using 11 speed tables - average of eastbound and westbound speeds - February 1992 before, August 1994 after |
| Briarcliff Dr (at Summerlin) | 61' and 81' tables | 34 | 32 | -6 | 8,329 | 4,747 | -43 | |
| Briarcliff Dr (at Mills) | 61' and 97' tables | 33 | 31 | -6 | 9,703 | 5,444 | -44 | |
| Briarcliff Dr (W of Ferncreek) | 62' and 102' tables | 35 | 30 | -14 | 9,916 | 4,904 | -51 | |
| **Tampa, FL** | | | | | | | | |
| Oklahoma Ave | 12' humps | 40 | 32 | -20 | 2,900 | 1,650 | -43 | |
| Manhattan Ave | 12' humps | 38 | 30 | -21 | 2,360 | 1,930 | -18 | |
| Parkland Blvd | 12' humps | 40 | 28 | -30 | 1,960 | 1,320 | -33 | |
| Azeele St | 12' humps | 42 | 33 | -21 | 3,260 | 2,650 | -19 | |
| Cleveland St | 12' humps | 40 | 34 | -15 | 1,890 | 1,220 | -35 | |
| Palm Dr | Closure one block away | N/A | | | 1,962 | 1,116 | -43 | Temporary closure removed due to diversion |
| **Thousand Oaks, CA*** | | | | | | | | |
| Kelly Rd | 12' humps | 43 | 32 | -26 | N/A | | | 4" high hump |
| Silas Ave (initial) | 12' humps | 38 | 34 | -11 | N/A | | | 3" high hump |
| Silas Ave (final) | 12' humps | 38 | 27 | -29 | N/A | | | 3" high hump |
| Cindy Ave | 12' humps | 27 | 23 | -15 | N/A | | | 3" high hump |

* J.P. Clement, "Speed Humps and the Thousand Oaks Experience," *ITE Journal*, Vol. 53, January 1983, pp. 35–39.

# 85th Percentile Speeds as Function of Hump Size and Spacing

| Community/Location | Measure | Spacing (feet) | Before Speed (mph) | After Speed at Midpoint (mph) |
|---|---|---|---|---|
| **Austin, TX** | | | | |
| Richcreek Rd | 12' humps | 431 | 37 | 30 |
| Pasadena Dr | 12' humps | 334 | 36 | 31 |
| Aspen Creek Pkwy | 12' humps | 257 | 38 | 26 |
| Woodland Ave | 12' humps | 238 | 40 | 28 |
| Roundup Tr | 12' humps | 365 | 39 | 31 |
| Cedar St or Ave | 22' tables (parabolic) | 445 | 35 | 28 |
| Broad Oaks Dr | 22' tables (parabolic) | 405 | 40 | 31 |
| Sunstrip Dr | 22' tables (parabolic) | 290 | 37 | 28 |
| Rockpoint Dr | 22' tables (parabolic) | 272 | 36 | 30 |
| **Beaverton, OR** | | | | |
| Hart Rd (at 142nd Ave) | 22' tables (parabolic) | 500 | 33 | 28 |
| Hart Rd (at Hart Pl) | 22' tables (parabolic) | 390 | 32 | 29 |
| Hart Rd (W of 130th Ave) | 22' tables (parabolic) | 435 | 34 | 30 |
| **Bellevue, WA** | | | | |
| Somerset  (#1-#2) | 12' humps | 340 | 37-40 (37 shown) | 28 |
| Highland  (#1-#2) | 12' humps | 923 | 30-36 | 27 |
| Highland  (#2-#3) | 12' humps | 218 | 36 | 27 |
| SE 63rd  (#1-#2) | 12' humps | 578 | 32-34 | 26 |
| SE 63rd  (#2-#3) | 12' humps | 509 | 36 | 30 |
| 166th/162nd SE  (#1-#2) | 12' humps | 613 | 34-37 (37 shown) | 27 |
| 166th/162nd SE  (#2-#3) | 12' humps | 960 | 34-37 (37 shown) | 27-32 |
| 166th/162nd SE  (#3-#4) | 12' humps | 584 | 34-37 (37 shown) | 29 |
| NE 39th Ave  (#1-#2) | 12' humps | 404 | 39 | 25 |
| 108th Ave SE (#1-#2) | 22' tables (parabolic) | 930 | 35 | 29 |
| 108th Ave SE (#2-#3) | 22' tables (parabolic) | 1,410 | 34 | 31 |
| 108th Ave SE (#3-#4) | 22' tables (parabolic) | 1,040 | 35 | 31 |
| **Ft. Lauderdale, FL** | | | | |
| SE 7th St | 22' tables (parabolic) | 625 | 36 | 32 |
| SE 9th St | 22' tables (parabolic) | 538 | 36 | 31 |
| SE 11th St | 22' tables (parabolic) | 437 | 38 | 29 |
| SE 11th Ct (E of SE 9th Ave) | 22' tables (parabolic) | 626 | 37 | 33 |
| SE 11th Ct (W of SE 9th Ave) | 22' tables (parabolic) | 372 | 36 | 31 |

| Community/Location | Measure | Spacing (feet) | Before Speed (mph) | After Speed at Midpoint (mph) |
|---|---|---|---|---|
| **Gwinnett County, GA** | | | | |
| Rocky Rd | 22' tables (trapezoidal) | 619 | 36 | 30 |
| Wakefield St | 22' tables (trapezoidal) | 439 | 38 | 29 |
| Gwinn Oaks Dr | 22' tables (trapezoidal) | 483 | 35 | 26 |
| Simpson Mill Ln | 22' tables (trapezoidal) | 451 | 36 | 30 |
| Oak Leaf Tr | 22' tables (trapezoidal) | 447 | 37 | 27 |
| Trotters Ridge | 22' tables (trapezoidal) | 704 | 40 | 34 |
| Valley Rd | 22' tables (trapezoidal) | 517 | 38 | 26 |
| Grandeus Ln | 22' tables (trapezoidal) | 453 | 38 | 30 |
| Rosedale Rd | 22' tables (trapezoidal) | 364 | 38 | 29 |
| Hillcrest Dr | 22' tables (trapezoidal) | 472 | 37 | 30 |
| Waterford Park Dr | 22' tables (trapezoidal) | 294 | 38 | 28 |
| Jane Rd | 22' tables (trapezoidal) | 387 | 36 | 28 |
| Fitzpatrick Way | 22' tables (trapezoidal) | 412 | 39 | 30 |
| Weston Dr | 22' tables (trapezoidal) | 395 | 37 | 27 |
| Clearwater Dr | 22' tables (trapezoidal) | 594 | 41 | 30 |
| **Howard County, MD** | | | | |
| Baltimore Ave | 22' tables (trapezoidal) | 450 | 38 | 28 |
| **Kirkland, WA** | | | | |
| 128th Ave NE | 14' humps | 373 | 36 | 28 |
| NE 90th St | 14' humps | 356 | 34 | 25 |
| NE 112th St | 22' tables (parabolic) | 290 | 35 | 27 |
| **Montgomery County, MD** | | | | |
| Durbin Rd | 12' humps | 265 | 33 | 25 |
| **Phoenix, AZ** | | | | |
| Clarendon Ave | 12' hump | 375 | 35 | 26 |
| **Portland, OR** | | | | |
| NW Cornell Rd | 22' tables (parabolic) | 310 | 34 | 30 |
| SE 67th Ave | 14' humps | 432-375 | 29 | 24 |
| N Bryant St | 14' humps | 400 | 32 | 24 |
| **Tampa, FL** | | | | |
| Oklahoma | 12' humps | 700 | 40 | 32 |
| Manhattan | 12' humps | 300 | 38 | 30 |
| Parkland | 12' humps | 560 | 40 | 28 |
| Azeele | 12' humps | 590 | 42 | 33 |
| Cleveland | 12' humps | 680 | 40 | 34 |

# Average Annual Accidents Before and After Traffic Calming

| Community/Location | Measures | Accidents | | | Volume | Comments |
| --- | --- | --- | --- | --- | --- | --- |
| | | Before | After | % Change | % Change | |
| **Boulder, CO** | | | | | | |
| Arapahoe Ave | Circles | 0 | 1 | + undefined | -4 | Intersection accidents only - 1994 vs. 1996 |
| Maxwell and 6th St | Circle | 1 | 0 | -100 | | Intersection accidents only - 1994 vs. 1996 |
| Evergreen and 9th St | Circles | 2 | 0 | -100 | -41 | Intersection accidents only - 1992/1993 vs. 1995/1996 |
| Balsam Ave | Circles | 2 | 0 | -100 | -24 | Intersection accidents only - 1994 vs. 1996 |
| Pine St | Circles | 6 | 12 | 100 | -16 | Intersection accidents only - 1994 vs. 1996 |
| **Dayton, OH** | | | | | | |
| Five Oaks Ave (between Richmond & Old Orchard) | 12' humps | 4 | 2 | -50 | | Closure at one end and STOP sign at other |
| Harvard Blvd | 12' humps | 8 | 10 | 25 | -12 | Annualized based on half of 1992 compared to half of 1993 |
| Homewood Ave (between Old Orchard & Forest Ave) | 12' hump | 0 | 0 | 0 | -46 | |
| Richmond Ave (between Five Oaks & Delaware Ave) | 12' humps | 10 | 0 | -100 | | Closure at one end and STOP sign at other |
| **Howard County, MD** | | | | | | |
| Baltimore Ave | 12' humps | 2.4 | .4 | -83 | | Average Annual based on 8 years before installation and 8 years after installation |
| Eliots Oak Rd | 22' tables | 5.7 | 1.7 | -70 | -5, -19 | Average Annual (3 years before and after) |
| Herperus Dr | 22' tables | 3.7 | 1 | -73 | -20, -22 | Over 3 years |
| **Montgomery County, MD** | | | | | | |
| Notley Rd | 12' humps | 0 | 0 | 0 | -37 | One year before installation compared to most recent 12 months |
| Aberdeen Rd | 12' humps | 0 | 0 | 0 | -44 | |
| Shorefield Rd | 12' humps | 3 | 2 | -33 | -23 | |
| Westbard Ave | 12' humps | 0 | 1 | + undefined | -7 | |
| Thayer Ave | 12' humps | 5 | 4 | -20 | -9 | |
| Burdette Rd | 12' humps | 1 | 1 | 0 | -17 | |
| Lilly Stone Dr | 12' humps | 0 | 0 | 0 | -38 | |
| Northwest Dr | 12' humps | 0 | 0 | 0 | -72 | |

| Community/Location | Measures | Accidents | | | Volume | Comments |
|---|---|---|---|---|---|---|
| | | Before | After | % Change | % Change | |
| **Montgomery County, MD** (continued | | | | | | |
| Stapleford Hall Dr | 12' humps | 1 | 0 | -100 | -21 | |
| Briardale Rd | 12' humps | 1 | 0 | -100 | -12 | |
| George Washington Dr | 12' humps | 0 | 0 | 0 | -13 | |
| Mill Creek Dr | 12' humps | 1 | 0 | -100 | -46 | |
| Wayfarer Rd | 12' humps | 1 | 0 | -100 | -52 | |
| Hermitage Rd | 12' humps | 2 | 0 | -100 | -35 | |
| Overlea Dr | 12' humps | 0 | 1 | + undefined | -56 | |
| Bel Pre Rd | 22' tables | 6 | 4 | -33 | 1 | |
| Morningwood Dr | 22' tables | 3 | 0 | -100 | -27 | |
| Brickyard Rd | Circle | 4 | 2 | -50 | -39 | |
| Sugarbush Ln | Circle | 1 | 0 | -100 | -11 | |
| Notley Rd | Circle | 6 | 4 | -33 | -43 | |
| Cherry Valley Dr | Circle | 4 | 2 | -50 | -49 | |
| **Omaha, NE** | | | | | | |
| 32nd St | 12' humps | 3 | 6 | 100 | | Midblock accidents - same number of months before and after installation |
| Erskine St | 12' humps | 6 | 11 | 83 | | |
| Burke St (between 121st and 122nd St) | 12' humps | 7 | 4 | -43 | | |
| Burke St (between 122nd and 123rd St) | 12' humps | 8 | 1 | -88 | | |
| 33rd St (between Mason and Pacific St) | 12' humps | 0 | 3 | + undefined | | |
| 33rd St (between Pacific St and Poppleton Ave) | 12' humps | 1 | 3 | 200 | | |
| 50th St | 12' humps | 1 | 3 | 200 | | |
| 55th St (between Pine and Hickory St) | 12' humps | 0 | 0 | 0 | | |
| 55th St (between Hickory and Walnut Sts) | 12' humps | 0 | 0 | 0 | | |
| 56th St (between Charles and Hamilton Sts) | 12' humps | 0 | 0 | 0 | | |
| 56th St (between Franklin and Seward Sts) | 12' humps | 0 | 0 | 0 | | |
| 76th St (between Burt and Webster Sts) | 12' humps | 0 | 1 | + undefined | | |
| 76th St (between Burt and Izard Sts) | 12' humps | 0 | 0 | 0 | | |
| 126th St | 12' humps | 0 | 1 | + undefined | | |
| Nina St | 12' humps | 3 | 2 | -33 | | |

| Community/Location | Measures | Accidents | | | Volume | Comments |
|---|---|---|---|---|---|---|
| | | Before | After | % Change | % Change | |
| **Omaha, NE** (continued) | | | | | | |
| Parkview Dr (between Grand Ave and Saratoga St) | 12' humps | 0 | 1 | + undefined | | |
| Parkview Dr (at Larimore Ave) | 12' humps | 0 | 0 | 0 | | |
| Parkview Dr (between Sahler and Sprague Sts) | 12' humps | 1 | 1 | 0 | | |
| Redick Ave (between Minne Lusa Blvd and 28th Ave) | 12' humps | 0 | 3 | + undefined | | |
| **Portland, OR** | | | | | | |
| NE 7th Ave | Circles | 18.3 | 10 | -45 | -15 | Average Annual (36 months before and after) |
| SE Clinton St (#1) | Circles | 33.5 | 26.8 | -20 | -17 | Average Annual (52 months before and after) |
| SE Clinton St (#2) | Circles | 8.1 | 4.6 | -43 | -43 | Average annual based on 52 months |
| NE Holman St | Circles | 4.9 | 4.7 | -4 | -21 | Average annual based on 74 months |
| NE 1st Ave | Circles | 1.8 | 1.6 | -11 | 0 | Average annual based on 61 months |
| NE 24th Ave | Circles | 3.7 | 1.2 | -68 | -9 | Average annual based on 61 months |
| NW 25th Ave | Circles | 3.9 | 1.9 | -51 | -17 | Average annual based on 76 months |
| NW Raleigh St | Circles | 0 | .2 | + undefined | -29 | Average annual based on 76 months |
| NW Cornell Rd | 22' tables | .4 | .8 | 100 | -1 | Average annual based on 29 months |
| NE 15th Ave (#1) | 22' tables | 12.8 | 6.4 | -50 | -20 | Average annual based on 15 months |
| NE 15th Ave (#2) | 22' tables | 12.5 | 7.4 | -41 | -20 | Average annual based on 26 months |
| SE Harold St | 22' tables | 9.6 | 8 | -17 | -39 | Average annual based on 15 months |
| N Macrum St | 14' humps | 1.2 | .9 | -25 | -23 | Average annual based on 41 months |
| NE Pacific St | 14' humps | 2.9 | 3.2 | 10 | 0 | Average annual based on 41 months |
| NE 108th Ave | 14' humps | 1.5 | .9 | -40 | -9 | Average annual based on 41 months |
| SE 55th Ave | 14' humps | 3.8 | 1.2 | -68 | -17 | Average annual based on 41 months |
| SW Boones Ferry Rd | 14' humps | 12.4 | 6.9 | -44 | -62 | Average annual based on 28 months |
| **San Diego, CA** | | | | | | |
| Aquarius Dr | 12' humps | 1 | 0 | -100 | -45 | Injury accidents - 1994 compared to 1995 - comparisons also on a million vehicle-mile basis |
| Avenida Del Gato | 12' humps | 2 | 0 | -100 | -58 | |
| Bootes St | 12' humps | 2 | 0 | -100 | -18 | |
| Capicorn Way | 12' humps | 13 | 8 | -38 | | |
| Libra Dr | 12' humps | 0 | 1 | + undefined | -52 | |
| **San Jose, CA** | | | | | | |
| Cinderella Ln | 12' humps | 2.3 | 1.5 | -35 | | Average annual based on 16 months |
| **Seattle, WA** | | | | | | |
| 1st Ave (76th and 77th Sts NW) | Circle | 3 | 1 | -100 | | Intersection accidents only - calendar year before treatment compared to calendar year after treatment |
| 11th Ave and 58th St NW | Circle | 2 | 0 | -100 | | |
| 14th Ave E and Olive St | Circle | 1 | 0 | -100 | | |
| 16th Ave and 55th St NE | Circle | 1 | 0 | -100 | | |

| Community/Location | Measures | Accidents | | | Volume | Comments |
| --- | --- | --- | --- | --- | --- | --- |
| | | Before | After | % Change | % Change | |
| **Seattle, WA** (continued) | | | | | | |
| 17th Ave and Trenton St SW | Circle | 1 | 0 | -100 | | Intersection accidents only - calendar year before treatment compared to calendar year after treatment |
| 18th Ave and 87th St NW | Circle | 0 | 0 | 0 | | |
| 18th Ave and Brandon St SW | Circle | 2 | 0 | -100 | | |
| 22nd Ave and 75th St NW | Circle | 4 | 0 | -100 | | |
| 27th Ave E and Fir St | Circle | 1 | 0 | -100 | | |
| 27th Ave E and Pike St | Circle | 0 | 1 | + undefined | | |
| 32nd Ave and Othello St SW | Circle | 2 | 0 | -100 | | |
| 35th Ave and 140th St NE | Circle | 1 | 0 | -100 | | |
| 39th Ave and Lucile St S | Circle | 2 | 0 | -100 | | |
| 39th Ave and Charlestown St SW | Circle | 1 | 0 | -100 | | |
| 40th Ave and Dawson St SW | Circle | 2 | 0 | -100 | | |
| 46th Ave and Alaska St S | Circle | 1 | 0 | -100 | | |
| 49th Ave and Oregon St S | Circle | 1 | 0 | -100 | | |
| 56th Ave and 58th St NE | Circle | 0 | 0 | 0 | | |
| 9th Ave and 56th St NW | Circle | 0 | 0 | 0 | | |
| Densmore Ave and 47th St N | Circle | 4 | 0 | -100 | | |
| Keystone Pl and 51st St N | Circle | 3 | 1 | -100 | | |
| Linden Ave and 87 St N | Circle | 1 | 1 | 0 | | |
| Minor Ave and Union St | Circle | 1 | 0 | -100 | | |
| North Park Ave &109 St N | Circle | 1 | 0 | -100 | | |
| Phinney Ave and 112 St N | Circle | 0 | 0 | 0 | | |
| Phinney Ave and 42 St N | Circle | 2 | 0 | -100 | | |
| Sunnyside Ave and 42nd St | Circle | 1 | 0 | -100 | | |
| Whitman Ave and 47th St | Circle | 2 | 0 | -100 | | |
| 1st Ave and 127th St NW | Circle | 2 | 0 | -100 | | |
| 1st Ave and 95th St NW | Circle | 1 | 0 | -100 | | |
| 12th Ave and 90th St NW | Circle | 3 | 0 | -100 | | |
| 12th Ave & Cloverdale St SW | Circle | 1 | 0 | -100 | | |
| 14th Ave and 90th St NW | Circle | 1 | 0 | -100 | | |
| 16th Ave and Howell St E | Circle | 3 | 2 | -33 | | |
| 17th Ave and Harrison St E | Circle | 0 | 0 | 0 | | |
| 17th Ave and 60th St NW | Circle | 1 | 0 | -100 | | |
| 17th Ave and 83rd St NW | Circle | 1 | 0 | -100 | | |
| 19th Ave and 107th St NE | Circle | 1 | 0 | -100 | | |
| 30th Ave & Henderson St SW | Circle | 4 | 0 | -100 | | |
| 34th Ave and 57th St NW | Circle | 0 | 0 | 0 | | |
| 37th Ave and Dakota St S | Circle | 4 | 0 | -100 | | |
| 37th Ave and Dakota St SW | Circle | 1 | 0 | -100 | | |
| 38th Ave and 88th St NE | Circle | 2 | 0 | -100 | | |

| Community/Location | Measures | Accidents | | | Volume | Comments |
|---|---|---|---|---|---|---|
| | | Before | After | % Change | % Change | |
| **Seattle, WA** (continued) | | | | | | |
| 4th Ave and 122nd St NW | Circle | 1 | 0 | -100 | | Intersection accidents only - calendar year before treatment compared to calendar year after treatment |
| 41st Ave and Findlay St SW | Circle | 1 | 0 | -100 | | |
| 44th Ave and Hinds St SW | Circle | 7 | 0 | -100 | | |
| 5th Ave and Prospect St N | Circle | 4 | 0 | -100 | | |
| 5th Ave and 70th St NW | Circle | 2 | 0 | -100 | | |
| 6th Ave and 73rd St NW | Circle | 2 | 0 | -100 | | |
| 6th Ave (81st & 82nd St NW) | Circles | 4 | 0 | -100 | | |
| 8th Ave and 115th NE | Circle | 0 | 0 | 0 | | |
| Ashworth Ave & 107th St N | Circle | 2 | 0 | -100 | | |
| Dayton Ave and 78th St N | Circle | 2 | 0 | -100 | | |
| Densmore Ave 103rd St N | Circle | 3 | 0 | -100 | | |
| Densmore Ave and 46th St N | Circle | 2 | 0 | -100 | | |
| Fremont Ave and 78th St N | Circle | 1 | 0 | -100 | | |
| Greenwood Ave & 45th St N | Circle | 1 | 0 | -100 | | |
| Interlake Ave and 107th St N | Circle | 3 | 0 | -100 | | |
| 1st Ave and 52nd St NE | Circle | 0 | 0 | -100 | | |
| 10th Ave and Rose St S | Circle | 0 | 0 | 0 | | Intersection accidents only - calendar year before treatment (1991) compared to calendar year after treatment |
| 11th Ave and Armour St W | Circle | 0 | 0 | 0 | | |
| 13th Ave and 90th St NW | Circle | 1 | 0 | -100 | | |
| 14th Ave and Hanford St S | Circle | 1 | 0 | -100 | | |
| 17th Ave and 107th St NE | Circle | 0 | 0 | -100 | | |
| 17th Ave and 75th St NW | Circle | 2 | 1 | -50 | | |
| 2nd Ave and 67th St NW | Circle | 4 | 0 | -100 | | |
| 20th Ave and Fir St E | Circle | 1 | 0 | -100 | | |
| 29th Ave & Washington St S | Circle | 1 | 0 | -100 | | |
| 30th Ave and 94th St NE | Circle | 1 | 0 | -100 | | |
| 30th Ave and Walker St S | Circle | 1 | 0 | -100 | | |
| 36th Ave & Cambridge St SW | Circle | 1 | 0 | -100 | | |
| 4th Ave and 44th St NE | Circle | 0 | 0 | 0 | | |
| 4th Ave and 62nd St NW | Circle | 2 | 0 | -100 | | |
| 40th Ave and 120th St NE | Circle | 2 | 0 | -100 | | |
| 41st Ave and Juneau St SW | Circle | 1 | 0 | -100 | | |
| 44th Ave and Dakota St SW | Circle | 2 | 0 | -100 | | |
| 46th Ave and Dawson St S | Circle | 1 | 0 | -100 | | |
| Ashworth Ave & 135th St N | Circle | 1 | 0 | -100 | | |
| Ashworth Ave & 36th St N | Circle | 0 | 0 | 0 | | |
| Densmore Ave & 44th St N | Circle | 1 | 0 | -100 | | |
| Evanston Ave and 107th St N | Circle | 2 | 0 | -100 | | |
| Evanston Ave and 115th St N | Circle | 1 | 0 | -100 | | |
| Evanston Ave and 92nd St N | Circle | 2 | 0 | -100 | | |
| Fremont Ave and 67th St N | Circle | 1 | 1 | 0 | | |
| Stone Ave and 103rd St N | Circle | 5 | 0 | -100 | | |
| Wallingford Ave & 51st St N | Circle | 1 | 0 | -100 | | |

| Community/Location | Measures | Accidents | | | Volume | Comments |
|---|---|---|---|---|---|---|
| | | Before | After | % Change | % Change | |
| **Seattle, WA** (continued) | | | | | | |
| 1st Ave and 51st St NE | Circle | 2 | 0 | -100 | | Intersection accidents only - calendar year before treatment compared to calendar year after treatment |
| 1st Ave and 110th St NW | Circle | 1 | 0 | -100 | | |
| 14th Ave and Forest St S | Circle | 2 | 0 | -100 | | |
| 14th Ave and Winthrop St S | Circle | 0 | 0 | 0 | | |
| 17th Ave and 61st NW | Circle | 1 | 1 | 0 | | |
| 22nd Ave and 58th St NW | Circle | 1 | 0 | -100 | | |
| 23rd Pl and 135th St NE | Circle | 1 | 0 | -100 | | |
| 25th Ave and Fir St E | Circle | 2 | 0 | -100 | | |
| 25th Ave and Newton St E | Circle | 3 | 0 | -100 | | |
| 30th Ave and 58th St NW | Circle | 2 | 0 | -100 | | |
| 34th Ave and Holly St SW | Circle | 1 | 0 | -100 | | |
| 38th Ave and 86th St NE | Circle | 1 | 0 | -100 | | |
| 41st Ave and Garfield St E | Circle | 3 | 0 | -100 | | |
| 42nd Ave and Hudson St S | Circle | 2 | 1 | -50 | | |
| 42nd Ave and Genesee St SW | Circle | 2 | 1 | -50 | | |
| 8th Ave and 120th St NE | Circle | 1 | 0 | -100 | | |
| 8th Ave and 47th St NE | Circle | 5 | 0 | -100 | | |
| 9th Ave and 67th St NW | Circle | 1 | 0 | -100 | | |
| Ashworth Ave and 97th St N | Circle | 0 | 0 | 0 | | |
| Corliss Ave (42nd & 43rd St N) | Circle | 4 | 0 | -100 | | |
| Dayton Ave and 84th St N | Circle | 0 | 0 | 0 | | |
| Densmore Ave and 97th St N | Circle | 5 | 0 | -100 | | |
| Division Ave and 67th St NW | Circle | 2 | 0 | -100 | | |
| Fremont Ave and 84th St N | Circle | 4 | 0 | -100 | | |
| Warren Ave and Fulton St N | Circle | 1 | 0 | -100 | | |
| Meridian Ave and 43rd St N | Circle | 1 | 0 | -100 | | |
| Ravenna Ave and 77th St NE | Circle | 2 | 0 | -100 | | |
| **Tampa, FL** | | | | | | |
| Oklahoma Ave | 12' humps | 7.4 | 8.4 | 14 | -43 | Average annual reported accidents - does not adjust for lower volumes after humps installed - accident increase understated |
| Manhattan Ave | 12' humps | 4.7 | 11.7 | 149 | -18 | |
| Parkland Blvd | 12' humps | 8.0 | 5.8 | -27 | -33 | |
| Azeele St | 12' humps | 11.3 | 5.6 | -50 | -19 | |
| Cleveland St | 12' humps | 9.7 | 11.0 | 13 | -35 | |

# Effectiveness of Education/Enforcement

| Community/Location | Programs | 85th Percentile Speed (mph) | | | Volumes (vehicles/day) | | | Comments |
|---|---|---|---|---|---|---|---|---|
| | | Before | After | % Change | Before | After | % Change | |
| **Austin, TX** | | | | | | | | |
| Mesa Dr (6500 blk) | Strict speed enforcement | 38 | 40 | 5 | N/A | | | Speed "after" treatment is actually during or after |
| Mesa Dr (7200 blk) | | 39 | 38 | -3 | N/A | | | |
| Highland Tr | | 38 | 34 | -11 | N/A | | | |
| Powell Ln | | 39 | 39 | 0 | N/A | | | |
| Lightsey Rd | | 43 | 38 | -12 | N/A | | | |
| Circle S Rd | | 41 | 38 | -7 | N/A | | | |
| Webberville Rd (1200 blk) | | 39 | 39 | 0 | N/A | | | |
| Webberville Rd (1900 blk) | | 40 | 38 | -5 | N/A | | | |
| **Boulder, CO** | | | | | | | | |
| N 26th St (between Iris and Kalmia) | High-enforcement zone | 34 | 37 | 9 | N/A | | | 4 weeks after enforcement - more impact 2 weeks after |
| N 26th St (between Norwood and Agate) | | 37 | 37 | 0 | N/A | | | |
| Baseline (between 13th and 14th) | | 34 | 34 | 0 | N/A | | | |
| Baseline (between Grant and 8th) | | 37 | 37 | 0 | N/A | | | |
| **Phoenix, AZ** | | | | | | | | |
| 71st Ave | Neighborhood speed watch | 36 | 36 | 0 | 1,016 | 737 | -27 | Speeds tend to return to earlier levels |
| Campbell Ave (E of 71st Ave) | | 39 | 39 | 0 | 878 | 861 | -2 | |
| Campbell Ave (W of 71st Ave) | | 36 | 33 | -8 | 940 | 970 | 3 | |
| Utopia Rd | | 32 | 33 | 3 | 993 | 872 | -12 | Most violators nonlocal |
| 24th St | | 41 | 40 | -2 | 8,403 | 9,189 | 9 | |
| **San Jose, CA** | | | | | | | | |
| Townsend | Photo-radar speed enforcement | 36 | 34 | -6 | N/A | | | Minimal traffic diversion |
| Yerba Buena Ave | | 39 | 39 | 0 | N/A | | | |
| Kingman Ave | | 40 | 34 | -15 | N/A | | | |
| Eden Ave | | 38 | 37 | -3 | N/A | | | |
| Serenity Wy | | 37 | 37 | 0 | N/A | | | |
| Kammerer | | 34 | 32 | -6 | N/A | | | |

# Effectiveness of Regulatory Measures

| Community/Location | Programs | 85th Percentile Speed (mph) | | | Volume (vehicles/day) | | | Comments |
|---|---|---|---|---|---|---|---|---|
| | | Before | After | % Change | Before | After | % Change | |
| **Boulder, CO** | | | | | | | | |
| 9th St (N of Evergreen) | All-way stops | 23 | 28 | 0 | N/A | | | Midblock speeds |
| 9th St (N of University) | All-way stops | 33 | 33 | 0 | N/A | | | |
| 13th St | All-way stops | 33 | 28 | -15 | N/A | | | |
| 9th St (Pine to Mapleton) | Speed limit signs Crosswalk striping | 32 | 31 | -3 | N/A | | | |
| **Charlotte, NC** | | | | | | | | |
| Charter Pl (between Thistle Ct and Sonata Pl) | All-way stops | 42 | 37 | -12 | 2,000 | 2,100 | 5 | Unwarranted stops 700' - 900' apart - posted speed of 25 mph; measurement taken immediately after; longer term volume impacts appear greater |
| Charter Pl (at Weber Ct) | All-way stops | 35 | 33 | -6 | 1,900 | 1,800 | -5 | |
| **Ft. Lauderdale, FL** | | | | | | | | |
| SW 7th St | All-way stops | N/A | | | 3,450 | 3,428 | -1 | Signal timing also altered to make cut-through route less attractive |
| SW 9th Ave | All-way stops | N/A | | | 5,553 | 4,314 | -22 | |
| **Gwinnett County, GA** | | | | | | | | |
| Brentford Lane (E of Hollybrook ) | All-way stops | 34 | 30 | -12 | N/A | | | Around midblock speeds |
| Brentford Lane (E of Brentforde) | All-way stops | 33 | 27 | -18 | N/A | | | |
| Brentford Lane (E of Baniff Ct) | All-way stops | 31 | 28 | -10 | N/A | | | |
| **Phoenix, AZ** | | | | | | | | |
| Orangewood Ave | All-way stops | 38 | 36 | -5 | 890 | 917 | 3 | Midblock measurement |
| 35th St | Turn restrictions (peak hours only) | N/A | | | 175 | 60 | -66 | Two blocks from a.m. turn restriction |
| Mercer Lane | Turn restrictions (peak hours only) | N/A | | | 178 | 41 | -77 | One block from a.m. turn restrictions |
| 37th St (same block as turn restriction) | Turn restriction (p.m. peak only) | N/A | | | 171 | 86 | -50 | Some volume reduction due to diagonal diverter a couple blocks away |
| Grenada Rd (same block as turn restriction) | Turn restriction (p.m. peak only) | N/A | | | 56 | 27 | -52 | Part of neighborhood-wide treatment |
| Palm Ln (same block as turn restriction) | Turn restriction (p.m. peak only) | N/A | | | 10 | 16 | 60 | |
| Holly St (same block as turn restriction) | Turn restriction (p.m. peak only) | N/A | | | | | | |
| **San Jose, CA** | | | | | | | | |
| San Antonio St | All-way stop | N/A | | | 19 | 23 | 21 | Same block as all-way stop |
| **Tucson, AZ** | | | | | | | | |
| Meyer Ave | One-way street | 21 | 18 | -14 | 368 | 164 | -55 | (Conversion from 2-way) |

# Effectiveness of Psycho-Perception Controls

| Community/Location | Programs | 85th Percentile Speed (mph) | | | Volumes (vehicles/day) | | | Comments |
|---|---|---|---|---|---|---|---|---|
| | | Before | After | % Change | Before | After | % Change | |
| **Eugene, OR** | | | | | | | | |
| W 18th Ave | Transverse markings at decreasing intervals | 37 | 35 | -5 | N/A | | | Installed on dangerous curve - accident reduction reported |
| **Howard County, MD** | | | | | | | | |
| Mayfield Ave | Transverse markings at decreasing intervals | 43 | 38 | -12 | N/A | | | |
| Sebring Dr | Centerline striping | 36 | 36 | 0 | N/A | | | Double yellow |
| Allview Dr | Centerline striping | 40 | 42 | 5 | N/A | | | Double yellow |
| Ducketts La | Edge line narrowing | 38 | 40 | 5 | N/A | | | |
| Wheatfield Wy | Edge line narrowing | 30 | 33 | 10 | N/A | | | From 38' to 22' - no centerline |
| **Orlando, FL** | | | | | | | | |
| Plaza Tr | Edge line narrowing | 32* | 33 | 3 | N/A | | | From 14' to 9' lane width |
| South Lake Orlando Pkwy | Edge line narrowing | 35* | 35 | 0 | N/A | | | From 18' to 9' lane width |
| **San Antonio, TX** | | | | | | | | |
| Independence Ave (location A) | Edge line narrowing | 35 | 35 | 0 | N/A | | | From 21' to 13' lane width |
| Independence Ave (location B) | | 33 | 34 | 3 | N/A | | | |
| Independence Ave (location C) | | 33 | 33 | 0 | N/A | | | |
| Independence Ave (location D) | | 36 | 36 | 0 | N/A | | | |
| Independence Ave (location E) | | 40 | 39 | -3 | N/A | | | |
| Independence Ave (location F) | | 38 | 39 | 3 | N/A | | | |

* Mean speeds

# Index

Page numbers in **boldface** refer to figures.
Page numbers followed by *t* refer to tables. Page numbers followed by *n* refer to notes.